Six Women

OF

SALEM

ALSO BY *MARILYNNE K. ROACH*

Gallows and Graves:
The Search to Locate the Death and Burial Sites
of the People Executed for Witchcraft in 1692 (1997)

The Salem Witch Trials:
A Day-by-Day Chronicle of a Community Under Siege (2002)

Records of the Salem Witch-Hunt
Bernard Rosenthal, editor in chief,
M. K. Roach, associate editor (2009)

CHILDREN'S NON-FICTION

In the Days of the Salem Witchcraft Trials (1996)

Six Women

OF

SALEM

The Untold Story of the *ACCUSED*
and Their *ACCUSERS* in the
SALEM WITCH TRIALS

MARILYNNE K. ROACH

Da Capo Press
A Member of the Perseus Books Group

Editorial production by *Marra*thon Production Services. www.marrathon.net

DESIGN BY JANE RAESE
Set in 12-point Adobe Caslon

Library of Congress Cataloging-in-Publication Data is available for this book.
ISBN 978-0-306-82120-2 (paperback)
ISBN 978-0-306-82234-6 (e-Book)

Published by Da Capo Press
A Member of the Perseus Books Group
www.dacapopress.com

Da Capo Press books are available at special discounts for bulk purchases in the U.S. by corporations, institutions, and other organizations. For more information, please contact the Special Markets Department at the Perseus Books Group, 2300 Chestnut Street, Suite 200, Philadelphia, PA 19103, or call (800) 810-4145, ext. 5000, or e-mail special.markets@perseusbooks.com.

10 9 8 7 6 5 4 3 2 1

I can say before my Eternal father I am innocent,
& God will clear my innocency.
—*Rebecca Nurse*

CONTENTS

Part Three: Afterword

PREFACE

The Salem witch trials consumed over twenty communities in 1692, dragged at least 162 people (and their reputations) before the law, tried 52, condemned 30, and put 20 to death—19 by hanging and 1 by pressing to induce a proper plea. At least 5 more died in prison.

In addition, at least seventy people were considered to be the afflicted victims of witchcraft—the suffering prey of evil magic—whereas three times that number risked their own lives by adding their names to petitions or speaking on behalf of the accused.

All of this stands as statistics, typical or atypical of witchcraft panics, based on records that are sometimes full, sometimes scanty. Not all the records have survived, although the Salem cases are often better documented than other cases elsewhere. Overlooked documents continue to appear—having been misfiled or transcribed in fragments from lost papers printed in obscure, rediscovered volumes.

The stories are preserved in the court documents and the contemporary commentary published soon after the trials. These have passed into American folklore as hardly believable events played out by incomprehensible characters who accuse one another (or several others) of unprovable crimes, all of whom are portrayed as symbols and stereotypes rather than real people like ourselves.

Yet the tragedy and turmoil of 1692 fed on basic human emotions and weaknesses, and the trials touched people personally as individuals—people with real stories, real lives, real suffering, and real deaths.

After each person affected had died—of old age, of illness, or by the hangman's rope—their families preserved the stories of their loved one's fortitude or fell silent with a willful forgetting that buried an inconvenient memory, bestowing ignorance on succeeding generations.

The relative obscurity of some of these lives challenges our ability to reconstruct them. Even the bare vital records of birth, marriage, and death are missing in many instances. Some were well remembered by their families and towns. Others would have escaped all written notice had it not been for their presence in the court records. Often the known lives of the people around them—such as the more public lives of fathers and husbands that suggest the private world of woman's work—give greater hints into their lives.

This book follows six such individuals, all women, for in Western culture most witch suspects were women. Although in 1692 several men were arrested for suspected witchcraft as well, as a few had been earlier, unlike most recorded historical events of the time, this one *centered* around the region's women—the bewitched, the accusers, the accused.

The six are Rebecca Nurse, Bridget Bishop, Mary English, Ann Putnam Sr., Tituba, and Mary Warren. Together they represent accusers and accused or both in one; married and single; rich, poor, and middling; free and slave; hopeful and desperate. The Introductions chapter presents them chronologically by (approximate) age, with the backstory of their lives up to the point when the witch scare began. Then their stories are woven throughout the events of that tragic year, with their individual experiences comprising the focus of the narrative.

All of this is based on fact, even the fictionalized sections recreating the characters' thoughts, and these are clearly marked by italicized text. Spelling is somewhat standardized in these fictionalized passages but kept close to the original in the body of the text. For example, "yᵉ" becomes "the" (as it was pronounced), and "yᵗ" becomes "that."

Old-style dates that indicate the year beginning in March, written 1691/92 for example, are treated as new style, with the year beginning in January of 1692.

I have made every effort to the best of my ability to obtain proper permissions and credits for the material presented here as noted in the endnotes, bibliography, and captions. If anything has been omitted, it will be corrected in future editions.

All lives are stories, and history is made of stories.

PART ONE

Introductions

Rebecca Nurse

Rebecca, holding the basket while her mother contemplates the fishmonger's display, listens, despite herself, to the market women's gossip.

"Black Shuck?" one says to a young sailor from somewhere else. "Oh, aye, you'd best be careful of that one. He roams the long sands, and those who meet the creature and live to tell the tale—and not all do, mind—commonly die within the year."

Rebecca, like everyone else in Great Yarmouth, has heard the tale of the spectral hound that haunts the barrier beach between the town and the waves. Such fearsome spirits prowl Britain's lonely places, the dark roads where travelers hear a quiet footfall behind them, moving when they move, stopping when they stop. Some brave enough to turn and face it report blazing red eyes. In other parts folk call them Bargest or Boggart, Padfoot or Pooka, and wonder if they are really devils in the shape of dogs.

A second woman nods in agreement, and the sailor looks alarmed.

"The creature doesn't always stay just on the beach," says the oldest of the fishwives. "When I was a girl there was a terrible day one summer. Storms rolled in with wind and tempests and lightning. And even though it was a Sabbath, Black Shuck rampaged through the countryside. Over the border in Sussex he burst into the church at Blythburg—during a service!—rushed up the nave between the people, and wrung the necks of two unfortunates as they knelt at prayer. Then he collapsed the church tower right through the roof. But that wasn't enough for the fiend. Within the hour he broke through the doors of the church at Bengay. And to this day both churches have the devil's fingerprints scorched into the wood of their north doors. Scorched!"

The sailor tries not to look frightened as the old women nod sagely. Locals know enough to fear Black Shuck.

Rebecca's mother drops a haddock into the basket and bids her with mild rebuke to come along now. It is impossible not to overhear—fishwives have loud voices. Rebecca follows, shivering a little at the thought

3

of spectral hounds. Fortunately, she has never encountered Shuck in all her fifteen years, and soon her family will be gone from Yarmouth. They are moving to New England, and things are different there.

The Great Yarmouth of *REBECCA*'s childhood was a long, narrow, medieval city crowded between its ancient walls and the River Yare. The mass of small brick and stone houses shouldered each other along a few streets that followed the curve of the river. The Rows, a multitude of alleys, connected these streets like teeth on a comb, fanning downslope westward so rain could wash household swill and cess to the Yare and outgoing tide on the one hand and allow easterly breezes to shift the air between the cramped Rows on the other. Passages were only five to three feet across (or less), so carts ran on two tandem wheels, and law required house doors to open inward to protect passersby.

More space opened up along the Quay and in the Market Place and even more around the parish Church of Saint Nicholas. Six hundred years old and larger than many cathedrals, it stood anchored on wooden piles sunk into the sandy earth, its stones built and rebuilt around its tower, its art and ornament periodically repaired, replaced, or swept away. Over three centuries before, a furious sea had broken over the town's protective dunes, surging over the walls and through-out the streets, four feet deep within the church itself. Human whims made their mark as well, when newer styles replaced old adornments on a caprice of fashion, disregarding the past enough to use old stone coffins in a staircase. In the middle of the previous century much of the art was removed or destroyed, considered too frivolous for a house of God, idolatrous distractions from true religion. When William Towne, a gardener, married Joanna Blessing here on April 25, 1620, the light of the North Sea fell through clear windows unencumbered by color, and only a pile of bright, shattered glass remained forgotten under a stair. And it was here that their firstborn was baptized Rebecca on February 21, 1621, in the ancient octagonal font of Purbeck marble—a limestone bearing ghostly fossils of fish and shells, ante-diluvian wonders.

Times were hard as Rebecca grew—learned to walk, learned to help with household tasks, learned to care for younger siblings as they were born, learned to read and attend to matters of her soul. Three years of heavy rains began the year of her birth, ruining harvest after harvest until 1623, when her short-lived brother John was born. By then, overseers of the poor could hardly help the aged and infirm of their parishes; poor families took to sheep stealing, and some folk ate dog. Crops improved eventually, but in 1625, when sister Susanna was born—and soon died—plague oppressed the region. Once that ended, harvests declined again beginning in 1628, when brother Edmund was born—and lived.

East Anglia's textile production—a cottage industry of independent spinners and weavers—languished as European wars disrupted old markets for the woolens. Merchants' storehouses filled with unsold cloth, and with no work to be had, weavers' families lapsed into malnutrition. Rising land prices squeezed small farmers off their holdings, and larger landowners found themselves caught between the government's mounting demands for taxes and increasingly desperate tenants who were unable to pay rent.

The price of grain doubled in the winter after Edmund's birth. Now desperate spinners sold their tools for food. During this three-year famine a mob in Colchester attacked a wagon transporting grain. In Yarmouth itself a merchant tried to ship out a load of chicken feed only to have a mob attack the boatmen and seize the once-despised buckwheat. In Malden a woman urged a band of men to break into a warehouse in broad daylight. "Come, my brave lads," she cried. "I will be your leader, and we will not starve." And they did not starve—for all were caught, tried for theft, and hanged.

Crops improved somewhat after 1632, when brother Jacob was born, but the bishops began to clamp down on Nonconformists like the Townes.

In the seventeenth century religion was as much a matter of national identity as it was of personal conviction—perhaps more so. Loyal subjects of most countries were expected to follow the forms of worship their monarchs approved, displaying solidarity as well as faith (or at least lip service). Few considered it possible that a nation could

separate church and state without weakening itself. (Although the
Netherlands had an official church, it allowed other well-behaved
faiths.) But over a century earlier Henry VIII of England had separated from Rome for dynastic reasons. Without a divorce from his first
wife, he could not hope to sire a legal male heir, and without one ready
to assume the throne upon Henry's death, the nation risked civil strife
from within and invasion from without. But Henry's national Church
of England did not change enough in its ideals and customs to match
the hopes of reform that many of his subjects longed for. This was especially so in East Anglia, the hump of land containing Norfolk
(where Great Yarmouth was located), Suffolk, and Essex counties opposite the Netherlands. Here the literacy rate (among men at least)
was higher than elsewhere in the realm, and here was the Puritan
hotbed of Cambridge University. Here folk hoped to improve the new
church further—to purify it from extraneous distractions and concentrate on the word of God. Their critics called them Puritans for that,
and East Anglia was full of them.

The Townes were among them, gathering every Sabbath in Saint
Nicholas to hear sermons from mostly sympathetic preachers. Rebecca
watched and listened from the congregation as the minister spoke
from the pulpit in the south transept—eight-sided like the baptismal
font (an "octagonal tub," said detractors). Gilt letters shone under its
book rest: "Feare God, Honour the Kynge 1 Pet 2." People sometimes
wondered which of these the government considered more important.

The bishop of London, who oversaw and managed the region,
eventually clamped down on just *what* was being said—or not said—
in his pulpits, and people began to think of leaving. The economy was
bad enough, and famine was a reality. But now their spiritual lives
were also under assault. The Book of Sports was only one insulting
example. In Lancashire in 1618, to solve the controversy between Puritans and gentry (most of whom were definitely *not* Puritans) over
what activity was suitable for a Sabbath, King James I issued a "Declaration of Sports," a definition of allowable Sunday pastimes. He ordered it be read from every pulpit.

The Declaration did have the decency to prohibit bear baiting, "in-
terludes" (theater was going *too* far), and bowling, which was "in the

meane sort of people by law prohibited" anyway. But lawful activities, according to the king, included dancing, archery, leaping and vaulting, plus seasonal May Games, Witsun Ales, and Morris dances, even Maypoles as long as these were conducted "in due and convenient time without impediment or neglect of divine service."

Even if none of this interrupted services, it surely interrupted the peace of the Sabbath and personal contemplation of the Scriptures. The Sabbath, to the reformers, was intended for the Lord, not for idle play or heathen crudities like Maypoles. The resulting outcry was severe enough that the king withdrew the proclamation.

Then, in 1633, James's son and successor, Charles, reintroduced the order everywhere in the realm and punished clergy who, in conscience, would not proclaim the Book of Sports (as its detractors called it) to their congregations and, thus, be a party to it. These men frequently digressed from approved procedure by omitting much of the church's ceremonies; elaborate vestments were another sore point. Largely Puritan parishes then found that conforming clergy were replacing their ministers. Ministers who were thus silenced—forbidden a voice from their former pulpits—delivered their sermons in other venues as lectures, with loyal listeners traveling considerable distances to hear them. When they were further threatened with arrest, jail terms, and fines, some went into hiding or fled oversea to the Netherlands.

The desperate economy combined with religious convictions impelled many in East Anglia to risk emigration. Land, they knew, was available in far-flung colonies among the savages of Northern Ireland and the New World. Some of those places, like Virginia, were dominated by leaders supportive of the bishops in the Church of England; others had been established by Puritans who sought to put as much distance as possible between the bishops and themselves. New England seemed a likely spot, and many Great Yarmouth folk were going there—whole families, not just young men seeking their fortunes. Removal required an investment: ship passage, supplies for the voyage over, and food to last until a farm or business could be made productive. But at least the place was no longer entirely a wilderness; others had already settled several towns and raised a few harvests.

Sister Mary was baptized in August 1634, and the family left Yarmouth for good, all except Edmund, who was still indentured to his shoemaker master. He could join the rest once he was free.

The year 1635 for their removal is approximate: after Mary's August 1634 christening, as recorded in Saint Nicholas's records, probably before September 1635, when the authorities cited as "Separatists, William Towne and Joanna his wife" for neglecting communion at St. Nicholas, and before the distribution of lots in Salem's Northfields that occurred before that town's records began in 1635. Northfields was the part of Salem across the North River from the peninsula where the town center was. William Towne's saltwater farm lay on the south shore of the Endicott River, where it met the Williston River. Their combined streams flowed south, met the North River, then rounded the peninsula of Salem town into Massachusetts Bay.

Edmund arrived in Salem two years later when his master, Henry Skerry, immigrated with his family *and* Edmund. (Skerry's wife, Elizabeth, brought old-country traditions with her for, as a great, great granddaughter related in 1802, she "always swept her hearth before she went to bed for the Fairies.") In addition, Rebecca's widowed aunt Alice Fermage (one of her mother's two older sisters) was also in Salem by 1638, along with two sons and four daughters. The eldest Blessing sister, Margaret, had died shortly before the Townes emigrated, but her widowed husband, Robert Buffum, and his new wife and her daughter from a first marriage soon immigrated and settled in Salem.

Joanna bore two more children in New England, Sarah and Joseph, but when is uncertain. Both were baptized in 1648, but that ceremony did not necessarily happen as soon after a baby's birth as it would in England. There, every loyal subject was expected to be a member of the Church of England and, therefore, eligible—if not required—to partake of the sacraments. New England churches, however, were each independent, and only full members were eligible for the sacraments of baptism and the Lord's Supper (the only two that Puritans recognized). What constituted a proper membership, however, became a bone of contention in the early days of Massachusetts. Influenced largely by the beliefs of the banished Ann Hutchinson and her followers, membership indicated a person who was considered saved, someone who, after much soul searching, felt (relatively) sure they were not damned.

Once applied, examined, and accepted, fully communing members could be baptized (if they had not been already) and have their children baptized.

While political and religious tensions between Royalist and Puritan factions worsened in England, leading to a civil war that the Puritans would win, Rebecca Towne married Francis Nurse in Salem on August 24, 1644. The earliest record of her future husband in Salem is a March 1, 1640 court case in which "Francis Nurse a youth" (he was about nineteen) was presented "for stealing of victuals & suspicion of breaking [into] a house." A note in the published record says that this entry was "crossed slightly," so perhaps Francis was exonerated. Some deeds describe Francis as a "tray maker." (Perhaps he was from Lincolnshire, where "tray" could mean a woven wattle hurdle—sections of temporary fencing used to pen sheep or make a gate, a handy skill for farmers.)

Presumably Francis rented his acres at first, while Rebecca began the constant work of keeping a house in order and bearing children about every other year, beginning in 1645, with son John. In 1648, a year between the births of daughter Rebecca and son Samuel, one Margaret Jones of Charlestown, a folk healer who frightened some of her patients, was tried for witchcraft and hanged in Boston.

Daughter Sarah was born around 1651, the year Rebecca's father, William Towne, moved the family to Topsfield—the year a Springfield couple, Hugh and Mary Parsons, were tried for witchcraft. Instead, the wife, a disturbed woman, was found guilty of infanticide, whereas the magistrates could not agree on the guilt of her moody husband, so he, unlike his wife, did *not* hang. In the years following, another woman—Ann Hibbins of Boston, a forceful widow whose arguments with difficult building contractors escalated into witchcraft charges—was found guilty of witchcraft and hanged in 1656 despite her kinship with Governor Richard Bellingham.

In the same decade the Society of Friends—Quakers, to their detractors, and even more nonconforming than other Nonconformists—began preaching views that the Massachusetts government found threatening: that because the non-Friends had religion all wrong and were going to Hell, none of their opinions counted. The legislature instituted draconian laws against the Quakers, who only protested more, even at the risk of their lives. One of Rebecca's female relatives, a distant Buxton cousin by marriage, demonstrated repeatedly and publicly—which was shocking enough in women—even appearing naked in the street to symbolize a point that the scandal of her nudity thoroughly obscured.

Francis once again had to enter a slander suit in 1651, this time against Jonathan and Eunice Porter. Once again the reason was not recorded, but Eunice Porter "made acknowledgement which the court accepted." Two years later Francis was "discharged from training"— excused, that is, from mustering with the local militia, the community's only defense. As he was still a young man of about thirty-three, perhaps he had been injured. Perhaps Rebecca had also been unwell. Later she would refer to the "difficult Exigences that hath Befallen me In the Times of my Travells" and the "fits that shee formerly use to have."

After an eight-year gap, around 1659, Rebecca gave birth to her next recorded child, Mary, followed by Francis Jr. in 1661. In England, meanwhile, the Puritan Commonwealth ended in 1660 with the restoration of the monarchy. Charles II's government now sided with the New England Quakers, requiring Massachusetts to tolerate sects other than orthodox Congregational only—although *all* Nonconformists were persecuted in England itself. Rebecca bore her daughter Elizabeth in 1665, the year of England's Great Plague, which killed 15 percent of London's population and compelled the king to evacuate the government to Oxford. Rebecca had her last child, Benjamin, in 1666, the year that marked London's Great Fire, which burned for five days over 436 acres, leveling eighty-seven churches and destroying 13,200 houses. Then, an attack up the Thames from the Dutch fleet compounded these disasters.

Meanwhile, Rebecca's seventy-five-year-old mother, Joanna Towne, twice spoke up publicly in a 1670 suit and countersuit that grew from Topfield's division over the suitability of its minister. Reverend Thomas Gilbert, despite claims from the Perkins family, had not been drunk one volatile Sabbath, she deposed in May. She had sat next to him at dinner and thought him "very temperate." If he acted oddly, then it was due to "his distemper" (a disorienting physical ailment that his supporters mentioned) but not from drinking "as some so uncharitably surmise against him." She repeated this in the November countersuit and added that he did not guzzle from the cup passed round the table but instead passed it to her, saying that "I needed it more than he, being older." Then when he did get a turn, there were only two or three spoonfuls of wine left in the cup. "He was moderate both in eating and drinking, and he knew what he said and did, and this I can safely testify upon oath."

Joanna's willingness to speak out may have caused lingering resentment, especially among Reverend Gilbert's critics. Her support of a man whom they considered wholly unsuitable to lead a church may have fueled the circulating gossip that hinted she may have been a witch. Gilbert, after all, had been in court repeatedly over slander suits. He allowed his personal resentment to intrude into his sermons (as when he remarked that "the necks of all who opposed the ministers of the Gospel should be broken"). More alarming were comments like "kings are asses and the scum of the earth," which could have serious consequences for all of Massachusetts if they ever reached London.

Unlike her Buxton kin, and after much soul searching and with the good report of her neighbors and fellow congregants, Rebecca joined the Salem Church in 1672, the year the General Court finally granted her rural neighborhood of Salem Village permission to begin to establish its own parish and hold religious services closer to home. William Towne, Rebecca's aged father, died in the following year.

In 1674 Elizabeth Clungen, a desperate woman who had been living in the neighborhood, left her four-year-old child at the Nurse household, then, according to the county records, "went away out of the jurisdiction privately." Elizabeth, whose own identity is obscure, had been married to one Thomas Clungen, who had earlier lived in Ipswich. She and Thomas were in Salem when their daughter, also named Elizabeth, was born in August 1670. Perhaps Thomas soon died. By the time her daughter was four, Elizabeth left a quantity of household furnishings stored at Goodman Richard Sibley's and entrusted the child to the Nurses—or, rather, to Rebecca. After Elizabeth did not return, Francis appeared before the authorities and "in charity took the child into his care and custody." The Essex County court ordered the Clungen property inventoried—iron cookware, bedding, a chest, and a silk waistcoat among other items—and granted a chair, a lamp, and a few other items to Sibley as payment for "house room, room & trouble about the goods." Francis paid the Clungen's debts with some of the other items and retained the rest "for the use of the child." Unfortunately, what became of mother or child is unclear. Such were often the fates of the impoverished and dispossessed.

Having been relieved of militia duty and having served a term as constable, Francis occasionally sat on grand juries and trial juries in Essex County's Quarterly Courts, gave evidence in land cases, and helped inventory the estates of deceased neighbors. In 1676 he was part of a coroner's jury that considered the alarming death of Jacob Goodall, a slow-witted man allegedly beaten to death by Giles Corey. (The court decided that Corey was not the sole means of the man's demise but set him a heavy fine nonetheless. This essentially favorable ruling made some folk conclude that Corey had bought his way out of a murder charge and its accompanying noose. Goodall's death and the "thwarted" justice would continue to be a topic of gossip.) In 1677 Francis was named guardian of the orphaned teenager Samuel Southwick, whose grandparents, Lawrence and Cassandra Southwick, had been exiled from Massachusetts years earlier as convicted Quakers.

While all this went on, worsening relations between the settlers and the native peoples erupted in 1675 into the conflict known as King Philip's War. Both sides suffered great losses, but the Indians lost nearly everything, including self-rule.

Once that disaster subsided locally—for skirmishes continued to the Eastward on the Maine and New Hampshire frontier—Francis made a down payment on a three hundred–acre farm to Reverend James Allen on April 29, 1678. (Francis had evidently rented that land or another farm nearby because the coroner's jury he had served on was made up of men from the same neighborhood.) Allen lived in Boston and had acquired the farm through marriage to the widow Elizabeth Endicott, whose first husband, John Endicott, had inherited the farm from *his* father, Governor John Endicott. The governor had once owned the whole peninsula between the Crane and Cow House Rivers with his Orchard Farm to the east and Governor's Plain to the west, where Francis and Rebecca settled. Endicott heirs still owned most of Orchard Farm, but lawsuits flared disputing the widow's right to let the land pass out of the family when there were no Endicott heirs from her first marriage. However, Nurse was not part of that legal tussle, and the courts eventually recognized Allen's right to the land. (Though conflicting boundary surveys did lead to disputes between Francis and Zerubabel Endicott, who cut wood on the disputed land. Francis twice sued him for trespass and twice lost.)

The terms of purchase were somewhat unusual in that the full price of £400 was not due for twenty-one years (and both Francis and Rebecca were already in their late fifties). Within that time Nurse would pay rent of £7 a year for the first dozen years and £10 yearly thereafter. He would be credited for improvements made to the farm and reimbursed, if he did not complete the transaction, for any improvements over the value of £150. Best of all, any proportion of the principal paid before the twenty-one-year deadline would count as the purchase of an equal proportion of the land, so that if he could not pay the whole £400, he would not lose the entire farm.

The two small rivers that bordered the Endicott lands narrowed inland into creeks as they reached the Nurse property, forming a peninsula called Birchwood. To the north was the Conamabsqnooncant, which the settlers called Duck or Crane River. To the south flowed the Soewamapenessett, called the Cow-House or Endicott River (Endicott's cow barn was near its shore), and it bordered William Towne's former farm. The road from Salem to Ipswich crossed these two salty streams near the Nurse property by Rum Bridge (at Philips's tavern) to the south and Hadlock's Bridge (named for the neighboring farmer) to the north.

Francis built a house here on a gentle rise above the fields and meadows. It probably had one room downstairs and one room above and faced south, with its back to the winter winds. (Another house stands there now, with some of its timbers recycled from an older building.)

In 1680 Elizabeth Morse of Newbury, an elderly woman formerly beset by poltergeists, was convicted of witchcraft, but because the branches of government could not agree on the degree of her guilt, she was spared from hanging and returned home to a form of house arrest instead.

Rebecca's mother, Joanna, died in 1682 after ten years of widowhood, and the Towne estate was divided among her children: land to the three sons, household goods to the three daughters. "Francis Nurs with the consent of Rebeka" made his mark on the agreement. Her two sisters made their own marks: "Mary Esty, formerly Mary Towne" and "Sarah Bridges." (This youngest sister would soon be widowed and marry a second time to Peter Cloyce.)

Shortly after this time Francis may have faced some manner of financial pinch, for he mortgaged the farm back to Reverend Allen in 1684, a situation apparently soon remedied. Not so quickly resolved, however, was the loss of the Massachusetts Charter that year. England revoked all charters in its realm, then restored them as each colony, business, and any other organization proved its loyalty to the crown. Massachusetts, however, resisted, so England combined all the colonies from Maine to West Jersey into one province, and in 1686 sent the royally appointed Governor Sir Edmund Andros to rule with the help of a regiment of redcoats.

In 1688 Goodwife Glover of Boston was hanged as a witch (under Andros's government). When news arrived the next spring that the Glorious Revolution in England had overthrown King James II and placed William and Mary on the throne, Boston rebelled, jailed Andros, and shipped him back to England. Unfortunately, his absence encouraged more frontier attacks from French and Indian forces.

Then, in the fall of 1689, someone's pigs dug up Rebecca's garden. This exasperated her enough that she, with her youngest son, marched over to Benjamin Holton's house and exchanged heated words about wandering swine and the damage they caused. Holton fell ill and died not long afterward, a circumstance that would later cause considerable trouble.

At the beginning of 1690 the aging Francis divided some of his fields into long, narrow strips of and conveyed them to his son Samuel

Nurse and to his sons-in-law Thomas Preston and John Tarbell, adding to the land he had already given them. The youngest son, Benjamin, and his wife were living at the homestead and working his father's farm. Then, in June 1691, Benjamin was called to militia duty Eastward (Maine and New Hampshire). Rather than risk his son's life, or lose his labor, Francis hired a neighbor to take his place, an arrangement that was legal at the time. John Hadlock had served his own term six months earlier but accepted the job in return for the military pay plus two shillings six pence a week from the Nurse family and the loan of a gun. Hadlock returned on leave the following December to collect twenty shillings from Francis, who had arranged payment through his friends Jonathan Walcott and Daniel Andrews.

Thus began 1692 for the Nurse family.

Benjamin was safe at home with his wife and their new baby. Rebecca was by now rather hard of hearing and not feeling her best. Nonetheless, she had her faith and her family around her, and what could be better than that?

Bridget Bishop

Bridget stands in the marketplace, glaring over the gag that muffles her mouth as she watches the people watching her.

Arms folded before her, she stares down the gawkers, those who gaze directly and smirk to see her there, the brats who shout insults, the adults who look shocked to read the caption pinned on the front of her cap, those who whisper to each other and glance away as if fearful of her glance.

With his black staff of office to show he is on duty, a constable stands by her to make sure that she does not leave before her time is up and that onlookers remain orderly. Now and then he gossips with his friends among the passersby, making nervous jests to keep his confidence, edgy about having to remain so close to such as she, as some folk think of her as more than merely a scold. Thus the constable is tethered here as well by her sentence and for the same amount of allotted time. This gives Bridget a modest amount of satisfaction.

She thinks she sees her daughter in the crowd, keeping to the edges and looking fearful. Her child's concern touches her, but she shouldn't have to see her mother mortified like this. Bridget catches the child's eye and shakes her head, motioning the girl to leave, to go home, which she does, with regret and relief competing in her face.

Bridget has been found guilty of fighting with her husband, of shouting terrible insults at him.

And so she had.

And so had he—*fought and insulted her in front of their little girl, and not for the first time. The county court had found him guilty as well, but he was not here to be stared at and made a mockery. No, he was one of the onlookers. His older daughter—Bridget's stepdaughter—had paid her father's fine to spare him this hour of humiliation.*

No one offered to spare Bridget.

Well, he *is* an old rogue and as bad as a devil to be married to, *she thinks as the interminable minutes unfold. The facts, damning as they might be, are no less true because Bridget shouted them in the presence of others. If she regrets anything, it is getting into* this *situation, having to endure the court's public punishment.*

Standing there, she is certain of one thing: fighting back she does not regret, nor landing a clout on his scowling face that resulted in such a satisfying smack!

B ridget's earliest record concerns her marriage to Samuel Wasselbe on April 13, 1660, at St. Mary-in-the-Marsh in Norwich, Norfolk County, England. Just what Goodman Wasselbe did and to whom he may have been related is another unanswered question. (The variously spelled Aslebee family of Andover would have two of their number accused of witchcraft in 1692—Rebecca (Aslebee) Johnson and Sarah (Aslebee) Cole—but presently there is no definite connection known between the families.) Samuel and *BRIDGET*'s son Benjamin was baptized in the same church on October 6, 1663. As this is the only record, presumably Benjamin died young.

Sometime between spring of the next year and the following winter Samuel himself died. Their daughter Mary was born in Boston, Massachusetts Bay, on January 10, 1665. The record there calls her a daughter of "Samuel dec[eased] & Bridget Wasselbee late of Norwich in England." Mary is not mentioned again and, like her brother, apparently died in infancy.

Had Samuel lived to set sail for New England?

If so, he could have died on shipboard or shortly after landfall. He certainly died before the birth of their daughter in Boston. Either way Bridget had endured the discomforts of pregnancy on top of the miseries of a long sea voyage. Crossings could take anywhere from six weeks (if the winds were favorable) to several months, with passengers crowded together on a lower deck or into the few tiny cabins, lurching with the roll of the vessel, dependent on slop buckets for latrines, risking disease from such close quarters or scurvy from inadequate diet, and hoping not to encounter either pirates or tempests that could send them to the bottom of the sea with no one ashore to know their fate.

(Later the bewitched girls would accuse Bridget of murdering her first husband, Goodman Wasselbe. What spiteful gossip had they absorbed?)

The following year widow Bridget Wasselbe was in Salem, where she married widower Thomas Oliver on July 26, 1666. He too was from Norwich, where he had been a calendar, someone who put a smooth finish on cloth, and had even returned there from New England for a time (without his first wife, who remained in Salem, refusing to join him). Thomas had three grown children by his late wife, Mary: two sons in their thirties and a daughter, also named Mary, now married to Job Hilliard. (His first wife had been a turbulent woman, a Sabbath breaker who was also given to showering insults and threats of bodily harm onto those who crossed her. She not only called New Englanders "theeves and Robbers" and uttered "divers mutinous speeches" before Captain William Hathorne but also "said the Governor was unjust, corrupt and a wretch" for fining her on insufficient evidence for stealing two goats.)

With Thomas, Bridget had a third child on May 8, 1667, Christian Oliver, and this daughter lived.

The marriage, however, was neither happy nor even compatible. Thomas had enough of a temper that he once openly defied a constable. (In 1669 he did, however, accept the official task of going "from house to house about the town once a month to inquire what strangers do come or have privily thrust themselves into the town." The town's poor fund could accommodate only so many, and not many at that, and Quakers were a constant headache.)

By January 1670 the couple's quarrels involved the neighbors and even the county court. Several times one or the other of the Olivers had called for their neighbor Mary Ropes to come witness the other's bad behavior. On these occasions Goodwife Ropes saw, as she testified, Bridget's "face at one time bloody and at other times black and blue."

But Bridget did not take such punishment meekly. Thomas also complained to Goody Ropes "that his wife had given him several blows." The county court ordered the contentious couple be whipped ten stripes apiece or pay a fine within a month. Presumably they paid the fine. (The same Quarterly Court heard several cases of Salem, Beverly, and Marblehead men living apart from their wives, some of whom had evidently not emigrated yet. Bridget may have preferred such a situation.)

However, the fines made no permanent improvement in the Olivers' relationship. In 1677 her husband so exasperated Bridget that she was heard even on the Sabbath calling him "many opprobrious names." Where shocked neighbors could hear she shouted, "Old rogue!" and "Old devil!" In those days, when a good name counted for everything, a person's reputation was taken seriously. What Thomas might have said or done on his part to make Bridget erupt or what the four neighbors summoned as witnesses might have said was not recorded when the matter reached court. However, they were *both* sentenced to stand for an hour "back to back, on a lecture day in the public market place," each gagged and each wearing a paper about their foreheads clearly inscribed with their offense.

LECTURES were optional sermons that local ministers delivered in rotation at the various area meetinghouses on Thursday afternoons, a custom evolved from the lectures given in England by clergy who were forbidden to preach by Church of England authorities. In New England these lectures became something of a social occasion (that occasionally interfered with work), in which eager listeners traveled to sample preaching styles. Salem could anticipate a crowd on such days, and anyone made to stand in public as punishment could expect a sizeable audience to pity or jeer them. Thomas's daughter Mary (now married to her second husband, William West) paid a twenty shilling fine to release her father from the impending humiliation. The stepdaughter, however, did not offer to spare her stepmother. Bridget had to stand at the crossroads by the meetinghouse and the town pump under the gaze of passersby, with the label pinned to her cap, stewing and steaming behind the cloth gag.

Name calling was taken seriously, but sentences varied. The same court that sentenced the Olivers also heard the case of Thomas Cooper, who had called Charles Phillips's wife "a blare eyed witch" and threatened to beat out Phillips's eyes. This case, however, was dismissed. Thomas Cooper likewise had called Samuel Eborne Sr. an "old rogue and old knave" and had threatened to "cuff his chops." The court only admonished Cooper "to order his tongue and carriage more regularly for time to come." And Richard Holman was fined for making "opprobrious speeches against Elizabeth Hooper" before several witnesses, "calling her base old baud and spiteful old witch."

Despite the similarity of "opprobrious speeches" with Bridget's outburst and the potentially fatal accusation of witchcraft, none of these men were subjected to public humiliation—only Bridget. She had insulted her husband, after all, whereas two thirds of the other cases had affronted only women.

Some people were already wondering if such a turbulent woman as Bridget might be a witch as well.

Samuel Gray had nightmares about her specter appearing in his room at night around the time his baby daughter sickened and died. Likewise, William Stacey, ill from small pox, was surprised by the concern Goody Oliver showed when she visited and "professed a great love for this deponent," as he later phrased it. Once he was well again, she paid him three pence for some work he did for her, but the money vanished from his pocket almost immediately. Not long after, when he encountered Bridget on her way to his father's mill, she asked if he thought his father would grind her grist, "Because," she had to explain, "folks counted her as a witch." He replied that his father would do the job, but the conversation caused him to wonder—especially when his wagon's off wheel suddenly slumped into a hole and stuck. Another man helped him dislodge it, but later he never could find the hole—as if it had simply disappeared. One midnight that same winter Stacey felt a pressure on his mouth and woke to see the form of Bridget sitting at the foot of his bed and the room as bright as if it were day. The specter then hopped about the room and vanished, leaving him in darkness. William did not keep the incident to himself, so the real Bridget confronted him, demanding to know if he had been telling such fanciful tales about her. He admitted to telling several people about the encounter and dared her to deny that it had indeed happened. Furious, she stalked away without replying; William took her silence as an admission of guilt.

By the summer of 1679 Bridget's life had improved—to the extent that her belligerent spouse Thomas died. He left no will, so the court granted the widow administration of the estate and allowed her use of the house during her lifetime, not just during her widowhood, as was more common. She was, however, responsible for paying his outstanding debts: £30 owed to parties back in England (as Thomas had admitted on his deathbed),plus sums due locally to the town, to Dr. Swinnerton, who had attended his last illness, and for his burial. There were also bequests owed to Thomas's children: twenty shillings each to the two sons of the first wife (no mention of daughter Mary) and twenty shillings to daughter Christian. The inventory, taken the summer before, included the house and its half-acre lot (big enough to include apple trees, a chicken run, and a pig sty) plus ten acres across the river in Northfield. The personal goods were sparse enough: Thomas's clothes, a rusty sword, and old bandoleers; a small bed with its bedding; one table and "three or four old chairs"; an iron pot and kettle, brass skillet, earthenware dishes, a few pails, tubs, odds and ends; and two pigs. The whole was estimated to be worth £76:8:0. Debts and bequests amounted to at least £39:0:11—a penny shy of £40.

In November 1679 the same court session that fined Goody Dicer for calling Mrs. Hollingworth a "witch and a thief" granted Bridget administration of her late husband's estate. But by February 1680 Bridget herself was arrested for witchcraft. Once again she had to stand before the county court and listen to the accusations, this time as John Ingersoll's slave Juan blamed her for spooking a team of horses out by Norman's Rocks and for making them run, sledge and all, into the swamp by Fish Creek. Then Juan told how he saw her specter, perched on a beam and holding a stolen egg, in his master's cow house. The apparition vanished when he tried to strike it with a pitchfork, he declared, but "it was the shape of Goody Oliver, as she now stands before the court." (Later at dinner he saw a spectral black cat and felt several painful pinches in his side.)

Other men, who had seen the panicked horses run into the swamp, commented that the animals seemed bewitched, but only Juan's testimony remains. The court ordered Bridget to be presented to the next Court of Assistants at Boston—the upper house of the legislature that tried capital cases. Meanwhile, she was to be jailed or to pay a bond as promise to appear. Bridget paid the bond, thus adding to her heavy debts. There is no further record of the case, suggesting that Bridget was not tried on the given evidence.

Nevertheless, Samuel and Sarah Shattuck thought she was a witch, especially after their son began to suffer seizures and act in a distressingly distracted manner in 1680. Bridget had brought some articles to Shattuck's dye works and paid him two pence for the work. Samuel passed the money to his assistant Henry Williams to put away, but soon afterward the coins were nowhere to be found. Henry *insisted* he had put the coins in a purse with other money and had locked it all in a box—only to have both purse and money vanish from the box "he could not tell how." They never did find it, and Samuel, rather than suspect Henry of theft, concluded that magic was behind the disappearance.

Hearing gossip that the Shattucks suspected she had a hand in the vanishing money, Bridget confronted Goodwife Shattuck in order to clear her already-tarnished name. She said Henry Williams should be beaten, but Sarah Shattuck preferred to believe her husband's assistant. Bridget left, muttering in a manner that Sarah thought sounded threatening.

Soon after, their son Samuel Jr., as normal as other children, was "taken in a terrible fit: his mouth and eyes were drawn aside and [he] gasped in such a manner as if he was upon the point of death." As the fits continued with crying jags, young Sam's "understanding decayed" and he became "stupefied and void of reason." After a year and a half of this terrifying ordeal, with the boy no better, a "stranger" advised Shattuck (as he later described it) that the boy must be bewitched. The stranger offered a way to break the spell: folklore suggested that scratching a witch "below the breath" and drawing blood would neutralize whatever spell was being cast.

Consequently, the stranger barged into Bridget's home, asking for a pot of cider as if she ran a tavern, in order to confront her. She replied curtly that he would have none there and snatched up a spade to make him leave. Following him outside and spying young Sam, she assumed that Shattuck had sent the two of them to plague her. Bridget smacked the boy's face, which bled. That she had drawn blood—instead of being bloodied herself—seemed all the more ominous to the Shattucks, especially as Sam's fits worsened. Now, if he were not lying as if dead, their son was rushing about and liable to fall into fire or water—a constant worry for his parents.

Nevertheless, schoolmaster Daniel Epps helped Bridget financially. In the summer of 1681 she sold him "two poles, or rods, more or less" of land between their houses in exchange for a sturdy fence, ten shillings in money, and other "considerable expense and cost, which Epps hath been at for said Oliver's use, amounting in all to five and thirty shillings which added to the former makes up the full and just sum of three pounds, ten shillings." Bridget consented to the arrangement and made her mark on the deed in the presence of Magistrate John Hathorne "in order to the further payment of debts which the estate of Thomas Oliver is liable to pay, and also for the present supply of my own necessities." She had already sold the Northfields lot the year before.

As time passed, more people suspected her of theft and witchcraft. Around 1682 Goody Whatford accused Bridget of stealing a spoon and felt threatened by Bridget's forceful reply. Goody Whatford then became unbalanced, "a vexation to her self, and all about her." She also thought the specters of Bridget Bishop and another woman named Alice Parker attacked her at night. (Might Bridget and Alice have been acquaintances or friends? They would both share a reputation for witchcraft. By 1685 the Shattucks suspected Goodwife Parker of worsening young Sam's fits.)

Bridget married for a third time around 1685 to Edward Bishop, a sawyer. Bridget still had lifetime rights to Thomas Oliver's property, and the couple appear to have demolished the old house and built a new one on the Oliver lot. They evidently hired John Bly and his son to remove the old structure. Although the workmen said nothing to her at the time, they may have regarded Bridget uneasily, for they found poppets enclosed within one of the cellar walls (as they would later relate), and everyone knew witches used such images to cast diabolical spells on their victims. (The poppets, if real, had more likely been built into the house when it was new, and Oliver had owned the place before Bridget immigrated to Massachusetts.) Perhaps the Blys gossiped about their find, for around this time several more local men had nightmares about Bridget creeping up on them in the night.

One of these was John Louder, the hired man at the Gedney family's Ship Tavern, which abutted Bridget's property. The Gedneys had already argued about Bridget's fowls getting into the Ship Tavern's orchard, and after the night apparition, John and Mistress Susanna Gedney spoke to Bridget about it over the back fence. This failed to improve Bridget's temper. John found her response menacing, followed (as he later testified) by daylight encounters with imps.

In May 1686 Bridget's daughter Christian married Thomas Mason, a mariner.

Bridget's own marriage to Bishop, meanwhile, although more peaceful than her marriage to Oliver, was not without problems. Edward sold a sow to John Bly (the man who had found poppets in the Oliver cellar) and had Bly pay the asking price to a third party to whom Edward owed money. Such involved transactions were not uncommon, but Bridget considered the pig and, therefore, the money, to be hers, even though husbands controlled their wives' property. She went to Bly's house and quarreled with him and his wife, but she could not correct the debt. Soon afterward the sow gave birth but refused to suckle her young or even eat, instead jumping and lurching about as if deaf and blind, foaming at the mouth. A neighbor advised a folk remedy, which eventually seemed to work but only after a frantic two hours, during which the sow bolted up and down the street between the Blys' and the Bishops' houses "as if she were stark mad."

Bridget's grandchild Susanna Mason was born on August 23, 1687, the same month that brought yet more trouble.

According to Bridget, she and her daughter were weeding her garden "by the northwest corner of her house" when Christian noticed a brass object on the ground. Not knowing what it was, Bridget asked her daughter to show it to pewterer Edmund Dolbier "when she went into town about any business." Two or three weeks later Christian did so, leaving it at Dolbier's shop to be evaluated. According to Dolbier, when he asked where she got it, Christian replied "that the said brass had lain about the house some years before her father died." Dolbier recognized the item as a "mill brass," a bearing in a mill's mechanism. Thomas Stacey (William Stacey's father), who operated the mill on the South River at the edge of Fish Flake Point, had told Edmund in July that one had gone missing and to keep an eye out for anyone trying to sell such an item for scrap. As agreed, Dolbier informed Stacey, who came to the shop, declared that the brass was indeed his, and took it back.

On December 14, 1687, Christian Mason was presented by the grand jury on "suspicion of taking away a piece of brass out of Salem Mill about five months since." Clerk of the Court Stephen Sewall issued summons for Dolbier and Stacey to appear the following day as witnesses.

According to Stacey, after fetching the brass from Dolbier, he went immediately to Edward Bishop's house to confront Bridget, "Whereupon," Thomas later testified, "the said Bridget Bishop kneeled down on her knees and asked him forgiveness and said she was sorry that she had taken the brass and that she would do so no more." In addition to this impromptu confession (according to Stacey), Bridget repeated her apology some while after this encounter at his mill. Once again she fell to her knees and begged forgiveness. (Perhaps, thinking she was a witch as well as a thief, he thought that this unlikely tale of Bridget's ostentatious remorse would encourage the court to be easy on her, thereby persuading her not to take spectral revenge on him.)

Yet Sewall issued a warrant for the sheriff or a deputy to "forthwith seize the person of Bridget the wife of Edward Bishop" and bring her to court "for feloniously taking away a piece of brass sometime last summer from Thomas Stacey."

Then later, on March 6, 1688, Deputy Jeremiah Neal brought Bridget before Justice John Hathorne at the next county court. There Stacey again charged Bridget with the theft. Thomas said she "twice acknowledged herself guilty," sticking to the story he had given in evidence back in December.

When the court questioned Bridget, however, she made it conspicuously clear that Stacey had *not* come to her house after fetching the brass from Dolbier. Furthermore, according to Bridget, Stacey had spoken to her about the matter only *once* at the mill, and she had certainly not admitted to *any* theft then or later—to him or to anyone else. She did not recognize the thing and did *not* know where it came from. Finally, she had *not* tried to sell the brass—she only wanted Dolbier to identify it.

Despite her assertions, the court ordered that she be committed to Salem jail until her trial at the next Session of the Peace in Ipswich. Fortunately, Edward Bishop and William Reeves posted £20 surety before Judge Hathorne so that Bridget could avoid jail—for the time being. Unfortunately, the record falls silent at this point. Presumably, for lack of convincing evidence, her case was dismissed.

This victory, such as it was, neither calmed nor cowed Bridget. She told Stacey that it was *his* doing that she had been arrested. He had already done her "more mischief than any other body," because "folks would believe him before anybody else." William found these recriminations most threatening and knew who to suspect when, one dark night en route to his barn, he found himself tossed bodily against a stone wall and down a bank. And when he passed Goody Bishop on the road by the brick kiln, his horse's tackle "flew in pieces and the cart fell down." More seriously, he suspected Bridget's malice after his

healthy baby daughter Priscilla died unexpectedly in 1690 after two
weeks of agonized crying.

So seldom is the appearance of *anyone* of the times described that
even a scrap of detail helps bring the character to greater life. With
Bridget, two witnesses mentioned articles of clothing worn by her alleged specter, items that prompted the supposed victims to identify
the apparition as hers. (Most people's wardrobes were seldom extensive.) Because two of the specified items were red, many assume that
Bridget was a flashy brazen character—or at least that the authorities
disapproved of her attire. Richard Coman had the waking dream of
seeing Bridget "in her red paragon bodice and the rest of her clothing
that she then usually did wear," whereas William Stacey would testify
that her specter wore "a black cap and a black hat and a red coat with
two eakes of two colors."

A woman's coat was a petticoat (a skirt) that could be worn in multiple layers for warmth. An eake is an addition. Bridget may have
added either decorative embellishments or just patches of whatever
she had available to mend an old garment that was growing older. A
bodice (from the word body) was an upper garment of a woman's
dress, generally boned or otherwise stiffened. Paragon was a heavy
wool or a wool mixed with either silk or linen, sometimes printed or
watered, used for clothing or furnishings. It was made in varying qual-
ities and was not necessarily expensive or, as people may have viewed
Bridget's attire, extravagant.

Red was actually a favorite color but was fairly expensive if the dye
could stand up to light and occasional washing without fading to rust.
Black dye—a soberly fashionable color—was also expensive and subject to fading unless it was of good quality.

Despite the stereotypes later generations would foist on their memory, Puritans did not confine themselves to black and gray; earth tones
were the most commonly available dyes. But inventories that specify
color contain such surprises as the occasional violet, orange, sky- or
lion-colored garments, for men as well as women.

Bridget was not necessarily flashy, but she was not a shy character
either. Although the courts had twice decided that Bridget was neither
a thief nor a witch, gossip and suspicion continued to dog her. Such

irritating rumors, she was all too well aware, could, under the wrong circumstances, prove deadly indeed.

Mary English

Mary sits by the light of a second-story window in a seaport town as she stitches. From outside she hears the cries of gulls, the thump and rattle of cargo being unloaded from ships, and the shouts and curses of sea-faring men. She holds a narrow linen strip nearly two feet long to the daylight and counts off the fine threads with the tip of her needle, then she draws a line of bright silk through this backing until it lies smooth and straight, making a tiny, perfect X.

She is fifteen and has been working on her sampler off and on for months. She has practiced and practiced again, pulled apart and done over the stitches she is learning until hand and eye and intention begin to work in concert and she can concentrate on the intricate interlaced designs—stylized flowers and fruit.

Once done, this strip that shows her skill will be a dictionary of stitches that skilled housewives need to know for making and mending the family's clothes and for marking the linens before entrusting such valuable items to a laundress.

When I'm grown and mistress of my own household, *she thinks . . . but she pauses and sighs.*

The breeze through the window is as damp and salty as tears. Just this spring Aunt Starr has died, leaving a family bereft and all her housewifely preparations cut short. Sorrow and death intrude unexpectedly even with the godly, even with the loved.

Mary sighs again and then turns to the work at hand.

Nearly done at last, she admires the rows of stylized strawberries and acorns, pansies and tulips, roses and honeysuckle. Across a ground of fine linen (grown in New England fields) twine flowery bands worked in lustrous blue, pink, and green silks from China.

China!

So far away, *she thinks, where silken strands are gathered from worms as skilled as spiders, passed from hand to hand by traders and then brought to Salem in ships like her father's.*

She checks the straightness of the stitches with a critical eye, while outside quarreling gulls squawk and swoop over the roof. Men's voices also approach, arguing in a lower tone. Running stitch, cross-stitch, Algerian eye, back stitch and double running, seeding and buttonhole, Spanish stitch, and long-armed cross.

She has worked the alphabet in ordinary cross-stitch and prepares to add her own name at the lower right, but the letters take up too much room to allow all of it on one line:

MARY HOLLINGWOR
TH

She secures and cuts the thread.

There . . . done at last.

The voices come closer, grow louder, and she recognizes the handyman's with another gruff and resentful voice right outside the gate. Then she hears her mother's voice, sharp and commanding, interrupt them. Father is away at sea, but he left Mother in charge at home. The arguing stops, and she hears the hired man mumble something subdued. Mary peers from the window in time to see the other man slouch off, grumbling toward the harbor. So that is over. Mother can always speak up when necessary, no matter what other folk might say.

Mary holds the sampler at length. So practical an item and how beautiful—she allows herself a rush of pardonable pride and then runs downstairs to show it to her mother.

Mary was approximately fifteen when she worked her sampler, which is real and still survives, nearly four centuries later—one of the few extant artifacts from the hands of one of the accused. The particularly rich stock of family lore her descendants repeated (some of it more fanciful than factual) claimed that *MARY* learned the needlework in Boston at the school of a Madame

Piedmont, so she may have stitched it in that city instead of at home in Salem. Certainly such institutions of female accomplishment were available for Mary's daughters at the end of the century. Generally students boarded with the schoolmistress or elsewhere; Mary had relatives in Boston with whom she might have lived, such as her father's half-brother William Hunter. The stories agree that she received a better education than did most girls of her time. She could certainly write—descendants preserved a scrap of her poetry—and her mother possessed a dictionary when few such volumes were published even in Europe.

At age seven, her father, William, had come to Salem in 1635 in the ship *Blessing* with his parents Richard and Susan Hollingworth, three Hollingworth siblings, and six Hunter half-brothers and-sisters from his mother's first marriage. (These included eleven-year-old William Hunter, for although sharing the same given name for half-siblings was not common, it was not unknown, especially if the name were important to both sides of the blended family.) His surname was variously spelled Hollingsworth, Hollinsworth, Hollingworth (as Mary stitched on her sampler), and Hollingwood, and it may have referred to a holly tree—or perhaps not, as the name was sometimes written as Holland.

The family settled on the Neck, a peninsula at the end of Salem's larger peninsula, at Point of Rocks. Salem Neck, with its narrow, easily fenced entrance, was mostly common land, reserved by the town as a Sunday pasture for local cattle. Granted, cattle had to graze, but the herdsman need not spoil his Sabbath driving them to more distant fields on a day when Scripture dictated that only the most necessary labor should be done. The Hollingworth shipyard stood near their home inside the Neck gate.

Attached by a narrow causeway to the southeast side of the Neck between Winter Harbor and Cat Cove lay Winter Island, also mostly common land. Fishermen rented space here from the town for their storehouses and stages, the wooden racks for drying and curing fish. Townsmen also built a fort at the tip to guard Salem Harbor from possible attack from French or Dutch warships and to serve as a

setting-out point for their own vessels sent against Canadian priva-
teers or "Turkish pirates."

The patriarch Richard prospered as a shipbuilder and property
owner despite occasional problems with the law, as when he traveled
unnecessarily on a Sabbath (and earned a spell in the stocks) or proved
prone to "much sleeping" during religious services (for which he was
admonished). His sons Richard Jr. and William also followed the maritime profession, trading from port to port in their own ships.

Sometime before 1661 William married a woman named Eleanor
and acquired a house on the shore in the neighborhood just outside
the Neck gate (likely a wedding present from his father). Eleanor's
family, whose last name may or may not have been Storey, remembered her as being unusually well educated and possessing a mind of
her own. The couple's eldest child, Mary, was born in the new house
or at Point of Rocks, depending on the account, around 1650 or 1651.
(Mary gave her age as thirty-nine in 1692 and was supposed to be
forty-two in 1694.) William and Eleanor also had two more children:
William Jr., who, like his father, would be a mariner and merchant,
and Susanna, who died young.

According to one source, the house burned in 1663, and the
Hollingworths spent the next decade living nearby. During this time
a Narragansett Indian called John was tried and ordered to be
whipped ten stripes in 1669 "for striking Mr. Wm. Hollingworth's wife
dead" (meaning unconscious). The court then had John whipped another ten stripes for being drunk (and it fined the man who sold him
the liquor). This may have been the same John who, with another Indian named Nimrod, was fined later that year for "the attempt of a
rape of two women." They had barged into various remote households
when the husbands were absent and bullied the wives into serving
them food while making bawdy, threatening remarks and gestures.
Fortunately those women escaped.

By 1672 William, who still owned land, built a fine new home on
the site of the burnt one. This new edifice boasted two rooms per
floor, a large stone cellar, and facade gables—a sizeable house for the
time. A storehouse stood nearby, and a wharf projected into Salem

Harbor just across the public way that bounded the property on the water side.

By this time William had business dealings with one Philippe L'Anglois, a French-speaking merchant from the Isle of Jersey who had recently settled in Salem. His surname—variously spelled as Langlois, Langloys, L'Anglais, Lengloz, LeEnglays, and Lenglois—meant "the Englishman." He soon anglicized it to Philip English.

Family lore would spin a tale of a Huguenot Chevalier's disinherited son who defied his parents and ran away to sea at age twelve seeking his fortune, who fetched up in Massachusetts utterly penniless until Eleanor Hollingworth spied him trudging past her gate and, taking pity on the lad, offered him beer in a silver mug and invited him to stay.

In fact, however, English was on good terms with his Jersey kin, Jersey law prevented him from being disinherited, he was not a Huguenot refugee, and he had already established a network of trading contacts in France, Sweden, and Spain before taking advantage of New World opportunities—so much for family lore. He evidently *did* board with the Hollingworths between voyages and certainly conducted business with William as they traded with the West Indies and Europe in Maine lumber, Virginia tobacco, and fish from Winter Island.

Nevertheless, William did not prosper as much as he may have hoped.

In 1672 he conveyed a house used as rental property to his unmarried daughter Mary—or rather Eleanor did. Although she was officially acting on his behalf in this transaction, how much she decided on her own when he was away at sea is unclear. Perhaps the transfer was a means to protect income property; after all, for a short time later, on June 1, 1672, Eleanor again acted as attorney to mortgage their own home to Philip Cromwell (a Salem butcher wealthy enough to lend money on the side) for £250 "in money and goods."

But William's string of bad luck continued.

In 1674, due to his losses at sea, the Salem selectmen granted his wife a license to keep an ordinary (a tavern where a set meal was offered) in her mortgaged house. Eleanor called it the Blue Anchor, and, as she had a brew house in the yard, she made the beer she sold. Such licenses were renewable yearly on the condition that the business remain respectable and the premises be available "to provide for the accommodation of the courts and jurors, likewise all other matters of a public concern proper for them."

The following year, on September 1, Mary (still in possession of the rental property) married her father's colleague Philip English. He would be remembered as being "of middle stature and strong physically . . . high spirited: not ungenerous, impulsive withal, and at times choleric [i.e., with a temper] . . . kind to the poor, yet not over conciliatory to his peers."

Philip was one of the first in a wave of Jersey immigrants to New England. Despite his anglicized name, he, like the others, generally spoke French as his first language and kept his accounts in French as well. Many of the Jersey families who settled in Salem would cluster conspicuously in the neighborhood outside the Neck. Some people distrusted them because of their sudden numbers, their foreign language, and their habit of suing for debt at the drop of a hat.

Jersey folk were Protestant—not Catholic like most French—but they were Anglican rather than any of the Puritan denominations. Nevertheless, their neighbors wondered if they might collude with the Canadian French raiders. Jerseyans were also largely Royalist; in fact, Philip's own godfather and possible kinsman, Sir Philip De Carteret, had harbored the fugitive Charles II from the Puritan forces. New England's Royal Governor Andros, from Guernsey—another Channel Isle—encouraged Jersey emigration in order to counteract the Puritan settlers' influence. More specifically, Philip English brought over many Jersey immigrants, most of them as bondservants—the men mainly working as mariners, the women as domestics in Salem and Marblehead.

Although Jersey and the other Channel Isles lay only a few miles off the coast of France, they were (and still are) part of British territory. The islands were once ruled by the dukes of Normandy, including the one called William the Conqueror who successfully captured England for his own. As England absorbed its conquerors, the Isles retained their Norman flavor, developing their own laws based on Norman and French traditions.

Mary gave birth to her first child on February 21, 1677, a daughter also named Mary. In the same year both Philip and William set sail again. William headed for Virginia, and Philip embarked on a complicated trans-Atlantic route. First, he sailed from Salem to Jersey, then he put his ketch in at St. Malo, the nearest French port. There he signed a contract with the agent of Jersey investor, Sire Moise Coubel, promising a 30 percent profit and itemizing his intended route. English would sail his ketch from St. Malo to Boston (presumably with French goods); then, loaded with New England cargo, it would sail to Spain, the Bay of Biscay, Bordeaux, England, and then back to Jersey or St. Malo, wherever the investor wished to collect his profits. Philips's complicated trading was successful, and he returned to Salem only to find that no one knew the whereabouts of his father-in-law.

When William's homecoming was more and more overdue, Eleanor inquired at every vessel that arrived at Salem, but no one could say for sure what had happened. Rumors suggested the ship had been lost at sea, and by November Eleanor had to ask the local court for help. The magistrates granted her power of attorney (as she had been acting all along), put her husband's estate in her hands, and ordered her to "act in the improvement of it as if her husband were yet alive until more information be received or the court order otherwise."

Eleanor had not only daily expenses to cover but also her husband's debts—the mortgage and unpaid bills to mariners and suppliers. Nevertheless, as she later told the court, she paid "out of my own labor not diminishing his estate" and took out loans "which I was trusted for and am in debt for most of it still." Some of these creditors threatened to arrest her for the debt, including Hugh Woodbury, her husband's kinsman.

Finally, in November 1678, the court assumed William must have died and granted Eleanor administration of his estate. The inventory of her husband's possessions included the still-mortgaged house and land; beds and bedding; her kitchen implements; tables and chairs; "Seven Framed pictures"; and her husband's black suit. The amount of unpaid debts far outstripped the worth of William's estate. No one ever did learn what happened to her husband.

While widow Hollingworth wrestled with the debts, applied for tax abatements, continued to operate the Blue Anchor, be deposed occasionally in court about fist fights that occurred there, and provisioned outgoing ships with bread and beer, Mary gave birth to a son on May 23, 1679. She named him William, but like his lost grandfather, the boy did not live.

Later that same year Goodwife Elizabeth Dicer, a neighbor from two houses east, got into a public argument with Eleanor. What provoked Goody Dicer's outburst is not preserved, but neighbors heard her shout that Eleanor was "an old baud" and wished "that the plague might take her." Then she accused Eleanor of being not only "a black mouthed whore," but also a "black mouthed witch . . . and a thief, and all her children" (which included Mary English as well). Goody Dicer found herself in court for her "railing words," abuse, and curses. Whether said in anger or out of conviction, such an allegation was serious, as witchcraft was a capital crime. Witnesses evidently spoke *for* Eleanor, and the court fined Goody Dicer. (During this same session the court granted administration of Thomas Oliver's estate to his widow, Bridget.)

Matters improved in 1681. When ashore, Philip served on county juries, and Mary, having examined her soul, applied to the Salem Church for full membership and was accepted. She received the sacrament of the Lord's Supper one spring Sabbath around the time the church was considering the problems at its feuding satellite congregation in Salem Village. "After some agitation," the church record noted, "the church agreed" to having George Burroughs preach there. The disagreement in the village would escalate in unexpected directions, but for now Mary celebrated by composing an acrostic based on her own name, using the "Y" as an ampersand (&).

May I with Mary choose the better part,
And serve the Lord with all my heart,
Rescue his word most joyfully
Y live to him eternally.

*E*verliving God I pray,
*N*ever leave me for to stray.
*G*ive me grace thee to obey
*L*ord grant that I may happy be
*I*n Jesus Christ eternally.
*S*ave me dear Lord by thy rich grace
*H*eaven then shall be my dwelling place.

Philip attended with her and at this point did not object to the lack of Church of England services. He had even signed the 1680 petition to the selectmen desiring a new, larger meeting house for Salem (as did Francis Nurse and Mary's brother William Hollingworth, among others).

On March 4, 1682, Eleanor paid off the last of the £250 mortgage to Cromwell "in money and goods in hand," and the Blue Anchor was wholly her own. In July Mary gave birth to daughter Susanna (who died young), and in the following year Philip was appointed a constable at the yearly town meeting. One of his duties was to collect taxes (Eleanor Hollingworth's was three shillings). This caused problems when Philip and some of the other tax collectors neglected to collect from fellow Jerseymen away at sea even though their families resided in Salem. Some of the men, he said, had moved away. Part of the problem may have been based on the fact that a medieval charter had exempted Jersey "from all manner of Taxes, Imposts, and Customs in all Cities, Market-Towns, and Ports of England," which a second ancient charter extended "to all Places within the King's Dominion beyond the Seas." Some Jerseymen, like Thomas Baker of Ipswich, were openly scornful of local law. When served with a warrant in 1679, he refused it, "saying he did not care for all the laws in the country." When told that he would be brought before Major William Hathorne for his refusal, he scoffed that "he would not be tried by that white hat limping rogue."

The Salem selectmen sued for the delinquent taxes in 1684 and confiscated a plot of land from English in lieu of payment. He bought it back in 1685 when he also purchased William Dicer's house-lot when William and the contentious Elizabeth moved to Maine.

Philip's tendency to sue others for overdue debts had already ruffled a few feathers. This practice was common enough in Jersey, where the laws made it more necessary, but in Massachusetts even when a debtor thought he had made arrangements to pay, Philip would sue and often had the debtor arrested—even other Jersey folk. In addition, the year before the selectmen's lawsuit, he had purchased the house and land once belonging to Mary's uncle Captain Robert Starr on the lot northwest of the Blue Anchor. Philip removed the old building and began constructing the largest mansion in town. During a time when most families lived in one room and a garret and the larger homes had two rooms on each of two floors, English's Great House (as it would be called) must have been a topic of fascination and envy.

Philip ordered an L-shaped house, with each of its upper levels projecting over the one below. House wrights raised an oak frame, filled the exterior walls with brick between the timbers, and then covered them with clapboards on the outside and plaster on the inside. Even the cellars were completely finished, from the stone floors to the plastered ceilings. Masons built many hearths leading to the great central chimney stack and constructed more than one oven in the kitchen. The ground floor contained pantries and parlors, a counting-house (Philip's business office), and possibly a shop (though that may have been added later). This allowed space for several rooms above and even in the attic, which was fully finished and plastered as well. A stone wall separated the front yard from the road to the Neck.

Over a century later the house still had the largest rooms in all of Salem. By then some of the facade gables had been removed, and the place was a bit worn, though still sound. Descendants would recall that there had been some sort of balcony with seats built outside the southern chamber over the shop, a sundial below this over the shop door, and tall roof ornaments at the peaks.

In September 1684, while Philip was at odds with the selectmen, Mary gave birth to Philip Jr. Meanwhile debt collectors plagued her brother William, who was back in Salem after sojourns as far away as Spain. For instance, Thomas Mudget, a co-owner of a ship William had hired, claimed the latter was responsible for part of the crew's pay and provisions. William disagreed and had evaded those creditors in both Virginia and Bilbao, Spain.

Then Deputy Marshal Philip Fowler appeared at the Blue Anchor, ostensibly to sell malt to Eleanor but in fact bearing an arrest warrant for William. Witnesses saw Fowler chase William across the yard toward the brew house, but the pursued got over the fence first and grabbed an ax to ward off his pursuer. Eleanor followed, shouting at Fowler that she would "stave out his brains," as she clouted him four blows and then seized him from behind, keeping him from following William, who bolted into the house to hide. Fowler entered a complaint before Magistrate John Hathorne but had to admit he had not yet taken his oath as deputy. (Philip English and others present testified to this.) The March 1685 Quarterly Court believed Eleanor's claim that she had not known Fowler was a constable, but she still had to pay costs of £1:7:4.

Perhaps Eleanor feared that her son's creditors would try to attach her hard-earned property, on the grounds that William was the only Hollingworth son and, therefore, heir. She had already taken the precaution in February of conveying "for divers good causes and considerations" and "my natural love and affection unto my daughter Mary English" the ownership of her house, outer housing and land, with the wharf and landing place. Eleanor apparently continued running the tavern.

Family tradition recalled that Mary had a good business head and was left in charge of Philip's business during his absences at sea. Given the example of her mother, this was very likely true.

Descendants also recalled the marriage of Philip and Mary in glowing terms—he certainly trusted her business acumen—but other descendants told a darker tale. In 1851 Philip's great-great grandson Ebenezer Hathorne told his cousin, the writer Nathaniel Hawthorne (who had added a "w" to his surname to distinguish and distance himself from his ancestor, the witch-trial judge, John Hathorne), that "This Philip left some bastards; but only legitimate daughters, one of whom married, I believe, the son of the persecuting John [Hathorne]; and thus all the legitimate blood of English is in our family."

But family lore can be more often dubious than undeniable. Although it is certainly possible that Mary's husband sired illegitimate offspring, court records credit all of the known children to Mary, with the dates of their births consistent with her being the mother of them all. Philip Jr. inherited the Blue Anchor, implying Hollingsworth blood. The births of the two Williams correspond to the deaths of Mary's own father and brother (also named William). Granted, however, some men had sired children with servant women. For example, Samuel Braybrook in Ipswich was ordered to bring up his child by the maidservant, and this must have been a strain, one imagines, on his childless wife. The English household had many servants, mostly indentured women from Jersey, but no mention of irregularities with them reached the court records. Ebenezer's anecdote may well have been baseless, though unsupported family stories usually tend to praise the ancestors.

Brother William's fortunes declined along with his health until he died, only thirty-three years old, on November 7, 1688. Eleanor saw to it that he had a proper funeral—£7 worth of wine and beer, £3:7:0 for three and a half-dozen pairs of gloves (as the usual favors to mourners), and fifteen shillings for the coffin and grave on Burying Point. Eleanor itemized these expenses along with others, all of which she billed to her son's estate: £1:10:0 to the doctor, ten shillings to the nurse, and £2:4:0 for providing meals to his apprentice for two months and three weeks. Most of the outlay went toward the funeral, and the whole claim amounted to £21:15:00.

No land or houses or ships appeared in William's meager inventory —"One small sea bed" with bedding, "two half worn hammocks," some chests and trunks, tankards and earthenware, but also silver buckles, a rapier, his clothing, fifty pounds of loaf sugar, and four remaining years worth of service from his apprentice. All this amounted to only £34:02:04.

Mary gave birth to another son that winter and named him William. On behalf of his mother-in-law, Philip took her son's inventory to the March Quarterly Court sitting at Ipswich, but he refused to administer the estate—or tried to refuse. Thomas Mudget, still trying to collect the old debt, soon sued Philip as executor of William's estate.

By the end of the year the indomitable Eleanor, "Old Mistress Hollingworth" (as Constable Philip Fowler had called her) died on November 22, 1689, at age fifty nine.

Unlike her husband and son, Eleanor left no debts.

In fact, her estate amounted to a surprising £467:18:00, mostly obtained through her own labor and perseverance. She had already transferred the tavern and the rental house to Mary but still owned part of another house and part of a warehouse on Winter Island. Her inventory listed more than the usual cooking implements and bedding: a copper furnace and other brewing equipment; quantities of wine and cider; several leather upholstered chairs; six chairs covered in Turkey-work needlepoint; cupboards, chests, and tables; dozens of yards of a variety of textiles; her own woolen and linen clothing and two pairs of silk stockings; two hammocks (her son's presumably); a dictionary; a flock of sheep and four swine; plus various sums of cash—£138:00:06 and £16. She also owned "one Indian servant" worth £25. All of this presumably went to Mary—debt free.

Mary must have been the one who commissioned the double gravestone to mark the graves of her mother and brother. It was a thick slate placed near the edge of Burial Point above the hush and wash of the tides. Carved with an inscription for each, it was decorated with garlands, stars, and the silhouette of an ornate classical urn as well as the more usual winged death's head.

Earlier that year Massachusetts had overthrown Royal Governor Andros, the action being a New England counterpart to the Glorious Revolution that ousted the openly Catholic King James II from England. James fled to the protection of his cousin, the king of France, who had designs of his own on the English colonies. While offering refuge to James, he ordered his governor in Canada, Count Louis de Buade Frontenac, to attack the English settlements. Thus, bands of Abenaki allies and *couriers du bois* (Frenchmen who ranged the forests, lived among the native tribes, and adopted their ways of wilderness warfare) made bloody surprise attacks over the snow. They struck

Schenectady, New York, in February 1690, killing about sixty colonists and kidnapping thirty, and then they hit Salmon Falls, New Hampshire, in March, this time killing thirty and marching more than fifty hostages off to Canada.

These sudden attacks spawned rumors of a Jersey plot to help Canadian French and local "negro and Indian servants" (i.e., slaves) to attack Massachusetts. (What Mrs. Hollingworth's "Indian servant" thought of this development is not recorded.) Jerseyman Isaac Morrell, the supposed ringleader, stood trial for treason, but fortunately for him, that rumor proved false. (The Huguenots of Frenchtown, Rhode Island, were not so lucky; their settlement was burned under suspicious circumstances in 1689 even *before* the frontier raids.)

It had been a disastrous year all around, though at least Massachusetts reacted by capturing Port Royal in Acadia (Nova Scotia) in April 1690. But a combined force of New Englanders and New Yorkers fell afoul of weather and smallpox when they were en route to attacking Quebec that fall. They succeeded only in ransoming a few captives from earlier raids, earning the contempt of the French, and losing many of their vessels in a storm on the return voyage. On the personal front, Mary's cousin Christian Trask of Beverly, after certain neighbors drove her to distraction, committed suicide by cutting her windpipe and jugular with a small, short-bladed pair of scissors.

Frontier attacks continued.

By December 1691 Massachusetts's General Court prohibited *any* French from living in the frontier towns or in the seaports—an order greatly resented and generally ignored. This, however, did not prevent Philip English from becoming a selectman in Salem in 1692.

Despite the constant threat of frontier attack and local resentment against the French, Philip and Mary English greeted the new year as secure and as well provided for as anyone could expect to be, and in fact, they were better than most—for the time being.

Ann Putnam Sr.

Ann jolts awake again—the baby is crying, a weak mewling that nevertheless slices into her sleep. She elbows herself up against the pillow and reaches down to the cradle beside the bed.

"Hush now, hush," she whispers.

Her husband does not wake but does stir slightly; the children in the trundle bed remain still. She drags a shawl around her shoulders, swings her legs out of the warm bedcovers, and picks up the child.

The mewling continues.

"Oh Sarah, will you never stop crying?" she murmurs over the tiny fretful head. Ann is so tired. Giving birth to this child did not ease her weariness, and six weeks of wakeful nights since then has drained her. Slipping her feet into cold shoes, Ann jounces the baby in her arms and stands in the drafty room so as not to jar the bed as well. But Sarah is not comforted.

Sighing, the mother pads to the door and makes her way to the other room, where the fire is banked low on the hearth but still giving off some half-hearted heat. The hired girl stirs in her pallet on the floor and grunts a groggy query but does not really rouse to offer help. She was of little use anyway.

"Stay there," says Ann to the hired girl, sitting in the great chair at hearthside. She opens her shift just enough in the chill December air to offer the child her breast, but Sarah nuzzles only briefly and then turns away, still making that thin constant fussing her mother feels powerless to stop and fills her with inarticulate exasperation. She knows that this is no fit emotion for a Christian woman, that it is an affront to God to resent this innocent child.

"Sarah, for pity's sake," she says, still rocking the infant in her arms and noting that Sarah's clouts are not soiled. So that is not the problem. She had already tried home remedies. Maybe tomorrow Tom would fetch a different doctor. She holds the child close in her aching arms and feels how warm the baby is—too warm. A fever now as well? So small and

so fragile a bundle and so demanding! *A child should not be coddled— her mother certainly never had coddled her—but they* must *be protected.*

The whining trails off, less frequent now, and Ann begins to doze, nearly quiet, at last nearly asleep. Would returning the infant to her cradle only wake her again? The mother slumps against the chair back, waiting until the child is truly, thankfully, still. Abruptly, the little body twists in her arms, slipping from her grasp, slipping away as if being pulled from her.

Ann is fully awake now, chilled from a drench of fear deeper than the winter cold pervading the house. Sarah jerks and arches, her crying now a weak, gasping wail. Ann grips the baby, desperate not to drop her, but Sarah bucks and writhes as if trying to escape from her mother, as if trying to evade something her mother cannot see.

Not again!

Even the hired girl rouses, looking aghast at the two of them. Sarah works her arms free of the blanket and flails them, fighting off . . .what?

"Sarah, no!" Ann cries, then calls, "Thomas!"

The baby twists like a snake and is as difficult to hold. But Ann does not drop her. She clings to the moving child and tries to hold her close. The spasms lessen, though they still ripple through the little body head to foot.

Thomas throws open the door from the other room. Holding a walking stick like a weapon as if expecting housebreakers, he stands there barefoot in his nightshirt.

Sarah quivers a few more times and then makes an odd little cry and stills at last. Thank goodness, *Ann thinks, cautiously resting the child in her lap to see her better. Sarah wears a look of surprise but makes no sound. Ann hears a sudden piercing scream like a distant fox in the night. She dimly recognizes it is her own voice at the same instant she realizes that Sarah is dead—another blessing snatched away.*

Born in Salisbury on June 15, 1661, the year before the marriage of her eldest sibling, *ANN* was the youngest of George and Elizabeth Carr's ten children. She grew up on Carr's Island near the mouth of the Merrimack River, named by the Algonquians for the great sturgeon that swam in abundance up its salty tides (a fish the settlers pickled and exported abroad). A timber bridge connected the north shore of the island to Salisbury, as her father's ferry service crossed the deeper water on the south side to Newbury.

Her father had immigrated to Massachusetts with his brother Richard around 1634 (about the same time the Townes settled in Salem), first to Ipswich, where they received land grants, then to Salisbury, a town with New Hampshire on the north and the Merrimack along its south shore. Besides being a shipwright, George owned a wharf in Boston and kept trading contacts there, owned part of a vessel in 1638 in partnership with colony leaders Simon Bradstreet and Richard Saltonstall (whose son Nathaniel would be the only magistrate to resign from the witch trial court of 1692), and, in 1649, traded a quarter share in another vessel to William Hilton for an Indian named James to be his "servant forever." Around 1641 he married a Boston woman named Elizabeth (possibly Elizabeth Dexter), who brought a not insignificant marriage portion of £200.

The December session of the Essex County Quarterly Court that same year appointed George to keep the Salisbury ferry by his island on condition he find "a sufficient horse boat and gives diligent attendance." He already operated some sort of vessel, but apparently he did not do so with sufficient diligence. Customers complained that he charged four pence just to allow cattle to swim alongside the boat with no help from him and that he obliged travelers to wait up to three hours on the shore "to the prejudice of their health." The court reproached him for these practices and itemized allowable fees as follows ("d" is a penny, of which pence is the plural):

man 2d
horse 6d
great cattle 6d each
calves and yearlings 2d
goats 1d
hogs 2d

"If present pay is not made," he could charge a penny more, but he was *not* to charge for cattle swimming alongside "for want of a great boat."

Elizabeth gave birth to their first child, also named Elizabeth, in April 1642, followed two years later by son George Jr., then Richard in 1645 or '46. At this point three-year-old Elizabeth was sent to her mother's relatives in Boston, where she stayed, with her childless uncle James Oliver and his wife taking her "as their own." The practice was not common in an era of large families and few childless couples, but it was not unknown. Why the Carrs gave her up is unanswered.

But life on Carr's Island had its hazards. When one Evan Morris of Ipswich sued George Carr over disputed wages in June 1646, George countered with the charge that the workman had threatened to kill him. Because Morris at some point not only tried to run from the constable but was also found to have committed "an action of a high nature done in England," the court fined him twenty shillings. Despite the seriousness of whatever he had done abroad, Morris remained in Essex County and continued to get into trouble. (He was sued for slander in 1656 for declaring that if there were "noe members of Churches there would be noe need of gallows" and charged in 1660 "for drunkenness, quarreling, and railing speeches" after a brawl that left his Topsfield employer fined for selling liquor without a license.)

Then in 1657 John Lewis's hired man, Henry Horrell, drowned near Carr's Island, and the body was not recovered for a month. Horrell and fellow workman Robert Quimby had gotten drunk in a skiff before dawn one Sabbath, lost an oar, and fetched up on Ram Island, where Horrell either fell or was thrown from the island's steep bank into the strong current. George Carr, his Indian, and a hired man rescued Quimby but strongly suspected foul play. When John Lewis arrived at Carr's house to collect Quimby, he noted that "Mrs. Carr was crying and wringing her hands and Mr. Carr very solitary." The case, being capital, went all the way to the Court of Assistants, which did not find Quimby guilty despite "some suspition thereof."

Elizabeth, meanwhile, gave birth to William in 1647 or '48. Her second son, Richard, died in 1649, at most just four years old. But she gave birth, in relentless and exhausting succession, the following spring to son James, in February 1652 to daughter Mary, and then the following December to daughter Sarah. After a three-year respite Elizabeth produced the next child, John, in November 1656. Three years later Elizabeth bore yet another son named Richard (like his dead sibling—not an uncommon practice). Sometime in 1660 eight-year-old Sarah was sent to live with her Uncle and Aunt Oliver in Boston, where she, like her eldest sister, stayed until she married. Finally Elizabeth gave birth to her tenth and last child—Ann—on June 15, 1661.

Less than a year later, in Boston, the eldest daughter, Elizabeth, married John Woodmancy, who stated that he thought of her as the Oliver's daughter rather than the Carrs'. Her uncle, James Oliver, evidently thought likewise, as he provided Elizabeth with a generous dowry of about £500. A short three years later, in December 1665, Elizabeth gave birth to a son, John, and subsequently died. Childbearing was not always a joyous event to welcome a new soul from God, for the risk of death for mother or child—or both—was very real.

When Ann was ten her twenty-one-year-old brother, James, met the widow Rebecca Maverick, who, since the death of her husband, Samuel Maverick Jr., had moved from Boston to the Salisbury home of her father, Reverend John Wheelwright. James was smitten with her, and when she suggested that he visit more often and not be such a stranger (at least as he later recalled it), he was sure she felt similarly toward him. When he returned a few evenings later, William Bradbury was there before him, evidently upset with young Mrs. Maverick, who treated William "coarsely" (again, according to James's view). William soon left, looking angry. He had, in fact, been courting the widow, and James interpreted the stormy exit to mean that Rebecca preferred himself. However, James soon fell strangely and alarmingly ill, with sensations running about his body as if some "living creature" were scampering invisibly throughout, "ready to tear me to pieces."

This ailment continued off and on for nine months, no matter what Dr. Anthony Crosby (the first physician in nearby Rowley) prescribed; not even a posset of steeped tobacco seemed to help. William Bradbury, meanwhile, mended his quarrel with the widow Maverick. He signed a renunciation to any claim against her late husband's estate on March 5, 1672, and married her a week later on March 12—discouraging news for James, whose condition failed to improve.

At last Dr. Crosby admitted that he believed James was "behagged" and urged his patient to tell who might have done it. James (as he

later claimed he said) hesitated to accuse anyone "counted honest," but
he suggested his romantic rival's mother, Mrs. Bradbury. Dr. Crosby
declared that "he believed that Mrs. Bradbury was a great deal worse
than Goody Martin" (referring to Susannah Martin of neighboring
Amesbury, an assertive woman who more than one resident in the area
suspected of being a witch).

Mistress Mary Bradbury, however, was a respectable matron married to Thomas Bradbury, town clerk, schoolmaster, and frequent
magistrate. One night soon after James had named Mrs. Bradbury
aloud, he felt a cat—or something else—hop onto his bed. He was
certain he was "broad awake," yet he could not move to strike it off. If
the thing was not Mrs. Bradbury in the form of some creature, surely
it was an imp or familiar that she had sent to plague him further.
When the thing came again another night, James *did* manage to move
and, he thought, hit it. From then on Dr. Crosby's medicine finally
worked, and James no longer doubted that Mrs. Bradbury was the
witch who had caused his ills on behalf of her son. (That both
William and Rebecca died in 1678, a mere six years after their union,
did not change his mind.) James never married and continued working for his father at his various enterprises.

Possibly around the same time Ann's brother John fell in love with
Mrs. Bradbury's granddaughter Jemima True. Despite his brother
James's experiences with the Bradburys, John convinced himself that
his father would approve of the match and would give him a marriage
portion—he lacked enough to start married life—but George Sr. most
certainly did *not* approve. Furthermore, "some in the family" persuaded
John's father that the boy was too young. The girl was a year younger
as it was, and the match evaporated. Soon afterward John became uncharacteristically melancholy, "by degrees much crazed," and so he
remained.

In 1672, some months after William and Rebecca Bradbury's wedding, when Ann was eleven, her third brother, William, married Elizabeth Pike (a daughter of Robert Pike, who had often opposed
Reverend Wheelwright's imperious tactics), and her sister Mary married James Bailey of Newbury. Bailey was a young man not long out
of Harvard (or "the college," as it was called). Two months after the

wedding a committee of men from Salem Village offered him £40 a year to serve as their minister.

Salem Village—also called Salem Farms—was a rural neighborhood of Salem itself, a long walk inland northwest of the harbor. The men there had petitioned the selectmen for years to have charge of their own security—rather than leave their families unprotected while they trudged into town to stand watch—and to establish their own church with their own minister. The same problem of distance had already whittled away Salem's outlying areas, and the town fathers were unwilling to lose any more. But the farmers were determined, so they took the matter all the way to the General Court, at last winning permission on October 8, 1672, to establish their own parish. Their victory meant that now they were responsible for building and maintaining a meeting house as well as paying a minister.

In the spring of 1673 the Village men, with a hired carpenter, raised a meeting house thirty-four feet long and twenty-eight feet broad on an acre donated by Joseph Hutchinson at a crossroad in the Village center. Like the courthouses and market houses in East Anglia, from where many of the settlers had started out, the plain, one-room structure looked more like a barn than a traditional ecclesiastical architecture and would serve as a space for civil as well as religious gatherings. ("Church" was used to indicate the people in full communing membership and did not refer to the building.) The Village decided on "plain" windows with no glass—shutters could keep out weather—and accepted a secondhand pulpit and deacon's bench that Salem's church donated.

Bailey's status as minister was not yet permanent, but in June the Village asked him to continue with them for another year. (And in July, back in Newbury, Mary Bailey gave birth to the couple's first child, whom they also named Mary, but the infant died in August.) The next winter the Village increased Bailey's pay by £7 worth of firewood and began to think of building a ministry house (otherwise known as a parsonage) for the young couple. In November the Village voted to build a house twenty-eight feet long by twenty feet deep with an eleven-foot lean-to at one end. Working together under a housewright's direction (probably the next spring), the men raised the timbers on the southern slope of Thorndike's Hill, some distance east of the meeting house and uphill from the road. It is possible that young Ann joined the Baileys here to help her sister; woman's work running a household usually needed more than one pair of hands.

In February 1674, in gratitude for his "coming amongst us to the ministry," brothers Thomas, Nathaniel, and John Putnam as well as Joseph Hutchinson and Joshua Rea deeded Bailey a parcel of thirty acres of upland on the slopes of Misty and Hadlock's Hills along with ten acres of lower-lying Cromwell's Meadow. However, not all the parishioners were as pleased or grateful; the Village had to sue fourteen taxpayers for not paying the ministerial rates. The Village already had its factions, for not everyone agreed with the Putnam family's choices. The disagreement over the choice of permanent minister simmered in the background as Bailey continued to preach and offer pastoral care. In the meantime his wife, Mary, gave birth to son John in 1675. Around that time her brother John Carr descended into melancholy and eventual madness. Also during this period the always-thorny relationship with the native peoples further deteriorated into King Philip's War, which, though relatively brief, was exceedingly brutal, destroying a nearly ruinous 10 percent of the white population. Yet the price paid by the native peoples in southern New England, who by now most of the colonists feared as fiends incarnate, was far greater in numbers as well as autonomy. Salem Village escaped attack as did Salisbury, where the General Court established a seven-man garrison in 1676 at Carr's Ferry. Ann's father, still a local leader, commanded the modest force at this crossing place on the Merrimack.

In 1678 Ann's sister Mary gave birth to another son, James Jr., and her sister Sarah, who had grown up in Boston, married blacksmith Thomas Baker. Ann herself, seventeen years old, was courted by Thomas Putnam Jr., the eldest son of Lieutenant Thomas Putnam, a prominent community leader and considerable landowner. Young Thomas had fought in a company of troopers in King Philip's War and had been one of the attackers in the Narragansett Campaign. Then, in the deep December snows of 1675, combined colonial and Mohegan forces, with their provisions spent and the nearest garrison populated only by the newly dead, attacked the Narragansetts' palisade fort on an island in a frozen swamp. The terrible hand-to-hand fighting in the burning fort left at least 80 colonists dead and 150 wounded, but they killed perhaps a thousand Narragansetts either directly or from exposure, as men, women, and children tried to flee the carnage.

Further, Thomas Sr. was not only prosperous but also generous. He built a new house east beyond Hathorne Hill for himself, his second wife, and the younger children (including eight-year-old Joseph, the only child from the second marriage) and then or soon after gave the use of the old homestead to Thomas Jr. The 150-acre farm included house, barns, orchards, uplands, pastures, and meadows. It stretched to the Ipswich River, its angles marked by a great rock and blazes on certain trees—white ash, white oak, red oak, and black oak, hornbeam, and maple.

Ann, aged seventeen, married twenty-six-year-old Thomas on November 25, 1678. If she had a hired girl to assist her in her new household, the servant could hardly have been much younger than her mistress. But she was *Mistress* Putnam now (Mrs. for short), not simply Ann (like a child, a servant, or a lower-class woman). Young as she was, as Mistress, she outranked even a Goodwife (Goody for short) like Rebecca Nurse. For both she and her husband were the children of wealthy men and began their married life with a fine material start. A prosperous future was a reasonable expectation. But expectations, either material or spiritual, however reassuring, are not inevitable in this mortal, earthly life.

Old controversies erupted the following winter when Nathaniel Putnam, whose support of Bailey had since soured, along with Bray Wilkins announced that Bailey was *not* qualified to be a minister. Their reasons—especially Nathaniel's change of heart—are now cloudy, but the allegation sparked a spate of charges and counter-charges. One side declared that only a few had invited Bailey to preach, that he sought to "carve out a considerable estate" in the Village when he was not their permanently ordained minister but there only "upon sufferance," and that Bailey did not even conduct prayers and Scripture reading for his own family. Thomas's father and several other men, including ten who lived outside the Village, defended Bailey's religious life. The slander of religious negligence escalated until it went to court, where witnesses gave conflicting accounts as to whether Bailey conducted family prayers and Scripture readings. (Ann was not called to testify, though she had lived in Bailey's household before her marriage.) With the Salem Church serving as mediator, Reverend John Higginson advised that the majority's wishes would rule, that the Village pay Bailey the salary due him, and that they "follow the things that make for peace." The last suggestion especially fell on deaf ears.

Thirty-eight men, including Thomas and his father, signed a letter supporting Bailey, but little changed. By July Salem Village's first minister announced, "I see no further grounds of hope for my future comfortable living amongst you in that work of the ministry in this place, and therefore am seriously thinking of my removal from you." In September a committee voted to raise Bailey's salary to £55 for the next year, granted him the freedom to leave if he found another place, and reserved the option for the Village to hire another minister at year's end.

In the midst of all this discord Ann was pregnant with her first child.

Her mother lived several towns distant; her sister was likely to move away soon. No doubt the older women of the neighborhood (Rebecca Nurse perhaps) or those skilled in folk medicine (like Elizabeth Procter) had plenty of advice for Ann—whether or not she appreciated or accepted it. Neighbor women as well as the midwife customarily gathered to encourage and aid when one of their own faced the travail of childbirth. Ann gave birth to a daughter on October 18, 1679 and named the child Ann.

Back in Salisbury around this time Jemima True had just married John March (rather than Ann's melancholy brother John), and Ann's father, George Carr, experienced a suspicious encounter. Riding home one Sabbath noon with his son Richard and young Zerubabel Endicott, they saw none other than Mrs. Mary Bradbury enter her gate. Immediately a blue boar (a gray hog) dashed from the same opening straight at Carr's horse. The steed stumbled, and in the confusion Carr and Richard lost sight of the creature. Zerubabel, however, thought it leaped into Mrs. Bradbury's window.

"Boys," Carr asked, "what did you see?"

They both described a blue boar and agreed that it came "from Mrs. Bradbury's gate."

Then, said Carr, "I am glad you see it as well as I."

All three concluded that the creature had been Mrs. Bradbury in spectral disguise, and no doubt she was up to more malicious mischief.

That same October, still disagreeing over who could vote for what minister (and still having trouble collecting the rates to pay Bailey), Salem Village petitioned the governor and General Court to ask just *who* among them *could* make such a choice. Ordinarily the full, communing members of an established church chose the minister, and then the whole congregation contributed to his salary. Although some of the villagers were members of the church in Salem town, the Village had not yet finalized the formation of their own church by ordaining a permanent minister who would (ideally, at least) serve the congregation for the rest of his career. Bailey provided preaching and pastoral care to the area but was not yet authorized to distribute the sacraments to his people; that privilege would come with ordination.

Maddeningly, the government ignored the actual situation and replied that "their inhabitants are to attend the law regulating voters in this and all other cases, as other towns are enjoined to do." This response ignored the facts that the Village was *not* an independent town, only a neighborhood of Salem, and that without a formally established church in the Village, there were no full members of a Salem Village church to vote on anything. (Settlers came to New England for a variety of reasons, but religion was definitely one of them. In the early days of settlement, towns did not establish churches so much as churches established towns.) Twenty-four village men explained that they were neither a church *nor* a town and again asked for some neutral party to consider the matter of the *next* minister (hoping that Bailey would indeed leave). But the General Court ruled that, as a majority wanted Bailey to stay, the Village should pay him £60 for the next year (two thirds in goods) plus fuel. Bailey, in fact, already contemplated removing his family from the contentious village.

By the spring of 1680 some of the minister's critics had a change of heart. At that time Nathaniel Putnam Sr. joined Thomas Putnam Sr.,

John Putnam, Thomas Fuller, and Joseph Hutchinson to deed meadow and upland lots to Bailey as well as part of the lot on which his house stood. Although an encouraging sign, the rest of the lot still belonged to the community. Bailey, who had acquired ownership of the parsonage, would later purchase the remaining land, which he rented out after he left the Village. For the time being, despite his concerns, he seems to have lingered, slowly collecting back pay.

The Village next approached George Burroughs to be their minister. Burroughs, also a Harvard graduate, was short, dark haired, and generally stronger than most expected. He had earlier taught school in Dedham (where he married his first wife, Hannah Fisher) and preached in Falmouth, Maine (until that town was burnt in King Philip's War, at which point he and other survivors evacuated to Cushing's Island in Casco Bay and lived on fish and berries until they were rescued). Since then he had been living in Salisbury, home of the Carr family. He and Hannah and at least two surviving children relocated to the Village and, without their own residence, boarded with John and Rebecca Putnam Sr., who thought the minister "a very sharp man to his wife." The Burroughs even quarreled over George's demand that Hannah sign "a written covenant . . . that she would never reveal his secrets" (as the Putnams would recall it), though what those secrets were remains unclear. How Burroughs got along with the Baileys, who were still living in the parsonage that might otherwise have been available to him, is another unanswered question.

By early 1681, when Ann gave birth in February to a son named Thomas, the Village asked Burroughs, not Bailey, to stay. Just off the road to Andover they also built a new parsonage, forty-two feet long by twenty feet wide, with two rooms in each of two floors, each with a hearth, plus a garret and a stone-walled cellar under the parlor. Mrs. Burroughs did not enjoy it for long, for she died that September. As he had not yet been paid, her husband had to borrow £7:1:10 from his former landlord for her funeral—a mortifying turn of events to be beholden to a man who did not trust him, especially as his lack of funds was due to the Village's default on their previously agreed-upon obligations.

In December Burroughs nevertheless agreed to stay—on the condition that, if differences arose, "we engage on both sides to submit to council for a peaceable issue." Salary was to be £60 a year and wood. The Village then voted to state that the ministerial house belonged to the Village, *not* to the minister. Burroughs was not settled permanently, however, nor did the Village have its own church yet.

Thomas and Ann still had to take their children to Salem town for baptism in its church, where Thomas was a member. Though Ann examined her soul, she did not yet feel reasonably certain that she was elect—saved—and worthy of full membership and the sacraments. Individuals, in the Calvinism that New England's Puritans inherited, either were saved or were, ultimately, irrevocably damned. Effort could not change that reality—though it took effort to discern it—nor could mortals comprehend why the Almighty chose to operate in such an unfathomable, fearsome manner. Although a Christian should engage in good works, no one should presume it as evidence of divine favor or assume it possible to buy or bribe one's way into Heaven.

The next year began with a dispute between the Village and neighboring Topsfield, for conflicting surveys had overlapped areas granted to different parties, none of whom would relinquish their claim to the contested land. The Putnam clan and their workmen faced off rival Topsfield men in distant woodlots, threatening each other with their axes in a decidedly un-Christian manner. Then, as winter ended, Ann's father fell ill in Salisbury. Newbury physician John Dole attended with a series of neighbors and relatives, each taking turns to watch at the sickbed, a neighborly custom that offered the family sickroom help as well as prayer. "At his earnest and continual desire," George Carr requested Reverend James and Mary Bailey to attend. (It is not clear if Ann was able to be present.) Father Carr, Bailey later said, "would not suffer myself nor wife to be absent from him," requiring "daily and nightly attendance."

Carr had no will and knew he was no longer able to make one. According to various watchers, he managed to state a few wishes, but this was hardly a substitute for a legal document. He desired that his brother Richard should continue to live in the household and that his

son James should carry on the family business and have Carr's Island.
James was also to be responsible for his "distempered" brother John
and was told to be fair to "your sister Mary, be sure do not wrong her,
she has been a good girl to me."

Dole, the physician, thought that "sometimes he seemed to be ra-
tional," but Carr was seldom *compos mentis* during his illness. "He
was," Dole would say, "not capable to settle his estate, but desired of
his children to agree amongst themselves." By the time George Carr
died on April 4, 1682, Bailey felt worn out from attending his father-
in-law's sickbed.

After the funeral (costing £17:4:0) the widow, her sons, and sons-
in-law met at Carr's house with a committee of appraisers—all local
men—to discuss the valuation of the estate. The widowed Elizabeth,
with sons George and James, presented to the court a list of £40:5:0
worth of the estate's outstanding debts to various parties along with
an inventory of Carr's possessions, totaling £1,100—household goods,
furniture, weapons, tools, lumber, and livestock as well as odd sums of
money, debts due and debts owed, the ferry, and a long list of scattered
meadows and pastures. "Some things, like sea instruments . . . were
not appraised," they noted. (The Indian named James was not listed
either.) The court ordered that £180 apiece be given to the widow, the
eldest son George, and son James (for his "several years service" in his
father's business) as well as £90 apiece to the younger sons and the
daughters.

Ordinarily, a widow would be granted a third of the estate (more
than she might expect under other governments), whereas the rest
would be divided among the children, with eldest son receiving double
portions. Elizabeth had other ideas.

Perhaps the Carr enterprises would not be economically viable if
they were divided in the traditional manner. Perhaps Elizabeth,
George, and James had been doing all the work of carrying on the
family business. Perhaps she was not fond of her sons-in-law. In any
case, she and the two sons found another set of appraisers—not local
this time—and produced a second untotaled inventory. (This one
noted that one of Carr's horses was "in the hands of Thomas Putnam.") Debts owed by the estate now included £23:1:0 due to "Mr.

James Bailey upon the account of the portion of Mary his wife which they had received" and £20:8:6 "paid to Thomas Putnam and Ann his wife on account of his wife's portion."

The sons-in-law and William Carr protested, and the matter went to court at Salem in June. Under a doctor's care from the rigors of attending his father-in-law and unable to perform "my necessary employment in order to the recovery of my health," Bailey penned a lengthy petition protesting the second inventory, stating that it was "suddenly obtained in the absence of some of the persons concerned," including himself, that it undervalued the estate, and that it omitted some things entirely. He had so far seen "little or nothing" of his wife's marriage portion, even though "my father Carr" was always especially fond of Mary and had said on his very deathbed that "she should not be wronged." But now, "by reason of the endeavors of some to get the estate into their own hands," it seemed she would be cheated of her rightful due. In his view "mother Carr" had shown "too much partiality to the case, viz. against the daughters in striving to get the estate (to the great damage of the daughters) settled upon the sons."

Widow Carr countered with her own petition that detailed *her* understanding of her late husband's wishes. George, William, and Richard were married, with families of their own. Having "been careful of his father's business and dutiful to him," living with and working for him even after he came of age, James was to have the Island and was to care for John, who was "crazed or distempered in his head these seven years and is not capable to govern himself." Her brother-in-law Richard Carr, who had long lived with them, was now "ancient and cannot provide for himself." Her husband had wanted his brother to have £10 or £11 a year, but the court would have to decide just how the estate could afford that. For herself, she wished to continue living in this household and for James to manage her part of the estate. She desired the magistrates "to leave something of the estate to be at my dispose at my decease among my children, for I did bring to my husband in that which was good estate to the value of two hundred pounds"—her marriage portion. As for the daughters, Elizabeth and Sarah had been raised as their uncle and aunt's children, who provided for them well (for instance, a £500 dowry to Elizabeth when she married Woodmancy). She could not see how the late Elizabeth's son John Woodmancy had *any* rights to George Carr's estate. (This countered her kinsman James Oliver's testimony that Carr had indeed promised that his grandson would inherit his mother's portion.) Her daughter Mary Bailey had received £23:1:0, whereas £20:8:6 went to "Ann the youngest, the wife of Thomas Putnam."

The sons-in-law—Thomas Putnam, James Bailey, and Thomas Baker—petitioned again in October, proposing as a conciliatory gesture, among other matters, "that our honored mother shall enjoy the Island and ferry during her natural life." They also offered to purchase the Amesbury ferry from George Carr Jr. at more than the appraised value and asked that the rest of the estate be proportionately divided so "that everyone may know his part." The Carrs did relinquish one of the horses to count toward Mary's inheritance, for Bailey rode it on a journey "southward" to negotiate with the Killingworth, Connecticut community about being their minister. The horse that Thomas Putnam had was no doubt considered part of Ann's portion. The estate's papers included several lists of differing amounts due to each party.

Although the first set of appraisers insisted that the widow and the two favored sons refused to show them all of the Carr estate, the court took the widow's side: the Carr enterprises remained with Elizabeth, George, and James.

(The same June court session also annulled Ralph and Katherine Ellenwood's marriage due to his "insuffiency." Katherine declared that she "would rather die than live with this man," whereas Ralph was reported to have blamed his problem on the presence of witches in the neighborhood.)

Perhaps forewarned by the contentious Carr probate, Thomas Putnam Sr. wrote a will of his own in February 1683, "being ancient and sensible of the declining of old age, and weakness, and symptoms of mortality daily attending upon me."

Meanwhile, as Burroughs's opponents circulated angry letters that led to slander suits and grievance committees, Ann gave birth to a daughter on May 29, 1683. Despite family resentments over the Carr estate, she named the child Elizabeth—her mother's name. The Putnams, however, evidently never cared for Burroughs and likely showed

no disappointment when he departed for Maine along with other returning refugees. After four Sabbaths bereft of a minister, several complained of the abandonment. Burroughs did return to the Village in
June, but he did so only to collect his back pay and then settle the debt
with John Putnam Sr. for his late wife's funeral. Part of the belated
pay was to cover what was owed, but even so, Putnam had Burroughs
arrested for debt. Other men posted a bond for his release, and the
suit was dropped when the Village voted to pay Burroughs £15, though
the embarrassing affair continued to gall him.

The Village next asked Deodat Lawson to preach, offering him £60
a year, but no wood. By April they added thirty cords of wood and reduced his pay to £40, then once again changed this sum to £60 with
no wood. This indecisiveness and arbitrary fluctuation would prove to
be a lasting thorn for all the Village ministers.

By now Ann's sister Mary was far away in Connecticut, where Bailey was minister of Killingworth. (Her brother Richard would visit
them there and marry a local girl before returning to Salisbury with
his bride.) Ann's mother, having seen the problems of dying intestate,
made a will of her own in March 1684, but she likely kept the details
of it to herself and the witnesses. In July 1685 Ann gave birth to another son and named him Ebenezer.

In January 1686 Thomas Putnam Sr., now over seventy, formally
deeded his eldest son, Thomas, the homestead and several parcels of
land that he was already using (reserving the right to cut wood on the
property during his lifetime). Two days later Thomas added a codicil
to his will and died by springtime. Once the older sons and sons-in-
law learned the particulars of the will, more trouble erupted: the lion's
share, as they saw it, went to the youngest son, Joseph, *not* to the eldest,
as was customary. Ann's husband, Thomas, petitioned Joseph Dudley,
then president of the Council of New England, asking that probate be
delayed until he could speak his piece. The matter went before the
council in July, with Daniel Wycom acting as attorney for Mary Putnam, widow and executrix. The will's witnesses, Israel Porter and John
Leach, verified that Thomas Sr. had indeed signed the document. The
sons and sons-in-law petitioned for the eldest brother, Thomas, to
serve as executor instead and "bring in a true inventory . . . so that each

of us may have the proportion of our deceased father's estate which by the law of God and man humbly belongs unto us." This was "the cry of the fatherless and motherless," for the will, as they saw it, "was occasioned to be made as it is by our mother-in-law [i.e., stepmother], by which instrument . . . we shall be extremely wronged."

However, the council let the document stand as it was.

The will detailed the approximately 150-acre farms that Thomas Sr. had already given to sons Thomas and Edward. All the sons were to share the ten acres in swampy Blind Hole Meadow. The 120-acre farm was to go to "Mary, my beloved wife, and to my son Joseph Putnam, born by her, my said wife." They were each to own one half, keep it in good repair, and on Mary's death the whole would pass to Joseph, who, meanwhile, would get all the farm tools (his mother would have half the use of them), "plow gear and cart, . . . mill stone and cider mill." He also specified that a house his wife had purchased from her first husband's family before she married Putnam was to remain hers for life; after her demise Thomas and Joseph were to divide it equally down the middle.

To the four children of his deceased daughter Ann Trask he willed £10 apiece on their coming of age at twenty-one. He had evidently promised the other daughters, Deliverance, Elizabeth, and Prudence, £100 each in household goods and "current pay," some of which they had already received in household items. Bond servant Joseph Stacey was to inherit eleven acres of upland and swamp once he served his allotted time.

Widow Mary Putnam was to receive £50 in plate and other goods (but not coins) that she could will as she wished to Thomas's children at her own decease. She and Joseph were to be executors jointly—an unusual stipulation, as Joseph was still only sixteen—and the boy would fully inherit at the age of just eighteen, *not* twenty-one, as was normal.

The codicil adjusted the sums due to the daughters and bestowed to sons Thomas and Edward a certain orchard in the event they lost another parcel to the Topsfield men in the ongoing boundary dispute.

The Topsfield dispute did in fact continue, as did the Village argument over whether or not to settle Lawson permanently as its minister. By February 1687 Salem town once again had to mediate, advising a year's cooling-off period. The mediators, Reverends John Higginson and Nicholas Noyes along with Magistrates Bartholomew Gedney and William Brown Jr., commented on the factions' contentious and un-Christian behavior. Such "settled prejudice and resolved animosity . . . have a tendency to make such a gap as we fear . . . will let out peace and order and let in confusion and every evil work." This too fell on deaf ears.

Instead, Lawson accepted a temporary (paying) post as chaplain in one of Sir Edmund Andros's frontier campaigns. Some in the Village criticized him for deserting his flock, though the flock had probably been slow in paying him. In his absence his wife and baby daughter sickened and died, so now Lawson had even less incentive to return to Salem Village.

Meanwhile, by the spring of 1687 Thomas, who wrote a fine, clear hand, finished the task of transcribing the Village records into a new volume, the old being full of crossings-out and marginal notes. The committee to oversee the copy, which had voted to omit certain "grievous" or "unprofitable" entries, paid him forty shillings.

In September Ann gave birth to another daughter, naming her Deliverance.

By the following June a new minister, Samuel Parris, and his family had been invited to the Village. This candidate seemed more acceptable to the Putnams and to enough of the others, even if they harbored silent doubts. In an October meeting the voters agreed to the choice, and with no heed to their earlier problem with Bailey over the first parsonage, they voted to give Parris "our ministry house and barn and two acres of land next adjoining to the house" if he "take office upon him amongst us and live and die in the work of ministry amongst us."

None of the earlier candidates had been ordained as permanent minister, even though the ideal situation was for a minister to remain with a particular flock. Ordination was not automatically bestowed at the completion of studies but was instead considered a reciprocal arrangement, almost a spiritual marriage, marking the occasion when a candidate joined in union with a particular church.

Given human nature, the ideal was not always realized.

While this matter proceeded, Ann heard of the death of her sister Mary Bailey far off in Connecticut. Less personal but distressing all the same was news from Boston that a certain Goody Glover had been found guilty of bewitching some children and hanged for the crime—a reminder that every family was vulnerable to spectral evil as well as to the many illnesses and material misfortunes that befell mortals. But Ann already knew firsthand about the fragility of families and the brevity of life.

The next year brought a successful—if risky—revolt against Governor Edmund Andros even as negotiations between Parris and the Village continued unabated. Ann, pregnant again, learned that her brother John, who never did recover his full senses, was failing in health. After two or three weeks of sickness he died peacefully in September, and his brother William (rather than James, as their father had wished) tended to him to the end. William claimed John never blamed anyone for his illness, but others (his sister Ann, no doubt) strongly suspected Mrs. Bradbury of foiling his courtship by driving him mad. Ann herself gave birth to a daughter in October and named her Sarah, likely to honor her sister Sarah Baker, who seems to have already died in Boston along with several of her children, as she was not named in their mother's 1684 will.

Parris's ordination in November promised a new beginning for the Village, but baby Sarah's death in mid-December was yet another loss, another occasion for grief and spiritual reflection. The child, "not quite two months," may have had an odd rash and may have convulsed as she perished.

To Ann, it did not seem quite natural.

Compounding this loss, news came of devastating frontier attacks from bands of French Canadian and Abenaki allies, striking Schenectady, New York, in February and Salmon Falls, New Hampshire, in March. A disastrous expedition against Quebec, foiled by weather and smallpox, soon erased any euphoria over a successful counterattack on the French town of Port Royal in Acadia (Nova Scotia to the English). And in the Village, factions again festered and erupted, as thirty-eight taxpayers withheld the minister's rates.

Ann's son Timothy was born in 1691. That same year her mother, Elizabeth Carr, died on May 6. Ann had been searching her soul and felt comparatively certain—as much as anyone could be—that she *was* indeed saved and worthy enough to partake of the Lord's Supper. Now that they had their own local church, the long process toward church membership finally led her, at age twenty-seven, to apply. Samuel Parris recorded her acceptance as the thirty-first member in the Salem Village Church book in both English and scholarly Latin:

1691 June 4—
At church meeting 4 June 1691
Admitted into the church:
31. Ann (wife to brother Thomas) Putnam. An Aetat 27
    [i.e. age 27 years]

By the end of the month her mother's estate was probated, and Ann learned of Elizabeth's bequests, somewhat outdated by other recent deaths: medical and funeral expenses; £1:10:9 to physician James Smith; the maid's wages; and £1:10:0 to "Mrs. Jackson for housework." Only two shillings each to sons George and William, one to the grandson John Woodmancy, only one to Mary (now deceased), "and to my daughter Anna Putnam one shilling."

One shilling—a mere token sum, commonly given as one step above disinheritance. The rest would go to John and Richard.

Ann was now the only living daughter, and in the absence of earthly riches, she would need to "store up treasures in Heaven"—spiritual gains.

Tituba

The girl kneels ahead of her mother in the canoe and watches the English sloop grow larger as they approach it across the salty Amacura River. Below, the sun casts nets of light crossed by the dark lines of little fish that dance in formation over the river bottom. She turns and smiles at her mother, who drives the canoe forward with sure, steady strokes of the paddle, first on one side, then the other. More canoes glide with them, bringing eight women and two children (counting themselves) to trade with the foreigners on the ship. The girl is pleased that she has been allowed to accompany the women to see how business is conducted. In the bottom of the canoes—scraped smooth and fire-hardened from single logs—are the goods they have grown or made themselves: casava bread, sweet potatoes, and sturdy woven hammocks.

What a fine day. What an adventure!

The child watches the bright birds flicker in and out of the trees along the banks, with their calls echoing over the water. She feels the sun warm her skin, for she and her mother wear only queyua slung around their hips, not the layers of heavy cloth the foreigners put on. If they are lucky, however, the men on the ship will have some European textiles to trade.

The sailors, jabbering welcome in their own tongue, let down a rope ladder to help the women and children climb aboard. As the eldest woman among them steps across the deck toward the head man of the crew—he wears more clothing and a fancier hat—his gestures of welcome suddenly become a lunge. He seizes her.

The other men grab three more of the women and then the two children. The girl cries out in terror.

"Dive for it!" the elder woman shouts. "Get help!"

Four women manage to leap from the rail and head for shore, with no time to climb into the canoes. They swim like otters, but the sailors scramble into the women's canoes to hunt them down—the swift craft that brought the band to the boat now proves their undoing. The men haul the women from the water, wrestle them into the canoes, clout them, and tie their hands and feet—no pretense of hospitality now.

The girl tries to cling to her mother. No one at home knows they were taken. No one is near enough to hear their shrieks and wails. The headman looks toward the shore as though he expects pursuit and then barks orders to his men, who bring out firearms and swarm the rigging to adjust the sails. As soon as the tide turns, the ship eases downstream.

No one comes to the shore.

No one rescues them.

How sharp the memory of that last day of freedom, of a normal life. How painful the last memory of home.

This incident may be the first sighting of *TITUBA*, the slave woman who was later a catalyst of the Salem witch trials—or perhaps not. The Salem woman called Tituba *may* have been one of the children kidnapped from the Amacura River, a tributary of the Oronoco in the Viceroyalty of Granada (now in Venezuela) by Captain Peter Wroth of the *Savoy* on August 2, 1674. His excuse was that, with England at war with Holland, the women were probably Arawak allies of the Dutch—unlike the large groups of men they had traded with downstream, whom they assumed were Carib allies of the British (as well as better able to resist capture).

Wroth took the captives as slaves to Barbados.

Although he evidently had only ten captives on board, and the distance was less than that of the transatlantic routes that slavers took from Africa, the journey had to have been harrowing and humiliating. African captive Olaudah Equiano, 150 years later, having gained both his freedom and a mastery of the English language in an era when many people, white or black, were illiterate, published an indictment of the slave trade. In it he described the captives' fear as they were packed below decks, unable to see where they were being taken and hardly able to breathe due to the "intolerably loathsome" stench of that hot, airless, confined space filled with "the shrieks of the women, and the groans of the dying." The only nod to sanitation were filthy "necessary tubs" used as latrines, awkward items into which small children often fell as they tried to balance on the rims. Some of the captives, allowed on deck for occasional exercise, managed to leap overboard in midocean. If they were lucky, they drowned. If they were rescued, they were "flogged . . . unmercifully" and obliged to live. Traumatic scenes like these introduced the captive girl to European civilization.

Finally the *Savoy* came within sight of Barbados and put in at Bridgetown, where merchants and planters came aboard to examine the cargo. In Equiano's description of his own arrival from Africa, the sight of strange buildings ashore and of the great ships in the harbor were alien enough, but the swarm of callous white men who prodded the captives like livestock and had them jump about made the captives fear that these strangers meant to eat them. Their terrified moaning and crying through the following night below deck was such that the whites ferried some old, long-enslaved Africans aboard to calm the captives. "They told us we were not to be eaten, but to work."

The Amacura captives would have then been herded into a slave merchant's holding pen "like so many sheep in a fold, without regard to sex or age." Over the next few days the merchant would signal with a drumbeat when sales began. Prospective buyers then rushed into the yard and examined the display of captives as they would examine cattle, causing even more alarm. "In this manner," wrote Equiano, "without scruple, are relations and friends separated, most of them never to see each other again. . . . Surely this is a new refinement of cruelty, which, while it has no advantage to atone for it, thus aggravates distress, and adds fresh horrors even to the wretchedness of slavery."

Thus the girl was separated from her fellow Amacurans and, in a waking nightmare, torn from her own mother forever (if her mother still lived). Taken to one of the sugar plantations, the girl learned to obey strangers, to work out the meaning of the new language through which the orders came, and would never again hear anyone speak in her own tongue. She learned to wear strange clothes and live with a gang of other slave children. Even those whose parents were owned by the same operation were often cared for by one woman day and night, fed all together, and set to tasks considered light—such as hand weeding a pasture.

On poorly run plantations owners skimped on their slaves' food and worked them "from earliest dawn to midnight, month to month without respite, or relaxation" at both high noon and on Sundays (as

William Beckford observed in eighteenth-century Jamaica). These owners even expected mothers to forage for their children's food. But these practices were not good for business, Beckford wrote, for overworked slaves would, in the long run, profit the owner as little as overworked livestock or exhausted land.

In the eighteenth century the recommended routine for a wellregulated sugar plantation included proper food, shelter, and medical care for the slaves and no more than thirty-nine lashes for serious infractions. Slaves began the workday at 6 a.m., paused a half hour or so for breakfast between nine and ten o'clock, then continued until dinner at noon, when the whole island rested for an hour and a half. Rather than spend this time on the main meal of the day, many slaves used the respite to talk among each other "or loiter away the time in useless inactivity"—a luxury in a life of constant toil. The ringing of a bell or the wail of a conch shell signaled the time to return to the fields, where work continued until sunset but no later than 7 p.m. The workers had evening and night to themselves, with the women cooking a supper of peppery pottage.

When the cane was "in crop" the slaves worked longer to harvest the stalks. Then men boiled the sap down and down in a series of smaller and smaller copper boilers until bright crystals of sugar formed around a sticky core of molasses. Shoveled into great barrels, both products were valuable commodities.

Some women were purchased for domestic rather than fieldwork, as the owners considered the lighter tasks around the house to be an honor of sort for the slave. This work, however, required a more "constant attendance." As a late eighteenth-century observer noticed, the women preferred fieldwork as "the more independent." If they lived in the slave-quarter huts, they at least had fellow captives around them and time to themselves. It was taken for granted that they would also produce children, one way or another, providing an increase of fieldworkers that only added to their owners' capital.

As Indian slaves were preferred for house work in late seventeenthcentury Barbados, the girl, as she grew, may have been trained for these tasks. (The Salem Tituba knew these duties and later referred to "her Mistress in her own Country" as one who taught her countermagic—

a lesson she would unlikely have received if she worked only in the fields.) For this she learned to wear the full set of European clothing: a shift, a long petticoat, a bodice, and a cap for modesty.

Two years after the *Savoy*'s raid, in 1676, a slave child called Tattuba was inventoried among the contents of a Barbadian sugar plantation owned by Samuel Thompson. *If* the girl from the Amacura were the same child, then *perhaps* she was the same young woman the merchant Samuel Parris purchased before he left the island in 1680 for New England, and thereby *may* have been the same Tituba involved in the Salem witch trials of 1692.

Or perhaps not.

For the reconstructed lives of slaves, the destitute, and social pariahs, words like "if," "perhaps," and "maybe" are needed when patching together the shreds of surviving fact. Slaves were counted first of all as property along with the tools and raw materials of whatever industry they were bound to rather than individuals with a lineage and identification in their own right.

What *can* be said for certain is that Captain Peter Wroth of the *Savoy* kidnapped eight women and two children from the Amacura River in the manner described above and took them as slaves to Barbados in one of the last such slaving raids into that region—an incident that Professor Elaine G. Breslaw uncovered as well as two lists of over sixty slaves belonging to the Thompson family's three hundred–acre sugar plantation in St. Thomas Parish, Barbados. At the end of the columns of "Boys & Girls" on each list, and apparently referring to an Indian slave, is the unusual name Tattuba.

Also certain is the fact that Samuel Parris was then a merchant, operating out of Bridgetown in Barbados from 1673 to 1680. Born in England around 1653, he moved to the island with his father, Thomas Parris, a merchant and landowner, and then attended Harvard in Massachusetts.

His father's death in 1673 required Samuel to cut short his time at college and return to Barbados to manage his inheritance: 20 acres in St. Peter's parish tied up in an eighty-two-year lease; 170 acres in St. James parish, which also included three servants, seventy slaves, cattle, sheep, and coppers to boil the sugar; a storehouse at Reid Bay; and land in Bridgetown. However, Parris then faced many challenges: competition from growers in Jamaica and the Leeward Islands depressed the price of sugar; poor farming practices exhausted and eroded the island soils; a near slave revolt was foiled in June of 1675, followed by a deadly and destructive hurricane in August. According to a census taken in October 1679, Parris was single, with a household consisting of an apprentice (who is not mentioned again) and one unspecified slave. In 1680 Parris sold most of his land and, as smallpox broke out on Barbados, relocated north to Massachusetts. By 1688, having married in Boston and changed his calling from merchant to minister, Samuel moved to Salem Village.

Amid all the uncertain maybes are the more uncertain questions of Tituba's name and origin. Spelling in the seventeenth century was still not standardized, so it depended on the creativity of the writers and how they heard a word. "Tituba" is the way that Samuel Parris, who most controlled her life, spelled her name. (Of course, he, like others, also used the alternate spelling of Putman for Putnam.) Boston jailer John Arnold used the spelling "Tituba" in his bills; Robert Calef and John Hale did likewise in their later narratives, as did Magistrate John Hathorne in his notes of court proceedings, though not consistently. Other variants include Tetaby, Titibe, Tittabe, Tittube, Tittapa, Titiba, Tittuba, and Titaba.

As Breslaw points out, *Titubear* is the Spanish for stagger or stammer, though Parris recorded no physical or speech impediment affecting his slave. *Titubo* and *titubabio*, furthermore, are the Latin for stagger and staggering in one's gait or other action. (Cotton Mather, who stammered in his youth and mastered the affliction through dogged determination and song, wrote about the "titubation" of stammers.) With his classical education, Parris *might* have bestowed a Latin name, but this seems unlikely.

More intriguing is Breslaw's suggestion that the name refers to the woman's people. The Tetebetana were an Arawak people living on the Amacura River in the area of Captain Wroth's raid. Their name apparently refers to their totem animal, a bird of the nightjar family, nocturnal birds like New England whip-poor-wills. (Another fiercer tribe, the Titetibe or Tivitivas, as different English explorers approximated the name, lived near the mouth of the Oronoco River.) In the Arawak language *Tetebetado* indicated a female, so Tituba possibly meant a Tetebetana girl or a woman of the Tetebetana.

Alternatively, Professor Peter Charles Hoffer is certain that the name is African, Yoruban specifically, and is nearly certain that Tituba was an African from Ghana or the child of a captive from Ghana. Breslaw notes that the "ba" ending *is* African but suggests that the African culture of the majority of Barbados's slaves influenced how her name was pronounced.

Others have speculated that Tituba was Carib or half Carib and half African, or they point out that her ancestry could have been any combination of Amerindian, African, and Caucasian—the three peoples populating the seventeenth-century Caribbean.

Some of the native Algonquians of New England *had* been enslaved locally after the wars between the indigenous tribes and the English settlers—mostly women and children, with the men shipped to slaving ports elsewhere. By century's end, apparently, few of the slaves in Massachusetts were Algonquian. The identities of Samuel Parris's John and Tituba Indian—or, for that matter, Mrs. Hollingworth's Indian servant or George Carr's Indian named James—is still open to question . . . many questions, in fact.

What *is* certain is that the white, largely English population in seventeenth-century Massachusetts *always* referred to Tituba as an Indian. Documents call her "an Indian Woman," "an Indian Woman servant," "an Indian Woman, belonging unto Mr. Samuel Parris of Salem Village," "the Indian," and "Tituba Indian." Some suggest that "Indian" meant West Indian—more of a geographic reference—and this supports Breslaw's interpretation. Hoffer, however, speculates that as Tituba was married to fellow slave John Indian, she was therefore known by her husband's name. Other non-Caucasian witch suspects like Candy and Mary Black, however, are called "Negro," and Candy was definitely from Barbados in the West Indies.

So *was* Tituba actually from Barbados? Although this is quite possible, facts about Tituba's life outside the witch trials are scant. Tituba herself referred to "her Mistress in her own Country" according to Reverend John Hale, who did not, unfortunately, record just what country that was. If it *were* Barbados, the mistress may well have been the widow Elizabeth Pearhouse, daughter of John Reid, who first married Edward Thompson, then Ralph Lane, and finally William Pearhouse. Mistress Pearhouse may have lived in Bridgetown rather than on the sugar plantation in the center of the island that she owned jointly with her son Edward Thompson. In addition, the family had business dealings with Samuel Parris, who worked from Bridgetown.

But *did* Parris buy Tituba in Barbados and then bring her to Massachusetts? After all, he may have purchased his slaves in New England. Cotton Mather, living in Boston, had, as he wrote, "bought a Spanish Indian, and bestowed him for a servant, on my Father" in 1681. (Spanish Indian meant an Indian from the Caribbean, generally.)

What is certain is that Tituba was an enslaved woman of color owned in 1692 by Reverend Samuel Parris of Salem Village. Earlier in her life she had lived elsewhere, owned by someone else.

Wherever she originated from, she was certainly in Boston, where Samuel Parris moved after renting out his remaining plantation and leaving the Indies. In Boston he continued as a merchant of West India goods and, in 1680, married Elizabeth Eldridge, a woman a few years older than himself and a fellow member of Boston's First Church. Their first child Thomas (named for Samuel's father) was born 1681; the second, Elizabeth (called Betty) followed in 1682. Parris sought to change his career to minister, and for a time he delivered sermons to the congregation at Stow, which was temporarily between pastors after a dispute with a former minister over ownership of the parsonage. (Salem Village's problems were not unique.)

Susanna Parris was born in Boston in January 1688, and by June the family seems to have moved to Salem Village. Now Tituba was responsible for keeping house (under Mistress Parris's authority) in the parsonage on the Andover Road originally built for Reverend Burroughs. Set back from this dirt track and facing south to put its back against the winter winds, the house, with two rooms on each of two floors, four hearths, plus a garret and a cellar, was larger than many of the area houses, but it was a constrained space nonetheless.

Parris used one of the upstairs rooms for his study—meaning that John would have to carry firewood up there in the winter. To the left of the front entry was the parlor, which was also used as the master bedroom. To the right was the hall (the main room), and at some point a lean-to was added behind this. A door led from the hall down field-stone steps into the storage cellar that lay under the parlor. Tituba and John Indian, being slaves, probably slept in the garret.

At this time Parris owned three slaves: John Indian and Tituba as well as a young boy who died the following March. Parris noted this in his records but omitted a name—breathing property that had ceased to breathe. Under March 25, 1689, he wrote in the list of Village deaths: "My Negroe lad," age fifteen.

There is some question whether, officially or informally, Tituba was married to John Indian, the other slave in the Parris household, or whether they simply worked in the same place. As Reverend Parris was unlikely to have countenanced extramarital goings-on under his roof, it is reasonable to assume that his slaves were properly married (as was legal, despite their vulnerable status). Reverend John Hale, an eye witness from the neighboring town of Beverly, referred to Parris's "Indian Man servant, and his Wife." (The presence of a "young John" in the same Barbadian inventory list of slave children as "Tattuba" invites speculation, but John was an exceedingly common name.)

The family had moved from Boston just when John Goodwin's children were acting bewitched, blaming an old woman in their neighborhood for sending tormenting spirits after them. News of Goody Glover's arrest and trial (in Governor Andros's courts) reached Salem Village along with news that she had confessed. The woman was hanged the following November, though the afflicted children did not recover for some months afterward.

What did Tituba think of this?

The native West Indians, Africans, Algonquians, and Europeans shared an acceptance of the spirit world's reality. How far any of the spirits might be trusted was another matter, however. The general Christian view was that good angels looked after humans in secret, that fallen evil angels (devils) worked their harm in a multitude of ways, that the souls of the dead went on to judgment, and that wandering spirits who were trying to get a mortal's attention were not to be trusted, no matter what they pretended. In folk belief, however, people assumed that occasional contact between humans and good (or, at least, neutral) spirits was safe enough. Living humans ran the gamut from good to evil, with most in between—so why not disembodied spirits?

In European and non-European cultures some experts trafficked in magic, with the intention to do good or at least to counteract someone else's harm. Some in England called them white witches or cunning folk. In New England that was too close to witches of the evil kind, people who allied themselves to the Devil and swore to do the Devil's work. But even people who did not think that what they did fell under the risky category of magic worked countercharms to ward off evil that others sent—to the exasperation of their ministers, who warned them that such foolery encouraged the imps they should avoid.

In Barbados once, at Newton Plantation in the southern part of the island, a slave woman about twenty years old died of lead poisoning. Her fellow slaves were allowed to bury their own dead, which they did in a series of mounds in the burying ground. Yet they placed her body apart from all the others, without a coffin or grave goods, face down in the earth, with the grave cut into the bedrock itself to prevent her from sitting up and escaping. In life she probably experienced painful cramps and spasms, which sound more like the symptoms of being bewitched than bewitching. Nonetheless, unlike the other mounds in that place, this one was never used to bury anyone else. Thus, witchcraft was feared in Barbados as well as in New England.

Besides avoiding the Boston witch scare, Samuel's relocation of his family allowed them to avoid the turmoil of April 1689, when the town revolted against Sir Edmund Andros. Parris, meanwhile, was negotiating a contract with the Village to determine what material support he would receive in return for ministering to the Village's spiritual needs on a permanent basis. Parris and the committees met again and again as they discussed firewood, provisions, and, at last, ownership of the parsonage, a recurring difficult matter not unique to Salem Village. Because Parris planned to remain with the Village permanently, the committee granted him ownership of the parsonage. He then purchased more acreage in the Village, probably building the lean-to off the back of the hall around this time.

Finally, on November 19, 1689, Parris was at last ordained in the meetinghouse. That cold day, if Tituba did not have to stay at home to tend the baby, then she may have sat in the gallery with the other slaves, servants, and hired help. Some chilled folk may have brought little foot-warmer fire boxes or a warm dog to ward against the un-compromising draughts as the Village watched the neighboring ministers—Nicholas Noyes of Salem, Samuel Phillips of Rowley, and John Hale of Beverly—place their hands upon Parris's head in blessing and charge him to serve faithfully before they offered the right hand of fellowship. Parris had to shorten his ordination sermon, however, because the weather was so bitter, in order to allow the new members of this just-formed church to sign their names in the church record book before the ink froze.

Later that same winter Canadian forces began making deadly for-ays against New York, New Hampshire, and Maine, leaving the rest of the region fearful of attack. While Sir William Phips led a fleet of Massachusetts militia to take Port Royal in April 1690, locals worried not only about possible raiding parties but also about the French-speaking Jersey folk among them and the possibility of a slave revolt. (Both Reverend Parris and Tituba would have been mindful of the thwarted slave revolt in Barbados.) Some people in Newbury thought Isaac Morrell, a local blacksmith, should *not* have been put in charge of one of the garrisons, and their worry grew into rumors that he and other Jerseymen intended to join with fellow French-speaking Cana-dians and local slaves to destroy the province.

Tituba and John must have heard these rumors as well as that "Isaac Morrell the Jerseyman" was arrested for treason. Several people from Newbury, both free and slave, testified against him, including thirty-year-old James, who had run away from Richard Dole. Caught by the watch, James claimed that Morrell and George Mosher, another Jer-seyman, had tempted him to join the rebels. "Mr. Moodey's Indian servant Joseph" likewise named Mosher and described how the man had said that a ship would sail into the river the following summer to take him to freedom. Twenty-year-old Robert Negro, nicknamed Robin, said that Morrell had told him in 1689 "that all the English should be cut off and the Negroes should be free." He also said that in

April, when the local fleet was heading for Nova Scotia, that Morrell and Mosher "persuaded me and all the Negroes to go away with him and George Mosher for they intended to take a vessel out of the dock at Newbury and go for Canada and join with the French against the English, and so come down with the French and Indians upon the backside of the country and destroy all the English and save none but only the Negro and Indian servants."

Despite these allegations, Morrell and Mosher were evidently *not* found guilty, and no such attack ensued. Was any part of it true? Or was it wishful thinking on the part of Robin Negro and his fellow slaves? Or did the story escalate when local slaves took what seemed a real opportunity to escape and then, once captured, spun a story built on current neighborhood fears in order to deflect punishment? Even if they did not believe the plot rumor themselves, their stories could work some kind of secondhand revenge or at least make life more difficult for a community who considered them chattel. After all, slaves could not easily play fair in so unfair a circumstance as enslavement.

This would give all the local slaves something to think about. Although servants, whether slave or free, could legally take their masters to court, this was seldom practical. Yet they had ample opportunity to make their masters' lives miserable. Some pilfered, some committed arson, and some slipped ratsbane into the family's food. But most did none of these things—the risks were too high; any rebellious servant, slave or free, could be "corrected" with a blow or a beating. Few masters, however, were as brutal as Peter Tufts of Malden, who tied a free, white, male servant to a tree and beat him with the thick end of an ox goad, a rod used to urge on cattle. (Neighbors reported this, and Tufts ended up in court.)

The term "servant" included any employee (like hired mariners and fisherman or shop clerks); field hands and domestic help; bond servants obliged to serve for a specified length of time, usually to repay a debt; apprentices learning a trade; and people permanently or indefinitely enslaved. Freedom *was* possible for this last category, though it was rare; a few free black families lived in Boston at least.

The number of slaves in Massachusetts was far fewer than in the West Indies, with its massive sugar industry, and their offspring were less an increase on an investment than just another mouth to feed. Some estimates suggest that, by 1700, there was one slave to every ninety free folk in Massachusetts. The earliest definite reference to their presence is 1638, when Governor John Winthrop noted that the Salem ship *Desire* had returned from the West Indies (where it had sold captured Pequot men, prisoners of war) and brought back "salt, cotton, tobacco and Negroes." Most slaves seem to have lived in the few towns, two or three at most in the households that owned them. The women worked at domestic tasks, the men at farming and crafts or as deckhands or cooks on fishing voyages. Owners might rent or lend a slave to friend, family member, or neighbor. Individual slaves are difficult to trace, with their presence known randomly in court records or probate inventories, itemized with other "property."

After an uneasy truce, more frontier raids struck Eastward in 1691, just as Tituba went about her work at the parsonage and John tended to the crops and livestock in the barn and fields.

Alongside Mistress Parris at times and always under her direction, Tituba worked in and around the ministry house. She cleaned for the family—swept and scrubbed floors, polished the copper pots in the lean-to, and boiled and scrubbed and wrung out laundry and spread it to dry over bushes. She worked in the kitchen garden in season, tended the hens and milked the cow, and set the milk in pans to separate the cream, which she then churned into butter.

Tituba cooked for the family—sallets and stews (but not the pepperpot of the islands), fresh peas in season, and pease porridge the rest of the year. She baked bread and maybe even set beer and cider to ferment in the cellar beneath the hall.

In Barbados the task was to keep a house and its inhabitants cool. In New England, however, though summer had spells of tropical humidity, keeping a household warm in the winter was the great concern.

That same year Parris discovered that the committees with which he had negotiated were no longer in charge, having been replaced by men who disagreed with what had seemed to be settled. Taxes everywhere in the province fell behind during the uncertain times, and the local rates that ought to have paid to Parris as his yearly salary went largely uncollected. By the fall of 1691 the parsonage began to run out of wood—the only fuel supply.

Parris had to remind his parishioners of this as the weather grew colder. Sleet and freezing rain at the beginning of November was replaced by bitter wind-driven snow at midmonth, followed by more snow and more hail. Fires in the parsonage hearths grew scant.

The rates committee decided that the parsonage did *not* belong to Parris after all and that his pay might be raised by *voluntary* donations instead of the agreed-upon amount, which was already in arrears. Tituba's master attended meeting after meeting with increasing irritation and suspicion. His ordination bound him to the Village Church, but a significant part of the congregation was acting against him.

If the master's future was uncertain, what could the slaves expect? Home was not secure, and the wilderness was full of unseen enemies.

Only the increasing cold was certain.

Mary Warren

Mary spits on the brass dial and gives it a final rub to make it gleam. . . . There.

She admires the nesting circles cut into the flat square plate, the arc of numbers, and the circling stars—wheels within wheels, beautiful and mysterious.

The sundial stands on a fence post set in the yard in front of the house on the farm that a large productive family works, and none of it is hers. Although she admires the beauty of the dial, she thinks also how extravagant it is. The thing won't show the time unless the sun shines, and if the sun shines, you can look at the sun itself to tell the time—or close enough.

"Mary!"

She realizes her mistress is talking to her, has been talking to her unheeded.

"*Mary! Stop woolgathering and fetch the water.*" (*Goodwife Procter sounds cross again. Little Abigail clings to her mother's apron whining for attention, the child's tone nearly as irritating as the mother's impatient voice.*) "*And be sure you close the lid so none of the children fall in.*"

"*Yes, ma'am.*"

No one has fallen in yet, *Mary thinks, feeling accused (though Goody Jacob's little girl did* die *in a well across the Village some years back, and her mother was never right in the head afterward, so it could* happen).

Mary stuffs the polishing rag into her pocket and fetches a pair of buckets and a yoke. As she walks away toward the well she hears the child droning on and on—"Mama, Mama!"—wanting attention. All this does is remind Mary of her own dead mother, and she thinks again how Goody Procter—when displeased—could sound so much like that other woman, that Alice Parker. She shrugs off the yoke, sets down her buckets, and hefts the wooden lid off the well.

There, far, far down, floats a circle of daylight and her own dim, ghostly reflection blocking the sun. Another bucket hangs from the long well-sweep, and this one she eases down the shaft toward the water until it shatters the surface into shards of light and dark.

As she lets the counterweighted sweep pivot to draw up the heavy bucket, she hears again in her memory Goody Parker's ranting as she berated Father, as if he were a servant and not a neighbor, and all this just before Mother grew worse, her illness strengthening as she herself grew weaker, she along with Mary's little sister. Mother died and the sister remained, though she is deaf now, locked into a silence that would not end in this life.

Mary pours the water into her other buckets and wrestles the well's lid back into place, securing it with a rock on top. Settling the yoke back on her sore neck, she steadies the slopping buckets at the end of their ropes and starts cautiously back to the house. If it were my house, she thinks, I would still face a constant round of work, but at least it would be *mine*. I would have something to show for it. *However, if there is a way to change her future, she cannot see it; no ambitious young man is courting her—and certainly no rich ones.*

She notices that someone is trudging up the road from Salem town. If they stop for a drink, she will have to serve the beer. Well, maybe there will be news from the harbor. Maybe someone new will come into her life, perhaps offering her a better future elsewhere rather than slaving here for someone else's family.

Maybe her fortunes, mysterious as they might be, will change at last.

Mary Warren's family is one of the less well documented, and her origin is still uncertain, for more than one family named Warren settled in seventeenth-century New England—in Plymouth, in Watertown, and elsewhere. The sketchy-yet-tantalizing details of the girl's life before 1692 exist only in the witch trial testimony, and her life afterward is presently unknown. But during the trials *MARY* played a reoccurring part in the documents, with her voice recorded in the surviving texts, where the words and actions of individuals more prominent in their own and later times do not survive, and her significant presence in those documents became an embarrassing reminder of the panic.

She was *not* the daughter of Abraham and Isabella Warren, who may have had ties with Ipswich and who lived in the Rial Side section of Salem near the Beverly border. (Abraham did have a daughter Mary, but in 1692 she was Widow Green.) Sarah Osborn, one of the first to be accused in 1692, may have been a Warren *before* she married Robert Prince and then Alexander Osborn. Again, the kinship, if any, is presently unknown.

Mary was "about twenty" in 1692, meaning that she was born around 1672, the year Rebecca Nurse joined the Salem Church, shortly before the outbreak of King Philip's War of 1675–1676. Just when the heart of Mary's own family disintegrated is not clear, however. Perhaps it was during one of the epidemics of smallpox, a disease deadly in its democracy, not long before the witch scare.

It began—as far as Mary was concerned—when Goodwife Alice Parker asked Mary's father to mow her grass. This meant to harvest the grass in a meadow, an important crop that would feed a family cow through the winter. Her husband, a fisherman, was likely absent at sea that haying season. Warren said he would if he had the time, but he did not make time to mow, so Goody Parker came to his house in a temper. On the one hand, Warren had his own work to do, and perhaps the illness was already in the household. On the other hand, if grass were not cut, dried, and properly stored in time, it would spoil and be useless, leaving the cow unfed and the owner facing the expense of buying hay. Mary was probably present when they exchanged heated words, thus witnessing the woman's tongue-lashing, an affront to her father. "He had better he *had* done it" was the phrase that stuck in Mary's mind, a threat for sure.

Shortly after this encounter her sister Elizabeth fell ill and, following quickly, their mother as well. Evidently, Mary escaped catching the disease—perhaps she was already employed elsewhere at that time—but Mother became weaker and weaker until she died. Elizabeth survived, but she lost her hearing. Engulfed in a terrible silence and overwhelmed by that silence, she ceased to speak.

Yes, Mary certainly remembered Goody Parker's words.

Alice Parker was married to fisherman John Parker. They lived just south of Salem Neck, not far from the Blue Anchor Tavern, and they rented their home from Mary English. Alice may have been a friend of Bridget Bishop, for their two spirits would be frequently reported committing mischief together. Goody Parker was also subject to fits of catalepsy, in which she suddenly fell unconscious, only to be discovered stiff and seemingly dead. Some of her neighbors were accustomed to this sight—it was a known malady, after all—but it unnerved others. Witches, according to folklore, were said to be able to leave their bodies behind and go about in spirit only to work their evil.

Where the Warrens lived and where the meadow was located remain unknown. The Parkers and the Warrens were likely neighbors, and the grass was perhaps in a rented meadow further out of town. What the shattered family did after their mother's death is also a mystery—where their father and Elizabeth went, whether they stayed in Salem (for they are alluded to only in trial documents), or what happened to the sister later. In the seventeenth century some individuals who lost hearing from childhood illness developed a system of personal signing that their families at least could use with them, but many others did not.

Mary was definitely working for John and Elizabeth Procter by 1692 and living with them inland just south of the Salem Village boundary. John Procter, about sixty years old at the time, was originally from Ipswich, where he still owned land and his brothers lived. He had been married twice before, first to a woman named Martha (possibly White), then to Elizabeth Thorndike. One son, Benjamin, the only one of the first wife's four children to survive, was now thirty-three and worked for his father. The second wife had born seven children, with at least two of them since dead and the eldest daughter now married and away. In 1674 John married Elizabeth Bassett of Lynn, whose grandmother Ann Burt had doctored her neighbors, and some had suspected her of being a witch. Healing skills were proper woman's work, but "cunning folk" claimed to heal as well. Although some of those suspicions went to court, Goody Burt was not found guilty of any of it. By 1692 Elizabeth was in her forties and had given birth to six children, only one of whom had died.

Procter rented a three hundred–acre farm named "Groton" from Emanuel Downing (whose London landholdings included the area where Downing Street was later built). The road from Salem ran uphill, dividing the farm as it ran before the house, while North Brook ran south of the road, heading for the North River and Salem Harbor. The bounds, marked by stumps and trees of black oak and white oak, encompassed plow land and a bit of swamp.

Procter obtained a license in 1666 to sell beer, cider, and liquors to passersby only (the neighborhood warned not to tarry there), as so many travelers stopped, hoping for refreshment. This meant that the women of the family served them while Procter and his sons and hired men worked the fields. There were problems in 1678, however, when John Procter was fined for selling "cider and strong water to Indians," but several neighbors testified in court that the Procters kept an orderly house. As for the charge, according to Zerubabel Endicott, "I fear it's out of ill will more than matter." But Giles Corey (whom Procter had mistakenly suspected of setting fire to his house some time earlier) and others described how they found an Indian lying drunk on the floor with a pot of cider. Corey's wife recalled that

Goody Procter had commented that "she might as well let them have drink as other folk." Unfortunately, that particular customer could not hold his liquor. Others said she had accepted items in pawn for a gill of liquor, a custom that could only encourage debt. Not only Procter but also Corey's son-in-law John Parker (a farmer, not the Salem mariner) were fined for selling to the Indians this time. Despite this and a few other fines for letting other people's servants get drunk, the courts renewed Procter's liquor license periodically.

Mary was the hired girl, earning an agreed-upon wage for a year at a time, plus room and board and whatever tips visitors might bestow. Any servant's situation depended on the mood of the employer. Some were treated as part of the family, and a few received bequests years later from grateful masters and mistresses. Others were mistreated, with the females sometimes at risk from predatory masters or other males in the family, or they dallied, unwisely assuming they could marry into the family only to be disabused of that notion once they had conceived. "Correcting" a servant included striking or even beating and was within a master's right if it were not overdone. For instance, Giles Corey went too far when, exasperated by the neighbor's slow-witted brother he had hired, he beat the man repeatedly with a stout stick. Even with a physician's attentions, the young man soon died. Corey was tried for murder, but because other people also frequently hit the deceased, he escaped the potentially capital charge and ended up only paying a stiff fine.

However, resentful servants could make employers' lives miserable, such as by pilfering their pantries, terrorizing their children in the parents' absence (as Reverend John Hale's family endured for a time), and even threatening to kill them. Kitchen help had the opportunity to slip poisons into the food, after all.

The Procters attended religious meeting in Salem rather than the Village, so Mary would have listened to sermons there from old Mr. Higginson or his assistant Nicholas Noyes when she was not left at home tending the youngest children.

She would have sat in the galleries with the other servants, for the seating was assigned by earthly rank and separated by sex, with women on one side of the center aisle and men on the other (rather than in family pews, as was the later custom). From up there Mary and the other hired girls could look down on the more favored seats below where the Procters and Nurses sat, and, unless they let their minds wander, listen to the ministers' long sermons and prayers.

The younger minister Nicholas Noyes frequently referred to the Book of Revelation with its strange imagery. The elderly John Higginson emphasized the uses of life's trials, for the troubles and sorrows we suffer may at least teach us something, may strengthen us spiritually. Mary's life had had trials enough for her to brood on—her mother's death, her own uncertain future—but what would she learn from them?

Between morning and afternoon services—or in whispered conversations when they should be paying attention—the girls and young women exchanged news and gossip. Mary would have heard the other hired girls' stories of growing up Eastward in Maine or New Hampshire until driven south to Massachusetts, fleeing the attacks of French and Indian forces that came out of nowhere with fire and sword; she would have heard of parents, siblings, and neighbors shot or axed or kidnapped. These raiding parties burned the remote towns, slaughtered the cattle, killed many of the townsfolk, and took survivors hostage. They moved some captives to their own native villages and marched others all the way to Canada, with many dying on the trail. Some captives were eventually ransomed, but others never returned home—melting into a Catholic life, forgetting their own faith, even, especially among the youngest children, their own language. The girls now in Salem had escaped, though many had lost close kin. One girl had slipped away with her family and Reverend George Burroughs to a little island off Falmouth and hid there until Massachusetts sent help.

Memories like that never faded for those who had endured them. For others, just hearing about those horrors increased the dread of what might yet happen.

Homelife with the Procters may have been tense. The older children seemed to have resented Elizabeth. Even in 1678, during the early years of her marriage, when the court questioned their liquor license, John's then sixteen-year-old daughter Elizabeth (by his second wife) was the one who kept the keys to the cellar and was responsible for serving the drinks. Goodwife Procter may have appreciated the help, though ordinarily the mistress of the house controlled the keys to all supplies. By 1692 stepdaughter Elizabeth was married to Thomas Very (whose sister Elizabeth married Francis and Rebecca Nurse's son John), but stepson Benjamin was part of the household still, more like an uncle in age to his youngest half-siblings. Years later, after the witch trials, he would state, "I was the eldest son of my father, and worked for my father 'til I was about thirty years of age, and helped bring up all my father's children by all his wives, one after another."

Perhaps a disagreement arose in the winter of 1688–1689, for on January 10, shortly before the birth of Elizabeth's fifth child, John submitted two deeds to probate judge Bartholomew Gedney. At least one had been written some years earlier, as it referred to his "purpose, if the Lord pleaseth, to make Elizabeth Bassett, of Lynn . . . my wife I having her parents consent thereunto." In the second she is Elizabeth Procter. The first stipulated that any children he and Elizabeth might have would inherit equally with his older children, and for this he put up, as bond, his land in the Chebaco section of Ipswich. The second states his intent "to make over and give unto my beloved wife Elizabeth Proctor and all my children . . . for their supply and maintenance" his Salem property, "house and land . . . cattle, swine, moveables and utensils." (The land here was a parcel adjacent to his rented farm.)

Judging from Mary's later testimony, John and Elizabeth quarreled as well, as she claimed that her master was nearly driven to make away with himself just to be rid of his wife's squabbles. Evidently Elizabeth knew her own mind and expressed it. She owned several books as well, even carrying one with her when she visited her sister in the nearby town of Reading. Just *what* that book was about Mary did not know. Elizabeth also seems to have doctored her neighbors (or offered to) as her grandmother had done.

Mary must have been anxious about her own future.

Besides domestic work, women earned money by doing laundry, baking, brewing, or running small shops or taverns—but all these services required equipment and, in some cases, a license. Married women or widows ran these enterprises, not young servant girls who possessed the desire but not the means. Women were sometimes paid to spin thread (helping a housewife deal with the flax she had grown or the fleece from her sheep), sew, or help with harvest, though the latter was seasonal or at least occasional work. By herself, she *might* earn enough with only those tasks and still have a place to live—but not easily. A few women who could afford it rented space in the corner of a room in someone else's house. Unless a woman had money or a strong extended family willing to have her be part of it, or if she worked as a domestic (as Mary did), she would need a husband to survive.

Mary was about twenty in 1692, the average age to marry.

But what prospects did she have?

She could be working in another woman's kitchen forever, unless the enemy captured her, dragging her off into darkness and wilderness, or if, like her dead mother and stricken sister, she were the victim of vengeful magic—another fearful possibility.

PART TWO

(1)
January 1692

From the meeting house gallery Tituba looks down on Mr. Parris as he speaks in the pulpit and down to on the heads of the congregation below—men on one side of the center aisle, women on the other, adults apart from the children. Up here above are the servants—free and slave—also sitting apart, the doctor's hired girl with the Putnam's maid. Tituba sees the heads of two young girls bend close, the children whispering when they ought to be listening: Mr. Parris's niece Abigail and the Putnam girl. Tituba hugs her cloak closer against the cold of the unheated building. Now what were they up to? At home Abigail—and Betty too—had been acting strange lately, though Tituba could not say exactly how. They seemed more nervous, moping or starting. She was almost certain that some eggs were missing from the larder. Had the girls taken them—though not to eat but rather to waste on fortune-telling? Girls that age might do that—and a little scrying was surely harmless if done right, *thinks Tituba, though she knows full well that Reverend Parris would not agree, and there would be an almighty trouble if he finds out*, if that was what was happening. If they are sickening for something, she would have to deal with that as well, but for now, with hands idle in her lap, she might as well enjoy not working. Even so, she needs to listen, to some extent, to what her master says to the people, for he will question her on it later. Tituba sighs. He expects her to understand what his sermons mean. If she can just catch the gist of his words, she can then let her mind wander to other subjects, have her thoughts to herself.

"Man, yea all mankind," Reverend Parris is saying, "the whole race of apostate Adam . . . even the very elect, are by nature dead in sins and trespasses . . ."

All mankind? *Tituba muses to herself.* Even the masters and mistresses who want to own you?

"*Consider the great sacrifices Christ has made for us," Parris continues, "and think how much that indicates that 'the worth of souls, is above all the world . . .'"*

Even the soul of a slave? *she wonders. Perhaps Christ thinks so, for slaves who felt they were saved, and thus among the spiritual elect, had joined churches in Boston. But they still remained slaves despite the passage in the Lord's Prayer her master had taught her: "May* thy *will be done on earth as it is in Heaven." God's will—not earthly property laws. These people were very definite about what they expected, yet there were so many contradictions.*

Down in the better seats among the matrons, Ann Putnam looks up from where she sits at Mr. Parris, at his head and shoulders that are visible above the edge of the pulpit's desk, with the cushion on the desk and the open Bible on the cushion. His breath makes little clouds just visible against the dark wood of the sounding board above the pulpit. She would take communion later with the other full members of the church, but even so . . . she does still wonder if she is really *worthy enough to do so.*

Christ, by "various troubles, afflictions, and persecutions in this world," tests and teaches his people, says Reverend Parris, as parents chasten children to get the point of obedience across. "Our lord Jesus seeing us often overbold and venturesome upon sin, suffers us almost to fall even as it were over head and ears, and for a time seems to desert us, and all is out of love to prevent a total fall . . ."

The little nagging dread stirs in the back of her mind that she might not be saved after all, that by presuming to take part in communion she is only thrusting in where she does not belong, snatching rudely and insultingly at the Lord's supper like a self-centered toddler grabbing at supper dishes that were none of its business. But no—she pushes that thought away. She has already done years of soul searching; she had not rushed into this grave matter of assuming herself to be saved. (Although one never knew, could never be sure in this mortal life but only try to live as if one were.) Her name was written among the elect—or at least written in the church record book's list of fully communing members.

"Afflictions are compared to a hedge of thorns," Reverend Parris con-
tinues, made to keep unruly livestock from bolting into dangerous terri-
tory. Because the elect are, in a way, separate from the world, others will
oppose them, for "great hatred ariseth even from nearest relations," and
"it is the main drift of the Devil to pull it all down," aided by "wicked
and reprobate men (the assistants of Satan to afflict the Church)." Even
the elect are endangered inwardly by their own soul lusts, outwardly by
persecutions and by "the power of Death."

Yet, says Parris, offering encouragement, Christ defends his Church
and his elect not only "by supplying them with renewed strength suitable
to their trials" but also "by hampering and fettering their enemies."

Ann concentrates again on the sermon instead of her pestering doubts.
She does not see her daughter whispering with the other girls.

Behind the minister that January day snow thickened and filled the scant view from the two high windows that flanked the pulpit. With the actual ceremony of the Lord's Supper for the full members still to do and the snow showing no signs of slacking, Mr. Parris finally cut short his sermon and dismissed the majority. Tituba would have taken the Parris children home to the parsonage while her mistress, Mrs. Putnam, and the other communing members stayed behind.

Samuel Parris's booklet of sermon notes, with his reference to the shortened meeting, has by chance survived. But what either Reverends John Higginson or Nicholas Noyes preached that day in Salem town has vanished unrecorded. As snow fell on Salem, on the wharves and the vessels moored at their wharves and on the larger Salem meeting house on the rise above the harbor, Mary English sat in the better of the women's seats, her husband among the favored men of the town, with her perhaps listening more attentively than he. Bridget and Edward Bishop occupied lesser seats in the men's and women's sides of the aisle, along with John and Elizabeth Procter. The Procter's maidservant Mary Warren watched from the gallery.

Rebecca Nurse and her family usually attended services in the nearer Village meeting house, but as she was a fully communing member of the church in Salem town, that is where her family took her to partake of the sacrament of the Lord's Supper. That winter would prove hard on her health, but she was not house-bound yet. Today she could also hear sermons and prayers from the elderly Reverend John Higginson and the younger Reverend Nicholas Noyes.

Reverend Noyes, known as a pleasant conversationalist among men of his own station, delivered sermons in a plain style, demonstrating his doctrine point by point. He was also perpetually curious and, some people thought, incautiously fond of the prophecies in the Book of Revelation.

Reverend Higginson, in the view of a recent visitor to Salem, "uses soft words but hard arguments, and labors more to shew the truth of his cause, than his spleen [i.e., his temper]." The old man was firm in the face of wrong, yet, as Noyes would describe it,

Reproofs, like lightning from him flew;
But Consolations dropt like dew.
The one broke Hearts as hard as Stone,
The other heal'd the Contrite one.

Higginson's "Touch-stone," Noyes added, was the use of life's hardships to teach and strengthen one's faith. One needed to be strong, for no one knew what they might have to face.

Bridget Bishop had heard the sermons too, but she left with most of the congregation after the regular service. Mary English and Rebecca Nurse, the richest woman in Salem and a farm wife respectively, remained for communion, to receive the sacrament and share the Lord's Supper with not only the other elect present but also as one in the long line of Christians, a fellowship reaching far into the past, back to the Apostles and to Christ himself.

This would have been important enough for Rebecca to make the effort to journey through the snow to town. But the rest of the time she stayed closer to home, where her extended family could keep her informed about the outside world—what families had sickness in them, who was near her time to deliver yet another child, what the situation was with Salem town and its quarrels.

Her husband, Francis, was on the committee the Village had chosen to represent their wish for more self-rule. So Francis was among
the rest who toiled down the muddy roads to the harbor on January 11
during a thaw to present their case before the Salem town meeting.
He returned with a story of town men treating the Village committee
like so many bumpkins when the Villagers asked to separate and form
their own town.

The Villagers had then offered an alternate request. (*They* were
willing to compromise and had also, just in case, petitioned the province's General Court in Boston for separation.) If they could not be
independent, could they be exempt from all charges that related
strictly to the town area in exchange for maintaining their own roads
and poor? The Salem men were no more agreeable to this, claiming
that the petitioners were not properly empowered to act for the Village; therefore they postponed the question—postponed indefinitely,
Salem hoped. But the Village committee, irritated at the dismissal,
were not about to let the matter drop.

At some point in January, when there was still snow on the ground
in Salem town, Bridget Bishop's friend Alice Parker suffered a cata-
tonic fit. She would not have remembered what happened during the
spell, but her neighbors had plenty to say about it. They found her
outdoors crumpled "upon the durt & Snow," looking quite dead. One
woman assured the men that this had happened before, that it was
an illness she had. Yet the men were skittish about touching her, and
the man who carried her home, slung over his shoulder like a sack of
meal, dropped her in his nervousness. Even then she did not wake,
but just when most everyone thought she was dead for sure—after
they undressed her and arranged her in bed—she came to and
laughed right in their faces. Alice may have felt relieved at waking,
but some of the neighbors suspected that she had parted her soul
from her body in order to spirit about who-knew-where and had just
returned to mock them at their efforts. Witches, they knew, could
do that.

People also knew full well that such afflictions, even if not understood, were natural. But gossip was dangerous. Bridget Bishop could
sympathize with her friend.

The Village folk also did not understand whatever worsening ailments troubled the girls at the Salem Village parsonage. Sighing and moping progressed to flinching and twisting, as if shying from something invisible—to others. Betty and Abigail gabbled nonsense no one could understand, huddled under the furniture as if hiding from . . . what? Mr. and Mrs. Parris first tried home remedies for ordinary illnesses. Then they called in the local physicians. When that did not ease the girls they added prayer, but the problem only grew. By January 20, according to Tituba's later testimony, Betty and Abigail spent the evening in the parlor (sitting room and master bedroom combined) with Mr. and Mrs. Parris, both of whom prayed over the girls. But prayer did not bring peace to them. Tituba, in the hall (the main room of the house) could hear the racket from the parlor across the entry, could hear their cries and shrieks as if they were being pinched.

The question persists to this day—what *was* the matter with the girls? Were they faking the whole thing? Would they have dared to? Had they genuinely frightened themselves by forbidden fortune-telling, or was something else wrong, some physical ailment?

Over the centuries critics and commentators, discarding witchcraft as a cause, have proposed that the accusers' so-called afflictions were the product of the Devil's deceptions, of their own conscious lies, of a natural mediumship, of clinical hysteria, of influenza, of ergot poisoning. "Fraud and imposture," wrote Thomas Hutchinson in 1750, a continuing view that in its more extreme form supposes a massive conspiracy.

The more popular explanations imagine a combination of lies and folk magic. In the nineteenth century Charles Upham described regular get-togethers of certain girls and young women to practice fortune-telling and other forbidden arts that Tituba taught them, as he assumed that, being a slave, she was likely to meddle in voodoo. *Nothing* in the contemporary record supports the idea that Tituba taught magic.

As Parris no doubt told his family and his flock, fortune-telling and other occult practices were an invitation to unauthorized spirits—devils. Nevertheless, the folk culture that was brought to New England from Britain preserved a strong current of folk magic that sought to counteract other people's evil magic, sought to deduce hidden information either by contacting angelic (or at least neutral) spirits or initiating some hazily understood natural process. Results, after all, appeared to show that *something* had happened. Although anyone might try to do this, the more proficient were called "cunning folk"—cunning men and cunning women. They knew something others did not.

In that winter of 1691–1692 some adults did attempt fortune-telling, and at least two unnamed girls tried to tell the future.

"I fear," Reverend John Hale of Beverly later wrote, "some young persons, through a vain curiosity to know their future condition, have tampered with the Devil's tools, so far that thereby one door was opened to Satan to play those pranks; *Anno* 1692.

"One of the Afflicted persons," he continued, "did try with an egg and a glas to find her future Husband's Calling." This was also called a Venus Glass, which is to say that she filled a clear beer glass with water and then dropped an egg white into it and watched the forms the thicker albumin made as it moved through the water until it suggested a shape that could be interpreted in relation to possible suitors. As a husband's condition in the world determined a wife's status, a girl might make out the hazy shape of someone she already hoped for or an object to serve as a clue: a fish for a fisherman or a sailing ship for a merchant. In this case "there came up a Coffin, that is, a specter in likeness of a Coffin. And she was afterward followed with diabolical molestations to her death; and so died a single person." (She died before 1697, when Hale wrote his account.)

"Another I was called to pray with," Hale continued, "being under sore fits and vexations of Satan," turned out to have "tried the same charm: and after her confession of it and manifestation of repentance for it, and our prayers to God for her, she was speedily released from those bonds of Satan."

In 1969 Chadwick Hansen suggested that the girl who saw the coffin and died young was Abigail Williams, and that the girl who confessed and recovered was Betty Parris. However, Mary Beth Norton pointed out in 2002 that girls older than nine-year-old Betty and eleven-year-old Abigail were more likely to have husbands on their minds, that Mary Warren or Susanna Sheldon were more likely candidates for the Venus Glass practice.

In Andover Goodwife Rebecca Johnson and her daughter, following a British tradition, turned a sieve to know if her absent brother-in-law was still alive. This involved two questioners suspending a sieve, its cylindrical wooden side made from thin, bent wood, with the bottom mesh woven of horse hair, between the blades of shears—blade and spring beaten from one strip of bent and sharpened metal—each person steadying the hoop with an index finger to the curve of the shear's spring. They then asked the question and waited for the spirits—or their own muscle twinges—to twitch the arrangement. "By Saint Peter & Saint Paul," Goody Johnson had recited, "if Haggat be dead Let this sieve turn round." And the sieve turned—though Haggat was actually still alive.

Or a searcher might place a large house key inside the pages of a Bible, tie the now-bowed book closed, then spin it around while asking a question. They might also first insert thin slips of paper bearing a question or a biblical verse into the key's hollow shaft. Thus, people sought information on lost loved ones, prospective husbands, strayed sweethearts, missing livestock as well as the identity of the thief who stole them.

Andover farmer and carpenter Samuel Wardwell told fortunes for his neighbors, revealing who would marry and who would die. It seemed a knack for him. "He was much adicted to that," a neighbor would recall, "and mayd sport of it." According to another neighbor, "said wardwall would look in their hand and then would Cast his Eyes down: upon the ground allways before he told Eny thing."

"An ancient woman" confided to Reverend Hale that she had seen her future husband in a conjuror's mirror back in England. Another parishioner, Dorcas Hoar, studied books of palmistry and physiognomy in order to see what the marks and forms of people's palms and faces indicated. She also had the disconcerting habit of declaring that apparently healthy children would not live long—to the grief of the parents when the prediction *did* come true.

Roger Toothaker of Billerica and Salem seemed the most professional of the local cunning folk, offering his services as a folk healer who used traditional medicines as well as charms and claiming that he could also find out thieves and witches. He boasted that he and his daughter had even *killed* a witch by using a charm that deflected the magic back against the source. Clearly he considered himself on the side of good spirits, regardless of whatever doubts that others might harbor for his methods.

But any answer, the ministers would explain, if not self-delusion, was the work of evil spirits—devils. Good spirits—angels—were better employed about God's business, and dead kin—ghosts—would have gone on to the next life in either Heaven or Hell. A wandering spirit was not to be trusted.

If the girls in the parsonage had been attempting magic, it was probably not a Venus Glass. They may have tried to find other information, but if they had not been involved with magic, then what did cause their odd actions and reactions that winter?

Might it have begun with a game of pretend that was later taken too seriously, either by the girls themselves or by adults who unexpectedly observed them?

The theory that it involved symptoms of ergot poisoning from tainted rye bread doesn't work. No one else in the household had convulsions, and convulsions occur only in cases of vitamin A deficiency, which is unlikely, given the available diet. Otherwise the symptom is gangrene, and no one reported that known malady. Any physical cause seems suspect, otherwise the cases of "bewitched" behavior would have been more widespread throughout the population.

As Chadwick Hansen proposed, clinical hysteria, now known as conversion disorder, seems to fit the situation. Fear and the reactions to great fear can match cultural expectations of what the symptoms would be, and prolonged terror and hopelessness can lead to death. In lesser situations a terrified person breathes too shallowly and, lacking enough oxygen, can fall unconscious, hallucinate, or convulse. The afflicted did all these things. Even if some of them only half-believed their situation, the reactions could become a self-fulfilling prophesy and, thus, apparent proof of evil magic to onlookers.

The times were uncertain. *If* the girls in Parris's household had been scrying the future on any matter, they would be anxious about

Reverend Parris possibly catching them at it, for surely he would not approve, considering the method an enticement to devils. The girls *knew* that yet did it anyway (or someone did). That alone would frighten them not just for being caught but also, if he were right and now that they had done it, they may have roused spirits best left alone. It was like striking a hornets' nest. They might fear the possible presence of baleful spirits *and* being caught and punished. In addition, they had other matters to worry them. At home in the parsonage the girls could have overheard enough of the parents' discontent to be uneasy.

Reverend Parris had not been paid his salary for a year, except what portions his supporters gave him themselves. His supply of firewood dwindled dangerously low in the freezing weather while the committee in charge of payment—Francis Nurse was on that committee—refused to collect it, never mind distribute it. They even disputed the promised transfer of ownership of the parsonage that Parris thought had been settled. Did he own his own home? Would he receive enough earthly substance to support himself and his family? Did he have the moral support of his congregation or not?

Beyond the Village problems, the times were uncertain for all of Massachusetts and New England: no one knew what London might decide to do to their government or what murderous attacks France and their Indian allies might inflict.

News at the end of January that York, Maine, had been attacked and burned on January 25 did nothing to calm anyone. Salem heard that seventy to a hundred survivors were kidnapped and about fifty people were dead, including the minister—shot through the head as he mounted his horse in front of his own door, and his corpse was mutilated as the town burned. All of this provided the attackers, as Cotton Mather would put it, with a "Diabolical Satisfaction."

As word of the York attack spreads through Salem Village, Ann Putnam's maid Mercy Lewis is struck by the news even more directly than the rest of the household, for she had lived through just such a nightmare when she had been a young child, surviving when so many others had perished brutally. Ann hopes the girl is not frightening the children with the bloody details. Thomas looks grim, and Ann forbears asking him about his own past experiences fighting such savages. To the whole household the frontier war has become an intimate and imminent threat.

The peril is real enough to the Nurse household, yet their relief that Benjamin at least has been spared frontier militia duty tempers their anxiety. Francis and Rebecca need his help more and more, as does his wife and child. Rebecca can be grateful for that mercy.

In the Village parsonage Tituba overhears her owners' worries. Reverend Parris sees the York attack as a scene straight from Hell, the violence not only leveling a whole settlement but also specifically targeting the minister, thus striking not only at the physical body of the community but also at its spiritual head. Tituba remembers the rumor from two winters before that the French would attack the English settlers but spare "the Negro and Indian servants"—the slaves. From what she and John have heard, however, nothing like that happened at York. They cannot expect a liberation from the Eastward—only more danger.

(2)

February 1692

Having finished overseeing the children's lessons, checking her embroidered marks identifying the freshly laundered linens against the household inventory to confirm none were missing, entering the latest rent receipts collected from her tenants, seeing that the kitchen servants have supper well in hand, and leaving milk from the bob-tailed cow cooling in the buttery, Mistress Mary English sits in her parlor and opens a book. The blue evening light in the diamond-paned windows contrasts with the coppery hearth fire and the clear flames of good beeswax candles.

No sooner does she settle to reading than the front door opens and her husband's voice fills the entry as he calls for one of the men to pull off his snowy boots. He surges into the parlor and sits down triumphantly.

"I've done it!" he announces. "The selectmen took a vote favoring my building and furnishing a proper pew for us in the meeting house"—for himself and two other merchants, Mary knows, suitable for their status.

He tosses his periwig onto another chair for the servant to carry out with the boots. No more wandering drafts along the meeting house floor, much less wandering dogs. And so much for Boston's insulting order that no French are to live on the coast. Obviously, Salem knows him better than that, knows he is not siding with the enemy. His native Jersey and its Protestant ways are at risk from Catholic King Louis as well. None of the other French in town are about to leave everything and depart either.

"That is a good turn of events," Mary agrees. With all the latest troubles, the neighbors' trust is a comfort—one less thing to worry about.

Elsewhere in Salem Goodwife Bridget Bishop stands by her fire to hook the iron lid off the Dutch oven and stir the stew within. Replacing the lid and the pan of coals on top, she looks sharply about the room for her granddaughter. Susanna is busy lining up little pieces of kindling and playing with them like dolls, well away from the cook-fire and the grease-filled Betty lamp that is casting a dim glow in the room. Bridget twitches the hem of her woolen petticoat away from the fire. Being woolen, it will smolder first, but there is no use risking flames and a burn.

She peers out the small window at the dusky street, wondering how long before Edward will return home with his muddy boots. Instead of seeing Edward, however, she sees the Shattuck woman with that strange boy of hers dragging behind, tugging on his mother's hand as if the street were full of obstacles. Bridget is never sure if he acts that way on purpose or not. Goody Shattuck pulls the lad along, her shoulders slumped, look-ing utterly weary. Feeling sorry for that family would be easier if they did not blame her for the boy's afflictions. She picks up her granddaughter and hugs her close. At least this child is well, but the threats that sur-round them are still out there—not least of which is the threat of neigh-borhood witch suspicions.

A woman at the lower end of the social scale arrived around this time at Samuel Parris's door, a pipe in her mouth, an in-fant in her arms, and a four-year-old girl in tow. She was Sarah Good, a married woman nevertheless reduced to begging for her children's sake. Having to ask galled her, for she had begun life as the daughter of a much better off innkeeper and then slowly de-scended into greater and greater poverty as first one husband died in debt and then a second proved inept at supporting his family, as her pride soured to resentment.

Tituba may have answered the door, but it was her master's place to decide on charity. He gave Sarah something for the child and watched the woman depart as she muttered in a tone more resentful than thankful. Betty and Abigail probably watched the encounter and heard the grumbling. Had the tattered woman uttered a curse? Did the girls frighten themselves all the more with speculations? Later the adults would recall that the malady the two suffered—whatever it was—grew worse around this time.

Sarah Good seldom attended meeting—"for want of cloase," she would say—but she could well have agreed with one of Reverend Parris's statements in his next sacrament sermon. "It is a woeful piece of corruption in an evil time, when the wicked prosper, & the godly party meet with vexations," he proclaimed, perhaps thinking of the stubborn rates committee or of the more vicious frontier attacks. (Tituba, in the gallery, might wonder about the wickedness of slave catching, of families lost and separated.) Yet misfortune, Parris continued, "teacheth us to War a good warfare, to subdue all our Spiritual enemies." It fell to him, then, as their minister to separate "the precious & the vile" within the congregation, "to encourage & comfort" those who followed God's laws and "to refuse & reject" those who did not. Within this struggle, however, no one should think that God had forsaken them, that they were overwhelmed like a sinking ship. "The Church may meet with storms, but it will never sink. For Christ sits not idle in the Heavens, but takes the most faithful care of his little Ship . . . bound for the Port of Heaven."

But why *did* the wicked prosper? After receiving communion that day Ann most likely joined many of the neighboring women at the home of her cousin-in-law Hannah Putnam, who was near her time of giving birth. Women would gather at such occasions to offer practical help and moral support, to share the tasks of easing the mother as well as the child during an event that displayed both the power and the utter vulnerability of women. It was Hannah's travail, a time of pain and effort and danger. Any number of complications, from a breech birth to the mother's convulsions, could end in the death of both mother and child—more reminders for Ann of her dead sisters and their dead children.

Hannah was no stranger to what she might expect, as this was her eleventh child (and there would be more in years to come). Her husband Jonathan's task was to fetch the midwife and then get out from under foot—this was women's work. Custom and modesty did not encourage the presence of men.

Whether Hannah's children were sent away for further privacy is likely, but many customs are not clear, being that they were what everyone knew and few wrote down. In the weeks before the birth

Hannah, besides preparing the childbed linen and baby clothes, would have brewed groaning beer and baked groaning cakes, traditional refreshments for her company. The birth was serious, but the women may as well enjoy what they could when they could.

If she were still well enough and if the weather not too severe, Rebecca Nurse may have attended as well, offering her years of experience in childbearing and childrearing. But Ann found no comfort in Rebecca's presence. What chance remark, quirk of personality, or misunderstanding had caused the original misgiving is lost; perhaps Rebecca had once commented on the deaths of Ann's children as being God's will, an unfathomable sorrow that had to be endured. In any case, Ann did not trust Goodwife Nurse for all that the old woman was supposed to be saved.

Of the other children born in the Village that winter, Ann had likely helped when Mary Putnam, wife of Thomas's brother Edward, gave birth to baby Prudence, but perhaps not a few days later, when Rebecca Nurse's daughter Mary Tarbell gave birth to a son, much less when the beggar Sarah Good had produced a second daughter back in December.

Hannah survived her labor and delivered a daughter. So much could go wrong, if not at birth then in infancy or, if the child survived that, then in young childhood and beyond from accident or disease, from any number of material ailments, and also from ailments from the Invisible World—from evil magic.

The girls at the parsonage certainly were not well and did not improve. Local doctors came and went, offering nostrums, until one of them, assumed to be William Griggs, who lived on the east side of the Village toward Beverly, spoke of the possible cause that must already have whispered in the backs of people's minds. The girls are "under an Evil Hand," he observed—under the spell of someone who directed evil magic toward them.

This was by no means certain, even to the fearful parents who accepted the reality of such a possibility, as was true of nearly everyone of the era. That it *might* be so in any particular case was a matter for caution, even doubt, and prayer was the proper course to take. Although word of this doctor's diagnosis spread through the neighborhood, both

Mr. and Mrs. Parris felt they could leave the children at home in the care of Tituba and John on the lecture day of Thursday, February 25.

On that day their neighbor Goodwife Mary Sibley visited the parsonage, but not to see Reverend or Mrs. Parris; rather, as she explained to Tituba and John, she had come across the fields out of concern for the suffering children. There was a method that might relieve them, she said, something that Reverend Parris had probably not tried—a little folk magic (she would not have named it so plainly), an *antidote* to someone else's harmful magic, a way to *repel* the hurt. Reverend Parris needn't know about this.

Tituba knew that Goody Sibley was considered a Christian woman and was a full member of the Salem Village Church. A bit of benign magic, or whatever the people in New England called it, surely could do no harm and might at last relieve the girls' symptoms by identifying their cause.

Under Goody Sibley's direction John and Tituba proceeded to concoct a "witch-cake," as the neighbor called it—an *anti*-witch-cake, more like it. Magic did not just happen—it was caused. So who caused *this* problem?

To make the witch-cake, one must take some of the victim's urine (a part of the sufferer easily separated from her body, a part imbued with the baleful magic sent against her), mix it with rye meal (a cheaper flour), and form it into a small cake. Bake this in the hot ashes on the hearth, and when done, feed it to the dog. This they did while Betty and Abigail (though their whereabouts are not specified) probably looked on, wondering what would come of the piss-pot recipe, likely realizing then, if they had not before, that adults were convinced that someone was sending *maleficia* at them—some witch—for who else could do it? The dog—whether the Parris dog or the Sibley's is not stated—ate the cooked dough. This biting and digesting of the cake that contained a part of the patient and, thereby, a part of the person who sent the magic against the patient ought to hurt the responsible witch. Ideally the guilty party would be drawn to the place where this was happening or at least would feel pain themselves.

The known result from Goody Sibley's advice was that the girls felt worse, frightened that there really *was* a witch or witches coming after them. (The records are silent on what Thomas and Susanna Parris did, saw, or where they were.)

Now Tituba had even more to deal with, and when the master and mistress returned she did not dare tell them of Goody Sibley's visit. The girls had seen her make the witch-cake after all and that magic had not helped a bit. Would they blame *her* for worsening the situation? For Betty and Abigail, in addition to feeling jabs and pinches, now said they saw shadowy forms and concluded that these were entities causing the pains. The sensations were not merely twinges to them but rather the result of someone actively pinching or striking them.

Perhaps when Betty and Abigail reported phantoms an adult asked if they recognized who it was and they blamed Tituba. They certainly reported that Tituba's specter followed them and clawed at them when she was nowhere near them. When she was out of the room and out of their sight, Tituba learned, the girls knew where she was and what she was doing, leaving her to wonder if Goody Sibley's charm *had* opened the girls' eyes to the Invisible World. Something was loosed, for now the girls contorted with arms, legs, necks, and backs, as they twisted from side to side under some force more fearful than epilepsy, or they gagged and gasped as if something invisible to all but themselves were choking them. Tituba herself was now in an even more precarious position than slavery alone could impose.

Alarmingly, two other Village girls were similarly afflicted on the day of the witch-cake: Dr. Griggs's niece Betty Hubbard as well as Ann Putnam Jr. How fast had word of the witch-cake charm spread, and by whom?

If Reverend Parris had not already consulted with other area ministers, he did so now, for soon after Goody Sibley's visit several ministers and town leaders assembled at the parsonage. They saw the girls' convulsions and saw how the choking stopped them from speaking, from answering their questions. The cause, they feared, was "preturnatural," as Reverend John Hale of Beverly noted, for they "feared the hand of Satan was in them." Satan's human agent was another matter, however. The ministers advised Parris to pray for an answer and to "sit still and wait upon the Providence of God to see what time might discover."

Then they questioned Tituba.

What about the witch-cake? they wanted to know. Tituba admitted that she had made such a thing, but she did not mention Goody Sibley. "Her Mistress in her own Country was a Witch," she said, as Hale remembered it, for Mistress Pearhouse was safely distant. That woman had taught her ways to reveal real witches, to *prevent* their evil magic. Tituba herself was *not* a witch, she insisted.

Apparently the accuracy of the children's accusations was not entirely believed just yet. Tituba remained in the same household, though the girls' maladies did not cease.

Tituba was accused, and Tituba had helped make the witch-cake, but she was not alone in the process. Parris, writing a few weeks later, after he had questioned his slaves and after he discovered the neighbor's involvement, referred to "the making of a cake by my Indian Man, who had his directions from this our Sister Mary Sibley."

Robert Calef, writing a few years later, noted that "Mr. Parris's Indian Man and Woman made a Cake of Rye Meal, with the Children's Water, and Baked it in the Ashes, and, as is said, gave it to the Dog; this was done as a means to Discover Witchcraft."

Reverend Hale of Beverly also noted the incident a few years later. Parris, he wrote, "had also an Indian Man servant, and his Wife who afterwards confessed, that without the knowledge of their Master or Mistress, they had taken some of the Afflicted persons Urine, and mixing it with meal had made a Cake, & baked it, to find out the Witch, as they said." After that was when the girls accused Tituba of pinching them.

John was mentioned more often than Tituba, but the girls did not cry out against him. As an adult left in charge of the children, Tituba would have had to discipline them from time to time, order them about at least. Yet as a slave with the status of property, she had no authority of her own. Were one or both of the girls showing resentment or a genuine, if misplaced, fear? Had one called for the woman and Parris interpreted the spoken name as the answer to the question of who hurt her? Did the girls identify the specters they claimed they saw before or after an adult suggested names for them? And once the parents took the remarks as accusations and seconded them with their own belief, the girls might well think that adult approval proved the supposition and came to believe what, after all, had been a question rather than a certain statement.

Gossip flew across the Village, spreading the word that the ailing girls were bewitched. Rebecca Nurse heard of the malady in the minister's family and remembered a time years beforehand when she too had suffered convulsive fits. Visiting the family would be the neighborly thing to do, but she feared that her own fits would reoccur if she saw the girls when one or both were in a seizure.

Beginning Thursday, the very day of the witch-cake, Dr. Grigg's niece Elizabeth Hubbard began to act afflicted as well. She would have heard of his earlier diagnosis of the evil hand, and this seemed to prove it. Also on Thursday, Ann Putnam witnessed her daughter, her namesake, begin to flinch away from some invisible menace, some spirit that neither she nor Thomas could perceive. They could only guess where it was by their daughter's reactions, guess what it was doing by their daughter's words and motions. Something, someone, kept pushing a book at the child, a book to sign her name in—the Devil's Book of his member witches, a base mockery of the church record book that listed Thomas and Ann's own names when they had joined.

On Saturday, February 27, a day of biting northeast wind, Elizabeth Hubbard arrived at the Procters' door, sent by her uncle, Dr. Griggs. The purpose of the errand was not recorded, but it would have been an opportunity for the girl to relate the latest Village news to Mary Warren, if to no one else. John Procter did his best to minimize the fears of possible witchcraft, but the maids were more apprehensive. Elizabeth left for the long trudge home, this time facing into the wind, and later word spread that a wolf had stalked the girl during her panicked walk.

On that same day Annie Putnam's agitation increased, until she had a name for the tormenting specter: Sarah Good.

So! Her identification of that disreputable beggar would come as no surprise to her parents. They could easily believe that that disagreeable and spiteful woman would cooperate with the Devil.

Annie's distress continued as she resisted the specter, with the weather matching the mood, lashing a tempest against the region.

Wind and cold rain drenched the still-frozen earth and flooded rivers already winter-full, drowning cattle westward and keeping many people from Sabbath services.

But it did not prevent the spread of gossip. Elizabeth Hubbard had reported specters not only of Sarah Good but also of Sarah Osborn, a sickly woman married to her former servant who now controlled his late master's farm.

By Monday Thomas Putnam had had enough. Resolved to put an end to the assaults from the Invisible World, he and his brother Edward, with neighbor Joseph Hutchinson and Rebecca Nurse's son-in-law Thomas Preston, braved the muddy roads and traveled into Salem town to register their complaint against Sarah Good, Sarah Osborn, and Tituba. They returned with news that the magistrates had issued arrest warrants immediately and ordered area constables to take the suspects into custody for questioning on the morrow at Ingersoll's ordinary.

Yet even this did not inhibit the specters. Although family and concerned neighbors gathered at Thomas and Ann Putnam's home to offer help and comfort, as was the custom in times of ordinary illness and hardship, Annie remained terrified all that evening, surrounded by spirits she said threatened her throat with a knife.

At the parsonage Betty and Abigail reported being pinched, but Tituba remained in the house. Parris ordered her to wash out the lean-to chamber, which was probably meant to keep her away from her supposed victims. Upstairs in the cold, low, slant-roofed room, which may have opened from her master's study, she worked under his suspicious eye. (Oddly, Parris did not seem to suspect John Indian, although he well knew the man had helped make the witch-cake.) Parris presumably gave consent for his slave to be named in the complaint. He must have questioned her himself after the gathering of ministers in order to inquire more forcefully just *what* she had been up to in his absence. It was a master's prerogative to "correct" a servant's ill behavior, and some were known to strike even their free white employees. However, she had not confessed to anything yet.

Tituba and John Indian kneel with the rest of the Parris family for evening prayers. They do this every day, but tonight concentration is impossible. Her master continues to address the Almighty aloud, but sudden shouts from Abigail and Betty drown out whatever he has to say. Betty and Abigail cringe and cower from specters they say are pinching them, stabbing them, tearing them away from prayer. Young Thomas and little Susanna are silent, the boy nervous but keeping apart from the girls, as Susanna starts to cry.

Abigail points to a swarm of invisible familiars that, to judge from the way she bats at the air, must surround her like a cloud of summer mosquitoes.

"The witches brought them!" she shouts.

Betty shrieks in terror again and again. Both girls topple as if struck, and they writhe under the table in a desperate attempt to escape . . . what?

Tituba's ears hurt from the piercing noises. She glances toward John, but his head is down. He is in no position to do much about any of this madness, much less to protect her. She cannot attend to Parris's prayers for fear of what these people mean to do next. None of the family trust her now. The girls react to her presence as they would to a rattlesnake in the house. She has no idea what to do about it.

(3)
March 1 to Mid-March 1692

Tituba learns what will happen early the next morning. While the girls are twitching as usual, the constable and some deputies arrive at the door, and Reverend Parris looks relieved but not surprised. She has barely enough time to snatch her cloak before they bind her hands and lead her outdoors into the cold. With a deputy on either side, she is marched down the road to the nearby ordinary—Deacon Ingersoll's home. They hold her arms firmly but seem jumpy, as if she might use magic to overpower them and escape. No one explains anything to her, but she gathers that the magistrates will question her here. So, she comes to understand, they do believe the children's accusations after all.

People are already loitering in the ordinary's yard, filling the tap room, where the magistrates will sit. They take her into another smaller room and leave her with Goodwife Ingersoll and some other women, but they stay within earshot. If Goody Ingersoll calls for help, they will rush in, but Tituba knows that no one will come if she cries out. She feels trapped and knows she must keep her wits about her if she is to find a chance to help herself.

She is to be searched for witch-marks and must remove her clothing. Shivering from more than drafts, Tituba removes her cloak and bodice and then pulls down her shift so Goody Ingersoll can look. No one seems to comment on any marks—something the Devil brands his witches with, Tituba understands, just as some slave masters brand runaways. There are no comments on anything from the waist down either. She tugs her clothes back together as Goody Ingersoll slips out. The two remaining women are also prisoners: an old woman who looks none too strong—Goodwife Sarah Osborn—and the ragged woman with a pipe who came begging at the parsonage—Sarah Good. Osborn looks desper-

ate. Good glares. Outside the door they hear the voice of Good's husband asking Goody Ingersoll if she saw a certain wart below his wife's right shoulder. He is precise when giving its location, though he is sure it was not there before. Good scowls all the more.

Sounds of the crowd increase, and time passes with no conversation among the three. They have nothing in common except their current captivity. At last a guard enters and tells them they're moving down the hill to the meeting house. Guards lead the three out, and the crowd parts but does not retreat far. Already too many people have swarmed to the site to fit in Ingersoll's ordinary, too many even for the large meeting house. Figures jostle at the windows as more pack the interior—more than those who attend on the Sabbath, Tituba notices.

Several strangers await them, men from Salem town: two magistrates, more deputies, and the constables. Reverend Parris and another man prepare to take notes. The four afflicted girls, clustered to one side, recoil at the sight of the prisoners. The magistrates say something, introducing the proceedings, then Good is brought forward to be questioned first while Tituba and Osborn are taken out of the room to wait their turns.

After a time Osborn is next. Nothing about the examination is a secret.

The rumble of voices carries through the unshuttered windows: demanding and questioning from the magistrates; lower tones from others in the room; higher tones of the accused women denying the charges, angry (in Good's case) or pleading (as Osborn is desperate to be believed); and the shrieks of the bewitched girls and thumps as they fall on the floor in convulsions.

Details trickle out, passed from one onlooker to another: neither woman confesses, neither admits she is a witch as charged, although Good is quick to believe that the other two may well be. Both say they are innocent, and neither is believed.

The court recesses for a noon meal, and with all three prisoners guarded together, it becomes plain that the other two think Tituba is the witch. Good glares daggers at her. Osborn cringes away fearfully. Even they, who know the charges against themselves are wrong, believe Tituba to be the Devil's servant. The magistrates must be even more convinced.

Soon enough Tituba is summoned to the meeting house. All eyes in the room fix on her, pinning her to the spot. She has sat in the gallery so many hours, as good as invisible to the better sort below, as she listened to Mr. Parris deliver his sermons. Now the crowd is looking at her, expecting her to speak in that place, before so many people. The four bewitched girls huddle to one side, witnesses, recoiling when she looks their way.

"Tituba," one of the magistrates demands, "what evil spirit have you familiarity with?"

"None." It is only the truth, but the magistrate regards the afflicted girls as they moan and flinch.

"Why do you hurt these poor children?" he continues, ignoring her denial. "What harm have they done unto you?"

"They do no harm to me. I no hurt them at all." She does not try to explain that whether the girls lie or if they are genuinely mistaken, their accusations cause her *prodigious harm. The magistrates must be made to believe that whatever is happening,* she *is not the cause of it. If evil spirits are at work, she knows nothing about it. But they do not believe her.*

"Why have you done it?"

"I have done nothing. I can't tell when the Devil works."

"What? Doth the Devil tell *you he hurts them?"*

"No, he tells me nothing." But this makes it sound as if she has at least encountered the Devil, so the magistrate pounces on it.

"Do you ever see something appear in some shape?"

"No. Never see anything."

"What familiarity have you with the Devil, or what is it you converse withal? Tell the truth. Who is it that hurts them?"

"The Devil for aught I know." From what she has heard from these people, the Devil does not need her *help to hurt anyone, being quite strong on his own.*

"What appearance or how doth he appear when he hurts them?" The man will not let up, will not listen to her. The afflicted witnesses continue to twitch and squirm. "With what shape or what is he like that hurts them?"

Slaves are expected not only to obey their owners' orders but also to conform to their expectations. This man—and her master, the whole room full of people—expect her to confess to what they already believe to be true. Very well then. She would obey their expectations if that would make the questions stop.

"Like a man, I think," she says cautiously. "Yesterday, I being in the lean-to chamber, I saw a thing like a man that told me serve him. And I told him no, I would not do such a thing." (Something she cannot say to Mr. Parris.) This is not a confession. She has not admitted to doing or seeing anything more than what the girls have described. Let them think the Devil also plagues her.

The girls begin to relax and be still, their pains stopping as Tituba speaks, as the court assumes she is confessing.

Had she seen anyone else? the man asks.

Four women, she says, and when pressed, she names the two other suspects. "Goody Osborn and Sarah Good, and I do not know who the others were." A tall man from Boston was with them, she adds. The room is hanging on her words, the afflicted remain quiet. Yes, Boston—they were there last night. The witches took her and brought her back. They told her to hurt the children, but she would not.

And then? The magistrates want to hear more.

The four witches and the man hurt the children, she says, and put the blame on her. This would explain why the girls said she hurt them, but when she continued to resist the witches' orders they told her flatly that they will do worse to her than they do to the girls.

"But did you not hurt them?" asks the magistrate.

"Yes," Tituba says, "but I will hurt them no more."

And then?

So Tituba continues her tale of how the spirit appeared more than once, many times in the past few months. Sometimes it took the form of a man, sometimes of a hog, and at least four times like a great black dog. The dog demanded she serve him and threatened violence if she refused, then turned into a man who threatened her again before trying bribery. A yellow bird accompanied him. He would give this to her, he said, if she would serve him; he would give her the bird and other pretty things. But he did not show her what those were.

"What also have you seen?" The questions would not stop.

Cats, she says, a red one and a black one, both demanding she serve them, demanding she hurt the children. Yes, she had pinched Elizabeth

Hubbard this very morning. The man in black took Tituba to the girl invisibly.

"Why did you go to Thomas Putnam's last night and hurt his child?"

She has heard the gossip about goings-on at the Putnam's.

"They pull and haul me and make me go," she says. She describes being dragged from the parsonage (as the guards had done that very morning) and flown through the air over the treetops to the Putnam's house. Concealed by a spell of invisibility, they entered seen only by the afflicted girl and ordered Tituba to cut off the child's head with a knife.

Men in the crowd speak up to verify that Putnam's daughter had described this very scene with the knife.

Yes, says Tituba, but she refused to comply with the witches even though they threatened to slit her own throat; instead, they flew her back to the parsonage. This was her spirit, of course. Family prayers were still in progress on her return, interrupted by a swarm of the witches' familiars: a bird with a woman's head, the yellow bird, a three-foot-tall creature on two legs and hairy all over, Osborn's yellow dog, Good's cat.

Abigail Williams interrupts to say that was the very bird-woman she saw last evening in her uncle's house.

"Why did you not tell your master?" the magistrate asks. Reverend Parris looks as if he wonders as well.

"I was afraid. They said they would cut off my head if I told."

Magistrate Corwin's own son had been hurt recently, but she denies any involvement.

"Did you never practice witchcraft in your own country?"

"No. Never before now." Somehow she has gotten around to confessing, to being not just the witches' victim but also a collaborator. Yes, she had seen Good and Osborn work evil magic earlier this morning but not now in court. Yes, Sarah Good sent the wolf to chase Elizabeth Hubbard. The questions go on and on. Yes, yes, to whatever they ask. She hardly hears what they say anymore.

"What clothes doth the man appear unto you in?"

"Black clothes sometimes"—not unlike a minister's garb—"sometimes a serge coat of another color. A tall man with white hair, I think."

"What apparel does the woman wear?" Who were the specters from Boston?

"I don't know what color." Would these questions never stop?

"What kind of clothes hath she?"

Tituba has to tell them something. *"A black silk hood with a white silk hood under it, with top knots. Which woman I know not, but have seen her in Boston when I lived there."*

"What clothes the little woman?"

"A serge coat," she says, meaning a petticoat, *"with a white cap, as I think."*

Despite her cooperation, the afflicted girls begin to writhe again.

"Do you see who it is that torments these children now?"

"Yes, it is Goody Good. She hurts them in her own shape."

The girls agree, and Elizabeth Hubbard contorts again.

"And who is it that hurts them now?"

"I am blind now. I cannot see." And she is mute as well to their endless questions. She too convulses in imitation or in fear, unable to go on, as afflicted as the girls. When she calms she tells them that Good and Osborn had attacked her, punishing her for her story.

The magistrates order Tituba and the other two prisoners held for future trial. Osborn and Tituba are to be taken to the jail in Salem town and Good to the other county jail in Ipswich on the morrow.

From her seat on a bench in the crowded meeting house Mrs. Ann Putnam has had an entirely different view of the proceedings from Tituba.

For days she has had to watch while her daughter fought off invisible spirits, as she cried in pain and terror at what her parents could not protect her from. Annie had been attacked again this morning before the hearing and then again in court when those three dreadful women came in. It breaks her heart to think her child has to endure this, yet she feels proud that Annie stands up to the witches even so. Stands up and speaks her mind—she is so like her father in that, like Thomas, who works tirelessly to bring the culprits to justice.

Those women—the first two with the brass to deny what was so obvious to all the onlookers, what was evident before their very eyes. Only the heathen slave had the decency to confess, which was a mercy, as it gave the victims some relief and verified Annie's tale of the knife. But the two unnamed women and the man from Boston—who are they?

The thought that more of the Devil's helpers are out there, somewhere, makes her shiver. Today's ordeal did not end the problem—what more must they face?

As the meeting house empties, Anne pulls her daughter to her, wishing she could protect her from the unseen terrors, as they watch the prisoners be taken away. A deputy struggles to balance Sarah Good on the back of his horse while she yells insults and resists, hampered by the infant in her arms. Will Good, looking sheepish, holds their older girl's hand. The child tries to break free, calling for her mother, then stamps her foot—her mother in miniature—demanding to be let go. As the deputy carries Sarah away, the little girl bursts into desperate tears, calling and calling. Watching the scene would break a heart of stone—if you didn't know what those Goods are.

At least four people took notes during the hearings of March 1: farmer Ezekiel Cheever, Thomas Putnam's young half-brother Joseph Putnam, and magistrates John Hathorne and Jonathan Corwin. The written records would be used in the women's eventual trials, whenever those could take place. Massachusetts would have to wait for its government to reform before it would be legal, or at least wise, to do more than a preliminary legal investigation while the original Charter of Massachusetts Bay was still in suspension and England deemed the province as lacking a recognized government. Some prisoners, found guilty of capital crimes back when Andros was in charge, still waited in the Boston jail for sentencing.

Rebecca Nurse's children brought the news home to her, who was likely still as concerned as the rest of the Villagers at the unusual prospect of multiple witches. Details of Tituba's confession describing the Devil as a black dog must have sounded alarmingly familiar. Four times the Devil had appeared to Tituba as the dog, they told their mother. The beast demanded that she serve him, but the slave had been afraid and resisted. "He said," Tituba had explained at the hearing, that "if I did not, he would do worse to me." It sounded all too plausible, so like the tales of Black Shuck back in Yarmouth.

Sarah Good was kept overnight at Constable Joseph Herrick's place before being transferred to the Ipswich jail, but Tituba and Goody Osborn were carted off to Salem.

Once the prisoners reached the harbor, word of their arrival would spread as swiftly as gossip, drawing idlers and concerned citizens alike to watch them pass through the gate into the jail's yard and leaving the town wondering at the presence of evil in their midst. Those who missed the hearing could quiz those who had been there for the particulars. If Bridget Bishop saw the cart pass, she would be right to wonder what comparisons her neighbors might draw between those prisoners and herself, considering her past problems with the law. Mary English, living further along the peninsula than the cart's path, would hear the news soon enough, but did she think of the insults long since flung at her own mother and worry about her own reputation, or did she worry only about the spiritual safety of her own small children?

Salem's jail was a square wooden building 20 feet to a side with 13-foot studs (so it may have accommodated two stories) set inside a yard measuring 70 feet along the lane and extending 280 feet back, with a fence surrounding it all. A brick chimney with one fireplace heated the building in winter. Iron bars on the windows and a lock on the door kept the prisoners in—although one man had dug himself free under the building's sill a few years earlier, suggesting the lack of a basement level. The dungeon mentioned in some records probably meant the common room on the ground floor. Judging from various testimony, the jail certainly had more than one room. The jailer, William Dounton, and his family lived nearby in the house of correction, where minor wrong-doers were taught the value of hard work and where the jailer rented a chamber or two to prisoners who could afford to pay for better lodgings. Less dangerous prisoners could exercise within the yard. Ordinarily prisoners remained incarcerated only until the next Quarterly Court sitting if they were not released on bail. The whole complex was only nine years old and in relatively good repair.

After a night in jail Tituba and Osborn again faced the magistrates, or at least Jonathan Corwin, who made extensive notes, joined by Reverend John Hale of Beverly as an observer. Each prisoner kept to her original story, with the older woman insisting on her innocence and Tituba obediently spinning further details of the Devil's demands. The specter had claimed to be God, but she did not believe him, saying, "I tould him I ask my maister & would have gone up but he stopt mee & would nott lett me." She told them that the Devil and his witches had met again the following Wednesday just before prayer time, and that was when they took her unwilling spirit and *forced* her to hurt the girls. "I would nott hurt Betty, I loved Betty, but [they] hall me & make me pinch Betty & the next Abigall."

The Devil brought his book in his pocket, she said, but Tituba's answers as to when and how she signed it were not clear. "I made a marke in the Book & made itt wth red like Bloud," she said, but she would not say what the red liquid was. The Devil "give me a pin Tyed in a stick to doe itt wth, butt he noe Lett me bloud wth itt as yett butt Intended another Time when he Come againe."

"Did you See any other marks in his book?" asked the magistrate.

"Yes," said Tituba, "yes a great many some marks red, Some yellow, he opened his book a great many marks in itt."

"Did he tell you the Names of [them]?" They knew she could not read.

"[Y]es of Two noe more Good & Osburne & he Say thay make the marks in that book & he showed them mee."

"[H]ow many marks doe you think there was?"

"Nine," said Tituba.

"[D]id thay Write there Names?"

"[T]hay Made marks, Goody Good Sayd she made hir mark, butt Goody Osburne Would nott Tell she was Cross to mee."

So now the magistrates had nine witches to worry about, not just the four mentioned earlier.

Then Tituba convulsed, being afflicted, the magistrates assumed, by some invisible spirit. When she came to she said that Good and Osborn had attacked her in retaliation for revealing their guilt. The magistrates took this at face value, and perhaps Tituba assumed it as well. Certainly the other two suspects resented her accusations. Good had made very public remarks about the worthlessness of testimony from a mere Indian; as low as Good was in the public esteem, Tituba was lower.

Now, however, the court valued Tituba's voice, as the magistrates believed her and considered the other two to be liars. Hathorne and Corwin were impressed that the stories Tituba told were consistent from day to day. The other two women seemed to be making excuses, with their statements contradictory.

According to Reverend Hale it was on this occasion that Tituba, "being searched by a Woman, she was found to have upon her body the marks of the Devils wounding of her." A few years after this, Robert Calef would write of Tituba: "The account she since gives of it is, that her Master did beat her and other ways abuse her, to make her confess and accuse (such as he call'd) her Sister-Witches, and that whatsoever she said by way of confessing or accusing others, was the effect of such usage."

Goody Ingersoll examined Tituba for witch-marks on March I, the day of her arrest and hearing, when she began by first insisting on her innocence and then confessing only after incessant questions. If Hale's account belongs on March 2 and refers to a second search (he was quite possibly present when the magistrates quizzed her again), the scars of beating would have to have been made between the hearing and the next day's questioning. The magistrates' record of the hearing does not note the result of Goody Ingersoll's search, and their record of the second interview makes no mention of a search.

In any case the laws of the time did allow masters to "correct" their servants, slave or free, just not with *excessive* force. "Correct" was understood to include hitting. Some men ended up in court for undue severity against free white employees. A slave, though not to be severely maltreated, in fact could be. Parris, indignant at this betrayal (in his eyes) by a servant in his own household, protective of his daughter's and niece's well-being, and all too aware of the scandal of a minister harboring a witch, especially during the current precarious state of Village tensions, may have taken it all out on Tituba in some way.

The magistrates questioned Osborn and Tituba again on March 3 in the Salem jail. Both kept to their original stories, though Tituba now added that witchcraft had killed Reverend Lawson's wife and child some years before, leaving the magistrates to wonder how long the enemy had been among them.

With the three suspects in custody, the four afflicted girls felt some relief. However, convinced that more witches were still at large, as Tituba had stated, they were not yet free of spectral threat. Also on March 3 Ann Putnam had to deal with her daughter's desperate attempt to resist attacks from both an unknown woman's specter as well as the spirit of Good's daughter Dorothy. The little girl could not have been more than six, yet according to Annie, the child had the Devil's book with her and kept shoving it at Annie to make her sign it, to sign away her soul. When she resisted, the child's specter pinched and even bit her.

On March 5 the law transferred Sarah Good from Ipswich to Salem with the other suspects—no easy task if she behaved as she had on the trip up, when she repeatedly flung herself from the horse and, in her guard's view, tried to kill herself. There the magistrates questioned both Good and Tituba. Both kept to their original claims, but Tituba, they felt, was again more consistent, especially in contrast to Good's evasions. Good seemed to be making up her account as she went, altering the story to put herself in a better light.

The three remained in Salem over the Sabbath. On Monday Tituba and the others were led out to a waiting cart and taken south to Boston. Witchcraft was a capital crime, and capital crimes were tried in Boston by the Governor's Assistants in their aspect of a higher court. The road led back toward the Village and then diverged from that route to circle the rocky terrain south of Salem town and pass through Lynn to skirt the wide extent of Rumney Marsh, with its salty tidal creeks and wide tussocky bog land that was dotted with the wooden staddles where farmers would stack salt hay to dry after summer harvest. They continued south to the mouths of the Mystic and the Charles Rivers and onto a ferry that would take them, wagon and all, across the water to the town of Boston on its peninsula between the open harbor and the tidal flats of the Back Bay. The jail here was stone and stood not far from the town house in a fenced yard where some prisoners could get air and exercise. The interior held a common room, which the majority of the prisoners used by day, and, opening off this space, smaller rooms with small, barred windows where some of the prisoners spent nights.

Prison keeper John Arnold received them, and two days later he brought shackles to further confine Good and Osborn. Their specters, he had been informed, still tormented the Village girls, so the authorities hoped the weighty iron might put a stop to that. No one reported having seen Tituba, however, as she had confessed—and been believed. So she remained unfettered—yet another reason for the two white women to resent her.

Back in Salem the annual town meeting convened on March 8 to elect town officers. Philip English was among the new selectmen along with merchant John Higginson Jr. (eldest son of the Salem's senior minister), their offices another indication of the town's trust. New constables included two Village men, Jonathan Putnam and Sergeant John Putnam Jr.

The constables' cousin Thomas Putnam still had a household beset by the Invisible World. Annie began to identify some of the specters she saw. Now that everyone knew from Tituba's account that there were at least nine witches lurking about, Ann and the other adults proposed names to help the girl identify the hazy figures she said she saw. They asked about identifying marks such as what clothes the specter wore (for people had small wardrobes). In offering help, they overlooked that these were leading questions. The suggested names would be of individuals whom Ann and Thomas did not trust, whom they may have half-suspected for years. Eventually Annie named Goodwife Corey.

Martha Corey, married to farmer Giles Corey as his third wife, had a son, Thomas Rich, from a first marriage, and a younger son Ben who was later described as "mulatto." For some years she had boarded in Salem town with young Ben, apparently apart from her husband, Henry Rich, yet since Henry's death she had Tom's inheritance in her keeping, waiting for his majority. She was, furthermore, a full member of the Village Church, had shared communion bread and wine with Ann Putnam, and sat in the congregation as one of the elect, one of the saints. Still, to Ann, she had an irritating knowing manner and a habit of referring to herself as a Gospel woman.

Because she was a member of the Village Church, allowing her to explain herself to fellow members was only proper. Consequently, around ten o'clock on the morning of March 12, Ann's brother-in-law Deacon Edward Putnam along with Ezekiel Cheever determined to speak with the woman and, if possible, resolve the matter. They evidently decided this at Thomas Putnam's house, for they asked Annie to take notice of what the specter was wearing when she next saw it in order to compare that with whatever Goody Corey proved to have on.

On their way to the Corey house about midafternoon, they stopped again at Thomas's house only to find that at noon the specter had struck Annie blind. It had identified itself as Goody Corey, said Annie, and told her "shee should see her no more before it was night because shee should not tell us what cloathes shee had on and then shee would come again and pay her off." (Whether this was blind to everything or just to the Invisible World is not clear.)

The men returned with a tale of Goody Corey knowing what they were there for before they had the chance to tell her, aware of their intent to ask about her clothing. They thought she seemed more scornful than concerned about witches in the community—and in the church—that their presence was a reflection on the whole Village. The Devil, she had replied, probably needed little effort to recruit the three prisoners, who were "idle sloathfull persons and minded nothing that was good," she said, not like *herself*, who rejoiced to hear the word of God. The men reminded her that joining the church did not guarantee election, but she dismissed this and began to lecture them on the Devil and his wrath.

Once the men left her father's house, Annie again felt distressing spectral symptoms and reported the vengeful specter of Martha Corey hitting and pinching her. According to her later testimony, Annie may already have identified another suspect as well: Elizabeth Procter.

On the following day, the Sabbath, specters seemed to be invading the Village meeting house. Goodwife Pope, a middle-aged neighbor of the Corey's, went temporarily blind during the service. Martha Corey was likely present, determined not to give in to local fears. Ann and Thomas along with Annie Putnam were probably in their accustomed places as well, but how they fared is not stated. It may have been today, after meeting, that Thomas Putnam invited Goody

Corey—who was, after all, a church member—to meet his ailing daughter directly. What Ann thought about the plan is not recorded.

That same day Annie reported a new specter: "the apperishton of a pale fast [i.e., pale-faced] woman that sat in her granmothers seat but did not know har name." Whether this referred to a seat in the meeting house or at home, nor which grandmother (or stepgrandmother), is not clear. Ann, joined by Mercy Lewis, the hired girl, questioned her daughter. They suggested names until Annie agreed to one of them: Rebecca Nurse.

With Uncle Edward and some other neighbors present, Thomas and Ann Putnam received Martha Corey at their home. The moment the woman crossed the threshold Annie thumped to the floor, with her head, hands, and feet twisted and contorted. It was Goody Corey doing this, the girl gasped, then she gagged as some invisible force pulled out her tongue and clamped her teeth into it. Ann watched frantically at this revenge inflicted on her own child and in her own home.

Once Annie began to recover she pointed at Corey. According to her Uncle Edward's notes, Annie exclaimed, "[T]her is a yellow burd asucking betwen your fore finger and midel finger I see it . . . I will Come and see it."

"[S]o you may," said Goody Corey,

As Edward would depose later, "I saw martha Cory put one of her fingers in the place whear ann had said she saw the burd and semed to give a hard rub." Annie exclaimed that the bird had disappeared, and "emediately she was blinded," unable to approach. As the girl struggled to reach the woman she "fell down blinded and Cold," contending, in her mother's view, against something unseen.

It was Goody Corey who made Goody Pope blind on Sabbath, Annie said, demonstrating with her hands over her own eyes only to then find that she could not remove them. Her parents and uncle tried to pull the panicked girl's hands away from her face, but they seemed stuck fast, and her family feared breaking them. Finally, somehow, Annie's hand came free, but what she then saw was the Invisible World, a vision of a man skewered on a spit and roasting over the fire of her home's own hearth. This matched stories of what some Indians were said to do to captives, a possibility well known to the maid Mercy Lewis, who had survived frontier attacks in her childhood. Everyone had heard stories of such tortures after the raid on Salmon Falls. (How had Mercy reacted to that? And what might Annie have expected Mercy to do now at this news of a man on a spit?)

"[G]oodey Cory," Annie shouted, "you be aturnning of it."

At that, Mercy grabbed a stick and struck a blow where Annie pointed. This made the vision vanish for a moment, but it returned almost immediately. Mercy swung again, and Annie warned, "[D]o not if you love your self," but it was too late. Mercy screamed from the pain in her arm. It was Goody Corey, said Annie. *She* had struck Mercy with an iron rod. Now both girls were in agony, and the Putnams begged Corey to leave.

"I won't. I won't!" Mercy screamed at the figures that menaced her—witch specters trying to make her sign the Devil's book.

At this point Martha Corey left, but Mercy's fits lasted for hours more. Menaced by the shadowy forms of women she could not identify, she resisted, shouting at the specters even when they threatened to twist her neck.

Her fits grew so bad that two or three grown men were sometimes needed to hold her, lest she fall into the fire or brain herself against the furniture. Late that night, when the clock was nearly at eleven, Mercy huddled in a chair opposite the hearth, resting. The chair began inching toward the fire. That got the watchers' attention. Two of the men grabbed the chair's back, only to find they could not prevent its slow, inexorable crawl, instead, the chair, with the girl in it, "her feat going formost," dragged them all toward the flames until Edward Putnam put himself between the fire and Mercy. Among the three of them they managed to lift the chair with its occupant—which stopped the movement.

So Edward later reported the incidents and swore to them the following September. (Later commentators assumed Mercy was using her feet to drag it forward, though it seems difficult for her to have moved a heavy chair *and* the two grown men pulling back on it. As with any of the year's testimony, events could have expanded with each retelling, like fish stories.)

As all this was happening, even if Mary Warren was not able to slip away against her master's wishes to the March 1 hearings, she would not have lacked for news of the goings-on at the Village when people stopped at the Procters' for a drink and gossip. Their stories included that of the wolf that Sarah Good sicced on Betty Hubbard (unless it was Sarah herself in disguise and not her familiar) right after Betty had left the Procters', of the nine signatures in the Devil's book, and of the many specters menacing the Village.

Then, one evening Mary Warren also reported shadowy forms. As she later described it, a shape, possibly Goody Corey's, drifted about the room, and as it passed her, Mary snatched at it and pulled it toward herself. Yet when she did, she found that the specter on her lap now had the appearance of her master, John Procter.

Procter himself stood elsewhere in the room, observing this suggestive mime. "[I]tt is noe body but I," he said, "itt is my shaddow that you see."

Mary tried to explain what she had seen, but Procter was disgusted. "I see there is noe heed to any of your Talkings, for you are all possest With the Devill for itt is nothing butt my shape."

Where Elizabeth Procter was on this occasion is not recorded

Despite her master's scorn, Mary felt more and more on edge. Who else in the neighborhood was malicious enough to have joined the Devil? And did every twinge herald a spectral attack?

Rebecca Nurse kept close to home now, feeling that the winter weather was too much to allow her to go abroad, even for neighborly errands. Her children kept her informed of the Village afflictions, Tituba's confession, and the threat of more unknown witches. Descriptions of the girls' convulsions alarmed her, and although she knew she ought to visit the families with illness in them, she feared to do so. Later, when asked why she neglected this neighborly duty, she replied, "Because I was afraid I should have fitts too." Stories of the reported familiars would also be alarming, especially that of the great black dog so like Black Shuck of Yarmouth's Long Sands: Yarmouth was far away, but the Devil was not.

Convulsions may be the result of physical ills (epilepsy, fevers, poisons, hypertension, etc.), emotions (hysteria), or a combination of the two. Convulsions from either means are actually contagious. A person sympathizing with another who suffers seizures can, as fear and excitement mount, also react the same way if they *expect* convulsions to be a logical outcome of the situation. In 1692 some—though not all—of the fits may have been, as critics have long stated, pretense, acting, and lies. But empathetic onlookers needn't know that to find themselves also convulsing, and the reaction in itself would be frightening enough to make the matter a self-fulfilling prophecy. Chadwick Hansen pointed out this fact in his 1969 study, *Witchcraft at Salem*. In addition, great fear can cause a person to breathe in shallow rapid breaths that, supplying insufficient oxygen to the brain, can cloud vision and cause convulsions and unconsciousness. But because the afflicted tended to recover quickly from their fits, the cause was not likely physical.

Mary Warren feels the dread close in 'til her panic rises as darkness seeps into her field of vision. It becomes harder to breathe, and she hears little shuddering gasps of distress that she knows are her own as she begins to tremble, the motion increasing violently. She half hears Goody Procter's voice commanding her to stop, half hears the disapproving tone more than the words.

The room and other inconsequential details fade from her notice as she heeds the shadowy specters that are rushing forward to overwhelm her and . . .

Suddenly, Mary is back in the Procters' kitchen. She reels, as if she has just been dropped into this familiar place from somewhere else. The side of her head stings.

Before her, Goodman Procter stands glaring, clenching his fists. She realizes he has just slapped her—hard—and is ready to hit her harder if necessary.

She clutches the burning side of her face. It takes her a moment to understand what her master is saying, but the tone of his voice is unmistakable. He is furious and does not believe that her fits are real, does not believe the specters she reports are real, does not believe that the pain she claims these spirits inflict is real. But if it's pain she wants, he will give it to her.

Mary tries to explain her fears, but he clouts her again, on the ear this time, his wife just standing there, looking grim and satisfied at the turn of events. Mary cries out at the pain. Procter grabs her arm and drags her across the room. Resistance only hurts the more, and Mary finds herself swung in an arc toward the spinning wheel. She collides with it and feels Procter's grip on both her shoulders as he shoves her down onto a stool. She nearly topples over, but he does not let go.

"You will work," he says, his angry face just inches from hers. "You will end this dangerous foolishness. You will behave and obey the both of us. Understand?"

Mary nods, unable to speak. She has often wondered what being this close to her master would be like, but this was not the sort of touch she had daydreamed about.

Procter straightens up. "Work," he says, kicking a basket of combed flax toward her. "Now."

Her hands tremble, but she nonetheless takes a handful of fibers and begins to turn the wheel. Both John and Elizabeth Procter stare at her, making sure she does what she is ordered to do.

March 18 to 31, 1692

Because her maid as well as her eldest daughter is bewitched, Mistress Ann Putnam has less help and more work. Now she has to tend to them, watch lest they topple too close to the open fire or an uncovered well—and this on top of her other children's demands, her husband's needs, the family and the hired men to feed.

In addition, she feels the familiar sour queasiness come morning, for she is with child again—her eighth—another to bear, to protect from all malevolent influences, both seen and unseen.

But weary as she is, there is no rest.

The day before, Ann, worn out by midafternoon, retired to her bed—just for a moment, just for a reprieve—only to have the vengeful specter of the Corey woman attack her. It was not enough that it tormented Annie and Mercy; now it pressed and choked Ann herself, threatening bodily harm if she did not sign away her soul.

Would the specter return?

Ann fears it will, for the witches are attacking other grown women now, not just children and maids. Her worries clamor ever closer, and every fear presses on her, one thing after another. She begins to glimpse shadowy forms flicker past the corners of her eyes.

Was it Corey?

Her fear surges into panic as the darkness increases, and she finds it harder and harder to breathe. A shadow congeals into the form of a woman—Martha Corey, back again with that red book and black pen, demanding Ann sign away her soul. Beyond the snarling Corey is another specter, an older woman.

Ann convulses; her scattered wits try to decipher who else would do this to her, who would send such terrors?

Rebecca Nurse. It must *be Rebecca,* she thinks. *It has to be.*

Amid the assault Ann clings to the strengthening thought that her soul is saved. Why throw away her own salvation and cast herself out of Heaven? How dare the witches think she would do that!

She cannot tell how long she struggles, but at last the room clears. The specters are gone—for now—and instead she sees Thomas, feels his strong grip on her shoulders, pulling her back, away from the darkness. With a sob of relief she clings to him, and they hold each other close, together a bulwark against witches and all the other unholy forces aligned against them.

By now perceived spectral threats had spread across the Village and beyond, attacking not only the girls and young women but matrons as well, for besides Ann Putnam, Mrs. Bethshua Pope had been struck blind for a time by specters, and Sarah Bibber, a laborer's wife, also suffered fits along with an "ancient woman named Goodall."

Matters in the Putnam household now looked severe enough for the family to resort to the law once again. Thomas's brother Edward along with Henry Kenny journeyed to town and made their complaint before Magistrates Hathorne and Corwin against Martha Corey. They named the suspect's supposed victims: Mrs. Ann Putnam Sr. and her daughter Ann Jr., Kenney's kinswoman Mercy Lewis, Dr. Grigg's niece Elizabeth Hubbard, and Reverend Parris's niece Abigail Williams. Parris's daughter Betty was not named and would not appear in any more complaints. (Her father may have sent her away from the turmoil to another household. She was certainly at Stephen Sewall's home in Salem town March 25, though it is only an informed guess that she stayed away.)

Because the following day was a Sabbath, Martha Corey remained free and probably attended services with the rest of the Village and the afflicted. Rebecca Nurse, feeling ill, remained at home. Reverend Deodat Lawson was a guest preacher this day, having come up from Boston after learning of Tituba's assertion that witchcraft had killed his first wife and their daughter. Some of the afflicted, including Ann's maid, Mercy Lewis, and Mrs. Pope, interrupted his sermon with loud comments; others in the congregation tried to calm the afflicted and keep their interruptions to a minimum. However, some of the afflicted reported Goody Corey's specter lurking up in the beams. After the service the real Martha Corey commented that the ministers and magistrates acted as if they were blind to what was going on but that *she* could open their eyes to the truth; after all, neither the girls nor the Devil could stand before a Gospel woman like herself.

It was another trying day for Mrs. Putnam, yet because it was the Sabbath, she found some solace in leafing through her Bible, dipping randomly into scripture. In Isaiah 40:1 she read, "Comfort ye, comfort ye my people, saith your God," and she applied that to her own situation. Reading further and skimming the chapter headings, she found Isaiah 49:1: "Listen, O isles unto me; and hearken ye people, from far; The LORD hath called me from the womb; from the bowels of my mother hath he made mention of me." This she applied to the state of her own soul, for, despite her continuing doubts, surely she was among the elect, called to God from even before her birth. Considering her new pregnancy, the metaphor may have given her hope about her child to come and certainly reminded her of this additional responsibility.

When she reached Isaiah 50:1 she applied *that* verse to the souls of Rebecca Nurse and Martha Corey: "Thus saith the Lord, Where is the bill of your mother's divorcement, whom I have put away? or which of my creditors is it to whom I have sold you? Behold, for your iniquities have ye sold yourselves, and for your transgressions is your mother put away."

Divorced, disowned, cast away by God—that was what happened to witches, to those cruel and foolish people who purchased the power to harm, with their souls as the price.

Now when neighbors came to pray with them for Annie's sake, the girl saw the shapes of her family's enemies among them: Goody Corey and Goody Nurse pretending to pray to God but actually praying to the Devil.

From the packed audience the next day Ann watched as her daughter and the other victims confronted Martha Corey, who had been arrested at last. The girls, shrieking in pain, crumpled at the sight of the woman, yet Corey insisted on her innocence as well as delivering a prayer before the assembly even though Reverend Noyse had opened the proceedings with prayer. Corey's forwardness (as others saw it)— her attempt to usurp a man's prerogative to deliver the public prayer— didn't impress Ann or the magistrates, Hathorne and Corwin. Instead, they noted her inability to answer *how* she had known ahead of time that the deputation would ask about her clothes.

The magistrates were insulted when the defendant sought to advise them, offended by her earlier boast that she would open their eyes to the truth. Her remark that her accusers could not stand before her now seemed like a threat to knock them down, as the afflicted fell if she even looked at them. Corey began to deny not only any guilt but also having said certain things that more than one witness had heard, having a familiar or seeing the yellow bird that her victims reported flying about the meeting house, and knowing anything about the Devil's book or about witches in the area. By then the afflicted were so susceptible to her every motion that they felt pain if she leaned against her chair or bit her own lip. Suddenly Mrs. Pope, feeling her bowels cramp, threw her muff at Martha Corey. The soft thing fell far short of the intended target, so the woman pulled off a shoe and hurled it at the defendant, striking the side of her head. Now the afflicted repeated every motion Martha made, moving when she moved, stamping their feet if she as much as shifted hers. To Ann and most of the rest of the audience she appeared to be magically manipulating the afflicted like puppets while everyone watched.

Finally the magistrates assigned Martha Corey to Salem jail to await trial, even as she continued to insist that she was a Gospel woman. Ann Putnam felt some relief that Corey would be in jail, and though she had suffered fewer seizures herself that day, Ann was exhausted, worn out by the ordeal.

But the next morning she was worse. Just at daybreak, as Ann later reported, Rebecca Nurse's specter appeared before Ann's bedside, clad at that early hour in a night cap and shift, threatening terrible tortures if Ann did not sign away her soul in the Devil's book. The specter held out a small, red bound volume, but Ann quoted scripture to

counter the witch's threats, perhaps Isaiah 50:1: "Behold, for your iniquities have ye sold yourselves . . ."

Neither God nor Christ could save Ann's soul, the specter sneered,
and then it threatened to rip that soul from her body. The spectral Rebecca may have brought the Devil himself to cajole and threaten, for
at some point around this time, as Ann later described it, her enemy
brought the dark, shadowy Fiend to persuade her to defy God. This
battle for Ann's soul lasted two hours.

This is how Ann remembered the incident. What it appeared like
to Thomas is not stated, but he believed his wife's interpretation of
the vision.

The real Rebecca Nurse knew nothing of this. She had been ill and
housebound for about a week as well as being frail and hard of hearing.
Rumor hinted that she was actually recovering from wounds dealt to
her specter, gossip that her family did not repeat to her. Toward the
end of March four neighbors arrived to visit: Rebecca's brother-in-law
Peter Cloyce, his neighbor Daniel Andrews, Andrew's brother-in-law
Israel Porter (Joseph Putnam's father-in-law), and Porter's wife, Elizabeth. Elizabeth Porter was Magistrate John Hathorne's sister, but the
four came as Rebecca's friends—not just to comfort but also to allow a
fellow church member to explain her side of a controversy. They would
later say that they were "desiered to goe," probably asked by the Nurse
family, but did not immediately introduce the purpose of their mission.

Noticing that she was in "A weak and Lowe condition in body,"
they asked how she was otherwise. As Porter wrote of the visit: "shee
said shee blest god for it shee had more of his presents in this sicknes
then somtime shee have had but not soe much as shee desiered but
shee would with the Apostle pres forward to the mark." She cited
other Scriptural encouragements, "and then of her owne Acord," she
brought up the topic of the afflicted, especially Reverend Parris's
daughter and his niece. She had heard the fits were "Awfull to behold."
She grieved for them, she said, "pittied them with all her harte" and
prayed for them all. But, she reported, she dared not visit any of them,
for in the past she too had suffered fits and feared a reoccurrence.
Nevertheless, she had "heard that there was persons spoke of that wear
as Innocent as shee was shee belived."

At that, the guests told her that some people *did* indeed suspect her.

This news took Rebecca completely by surprise, and she needed a few moments to take it in.

"[W]ell," said Rebecca. "[I]f it be soe the will of the Lord [be] done." She sat still for a space looking, her visitors thought, amazed. Clearly the information was unexpected.

"[W]ell," she repeated, "as to this thing I am as Innocent as the child unborne but seurly," she added," "what sine hath god found out in me unrepented of that he should Lay such an Affliction upon me In my old Age."

Ann Putnam, meanwhile, continued to suffer convulsions. On Wednesday, March 23, as Ann, attended by concerned kin and neighbors, rested on the bed recovering from her latest seizure, her former pastor Deodat Lawson paid a call on the ailing household. The tormenting specter, Ann and Thomas told Lawson, had boasted earlier that the minister would not pray for Ann—or would not be allowed to. Nevertheless, they asked Lawson to defy the specter and pray with Ann while she was still conscious. As Lawson later wrote,

At the first beginning she attended; but after a little time, was taken with a fit yet continued silent, and seemed to be Asleep; when Prayer was done, her Husband going to her, found her in a Fit; he took her off the Bed, to set her on his Knees; but at first she was so stiff, she could not be bended; but she afterwards set down; but quickly began to strive violently with her Arms and Leggs; she then began to Complain of, and as it were to Converse personally with, Goodw[ife] N[urse].

Lawson must have been scribbling notes as Ann argued.

Goodw[ife] N[urse]. Be gone! Be gone! Be gone! are you not ashamed, a Woman of your Profession to afflict a poor Creature so? [for Rebecca was a professed Christian and thus considered elect.] what hurt did I ever do you in my life! you have but two years to live, and then the Devil will torment your Soul, for this your Name is blotted out of Gods Book, and it shall never be put in Gods Book again. be gone for shame, are you not afraid of that which is coming upon you? I Know, I know, what will make you afraid; the wrath of an Angry God. I am sure that will make you afraid; be gone, do not torment me, I know what you would have (we judged she meant her Soul) but it is out of your reach; it is Clothed with the white Robes of Christ's Righteousness.

Lawson and the others watched while Ann, her eyes "fast closed all this time," disputed with the specter over the existence of a certain passage of Scripture. Evidently the spectral Rebecca denied its existence yet tried to prevent Ann from citing it. Ann insisted that there *was* such a passage and that it would vanquish the specter, at least for the time being.

"I am sure you cannot stand before that Text!" Ann exclaimed, but she was immediately "sorely Afflicted; her mouth drawn on one side, and her body strained for about a minute.

"I will tell, I will tell," she managed at last. Then she repeated, "it is, it is, it is!" before being choked off again. At last she pulled free. "It is the third Chapter of the Revelations."

Lawson hesitated, for the Devil might mean to use the scripture against them by encouraging its use as a superstitious charm. He agreed, however, as an experiment, presumably using a Geneva translation of the Bible favored by Puritans rather than the Church of England King James version.

Before he finished the first verse, which ended, "I know thy works; for thou hast a name that thou livest, but thou art dead," Ann opened her eyes and relaxed as Lawson continued: "Be awake, and strengthen the things which remain, that are ready to dye, for I have not found thy works perfect before God. Remember therefore, how thou hast received and heard, and hold fast, and repent. If therefore thou wilt not watch, I will come on thee as a thief, and thou shalt not know what hour I will come upon thee."

And this comforted Ann, who assumed that Rebecca did not know what well-deserved punishment was in store for her or when it would happen.

Lawson continued to the section about the triumphant soul that Ann had referred to in her fit as concerning her own: "He that overcometh, shall be clothed in white array, and I will not put out his name out of the book of life, but I will confess his name before my Father, and before his Angels"—unlike Rebecca's name, which, according to Ann's remark, was blotted out of God's Book forever.

When Lawson finished, Ann addressed the specter triumphantly: "Did I not say he should go to Prayer?"

This particular fit took half an hour, Lawson noted: "Her Husband and the Spectators told me, she had often been so relieved by reading Texts that she named, something pertinent to her Case; as Isa. 40. 1, Isa 49. 1, Isa. 50. 1, and several others"—including the Book of Revelation, it seems.

Revelation is a highly symbolic work traditionally ascribed to the disciple John; it is framed as a vision the writer experienced and addressed to seven early Christian churches in the Near East. Its meaning is still debated, with interpretations ranging from a literal description of the world's eventual end to first-century comments on Nero's regime that were too risky to discuss openly. In seventeenth-century Massachusetts the book especially intrigued Reverend Nicholas Noyes of Salem, who was hardly the only one who found it fascinating. If the Devil were actually making an organized assault on their churches and communities, this possibility too closely matched the action in Revelation.

Edward and Jonathan Putnam were probably among the onlookers, for on the same day they journeyed to town and entered complaints against not only Rebecca Nurse for tormenting Mrs. Ann Putnam, her daughter Annie, Abigail Williams, "and others" but also against little Dorothy Good as well.

So at some point before eight o'clock the next morning Rebecca heard a knock on the house door, and this time the family opened to find Marshall George Herrick with his official black staff of office confronting them. Rebecca had not yet recovered from whatever her illness was, but in spite of her angry relatives, Herrick produced and read the warrant for her arrest. Francis had to have been furious at that, protective and protesting. But nothing he or his sons could do prevented the marshall from bundling Rebecca off to Ingersoll's. To judge from their later actions, Francis and much of her family followed, frustrated and fuming at the idea anyone could seriously suspect his wife, their mother.

The child Dorothy Good was also brought to the ordinary under arrest. Deodat Lawson saw her there, where she seemed "as hale and well as other children." Who knows what she might have understood of the events. Perhaps the grandmotherly presence of Goody Nurse was some comfort.

Also about was Mary Warren, having escaped from Procter's fiercely watchful eye. Besides clouting her back to attention, Procter may have beaten her more than that. But once being forced to focus on her spinning, Mary had calmed, and for a time she had no more hysterical episodes. Eventually, however, Procter needed to be away from home for a few days to attend to business elsewhere, and Mary, brooding on the apparent plague of witches, began letting her nervousness get the better of her. Without her master's warning blows to jolt her, she started experiencing fits again. If Goodwife Elizabeth Procter tried to slap some sense into the girl, it didn't work. Mary already resented her mistress, behind her back referring to her slightingly as Betty Procter. (That much she would say to the magistrates; how she may have referred to her mistress when sharing gossip with the other hired girls is another matter.)

The Thursday of the hearing was also lecture day and the Village's turn to host the talk—a respectable excuse to slip away from work early enough to watch the questioning of suspects as well. Mercy's name does not appear in the notes of this day's hearings or on any of the surviving indictments. Mrs. Ann Putnam was definitely an afflicted witness named in the complaint. She had already convulsed that morning before court convened.

Once again Ingersoll's ordinary was too small for the crowd of onlookers. So at ten o'clock Rebecca stood alone between guards in the packed Salem Village meeting house. She faced the Magistrates John Hathorne and Jonathan Corwin along with the array of accusing afflicted witnesses. Besides Mrs. Ann Putnam, her daughter, and Abigail Williams (all named in the warrant), Ann's maid Mercy Lewis, Mary Walcott, Elizabeth Hubbard, and Mrs. Bethshua Pope were also present. These witnesses were agitated from the start, nervous through Reverend John Hale's opening prayer and the magistrates' remarks. Some of them had only seen Goody Nurse's specter, though it had not harmed them.

Hathorne gestured to some of the younger accusers, asking, "Goody Nurse, here are two An Putman the child & Abigail Williams complains of your hurting them What do you say to it[?]"

"I can say before my Eternal father I am innocent, & God will clear my innocency."

"Here is never a one in the Assembly but desiers it," said Hathorne, sounding almost sympathetic, "but," he added, "if you be guilty Pray God discover you."

Henry Kenny, Mercy Lewis's kinsman, "entered his complaint," then "said that since this Nurse came into the house we was seiz'd twise with an amaz'd condition." But Parris's notes do not explain just what had happened, and it is not clear if the incident happened at Kenny's house or at the meeting house.

Building on this, Hathorne again indicated the afflicted. "Here are not only these but, here is the wife of Mr Tho[mas] Putman who accuseth you by credible information & that both of tempting her to iniquity, & of greatly hurting her." (The "credible information" was presumably other people's accounts of what Ann said and did during her fits, the iniquity being the specter's attempts to recruit Ann's soul to witchcraft. Other people had witnessed that one-sided conversation.) Not all of the afflicted witnesses were certain that Goody Nurse had hurt them, however, even though they reported seeing her specter at the witches' meetings.

Rebecca did not associate herself with any specter. "I am innocent & clear & have not been able to get out of doors these 8 or 9 dayes."

Edward Putnam related an account of Rebecca's supposed acts of torture.

Hathorne asked Goody Nurse if it were true.

"I never afflicted no child never in my life."

"You see these accuse you, is it true?"

"No."

"Are you an innocent person relating to this Witchcraft[?]"

At this point Ann Putnam had had enough of what she saw as lies. Before Rebecca could deny this as well, Ann began shouting, "Did you not bring the Black man with you, did you not bid me tempt God & dye[?] How oft have you eat & drunk y[ou]r own damnation[?]" (How often, that is, had Rebecca taken communion under false pretenses, partaken of the Lord's bread and wine when she was actually pledged to the Devil?)

"What do you say to them[?]" said Hathorne.

"Oh, Lord, help me." Rebecca cried. She spread her hands imploringly—and the afflicted flinched away, groaning as if she had thrust some invisible force at them with the gesture.

"Do you not see what a Solemn condition these are in?" the magistrate demanded of her. "[W]hen your hands are loose the persons are afflicted."

The guards grabbed Rebecca's hands to hold them still. Across the room she saw the surging mass of the afflicted, and two of the young women were shouting. She may not have heard them clearly, but they accused her specter of attacking them as well. Mary Walcott and Elizabeth Hubbard had not accused Rebecca of actually hurting them before, but now Mary cried out that she had been bitten and raised her arm to display tooth marks on the wrist. Elizabeth Hubbard also accused Rebecca of hurting her now.

"Here are these 2 grown persons now accuse you," said Hathorne (that is, not children like Abigail and Annie). "[What] say you? Do not you see these afflicted persons, & hear them accuse you[?]"

"The Lord knows I have not hurt them. I am an innocent person."

But the afflicted cried that the Devil himself stood by Rebecca, whispering in her ear amid a swarm of imp familiars. Many of them convulsed, twitching and flailing in terror at such a sight, causing several people in the audience to burst into sympathetic tears.

"It is very awfull to all to see these agonies," said Hathorne, and she a woman who had so long professed to be a Christian acting with the Devil right in front of them all by the look of it, "& yet to see you stand with dry eyes when these are so many what [i.e., wet]."

"You do not know my heart," Rebecca answered.

"You would do well if you are guilty to confess & give Glory to God."

"I am as clear as the child unborn."

"What uncertainty there may be in apparitions I know not," he continued. But what about the familiar spirits? The afflicted could see them right there in court, all flocking to her. "Now what do you say to that?"

"I have none Sir."

"If you have," he chided, "confes, & give glory to God. I pray God clear you if you be innocent, & if you are guilty discover you. And therefore give me an upright answer have you any familiarity with these spirits?"

"No, I have none but with God alone."

"How came you sick?" Gossip had speculated that, rather than being ill, she may have been injured when people struck back at her specter.

"I am sick at my stomach."

"Have you no wounds?"

"I have none but old age."

The afflicted again said they saw the Devil and the imps and flocking spectral birds, and they shrieked at the sight. Rebecca leaned back against a support—a chair or a pew—and the afflicted arced backward as if their spines would break. She moved her hands, and they shied away as though they were being hit. To the magistrates and to much of the audience, the cause and effect of her movements and the afflicted's reactions seemed painfully obvious.

"It is all false," she insisted. "I am clear."

"Possibly you may apprehend you are no witch, but have you not been led aside by temptations that way[?]"

"I have not."

"What a sad thing is it that a Church member here & now another of Salem, should be thus accused and charged," he observed, referring both to Martha Corey and Rebecca Nurse.

"A sad thing sure enough!" Mrs. Bathshua Pope shouted, but evidently she did not throw anything this time. She and the others then fell into "grievous" and "lamentable fits."

According to some of them Rebecca's specter detached from her body and hit them on its way out of the meeting house. Outside, her spirit mounted a horse behind the Devil and galloped around the building in mockery. The afflicted screeched so much so that folk up the road heard them, while inside the meeting house people wondered who in the audience would convulse next. Instead of trembling, Ann Putnam froze, locked in paralysis. The magistrates gave Thomas permission to carry her outdoors, and once away from the commotion, she relaxed and began to recover.

The court, however, was not through with Rebecca Nurse. "Tell us have not you had visible appearances more than what is common in nature?"

"I have none nor never had in my life."

"Do you not think these suffer voluntarily or involuntarily[?]"

"I cannot tell."

"That is strange everyone can judge."

"I must be silent."

"They accuse you of hurting them, & if you think it is [not] unwillingly but by designe you must look upon them as murderers"—that is, did she think her accusers lied, doing so in a charge that could take her life?

"I cannot tell what to think of it."

The magistrates insisted, so Rebecca admitted she had not understood all that was said. She was hard of hearing, after all.

"Well then give an answer now, do you think these suffer against their wills or not[?]"

"I do not think these suffer against their wills."

"Why did you never visit these afflicted persons?"

"Because I was afraid I should have fits too."

"Is it not an unaccountable case that when you are examined these persons are afflicted?" For the afflicted were reacting to her every movement.

"I have got no body to look to but God." She moved her hands as she spoke, and as she did, the afflicted responded with "violent fits of torture."

"Do you beleive these afflicted persons are bewitcht[?]"

"I do think they are."

"When this Witchcraft came upon the stage there was no suspicion of Tituba," Hathorne continued. "She profest much love to that Child Betty Parris, but it was her apparition did the mischief, & why should not you also be guilty, for your apparition doth hurt also."

"Would you have me belie my self [?]" Rebecca cocked her head, and Elizabeth Hubbard's neck bent sharply to the side.

"[S]et up Goody Nurses head," Abigail Williams cried, "the maids neck will be broke."

"What do you think of this?"

"I cannot help it. The Devil may appear in my shape." The magistrates ignored her logic and instead directed Reverend Parris to read the shorthand notes he had taken of some of Mrs. Ann Putnam's fits. (These have not survived but must have been close to Reverend Lawson's account of the same or a similar episode.) Mrs. Putnam's spectral dialogues with an invisible Rebecca along with the courtroom convulsions of the afflicted impressed the magistrates more than the real Rebecca's Scriptural argument about the Devil's deceptions. The magistrates then ordered that Goody Nurse be held for later trial.

If Mary Warren had had any doubts about her interpretation of her symptoms, the sight of two grown women convulsing—respected married women, not just unregarded hired girls—accusing their neighbors of bewitching them must have seemed to prove her worst fears. Mrs. Putnam looked half dead as her husband carried her from the meeting house—a fearful sight.

The examination of Sarah Good's child Dorothy is lost, but as young as she was, she also was held for trial. What the child thought it was all about is anyone's guess. The afflicted reacted as though Dorothy's specter attacked them every time the girl looked their way. Some of them claimed her specter bit them, showing little teeth marks on their skin. This must have impressed Mary Warren.

(The little girl may have been placed in the house of prison keeper William Dounton rather than in the common jail, for it was there, on March 26, that Hathorne, Corwin, and Reverend Higginson would question Dorothy further. They must have asked her about familiars, for, according to Deodat Lawson, the child "told them . . . it had a little Snake." Pointing to "a deep Red Spot, about the Bigness of a Flea-bite" on "the Lowest point of [her] Fore-Finger," she said that was where the snake would suck nourishment. And no, "the great Black man" [i.e., the Devil] had not given her the snake—her mother had.)

After the midday meal on March 24, visiting minister Deodat Lawson delivered the afternoon lecture, which was intended as a warning against jumping to conclusions. Was Rebecca Nurse present under guard as an example, or was she confined to the watch-house prior to being taken to Salem jail? Ann Putnam may have recovered enough to listen (the afflicted tended to recover fairly quickly, especially if they had won their point). Mary Warren was almost certainly present.

The text, Zachariah 3:2, concerned a man who Satan himself had accused, only to have his sins forgiven. Lawson himself had to have had his dead wife and baby daughter in mind, supposedly, according to Tituba, killed by witchcraft. But he reminded his audience that the Devil had malice enough against humanity and could act against them both physically and mentally without the help of mortal witches. He warned against the Devil's "Mists of Darkness, and ignorance, in the Understanding" and "false Representations to the Eyes" (as Rebecca Nurse had warned the court), advised them to look into their own hearts and consider what they were doing that would please the Devil, and reminded them that no one had yet been *proven* guilty. "Give no place to the Devil," Lawson warned, "by Rash Censuring of others, without sufficient grounds, or false accusing any willingly." He reminded the courts to consider the cases by *lawful* means—that is, no folk tests or torture—and reminded the people against trying to use supposedly protective folk charms, which is so close to harmful magic. If John Indian sat in the gallery listening, he likely worried about the witch-cake Goody Sibley had encouraged him and Tituba to make to help the girls. If Goody Sibley heard this part, she had reason to worry about her association with magic of any kind.

But Lawson's listeners apparently paid most attention when he described the dangers of the times as well as his description of how actual witches allowed the Devil to "use their Bodies and Minds, Shapes and Representations to Affright and Afflict others, at his pleasure."

And in that time of very real frontier attacks leveled at the towns from Canada, they paid more mind to his military metaphor to "ARM! ARM! ARM!"—which he clarified as meaning, "PRAY! PRAY! PRAY!" "Let us admit no parley," he said, "give no quarter, let none of Satan's Forces or Furies, be more vigilant to hurt us than we are to resist & repress them." *Yes*, audience members like the Putnams and Mary Warren thought, *resist and repress*. The danger seemed so obvious to them.

Rebecca Nurse was taken off to Salem jail, while Ann Putnam returned home with her family, probably feeling somewhat (but not entirely) safer.

Mary Warren, however, did not return to the Procter farm but instead stayed somewhere in the Village overnight. She and the other afflicted girls still experienced fits and visions despite the capture of the latest suspects. Mary could not help noticing how differently the Putnam and Williams and Walcott girls were treated than she had been, how the adults offered sympathy and consolation, whereas Elizabeth Procter criticized and John Procter beat her. Even the maids, Lewis and Hubbard, were treated sympathetically by *their* masters. And in all cases the magistrates themselves took what the afflicted said seriously instead of dismissing their complaints as the foolishness of mere girls, paid attention to them who had, until then, been ignored.

Before she could return to the Procter farm the next morning, Mary's infuriated master appeared. Not only had she disobeyed him, but he had also lost a day of her work, lost his own work time fetching her back, and would lose more time while she got over her latest spell of fits. He hauled her home, no doubt telling her, as he had already told Walter Phillips on his way to the Village, that he would rather have paid forty pence than let her go to the court. "[W]e should all be Devils & Witches quickly," he had said to Phillips. Those supposedly afflicted accusers "should rather be had to the Whipping post," he proclaimed—whipped like common liars, that is. Now he had to "fetch his jade home and thresh the Devil out of her." He called her *jade*, as though she were a wanton woman, and he made it clear that her actions would only lead to more accusations. He doubtless repeated it all to Mary on the difficult trip home.

That John called Mary a jade, taken with Mary's disjointed testimony about pulling a specter into her lap and finding it was her master's spirit, suggests a sexual undercurrent to the problem. Had Mary done more than fantasize a romance with her master? Had she made any sort of advance toward him—the potential strong protector—or indicated that she would not rebuff such an advance from him if he offered one? Her statements never hint that he showed any desires toward her. His only stated reactions seem to be disgust and anger. Whatever he felt about the maid, the situation had to have caused an awkwardness between him and his wife. What did Elizabeth think, and did any of this refer to the couple's quarrels that Mary would mention?

So on that day, while the specter of Rebecca Nurse reportedly lashed Annie Putnam with a chain as invisible as the specter yet raised visible welts, John Procter whipped Mary Warren with a firm hand. Gradually she responded to the beatings and quieted again. Nevertheless, others in the Village had already named Elizabeth Procter as a witch, and Mary, in the past, must have complained about her mistress to the other afflicted girls and probably in terms more disrespectful than just to call her "Betty." Now insults like "hag" or "old witch"—if she used those terms—could have grim consequences. Soon others reported Goody Procter's specter more and more often.

If Rebecca Nurse's family attended the Village Church's next Sacrament Sabbath on March 27, Reverend Parris's choice of sermon text would not have pleased them, but they would have had plenty to report to their mother when they next visited her in jail. "Have I not chosen you twelve," Parris quoted, "& one of you is a Devil?" The text cited Christ's remark to his disciples after Judas had betrayed him to the authorities, and Parris intended it, as his notes show, to parallel the "dreadful Witchcraft broke out here a few weeks past." The two examined "by Civil Authority" and "vehemently suspected for shee-witches" were not merely local; they were members of the Salem town and the Salem Village Churches (Rebecca Nurse and Martha Corey). The comparison was certainly clear to the congregation, for as soon as he announced the text a woman stood up from among the women's benches, stalked out of the meeting house, and slammed the door behind her: Goodwife Sarah Cloyce, Rebecca's youngest sister and a communing member herself. Apparently the rest of the Nurse and Cloyce kin present remained, as Parris's notes mention no one else leaving. The afflicted grew agitated, and later they would say that Goody Cloyce curtseyed to the Devil at the gate outside.

The remaining congregation then heard Parris's sermon, in which he somewhat qualified his remarks. Christ's "Church," he said, "consists of good & bad, as a Garden that has weeds as well as flowers." But there were many ways to commit evil other than outright witchcraft: drunkenness, slander, lies, pride, envy. Even church members should examine their own hearts for the weaknesses that let the Devil in even as they pray for a solution to the present crisis of the Devil's invasion.

"Pray we also that not one true Saint may suffer as a Devil, either in name, or body. The Devil would represent the best Saints as devils if he could," he said—as Lawson had warned and as Rebecca Nurse had tried to explain to the court—"but," he added, "it is not easy to imagine that his power is of such extent." Rebecca's family realized that Parris was convinced that the current suspects—including their own mother—were indeed allied with the forces of evil.

The term "devil," Parris explained, included humans as well as "wicked spirits," those "vile & wicked persons . . . who, for their villany & impiety do most resemble Devils."

Being a full member of the church, Parris continued, and assuming one was saved did not guarantee that one was correct in the assumption. "This you & I may be, & yet Devils for all that." He also warned the devilish hypocrites among the membership that taking communion under such lying circumstances made them deserving of "the hottest of God's wrath." So "if there be any such among us, forbear to come this day to the Lord's Table, lest Satan enter more powerfully into you." Sarah Cloyce had already left, but the rest of the full members must have feared what the neighbors might think if they did *not* come forward. Parris's notes say nothing of any abstentions, and what the communing members of Rebecca's family did is also not recorded. Francis was not a full member and would have left with the rest of the congregation after the main service. His daughter Mary Tarbell and her husband, John, son Samuel Nurse and his wife, Mary, were all communing members along with his sister-in-law Sarah Cloyce's husband, Peter. Ann Putnam would likely have quashed her own reoccurring doubts of worthiness to take communion, applying all of Parris's remarks to Rebecca Nurse.

Before the communion service itself, the full members heard Parris read aloud Mary Sibley's apology for her "rashness" of using the countermagic of the witch-cake. The voting members (only male) agreed to accept it by raising their hands—unanimously. Although the charm was admittedly magic, even if countermagic, it was not magic enough for Goody Sibley to be considered a witch. This may have caused more resentment among Rebecca's kin: Why was *their* mother chained in jail and Goody Sibley—who had *confessed* to the charm—not even charged? Yet the men's vote had been unanimous, indicating that Peter Cloyce, Samuel Nurse, and John Tarbell had voted to forgive Goody Sibley.

Nevertheless, on the following day, March 28, members of Sarah's and Rebecca's families investigated the accusations for themselves. There was still time to clarify the facts of the matter. Samuel Nurse and his brother-in-law John Tarbell visited Thomas Putnam's house to speak with the afflicted. Ann, her daughter, and the maid were well enough at the time that no one suffered any fits. Who, Tarbell asked, had first named his mother-in-law Nurse as one of the specter witches?

As Tarbell later reported, Annie said that at the beginning of her problems, back before the others were affected, she had seen "the apperishton of a pale fast [i.e., pale-faced] woman that sat in her granmothers seat but did not know har name."

But who *named* Goody Nurse? Tarbell persisted. Mercy Lewis said that her mistress had. Ann Putnam said Mercy was the one who had told her daughter. Each thought the other had first identified the spirit.

"It was you," one said, and "It was you that told her," said the other.

"[T]hus they turned it upone one another," Tarbell noted, and he noted also that it had happened "before any was afflicted at thomas putnams besids his daughter" and that either Mrs. Putnam or the maid or both had "told his daughter it was goody nurs."

On the same day Sarah Cloyce's stepson-in-law Daniel Eliot also questioned some of the afflicted (unfortunately not named) when he and William Rayment Jr. encountered them at Ingersoll's. Whoever they were, they were free of fits. Rayment, discussing the hearings, mentioned a rumor that Elizabeth Procter would be questioned the following day.

Goody Ingersoll declared that she did not believe it. She had heard nothing about it.

"[T]here goody procter," cried one of the girls, pointing at empty air. "[T]here goody procter." Then, "[O]ld wich Ile have her hang."

Rayment said they lied, for he could see nothing. Goody Ingersoll also called them liars, reproving them sharply for such dangerous talk, "for there was nothing."

"[T]hey semed to make a Jest of it," Rayment later reported. As Eliot remembered it, "the garl said that she did it for sport they must have some sport."

Did those girls mean sportive jests at *that* moment, or were they doing this at other times when they were believed? Rebecca Nurse's supporters, who had no doubt of her innocence, considered the accusations not so much mistaken as malicious lies.

But not all untruths were necessarily conscious. When neighbors arrived to help tend the afflicted, Thomas and Ann Putnam told them that Mercy Lewis had named Elizabeth Procter among the tormenting witches. However, as Samuel Barton would report, "mercy lewes said that she did not Cry out of goody procter nor nobody she said she did say thear she is but did nat teel them who and Thomas Putnam & his wife & others told her that she Cryed out of goody pro[c]ter," To that, Mercy answered that "if she did it was when she was out in her head for she said she saw nobody."

John Houlton likewise remembered how when Thomas and Ann Putnam said Mercy had seen or named Elizabeth Procter, "we heard the sayd mercy Lewis affirme that she never sayd that ever she saw her."

Thus, listeners heard what they expected and remembered what seemed to fit their fears and assumptions.

Others were reporting Elizabeth Procter's specter as well, for gossip had spread that news. The real Procters, however, kept Mary Warren under close watch at home, keeping her hard at work, with no time for gadding and wool gathering.

John and Elizabeth watched their hired girl with disapproving eyes, suspicious of any odd behavior. They assigned Mary Warren tasks during which they could watch her, and John likely beat her again as promised, especially if she seemed about to fall into convulsions again. Perhaps even Elizabeth slapped the girl back to attention. Both of them made it clear to her that if she *did* have a fit and if she seemed as though she were about to hurt herself falling into the hearth fire or down the well, they would *not* save her. He may have even threatened "to burn her out of her fitt."

At one point, according to Mary's later testimony, John exclaimed that "if [they] are Afflicted"—and he doubted it—"I wish [they] were more Afflicted & you and all."

Mary, puzzled, asked, "[M]aster, w[ha]t make you Say soe?"

"[B]ecause [they] goe to bring out Innocent persones."

"That could nott bee." But Mary pondered on the possibility and evidently considered whether or not witch-specters really caused her symptoms.

The more Mary mulled over exactly what she had been feeling and experiencing, the more her symptoms calmed. She now resisted the urge to panic until it faded and no longer overcame her. She thought how her symptoms were more the confusions of a truly distracted mind and not what they had seemed. As embarrassing as that might be, Mary was relieved and thankful to have escaped the turmoil she had fallen into.

The following Thursday's lecture on March 31 took place in Salem town, and the day was observed as a public fast on behalf of the afflicted. Either before or after the lecture, according to Parris's niece Abigail Williams, about forty witches held a mocking sacrament in her uncle's parsonage at the Village, where Sarah Cloyce and Sarah Good acted as deacons to serve a sacrament of red flesh and blood in a mockingly literal parody of the Lord's Supper. Now Reverend Parris had that invasion to worry over, this contemptuous assault carried out in his own home at a time when his opponents questioned his fittingness to serve the church's Sacraments. In Salem town old George Jacobs (as would later be reported) made some small disturbance from the audience, most likely snorting disagreement as to how much sympathy need be extended to the supposed afflicted.

Mary English, seated in a pew on a cushion and trying to attend to Reverend Noyes's fast day lecture, cannot help remembering the insults once leveled against her late mother, when that Dicer woman had called Eleanor Hollingworth a "black-mouthed witch . . . and a thief and all her children." At least that outburst had led to a slander suit rather than a witch trial, and it had happened years ago, but one never knew. Surely Dicer's display of vulgar ill humor and choice of words (the insult "whore" was hurled about then as well) needn't be taken seriously after all this time—certainly not in comparison with the present spectral goings-on.

Mary hears Reverend Noyes describe the sufferings of the afflicted folk—nothing like that had been happening when Goody Dicer lost her temper—and hears a snort of derision from the rear of the meeting house. People turn to gawk, and a ripple of whispers identifies old George Jacobs as the source. Evidently not everyone believes it is happening now either.

This tangle will be sorted out soon. *Mary composes herself to listen.*

Elsewhere in the meeting house Bridget Bishop, seated on a bench, looks straight ahead toward the pulpit, but she cannot concentrate on Reverend Noyes's words. She can feel people in the audience watching her, brief furtive glances when they think she isn't looking. Earlier she had caught the gaze of her friend Alice Parker, but neither spoke. Both know how neighbors gossip about them, exchanging old suspicions of possible witchcraft, but only Bridget knows what it is like to be formally accused and arrested, to be questioned before the magistrates and made to listen to dangerously nonsensical accusations against herself, to be jailed awaiting a trial that could bring about her death. She has endured all that—and survived. She does not wish ever to endure it again.

Bridget does not want to attend today's lecture either, but staying away could seem suspicious. With some neighbors, *she thinks*, anything I do seems suspicious to *their* minds.

To judge from the crowd, others have taken the same precaution of showing up. She shifts on the hard seat and realizes that even with the great number of people in attendance, she has a comfortable amount of room on the bench—the women to either side are making sure they do not sit too near.

Are they afraid of me, or are they afraid of being seen with me?

The knot in her stomach tightens, and she feels an all-too-familiar sick emptiness. She knew it, but now she feels it. She can no longer pretend the nightmare is not happening again. Although so far the afflicted live at a distance in the Village and not in town, news from the Village is hardly encouraging—girls, young women, and even married matrons are shouting and tumbling down in public while yelling accusations. It is only a matter of time before all this creeps closer to home.

She hazards a look about and sees two women she knows only by sight, their heads together, whispering. One glances over her shoulder in Bridget's direction but snaps her head back when she sees Bishop looking at her. They are afraid.

Fear makes them dangerous.

Surrounded by this doubtful swarm of people, hemmed in by potential enemies, Bridget feels utterly alone.

(5)
April 1 to 19, 1692

Mary Warren walks up the muddy road, past meadows newly green with spring to the center of Salem Village. In the distance a farmer urges his yoked oxen onward as they plow a dark furrow. The air holds the scent of new leaves, freshly turned earth, and dung enriching the plowed fields.

Ahead, where the road parts, is Ingersoll's ordinary, but Mary passes that as well. Others are gathered there, including some of the still-afflicted girls. Their occasional shouts and cries float from the open windows along with the murmur of onlookers.

Mary continues east and downhill toward the meeting house, where the road branches again. Outside the building stands a notice board tacked with fluttering notes—notices of committee meetings and requests for prayers of thanks or supplication. Tomorrow Reverend Parris will read these to the congregation so that neighbors may pray for one other.

She digs into her pocket and finds the scrap of paper with her own semiliterate request for prayers of gratitude to God for her deliverance. The fits have receded and ceased. Her own fears and foolishness had caused them, she now knows. How like the delirium of the mad the symptoms had been—a sobering thought. What a relief it is not to feel the cloud of plaguing uncertainty always pursuing her. She takes a pin from her pocket, presses it through the paper into the wood, and taps it in with a rock. There!

She has been mistaken, gravely mistaken, but now she feels clear and free.

She turns and begins the walk back to the Procter farm, as the wails of the afflicted drift behind her, faint in the distance. She does not see the figures step from the ordinary and watch her for a moment before heading toward the notice board.

Putting up a note to request neighborly prayers for help or thanks was a common custom into the nineteenth century. Once Mary Warren was well enough for the Procters to allow her out of their sight now and then, she wrote a request for prayers of thanks for her deliverance from the fits (or had someone else write it, for though she could read after a fashion, writing was taught after reading, and not everyone learned the skill). She posted it on the notice board at the Village meeting house on Saturday, April 2. But the Procters, when they learned what she had done, were anything but pleased to hear about their business being thus announced to local gossips. Elizabeth Procter, to judge from later descriptions, rousted Mary from sleep that night with sharp and angry words regarding what she had done.

However, the note was already posted, so Reverend Parris read it along with any other prayer requests the following day. Although Mary thanked God for her recovery, other people remembered that the witch-specters had promised an end to pain if the victim joined them on the Devil's side. Mary's pain had stopped, so what were they to think?

After the services some questioned Mary. (The records don't say who spoke with her, but Elizabeth Hubbard later seemed most insulted by the idea, giving the Putnams reason to wonder. Only two days beforehand Thomas and Ann had watched while their maid Mercy Lewis resisted joining a bloody witch-sacrament, saved, the girl told them, by the sudden appearance of a shining angelic-like figure of a man. Once the witch-specters fled, Mercy had heard a choir of angels singing psalms, as the Village congregation had recently done, including Psalm 110, which had been the text of Reverend Parris's January Sacrament sermon, as well as a song from the Book of Revelation, which her mistress so often consulted.)

If Mary Warren had been mistaken, what about the other afflicted girls? They "did but dissemble," said Mary. (The *Oxford English Dictionary* presents a thorough definition of the word "dissemble" through the centuries: to disguise, to pretend, to feign, to conceal a true intention, to deceive, to shut one's eyes to a fact.)

Ann Putnam was convinced of the cause of her own troubles, and she trusted Annie's statements. Was Mary Warren calling them all *liars*? Had the Procters *told* her to say this?

As gossip focused on Mary's request just as they had predicted, the Procters had more reason to be angry with the girl. The evening after the Sabbath service an exasperated Elizabeth Procter exclaimed—if accurately recorded—that both Mary and stepson John would be called witches soon. This might imply that Mary was involved with the master's son, as he showed more sympathy for the maid's fits than the master and mistress did or because he helped her write the prayer request. However, the earlier incident of John Sr.'s specter sitting on Mary's lap suggests carnal thoughts toward her master. (Mary would relate that incident in the course of an afflicted confession, so the whole episode is uncertain and inconclusive.)

Perhaps Mary fanaticized about becoming the fourth Goodwife Procter—*if* Elizabeth died. Or, more realistically, of marrying John Procter Sr.'s son, twenty-four-year-old John Jr. Elizabeth, of course, did not relish the idea of having that maid as a daughter-in-law, much less of dying to leave her husband an eligible widower. For now, however, the maid seemed to be in her right mind.

Word must have made its way to the Procter and Nurse households that Captain Jonathan Walcott and Lieutenant Nathaniel Ingersoll had entered a complaint on April 4 against both Elizabeth Procter and Sarah Cloyce. But because the witch problem had escalated so unexpectedly, the Salem magistrates needed to consult Boston before issuing any further arrest warrants.

In the meantime the afflicted reported the specters of both new suspects and of John Procter Sr. At the parsonage Abigail Williams wailed that Goodman Procter pinched her, similar turmoil ensued at Thomas Putnam's house, and on the next Sabbath Tituba's husband, John Indian, made a commotion during services, crying out that Sarah Cloyce's specter bit him.

But not all the supposed sightings were definite. On the same Sabbath, at Ingersoll's, Ann Putnam's maid Mercy Lewis had a seizure, during which she too called the name of Goody Cloyce—or so the bystanders heard. As Mercy came to, according to Ephraim Sheldon (a Maine refugee, like herself), "she was asked who she saw. she answered she Saw no body they demanded of her whether or noe she did not see Goodwife Nurse or Goodwife Cloyce or Goodwife Gory [Corey]. she answered she saw no body."

Where her mistress, Ann Putnam, was at this time is not stated. Although she had tried to contradict their statements before, Mercy perhaps admitted doubt more easily if her master and mistress were not present, and their whereabouts is not always clear. Mercy spoke more certainly at other times, as when the angelic figure rescued her from the invisible witch-specters and their bloody mock-sacrament.

A week passed, giving time for Thomas Putnam to worry about witch attacks, time for the Procters to resent neighborhood suspicions while they kept sharper watch over Mary Warren, and time for Rebecca Nurse's family to worry about the accusations spreading against their kin.

Suspense ended for the Procters on the morning of April 11, when Marshall George Herrick and his constables appeared at their door, reading an arrest warrant for Goodwife Elizabeth Procter on the charge that she and Goody Cloyce were suspected of committing "sundry acts of witchcraft" against Abigail Williams and John Indian at the parsonage as well as Mary Walcott, Thomas Putnam's daughter Ann, and his maid Mercy Lewis.

Herrick's orders included not only summoning Elizabeth Hubbard but also Mary Warren to give evidence. As the complaint had been entered the day after Mary's note of thanks was read in the meeting house, clearly Walcott and Ingersoll still lumped her among the afflicted. So Mary must have had to accompany her master and mistress to Salem town and probably some of the sons as well, leaving the youngest children behind, who surely wanted to know why their mother was being taken away.

Ann Putnam may well have attended the hearings in the Salem meeting house, as Annie was one of the afflicted witnesses. Bridget Bishop would have had to decide whether it was safe to be present. She needed to find out exactly what the dangers were without reminding anyone of her earlier narrow escape from just such an accusation.

Mary English may have thought that her husband's position in town made her safe enough—if she thought herself in danger at all.

Rebecca Nurse, locked in the Salem jail with Martha Corey and young Dorothy Good, learned soon enough what the danger was when guards brought in her sister Sarah Cloyce and both Procters later that day. Sarah could tell her that Deputy Governor Thomas Danforth had presided at the day's hearing along with four of the Governor's Council. If any of the witch cases came to trial, the councilors would likely act as the higher court for capital matters once the province received its new charter.

Sarah could also relate the terrible racket of the accusing witnesses, their fits and shouts. The Putnam girl was one of them, Thomas Putnam's maid, Abigail Williams, Mary Walcott, Elizabeth Hubbard, even Mistress Pope and Sarah Bibber, both grown women, *and* John Indian—a grown man, Reverend Parris's slave, and Tituba's husband. John Indian accused both Goodwives Cloyce and Procter to their faces of bringing him the Devil's book to sign and then of choking him for his refusal. When Sarah called him a liar, he claimed her specter had bit and pinched him hard enough to draw blood the day before—on a Sabbath and in the meeting house. Sarah had fainted at one point, but instead of sympathy, the afflicted said, "Oh! her spirit is gone to prison to her sister Nurse." And now she was in prison for real.

John Indian also accused Elizabeth Procter, at which her husband remarked that, given the chance, he would *beat* the Devil out of the slave. For a time most of the afflicted girls seemed unable to speak. Elizabeth Hubbard remained mute throughout, though they seemed to struggle to speak. Abigail Williams and Annie Putnam found their voices soon enough to claim that Goody Procter often tormented them for refusing the Devil's book. "[S]he saith she hath made her maid set her hand to it," said Annie Putnam. When the magistrate asked Abigail Williams what Goody Procter wanted her to do with the book, the girl replied, "To write in it and I shall be well"—as well as Mary Warren was on her recovery. Then Abigail had turned to Elizabeth and asked, "Did you not tell me that your maid had written?"

Elizabeth warned the girl against lying: "Dear child, it is not so. There is another judgment, dear child." But after that, the girls saw only Elizabeth's specter taunting them from the beam overhead as well as a specter of John Procter stalking among them. They shouted a warning to Mrs. Pope, who collapsed—the specter tipped her over, the girls said.

"What do you say Goodman Procter to these things?" the magistrate demanded.

"I know not," answered Procter, "I am innocent."

When Mrs. Pope fell into a fit, the magistrate continued: "You see the devil will deceive you; the children could see what you was going to do before the woman was hurt. I would advise you to repentance, for the devil is bringing you out." He ignored the fact that Mrs. Pope could hear the warning *before* she fell, as could Goody Bibber when Abigail shouted another warning—"[T]here is Goodman Procter going to hurt Goody Bibber!"—just before that woman began to convulse.

Then the court placed John Procter himself in custody.

Benjamin Gould, who was not afflicted, described his sighting in his bedchamber the previous Thurday of both Coreys and Procters as well as Goodwives Cloyce, Nurse, and Griggs. (The latter was Elizabeth Hubbard's aunt, but nothing would come of this suspicion.)

Both Annie Putnam and Abigail Williams tried to strike Elizabeth, only to be repelled by a force invisible to everyone else. Abigail did get close enough to connect with the lightest touch, but she shrieked, saying that her fingers burned. Annie collapsed, clutching her head.

None of this could encourage the prisoners or their families. It certainly could not have encouraged Mary Warren. The warrant named her as a witness and made no mention that she had tried to evade the summons (as others would try to do), yet none of the surviving records—Samuel Parris's notes of the questioning, depositions from various parties—mention her at this hearing at all. She must have remained silent amid the turmoil, still free from fits, still resisting the urge to join in, but nonetheless hearing Abigail Williams and Annie Putnam both accuse her of signing the Devil's book.

Nearly everyone present must have been aware of Mary's recovery from her fits and afflictions, all too aware that the Devil had promised the others to stop hurting them if they signed on to his side. The law did nothing about the matter for the time being, and Mary presumably returned to the Procter farm with the resentful sons to face the younger Procter children, who had to be told that neither parent would be returning any time soon.

And it was all her fault, as the Procter sons would remind her. Every choice she made had turned disastrous, even the realization that her visions were false, deluded. If she had had foolish dreams of John Procter being her loving protector—or *any* sort of protector, for that matter—the court had ended that as well.

However much the sons of the first two marriages may have resented stepmother Elizabeth, they now could have hated Mary all the more for getting their father arrested. Yet she had nowhere else to go and had to live with the Procters, working for people who had no respect or even affection for her and carrying no notion of what her future held except the dread that matters would only worsen. She was utterly alone.

Notes for John Procter's hearing are lost. He may have been questioned in Salem on April 12, the day after his arrest. The afflicted certainly reported his specter that day in town along with specters of all the other suspects then in Salem's jail, including the Good child. According to John Indian they even tormented the dog that reclined under the table where Parris was writing.

All of the new prisoners—John and Elizabeth Procter, Martha Corey and little Dorothy Good, sisters Rebecca Nurse and Sarah Cloyce—were led from the jail that day or the next and carted to Boston to await trial. Despite the welcome fresh air, the jolting journey, which took the better part of the day, must have exhausted the elderly Rebecca. Giles Corey accompanied them as far as the ferry that would take them to Boston. Other relatives may have straggled along as well, such as the Procter sons, Peter Cloyce, and loyal Nurse kindred. The rest of the party crossed the water and ended at Boston's jail. There young Dorothy could at least join her mother and sister.

The suspects' specters, however, still roamed the Village, according to the afflicted, who expected the accused to resent them. Constable John Putnam thought so when, on April 13, his two-month-old daughter began to sicken and fall into convulsions. Back when Rebecca

Nurse and Sarah Cloyce were arrested he had commented that it was not surprising that *they* should be suspected, as their mother, Joanna Towne, had been a witch before them, even if not prosecuted. Soon after saying this he was "taken with strange kinds of fits," as he later said. Now the baby was sick. By nightfall the situation was so serious that he and Hannah sent for a doctor and for his mother as well. Despite the late hour Mrs. Elizabeth Putnam arrived to look upon her suffering granddaughter. The child, she feared, was under an evil hand. The doctor agreed. If he were William Griggs, this was the diagnosis he had given of the first afflicted girls. Two days later, on Friday, the baby died. News of this development would not have calmed Ann Putnam, fearing for her own children and convinced of Rebecca Nurse's enmity.

So, imprisoned or not, the suspects' specters could still do their work. The afflicted still convulsed, were still tormented by the same apparitions plus more—including those of Bridget Bishop and Mary Warren. On Monday, April 18, a week after John and Elizabeth Procter's arrest, John Putnam Jr. and Ezekiel Cheever entered a complaint against Warren, Bishop, Martha Corey's husband, Giles, and Abigail Hobbs. The victims of these "sundry acts of witchcraft" were listed as Ann Putnam Jr., Mercy Lewis, Abigail Williams, Mary Walcott, and Elizabeth Hubbard, all of Salem Village.

Constables arrested all four the same day and brought them to Salem Village for questioning on the morrow, probably keeping them in the watch-house over night.

Bridget Bishop might have felt a cold flood of fear but not surprise to see the marshall with his staff of office, his men, and an arrest warrant at her door. She knew she was suspected again or, rather, still. The stain of witchcraft never faded—certainly not from *her* neighbors' minds. Yet the afflicted and their fits lived far off in the Village, and she did not know any of them. She possibly had heard of the supposed victims named in the warrant only in recent gossip. Their lives had not rubbed together over daily tasks, so there was no opportunity for resentments—justified or fancied—to grow.

Yet there she was, hands bound, balanced on a pillion behind one deputy, eyed sharply by the others, riding to a part of town she had never seen before, past fields and rough pastures, along the muddy road, deeper into the country to a crossroads with a tavern, a small meeting house, and even smaller watch-house. Loiterers from the tavern stared as a deputy hoisted her down from the horse and led her into the watch-house.

By nightfall three others beside Bridget shared the little room: an angry old man and two frightened young women.

After a comfortless night and a sparse breakfast, they were escorted, one by one, down to the meeting house, which was crowded with everyone who could steal away from work, barely leaving room for the magistrates and the afflicted witnesses.

Giles Corey was taken first, then the Hobbs girl, then Mary Warren. Bridget might cling to hope, knowing that she was innocent of the charge and that the courts had dropped the earlier cases against her. While the guards hovered around, looking nervous, Bridget remarked to one of them that she had been suspected of witchcraft for ten years but that she was *not* a witch, so the Devil could not touch her.

Mary Warren faces the magistrates and her accusers, very near panic, hardly able to make sense. She claims innocence, but the afflicted fall into such fits that they cannot speak even to accuse her, all except Elizabeth Hubbard, the Griggs' hired girl, who had said a wolf chased her after an errand to the Procters'.

"What do you say for yourself?" Hathorne asks Mary. "Are you guilty or not?"

"I am innocent."

Some of the afflicted girls seem struck dumb, but Elizabeth Hubbard accuses Mary before falling into a violent fit.

"You were a little while ago an afflicted person," Hathorne reminds her. "Now you are an afflicter. How comes this to pass?"

God alone could understand this tangle. "I look up to God," says Mary with some confusion, "and take it to be a great mercy of God."

"What," Hathorne demands, "do you take it to be a great mercy to afflict others?"

Elizabeth Hubbard says that soon after Mary recovered from her fits, she had stated "that the afflicted persons did but dissemble." Then all the afflicted convulse—convincingly—including Mrs. Pope and John In-dian. Mary's specter, they say, causes these violent fits.

The specter of prisoner Abigail Hobbs, Hawthorn says, was also re-ported to be torturing the witnesses, and she has confessed. "She owns that she had made a league with the Devil."

At that, Mary collapses, convulsing.

Goodwife Corey and the Procters knocked her down, the afflicted cry, so she could not confess.

Mary writhes on the floor, unable to hear, see, or speak. Finally she chokes out some words. "I will speak!" She recovers a little and wrings her hands. "Oh, I am sorry for it, I am sorry for it." But her jaws clamp down, bite off the words, and grind her teeth to prevent speech as she convulses again. "Oh, Lord help me, Oh, good Lord save me!" she sobs, then gags again. "I will tell, I will tell," she manages, but she faints before she can continue.

Mary regains consciousness enough to mutter, "I will tell, I will tell, they brought me to it," and the packed roomful of watchers assume that the "they" are vengeful Procter specters (rather than resentful afflicted). The convulsions continue, then: "I will tell. They did, they did, they did." But the seizures begin again, worse than before, and the magistrates or-der her to be removed for the time being.

With so many against her, Mary is utterly confounded, not knowing what to believe. For the moment. at least, she may think that she really has stumbled into the Devil's snare. Whatever she had said, whatever she had meant, she realizes, as she waits back in the lock-up, just what the court will accept, which possibility is currently the safest.

(6)
April 19 to 30, 1692

Bridget Bishop is next. The guards have brought back Mary Warren, who looks like death warmed over, nearly stunned with terror and showing the whites of her eyes like a frightened horse.

The guards now escort Bridget to the waiting court. Whatever they say to her she ignores, preoccupied by the puzzle of who has accused her this time, here in a place of strangers.

Except for the magistrates, John Hathorne and Jonathan Corwin, whom she has faced before, she recognizes no one in the packed meeting house—certainly not the cluster of afflicted witnesses—young chits, women old enough to know better, and an Indian man. All of them fall in fits at her approach.

She answers the charges firmly. "I am innocent. I know nothing of it. I have done no witchcraft." She looks from side to side out over the audience crowding the room. "I take all this people to witness that I am clear."

Hathorne, who does most of the talking, orders the afflicted to look carefully at the defendant and see if she is the same whose specter has been hurting them. Occasionally the afflicted will admit doubt when he asks the same question, but Abigail Williams, Mercy Lewis, and Annie Putnam all affirm that Bridget is the same.

"I never did hurt them in my life. I did never see these persons before," Bridget protests. "I am as innocent as the child unborn."

But the afflicted insist otherwise. Mary Walcott tells how she had pointed to Bridget's specter so her brother Jonathan would know where to hit at it with his sword, and when he did she heard its petticoat tear.

"Is not your coat cut?" Hathorne asks.

"No," she says, but the officers examine the garment and find a rent, a little two-way flap hanging loose, that looks, to them, like the tear *described. Jonathan explains that his sword had been in its scabbard when he struck.*

"They say you bewitched your first husband to death," says Hathorne.

That would be Samuel Wasselbe, so many years ago now. "If it please your worship I know nothing of it." *The afflicted insist that she hurts them for sure, that she has been foisting the Devil's book on them. Bridget shakes her head angrily at that and tells the afflicted that everything they say is all false. In response, their heads all wrench back and forth.*

Samuel Braybrook describes how, earlier that day, Bishop told him that "she had been accounted a Witch these ten years, but she was no witch, the Devil cannot hurt her."

"I am no witch," Bridget repeats.

"Goody Bishop," asks Hathorne, "what contract have you made with the Devil?"

"I have made no contract with the Devil. I never saw him in my life."

"She calls the Devil her God," Annie Putnam shouts.

"Can you not find in your heart to tell the truth?" asks Hathorne.

"I do tell the truth. I never hurt these persons in my life. I never saw them before."

Mercy Lewis cries out that Bishop's specter had come to the Putnam house the night before and admitted that her master—the Devil—was making her tell more than she wished to tell. Hathorne, believing the accusations, orders Bridget to explain how the afflicted were tormented. "Tell us the truth," he demands.

The afflicted continue to shout at her and convulse, jerking like puppets at Bridget's every move. "I am innocent," Bridget insists. "I am not come here to say I am a witch to take away my life."

"Why you seem to act witchcraft before us, by the motion of your body," says Hathorne. "Do you not see how they are tormented? You are acting witchcraft before us! What do you say to this? Why have you not an heart to confess the truth?"

"I know nothing of it. I am innocent to a Witch. I know not what a Witch is."

"How do you know then that you are not a witch?"

"I do not know what you say."

"How can you know, you are no Witch, and yet not *know what a Witch is?"*

"I am clear," she snaps. "If I were any such person you should know it."

"You may threaten, but you can do no more than you are permitted." He acts as though God would not permit me to hurt *him*, even though I can hurt the girls, *she thinks.*

"I am innocent of a Witch." And no, she continues, she did not give the Devil permission to use a specter in her likeness to harm people.

Marshall George Herrick, whose trade is upholstery, chimes in to ask, "How came you into my bedchamber one morning then, and asked me whither I had any curtains to sell?" He must have dreamed that, *thinks Bridget, just as the afflicted break in with accusations of Bridget's specter killing people.*

"What do you say to these murders you are charged with?"

This was too much. "I hope I am not guilty of Murder." She rolls her eyes and then the eyes of the afflicted roll back into their sockets. She denies causing this to happen or knowing who might have done it. "I know nothing of it. I do not know whither there be any witches or no."

"Have you not heard that some have confessed?"

"No. I know nothing of it."

John Hutchinson and John Hewes contradict this, for they had told her just that.

"Why look you, you are taken now in a flat lie," says Hathorne.

"I did not hear them." Bridget protests, but she is held over for trial. As the afflicted writhe in a painful commotion, the guards march her out, back to the lock-up, past the gawking onlookers, with Will Good among them. Surely, asks Samuel Gould, it must trouble her to see how the afflicted suffer.

"No," says Bridget.

But does she think someone bewitches them?

Bridget answers only that she does not know what to think. She knows that she is innocent, but she also realizes that no one there is listening to her side of the story. If the law won't listen, then what recourse has she?

What Mary Warren had said in court earlier was not taken as conflicted confusion but rather as a confession. She had had time to collect herself but convulsed at the very start of this round of questions.

"Have you signed the Devil's book?"

"No."

"Have you not toucht it?"

"No."

The afflicted, who were calm enough when the suspect seemed to be confessing, reacted the while to her denials. Mary too fell into seizures again, and they were severe enough that the court sent her out into the fresh air.

"After a considerable apace of time," according to Parris's notes, the officers brought her back inside. But her fits prevented her from answering anything, and the court ordered her taken out a third time.

For the fourth attempt the magistrates questioned Mary "in private" with the ministers attending (including Parris, who took notes) but not the noisy audience and evidently not the noisier afflicted either. This time Mary managed to talk between convulsions.

"She said, I shall not speak a word but I will speak, I will speak satan—she saith she will kill me. Oh! she saith, she owes me a spite, & will claw me off." This spiteful revenge was taken to mean Elizabeth Procter's, but Mary seemed to be addressing the Devil himself. "Avoid Satan," she shouted, "for the name of God avoid." She fell into convulsions. Recovering, she cried, "[W]ill ye; I will prevent ye, in the Name of God."

The magistrates wanted to hear directly if Mary had actually signed the Devil's book. "Tell us, how far have you yeilded?" But her fits were too severe for much clear speech. "What did they say you should do, & you should be well?"

But she bit down on her lips to keep them closed, so the magistrates gave up for the time being.

Mary's whirling thoughts probably centered on survival. Although the magistrates believed she had joined the witches, she had not actually admitted that but rather blamed an unnamed woman of torturing and tempting her to do so. Everyone assumed she meant Elizabeth

Procter, for the other afflicted reported that the specters of both Procters were present in court.

Perhaps she consciously lied, hoping to buy the court's forgiveness, although by then she may have believed the magistrates and accusers were right after all and then given voice to her conflicts with her mistress. As other confessors would later report, they had been frightened into confessing, some even doubting their own innocence. One woman's brother would repeatedly tell her "that God would not suffer so many good men to be in such an errour about it."

The four prisoners were taken to the Salem jail where, later that evening, Mary brooded over the fact that more and more suspects were being arrested and that she was locked in with people she had accused, people with reason to resent and possibly torment her. She may have dreamed of an angry Giles Corey.

Mary was more able to talk the following morning, and at that time the magistrates interviewed her again, but this time in the jail. In answer to their questions she spun a tale of John and Elizabeth Procter trapping her in a web of witchcraft.

She had not realized they were witches until they *told* her they were, she said. Goody Procter declared as much the night after Mary posted her prayer request. The angry woman had pulled her out of her bed to berate her, for neither her master nor her mistress wanted her asking for public prayers. "The Sabbath Even after I had put up my note for thanks in publick," said Mary, "my Mistris appeared to mee, and puld mee out of the Bed, and told mee that she was a witch, and had put her hand to the Book, she told mee this in her Bodily person, and that This Examinant might have known she was a Witch, if she had but minded what Books she read in." As it was, Mary had marked the Devil's book herself without realizing what it was until afterward. Goody Procter—in person, not a specter, Mary said—predicted the following night "that my self and her son John would quickly be brought out for witches."

Mary grew more agitated as she described Giles Corey's resentful specter threatening her the night before with news "that the Magistrates were goeing up to the farms, to bring down more witches to torment her." She fell "in a dreadful fit," caused, she said when she recovered, by Corey, although the man himself was locked in another room being questioned. She described the apparition—his hat and coat, the white cap, the chains, the rope around his waist. The magistrates ordered Corey taken from "close prison" and brought before them. As soon as he clanked into the room, Mary collapsed in a seizure, and the magistrates could see that the old man was dressed exactly as she had described. (The implication is that he was wearing something different from whatever he wore the day before at the examination, though a change of clothes seems unusual.) The magistrates—and probably Mary as well—had heard that old Corey had recently threatened to "fitt her for itt because he told her she had Caused her Master to ask more for a peice of Meadow then he was willing to give." Procter and Corey, living in the same area, had been at odds before. When one of the Procter sons was careless with a lamp that burned Procter's roof, his father blamed Corey for setting the fire out of spite over another quarrel—upon which Corey sued Procter for slander.

Other specters rioted through the Village that evening of April 20, with one of them attacking Annie Putnam: "[O]h dreadfull: dreadfull," Annie cried, "here is a minister com[e] what are Ministers wicthes to[o] whence com you and what is your name for I will complaine of you tho you be A minister if you be a wizzard."

Her father and attending neighbors watched as Annie writhed and gagged, appearing to fight off the specter as it tried to make her sign the Devil's book. The girl resisted, shouting that ministers were supposed to teach children to fear God, not drag them to the Devil's cause. "[O]h dreadfull dreadffull tell me your name that I may know who you are."

The specter persisted, torturing her to sign the book but at last admitting he was George Burroughs, the former minister in the Village and the Putnams' adversary. According to Annie, he said that he had not only killed his own first two wives and several locals soldiering Eastward; he also killed Deodat Lawson's wife because she did not want to leave the Village and the Lawson child in retaliation for Deodat's chaplain service Eastward. This only seemed to verify what Tituba had said earlier. And, yes, the specter told the girl, he *had* recruited Abigail Hobbs—who had confessed as much. Annie went on to report, "[A]nd he also tould me that he was above a wicth for he was a cunjurer."

Ann and Thomas may have expected something like this to happen. They wouldn't put it past Burroughs to join the Devil, for it only confirmed their dislike of the man, this minister whose replacement of their brother-in-law Reverend James Bailey drove Bailey and Ann's sister Mary to Connecticut, where so many of the Bailey children died. The thought that Burroughs was capable of killing *children* could only further frighten Ann, who was still grieving for her own dead infants.

The following day Thomas Putnam took action. Mirroring the language of Ezekiel 1:16, he composed a letter to the magistrates about these new developments that "we conceive you have not heard, which are high and dreadful—of a wheel within a wheel at which our ears do tingle": the shocking news that a minister's specter was now abroad among the witches. Thomas joined fellow Villager John Buxton to enter complaints in Salem against nine suspects. Five were from Topsfield: Sarah Wildes, William and Deliverance Hobbs (the father and stepmother of the confessor Abigail Hobbs), Nehemiah Abbott Jr., and Mary Esty (sister of Rebecca Nurse and Sarah Cloyce). Three were from Salem Village: Edward and Sarah Bishop (a stepdaughter of Sarah Wildes, no relation to Bridget Bishop's husband), and Mary Black (Nathaniel Putnam's slave). One was from Salem town: Mary English.

Thomas Putnam also submitted his letter to Magistrates Hathorne and Corwin. As the surviving part of the note does not name the new suspect, perhaps Thomas included it as a request to discuss the matter directly with the magistrates, for the day's complaints and arrest warrants did not include Burroughs.

The magistrates again interviewed Mary Warren in Salem jail on April 21, accompanied by Reverend Nicholas Noyes and Simon Willard, who took notes. They wanted to know: the book that she had touched and saw the "flourish" in, might it have been a Bible?

No, she said, she had been deceived. And no, she had *not* told Mercy Lewis that she had signed.

Had Goodwife Procter brought the book? they asked.

No, her master had. She was sitting alone eating a meal of buttered bread and cider when her employers entered the room with a book that looked *something* like a Bible—but it was not. They had held the volume open before her and told her to read from it. Mary made out the word "Moses" but could not read the rest, so John Procter handed the book to her. As soon as her fingertip touched it—*barely* touched the page—a black mark appeared. This frightened her, and when she moved her hand to place her finger on another line, her hand was drawn back to the stain. She knew there was nothing on her hands except perhaps butter or sweat—but not blood. She had not signed in blood, but when she picked up her bread, the darkness from her finger smudged it.

And now, in jail, she cried out that she was "undon body and soul and cryed out greivously." The magistrates were not sympathetic, however, and told her that if the Devil could use her specter to torment others, then she *must* have agreed to sign the book willingly.

The Procters had *tortured* her, she protested, "threttoned with the hott tongss" and "thretned to drown her & to mak her run through the hedges."

To ease her mortal body's pain, the magistrates replied, she had sold her immortal soul. They then asked if Mary had seen her master and mistress, as she too was sent to Salem jail. She thought she had seen her master (though in person or as a specter is not clear from the notes), saying, "[I] dare say it was he."

When asked if he then said anything to her, she replied, "[N]othing"—John Procter had said nothing to her.

Then Mary convulsed, as if fighting off spirits. "I will tell I will tell," she cried. "[T]hou wicked creature it is you stopt my mouth but I will confess the little that I have to confess."

The magistrates wanted to know who she was trying to tell them about in spite of Goody Procter.

"[O] Betty Procter," Mary addressed the specter rudely, then explained to the magistrates: "[I]t is she it is she I lived with last." Turning back to the specter, she cried, "It shall be known thou wrech hast thou undone me body and soul." To the magistrates Mary then said, "[S]he wishes she had made me mak a through league."

Her mistress did not want her to tell anyone that she was a witch. The Procters didn't want anyone to know what went on in their household with that termagant of a woman. John Procter had threatened "to make away with him self becaus of his wives quarrilling with him"—his specter had just now reminded her of that.

How had Mary known that her mistress was a witch? asked the magistrates.

Mary, rising from yet another fit, repeated her desire to tell: Goody Procter had said that Mary might have realized "she was a wich if she herkend to what she used to read," for her mistress had many books and even carried one in her pocket when she visited her sister in the nearby town of Reading.

Then the magistrates asked: Before Mary touched the book and made the black mark, had she known her mistress was a witch, and how did she know it?

Goody Procter told her "that same night that I was thrown out of bed," said Mary. It happened the night after Mary posted the "note of thanks giving . . . at the meeting hous." And it was her mistress in her bodily form, not her specter, as far as Mary knew.

The specters of Giles Corey and Sarah Good had pestered her with the book since she came to prison, and "she afirmd her mistris was a witch," wrote Simon Willard. Yet Mary tried not to accuse John Procter directly. Despite what she had already said, "she would not own that she knew her master to be a wich or wizzard."

As for Mary's claim about ignorantly signing the book with a mark, the magistrates still did not believe that she *had* been ignorant. Mary denied any willingness, denied giving the Devil permission to afflict with her counterfeit appearance, and denied sticking pins into images. The Procters had spoken of such magic, but Mary had never seen images in their house. As for magical potions, Goody Procter did use a vile-smelling green salve on Mary for a past ailment—it had come from Elizabeth's mother, Goody Bassett in Lynn—but that was the only ointment she knew of.

Reverend Noyes pointed out that as she had touched the book twice—hadn't she suspected it was the Devil's book before she touched it the second time?

"[I]t was no good book," she conceded.

What did she mean by that?

"[A] book to deceiv."

The magistrates issued the latest batch of arrest warrants for suspects to be questioned the following day in the Village. Different branches of Mary English's descendants would relate various—and possibly embroidered—accounts of her arrest. In one version the household had retired for the night when Mary and Philip heard the loud rap of the front door's brass knocker, followed by the sound of footsteps on the stairs. Assuming it was someone calling about a business emergency, Philip got up to pull on his clothes and attend to the matter. But when the servant entered, officers of the law followed close on the man's heels, filling the room. They flung back the bed curtains, read the arrest warrant to Mary, and ordered her to get up and come with them.

Philip was furious. Mary remained where she was. She was not about to appear before these men in her shift, and she was not going to leave in the middle of the night. She remained calm while her husband fumed, and the officers, nonplussed, reconsidered, as they were reluctant to lay hands on a gentlewoman in her own bed. They compromised: they would leave a guard about the house, but she must come with them in the morning. Once they withdrew, Philip spent much of the night pacing angrily while Mary remained in bed.

The officers returned at an early hour. This time Mary told them firmly that it was not her usual time to rise, and they retreated again. Finally she rose and dressed properly, breakfasted with her family, and told the servants what needed to be done. The servants were grief-stricken and would have tried to protect her from the arrest party, but she forbade it. Then Mary instructed her children to attend to their studies and bade farewell to them all. Only then did she consent to leave, informing the guards that she was "ready to die."

All of this prompts questions. If the law arrived so late at night to make the arrest, did they fear Mistress English might try to flee? In one family version Philip was present, fuming powerlessly, but in another he was out of town at the time of her arrest and absent during her examination as well. As for being "ready to die," no one had yet been tried, much less condemned, but the crime carried a death penalty, as everyone knew.

Some of Mary's descendants thought that some neighbors held Mary's upper-class demeanor against her. Other descendants would blame the ignorant rustics at the Village for all the suspicions and accusations; apparently rumors clung to Mary and her deceased mother, who had sued the angry neighbor who called her a witch.

The latest batch of suspects were brought to Ingersol's in Salem Village to be examined by ten o'clock in the morning of April 22. Like Bridget Bishop, Mistress Mary English may never have been in the Village before or known anyone there. Now she found herself elbow to elbow with nine other prisoners, farmers and farmwives for the most part: Nehemiah Abbott, William and Deliverance Hobbs, Edward and Sarah Bishop, Sarah's stepmother, Goodwife Sarah Wildes, Goodwife Mary Esty, and a slave woman called Mary Black.

Mary English would have known the Bishops, at least by reputation. They ran an unlicensed tavern from their home that was the bane of their neighbors, one of whom had been Mary's cousin Christian Trask. After quarreling with the Bishops, Christian committed suicide by cutting her own throat with a pair of tiny sewing scissors. This led many to believe that Sarah Bishop had bewitched Christian.

As the court assembled in the Village meeting house, the afflicted were already in a state, witnessing, they reported, a large assembly of witches in Parris's nearby field. (Their proximity to Parris's home was threatening enough for the minister, but as the field was part of the disputed parsonage land he had thought he owned, we can only speculate what additional fears for his reputation that incident may have caused.) According to various spectral testimony, male and female witches flew in from all the region to receive a Hellish sacrament of bloody bread and wine administered by Reverend George Burroughs with the assistance of female deacons Rebecca Nurse, Sarah Osborn, Sarah Good, and Sarah Wildes. At some point a trumpet sounded from somewhere—apparently this was not spectral, for everyone could hear it—and the afflicted said that Burroughs was summoning his crew. No one ever discovered who blew that horn.

As she waited among the other prisoners, Mistress English learned how the others fared as they were returned from questioning one by one. Goodwife Deliverance Hobbs, like Mary Warren, had been afflicted, but now the other afflicted witnesses accused her. She admitted seeing spectral birds and cats and dogs as well as the shapes of people, including Sarah Wildes, who was also accused, and Mercy Lewis, who stood among Goody Hobbs's own accusers. Gradually she weakened in her answers and, like her stepdaughter, Abigail (and Mary Warren), confessed. Deliverance's husband, William Hobbs, did *not* confess despite the statements of the afflicted and of his own daughter, nor did Sarah Wildes or her stepdaughter, Sarah Bishop, and her husband, Edward Bishop. All were held for trial. Although Parris's notes include the Mercy Lewis specter, the court did not take this accusation seriously, although the accusation must have troubled Mercy.

Nehemiah Abbott Jr. was also returned to the lock-up, but only temporarily. As the other prisoners learned, he too had insisted on his innocence, but for some reason only Annie Putnam was certain he was the spectral perpetrator. Then Mary Walcott said he looked like the pursuing specter that, she added, was seated on the beam above them. The magistrate reminded Abbott that the defendant before him had confessed.

"If I should confess this, I must confess what is false," said Abbott, insisting as "I speak before God that I am clear from this accusation."

For some reason Abbott's insistence impressed the magistrates enough that they cautioned the afflicted: "Charge him not unless it be he." Annie Putnam was certain Abbott was the same, Mary Walcott was doubtful, and Mercy Lewis said he was *not* the man.

All three agreed that the specter "had a bunch" or "a wen" by his eyes—a growth.

"[B]e you the man?" Annie moaned in a fit. "[A]y, do you say you be the man? Did you put a mist before my eyes?"

With even Annie uncertain, the court sent Abbott out for the time being. That must have encouraged the other prisoners.

Mary Esty, whose sisters Rebecca Nurse and Sarah Cloyce were already jailed, did not confess either. "I can say before Christ Jesus, I am free."

And when the magistrates pointed out that she could see how the afflicted were tormented, she replied, "Would you have me accuse my self?"

Because even John Indian said that he had seen Goody Esty's specter with Goody Hobbs, one of the magistrates asked how much she had cooperated with Satan in order for the Fiend to use a specter in her shape.

"Sir," she answered, "I never complyed but prayed against him all my dayes. I have no complyance with Satan, in this. What would you have me do?"

"Confess if you be guilty."

"I will say it, if it was my last time, I am clear of this sin."

The magistrates seemed undecided enough to ask the accusers: "Are you certain this is the woman?"

The afflicted were speechless from convulsions, though Annie managed to say, "[I]t was like her, & she told me her name."

But that slim doubt began to evaporate when the afflicted began mimicking Goody Esty's gestures: their hands were clenched when she clasped her hands, Elizabeth Hubbard's neck seemed pushed down when Goody Esty hung her own head. "Oh. Goody Easty, Goody Easty you are the woman," Elizabeth wailed, "you are the woman."

"What do you say to this?" the magistrate demanded.

"Why God will know."

"Nay God knows now."

"I know he dos." Mary Esty, like her sisters, was not about to accuse herself.

"What did you think of the actions of others before your sisters came out?" asked the magistrate. "[D]id you think it was Witchcraft?"

"I cannot tell."

"Why do you not think it is Witchcraft?"

"It is an evil Spirit, but whither it be Witchcraft I do not know."

And like her sisters, Mary Esty was held for trial.

Mary Black, a slave belonging to Nathaniel Putnam, denied hurting by image magic, but when she pinned her neck cloth as the magistrate instructed, the afflicted reacted as if stabbed. Her case is hazy, but she too was held for trial. Sarah Wildes did not confess either, nor did Edward and Sarah Bishop, whose paperwork is lost.

Abbott was taken back to the court, but he did not return. The waiting prisoners learned that he had been released, with the charge dismissed. When the afflicted were told to look at him outside by daylight they had stared at the man's knobby features and the swath of hair falling over his eyes, then decided that he was *not* the same person as the specter. Abbott lacked a wen next to his eye; this was even more encouraging.

No examination papers for Mary English have survived, only a family tradition of her attitude. Taken into the thronged meeting house, its interior dimmed by the crowd that blocked the windows, she faced the afflicted accusers: two girls, two young women, and a grown man—Annie Putnam, Mary Walcott, Elizabeth Hubbard, Reverend Parris's niece Abigail Williams, and his slave John Indian. Presumably the fits and questioning proceeded as it had for the other suspects but without the doubts that freed Abbott. According to tradition, Mary, having learned what the questions were for the other prisoners, questioned the magistrates herself, demanding to know whether such proceedings "were right and lawful." There were higher courts than the one she addressed, and she intended to inquire of *them* whether the current proceedings "were law and justice" and see "that their decisions should be reviewed by the Superior Judges"—or so her family would tell it. She may also have alluded to a Heavenly court where false witness would not deceive the Almighty.

Nevertheless, the magistrates held Mary English for further trial. Unless he had been out of town during his wife's arrest (as one family story said), Philip English was presumably in the audience along with Isaac Esty for their wives, just as Francis Nurse had been present for Rebecca. Philip evidently kept his temper, for there were apparently no hotheaded objections like the ones that resulted in John Procter's own arrest.

Hathorne and Corwin ordered Marshall Herrick to take all of the day's defendants, except for fortunate Goodman Abbott, from the Village to the Salem jail.

But the afflictions did not cease. On the day after the latest hearings Annie Putnam recoiled from the specter of neighbor John Willard as he brought the Devil's book and threatened her if she refused to sign. Ann and Thomas heard her beg the persecuting specter for mercy, promising not to complain of him if he would only stop hurting her. But on the next day, April 24—and a Sabbath at that—the specter hurt her so much that she cried out his name with all the visiting neighbors to hear.

Willard had been in their house in person, along with other neighbors, helping them and showing sympathy for the afflicted. He had even served as a deputy to convey arrested suspects before losing patience with the afflicted and refusing to help in the escalating arrests. "[H]ang them," he had said of the afflicted. "[T]hey ar all witches." And now, according to Annie, here *he* was among the witches, actively opposing the afflicted. His own relatives were suspicious of the man.

Word of Annie's accusation reached the real Willard, who, then, like Martha Corey, determined to solve the problem by facing the girl directly to sort out the truth—and with no greater success. Ann Putnam watched as Thomas let Willard into their home and saw how the encounter only worsened her daughter's continuing distress. Annie begged the man to stop tormenting her. She still refused to sign the Devil's book but weakened enough to bargain, begging that if he would only stop hurting her, she would not complain against him. Willard, in response, denied he had anything to do with specters, but nothing was solved.

That was Monday, April 25. Annie actually had an easier time for the next few days, as if her pleading had yielded results. By Thursday the Willard specter was back, throttling the girl, beating and pinching her and threatening to kill her if she would not sign his book, just as he had whipped her little sister to death. Annie continued to resist, and, as she would later testify, "I saw the apperishtion of my little sister

Sarah who died when she was about six weeks old crieing out for vengance against John willard." Then, according to Annie, the ghost of Willard's first wife appeared also in her winding sheet, right from the grave, to accuse her husband of killing her as well.

Ann could not see her dead child's ghost, but such a revelation could only stab her heart with cold fear, fear for Annie, crushing sorrow for the lost Sarah, and fear for the baby to come. For some reason, however, the Putnams did not yet enter a complaint against Willard.

In Salem town, meanwhile, Philip English visited his imprisoned wife daily (according to family lore). This at least allowed her to get news of and make plans for the children. But confined as she was, her specter, like those of the other prisoners, was reported harming the afflicted along with the specters of Bridget Bishop and Giles and Martha Corey. A newly bewitched girl, Susanna Sheldon, was at this time beleaguered by all of them—pinched, bitten, prevented from eating, and threatened with the book. Mary English, she said, had a yellow bird familiar, while Bridget's was "a streked [i.e., a streaked] snake creeping over her shoulder and crep into her bosom."

She said she saw Philip English among the witches as well, first when his specter climbed over his pew on the next Sabbath in the town's meeting house to pinch her—while Philip himself probably sat in his newly refurbished seat. It followed her home along with "a black man with a hy crouned hatt on his head" who seems to have been either the Devil or the black-haired Reverend Burroughs, who kept presenting a book to her. The English specter told Susanna "that black man were her god and if shee would touch that boock hee would not pinsh her no more nor no bodie els should." She continued to refuse the book, so the next day English's specter pinched her again and threatened to kill her if she would not comply.

Philip's sharp business practices had certainly made him unpopular, especially among people who owed him money. He had also spoken against the current government, for he much preferred Andros (a fellow Anglican and fellow Channel Islander) to Phips.

On Saturday, April 30, a week and a day after Mary's examination at the Village, Thomas Putnam and Captain Jonathan Walcott swore out complaints against six more suspected witches: Salem Village's former minister George Burroughs, who was now in Maine; Susannah Martin of Amesbury; Lydia Dustin of Reading; Sarah Morrell and Dorcas Hoar of Beverly; and Philip English of Salem (but not John Willard—not yet). Their victims were listed as Captain Walcott's daughter Mary, Thomas Putnam's maid Mercy Lewis and his daughter Annie, Abigail Williams, Elizabeth Hubbard, and Susanna Sheldon. Hathorne and Corwin issued arrest warrants for all of the suspects and scheduled the next examination for the following Monday at Ingersoll's in the Village.

Perhaps the Sabbath gave Philip English the opportunity to hear of this development in time and, if he had not already left town, flee. Whenever Marshall George Herrick arrived at English's house, he discovered that the suspect was not to be found.

While Philip found a hiding place, John Arnold began making repairs to Boston's jail and to the "prison house" where he and his family lived: five hundred board feet of lumber, two hundred nails. He added the cost of these to the list of out-of-pocket expenses, which included chains made for Good and Osborn and the two blankets provided for Sarah Good's infant child.

Tituba overhears scraps of news from the visiting families of Rebecca Nurse and Sarah Cloyce. Husbands and children make the long journey to Boston, which takes at least a half a day or more. They bring supplies and news and what comfort they can offer, but the arrest of the third sister, Mary Esty, is no comfort at all. Corey and Procter kin visit when they can. No one comes for Sarah Good. That woman has young Dorothy—the child clings, barnacle-like, to her mother—as well as the infant, who seems to be growing weaker. On the day Dorothy Good arrived with the latest prisoners, what relief and tearful joy on the child's face when she saw her mother! But what despair on the mother's face when she saw her daughter here in prison.

Sometimes an offended relative of the accused speaks directly to Tituba, but the words spoken are seldom more than an accusation. Yet even this, their outrage, can be viewed as an improvement. Not too long ago they never would have deigned to address her at all.

Her husband, John Indian, now among the afflicted accusers, convulsed during the hearings and between times in the taverns. Frustrated family members blame Tituba for her confession and the direction the courts have taken because of it. Did she know what that John Indian did? He accused our Sarah of biting him—her specter, that is—but a barbarous accusation nonetheless. And do you know how he rolls about on the floor with the afflicted white girls? What does that mean?

After the hearings for Goodwives Cloyce and Procter in Salem, Tituba learns, her John was given a ride back to the Village behind another man, two to a horse. Partway there he had a fit (or whatever it was the so-called afflicted had), during which he bit the man before him. Edward Bishop (the tavern owner, not Bridget's sawyer husband), riding nearby, clouted John with his stick to make him let go, which he did. John claimed he was trying not to fall off the horse, for the spirits had bound his wrists. But Bishop was not impressed, even though others present wondered how the slave's hands got tied so tightly that the cord bit into the flesh. After that, in a hardly surprising development, the afflicted named Goodman Bishop among their specters.

What can Tituba make of this morsel of information? Biting a white man—how satisfying that must have been for John. But how John's inclusion with the afflicted might affect her own case—as an admitted witch not yet tried—that is another matter.

(7)

May 1 to 12, 1692

Mistress Mary English and hired girl Mary Warren both wait in the Salem jail along with Mary Esty, Edward and Sarah Bishop, and Abigail Hobbs, with her father, William and stepmother, Deliverance for the next stage of the court's proceedings. Philip is not there. His visits to Mary had stopped abruptly, and his absence is troubling. Finally word came to her that he too had been accused and had run away a step ahead of the arrest warrant. So far he eludes capture. She prays the servants are taking proper care of the children.

Goodwife Hobbs, earlier besieged by specters, had been herself accused and then confessed that she too was a witch—then thought better of it. Yet once she denied the confession, her specter began to torment the afflicted once more. Now the magistrates question her again in the jail. Jonathan Corwin takes notes.

Just what has she done to cause her specter to torture the afflicted again? they want to know.

"Nothing at all."

"But have you not since been tempted?"

She begins to weaken. "Yes Sir, but I have not done it, nor will not doe it."

"Here is a great change since we last spake to you, for now you afflict and torment again."

The magistrates are still convinced that if a confession gives the afflicted victims temporary ease, that shows the suspect has renounced a previous pact with the Devil. But, as Mary Warren knows all too well, if a suspect tries to withdraw a confession—and her specter again attacks the girls—then the suspect must have rejoined *the Devil's side, the recantation being only half-hearted or a lie. Honest people tell the truth.*

The Devil is the Prince of Lies. "Now tell us the truth. Who tempted you to sign again?"

"It was Goody Oliver," Goody Hobbs says, referring to Bridget Bishop by her second husband's name, a woman already arrested. "She would have me to set my hand to the book, but I would not, neither have I, neither did consent to hurt them again."

The magistrates seize on the capitulation and ignore her denials. What about her earlier accusations? Had not Goody Wildes appeared to her and tempted her to sign the Devil's book?

Off to the side among the other prisoners, Mary English understands how the magistrates interpret the matter but wishes the woman would stand up to them. Mary Warren knows too well what the magistrates expect and what they will do about it.

Goody Hobbs's resolve wilts further. Yes, she saw those things. Yes, she was tempted. Yes, the specters ordered her not to tell about them. Yes, she did confess before. Yes, yes, yes. Yes, she signed. "It was Goody Oliver that tempted me to deny all that I had confessed before," she says, defeated at last. "All that I confessed before is true." She names her fellow witches— Osborne, Good, Burroughs, Oliver, Wildes, Nurse, the Coreys, and the Procters—but she does not know who the man with the wen is.

Someone had overheard her talking with disembodied voices. The witch specters, she says, brought a feast of roast and boiled meat to the jail, but she did not eat any of it.

Yet the magistrates clearly account her a confessed witch.

Later, after the magistrates leave, Mary Warren tries to explain what it is like for a confessor. "The magistrates might as well examine Keysar's daughter that had been distracted many years," she says, naming an odd woman well known in Salem town, "and take notice of what she said as well as any of the afflicted persons."

"When I was afflicted I thought I saw the apparitions of a hundred persons" for "my head was distempered." She did not know what she said then in her fits. And when she was well again she could not say that she had seen the apparitions at the times she said she had seen them.

Distempered, distracted, or dissembling? Mary English and the other prisoners listen and remember.

Although it is not clear whether the other suspects in Salem's jail witnessed the magistrates interviewing Goody Hobbs on May 3, the gist of the encounter would soon become common knowledge there and in the town at large.

The magistrates did not believe Mary Warren's attempted recantation, and they told her firmly that they did not. Had not she herself told them that the specters promised to stop hurting her if she joined them? Now that her pains had stopped, what else were they to think? She *must* have agreed to join her tempters. That made her a witch, did it not? And being an admitted witch—for she had said she was— she would be locked up with the rest of the prisoners, people *she* had accused, people whose guilt *she* had revealed. How would she like that? And how did she think the other witches would receive her after her betrayal? Her thin retraction would hardly help her with *them*, now would it? She would be locked up with the likes of Burroughs, the ringleader of them all.

To judge from what other reluctant "confessors" would say, Reverend Noyes may have lectured her on what she had done, as he saw it, until Mary realized that he and the magistrates would believe a damning confession of witchcraft but would not believe a retraction of the confession, no matter how often she repeated it.

Some local families had journeyed to the capital for the election, staying with kin to enjoy the festivities. By week's end all were back, and news filtered through the region: of the fast day that the General Court had ordered for May 26 to ask Heaven's mercy on the time's troubles, but without specifying the witch scare; of the second arrest warrant for the elusive Philip English; and of old Bray Wilkins's illness and his grandson Daniel Wilkins's odd behavior.

Ann Putnam perhaps contented herself with getting much of the news from Thomas, who still escorted Annie and the maid Mercy to the hearings. It was safer that way for her and the child to come, posing less risk of having further fits and seizures. Although the afflicted discovered more and more witches, the Putnam household was not backing away from their perceived duty in opposing them.

Ann Putnam could only watch as specters besieged Annie. Though Rebecca Nurse was bodily imprisoned, the girl said that the woman's specter still roamed freely to attack the afflicted and brag of her many murder victims.

On May 2 Annie and Mercy had stood with the other afflicted girls, Goodwife Sarah Bibber, and John Indian against yet more suspects, two of them defiant widows. The light-fingered Dorcas Hoar, known to consult books on fortune-telling, muttered imprecations against her accusers. Susannah Martin was openly scornful, laughing when Annie threw a glove at her. She labeled the afflictions "folly," and although she claimed some concern for the afflicted, she nonetheless addressed Mercy with dripping sarcasm and talked back to the court. Not only did she *not* believe that her accusers were bewitched, but she also made sinister reference to their master, as if the afflicted were the witches.

"You said their Master," the magistrates observed. "Who do you think is their Master? "

"If they be dealing in the black art, you may know as well as I."

This only drove the accusers to worse convulsions, and when the bench asked her to explain how it was that her appearance hurt the girls, she countered with a reference to the story of a spirit counterfeiting the form of the Prophet Samuel. "He that appeared in [the] same shape as [a] glorifyed saint can appear in any ones shape." Others had pointed out the parallel, but again the court brushed it aside.

"Have not you compassion on these afflicted?" the magistrates asked.

"No, I have none."

The magistrates ordered the latest prisoners, none of whom had confessed, straight to Boston to await trial. The law had to send someone to Maine to apprehend Reverend George Burroughs. Philip English, as Marshall Herrick reported, was still not to be found.

Burroughs himself arrived in Salem May 4, escorted from Wells, Maine, then locked by himself into an upstairs room of Thomas Beadle's tavern. But no further hearings would happen yet, for Hathorne and Corwin were in Boston, representing Salem in the annual election.

The Burroughs specter, meanwhile, still besieged Ann Putnam's household.

Ann watched helplessly as specters attacked Annie and the maid. On Saturday, May 7, Thomas and Edward Putnam along with visiting neighbors witnessed Mercy Lewis, who had worked for the Burroughs family in Maine, flinch away from an invisible specter. Her former employer, she told them, continued to push a book at her to sign. It was not the same volume the specter had brought earlier but rather a new sort of book, one she had never seen before. The specter claimed there was no harm in it. "I tould him I did not beleve him," said Mercy, "for I had been often in his studdy but I nevr saw that book their but he tould me that he had severall books in his studdy which I never saw . . . counjuring books . . . and he could raise the divell and that he had bewicthed his Two first wives to death."

When Mercy asked the specter how he could torment people when his body was locked up in Salem, the specter boasted, "that the divell was his sarvant and he sent him in his shap to doe it." Then the specter fell to tormenting Mercy "most dreadfully," but the girl would not give in. Thomas and Edward heard her shout, "Mr. Burroughs I will not writ in your book tho you doe kil me." As Thomas wrote soon afterward: "we ware redy to fear that every joynt of hir body was redy to be displaced."

Nor did Mercy and Annie give in the following day, a Sabbath, and a Sacrament Sabbath at that; although they, along with the Williams and Walcott girls, were sorely tortured.

"We cannot drink of the cup of the Lord and the cup of Devils," said Reverend Parris, stating his sermon's text. "You cannot be partakers of the Lord's Table and the table of Devils."

As Thomas and Ann Putnam shared in the Lord's Supper with the other full members, they, like many others, must have wondered about the apparent swarm of neighbors who *had* drunk the Devil's sacrament, pledging themselves to evil, a situation serious enough that Thomas and John Putnam Jr. headed to town that same day to enter complaints against a brace of new suspects from Reading and Woburn.

But that was not the last of the specters, because Annie now reported one of an old gray-haired man calling himself Father Pharaoh and claiming that even her own father addressed him so, as unlikely

as that was. Annie refused to call such a wizard her grandfather.
Thomas Putnam and Robert Morrell witnessed "her hellish temtations" and heard her shout, "I will not writ old pharoah I will not writ
in your book."

But once again the Putnam household witnessed the most vicious
assaults from the George Burroughs specter. It threatened to kill
Mercy Lewis if she dared to witness against him. "[H]e tould me,"
said Mercy, "I should not see his Two wifes if he could help it."

But Annie saw the two dead Burroughs wives, and the sight of
them terrified her even more than the sight of their husband's specter.
They looked like corpses, Annie told her parents, dead women
wrapped in winding sheets ready for the grave. The two ghosts, from
what Annie said, grew angry at their husband, reminding him how
cruelly he had treated them, telling him that they would be in Heaven
when he was in Hell. At this insubordination, Burroughs's spirit vanished, leaving the wives to speak their piece.

The first wife told Annie how her husband had killed her in the
Salem Village parsonage, stabbing her under one arm. The ghost drew
her sheet aside to display the wound. The second wife said that Burroughs and his present wife had murdered her in a boat going Eastward "because they would have one another." The ghost wives pleaded
with Annie to bring their complaints to the magistrates and charge
their husband with their murders right to his face. If he still wouldn't
admit the crimes, they might have to appear in court themselves, Annie reported.

Ann remembered the first wife, buried now in the Village; the second had been a Hathorne widow when she married him. Such terrible
developments likely seemed chillingly logical to Ann and Thomas:
What would murder mean to someone who threw away his own soul?

The following morning, the day of Reverend Burroughs's hearing,
Mercy Lewis, recovering from "a kind of a Trance," said that his
specter snatched her away (in spirit, presumably) to "an exceeding high
mountain" from which he showed her "all the kingdoms of the earth."
Burroughs "tould me that he would give them all to me if I would
writ in his book," Mercy told the Putnams, "and if I would not he
would thro me down and brake my neck." Yet she defied him, answer-

ing that "they ware non of his to give and I would not writ if he throde me down on 100 pichforks."

However, Mercy survived these threats and was well enough to go off to the Village meeting house with Thomas and Annie to serve as a witness in the day's hearings. At some point Thomas wrote a summary of her vision to show the court, a document that refrained from commenting on the obvious parallel to the Scriptural episode in which Satan tempted Christ in similar manner and in which Christ—like Mercy Lewis—refused to be tempted.

Considering how Ann and Thomas felt about Reverend Burroughs, the man's hearing was probably too enticing to miss, regardless of whatever precautions against more convulsions she may have taken previously.

With a minister accused of going over to the enemy, two assistants, William Stoughton and Samuel Sewall, had journeyed north from Boston to preside over Burroughs's hearing in Salem Village along with local magistrates John Hathorne and Jonathan Corwin. Stoughton, aged about sixty, a Dorchester landowner and career politician, had, like Sewall, studied for the ministry before turning to secular pursuits. He had served on the Governor's Council even under Sir Edmund Andros (when Goody Glover was condemned as a witch) and, despite the unpopularity of that regime, retained his same position as assistant. Samuel Sewall, twenty years younger than Stoughton, was a Boston merchant and office holder who had quit his position in the Boston militia under Andros over a matter of conscience. Both men had reputations of fairness. Stoughton expressed no doubts about the validity of spectral evidence. What doubts Sewall had of the situation at this point he kept to himself.

Ann and the rest of the onlookers in the meeting house had to wait while the magistrates first questioned Burroughs privately, "none of the Bewitched being present" (as Samuel Parris recorded), which was a professional courtesy. Once the magistrates and the prisoner repaired to the packed meeting house the racket began.

Right at the start Susanna Sheldon declared that Burroughs's two dead wives had appeared to her to accuse him of killing not only three children when he was Eastward, two of them his own, but of murdering them as well, the first smothered, the second choked. The magistrates ordered Burroughs to turn and look at his accuser, which resulted in Susanna and most of the other afflicted falling to the floor. If someone even spoke his name, they were affected.

As someone was about to read Mercy Lewis's statement of her recent tortures—probably Thomas Putnam, who had written it out—Burroughs looked at Mercy, who then "fell into a dreadful & tedious fit." The afflicted witnesses were, for the most part, overcome by fits that prevented them from speaking against Burroughs until the convulsions subsided, making the whole process more difficult than usual. To the magistrates, the "Preternatural Mischiefs" convulsing the afflicted were such as "could not possibly be Dissembled." Mrs. Ann Putnam certainly accepted their reality.

Mary Walcott also reported that the ghost wives demanded vengeance, adding that Burroughs had unsuccessfully tried to kill his first wife and their child while she was in labor. (This surely reminded Ann of her own dead children.)

Elizabeth Hubbard had not seen the ghosts but, like all the others, had been tormented because she would not sign the book. Annie Putnam and the rest affirmed that Burroughs's specter was most insistent with the book. The magistrates asked Burroughs what he made of all this.

He replied that "it was an amazing & humbling Providence" but that he did not understand it. "[S]ome of you may observe," he noted, "that when they begin [to] name my name, they cannot name it."

Who, Stoughton asked him, did he think "hindered these witnesses from giving their testimonies?"

The Devil, Burroughs supposed.

"How comes the Divel so loathe to have any Testimony born against you?" Stoughton countered, and this, the magistrates thought, greatly confused Burroughs.

Sarah Bibber, a married woman, was tormented during the proceedings and said she witnessed the other spectral afflictions but that Burroughs's specter had not hurt her nor had she even seen him in person, though his spirit had tried to lure her away from attending court that morning.

Susanna Sheldon had more to say, and in the confusion no one seemed to heed that Annie's story of Burroughs's dead wives being stabbed under the arm and killed in a boat contradicted not only Susanna's tale of the ghosts telling her they were smothered and choked but also Mercy Lewis's earlier account that Burroughs had killed them through witchcraft. It was enough that the women's ghosts and now the ghosts of two children, according to Susanna, accused the man; attention to such crucial details was lost in the rising clamor. As Parris noted, some of "The Bewitched were so tortured that Authority ordered them to be taken away" to recover. If Annie Putnam was one of these, her anxious, watching mother would not have had much sympathy for the accused, certainly not for a man who was notoriously harsh to his first two wives, who supposedly kept one of them working even after the birth pangs came upon her.

Others testified, including confessors Deliverance and Abigail Hobbs as well as John and Rebecca Putnam, who recalled that, when he boarded with them, "he was a very harch sharp man to his wife." He also had wanted his wife to sign and seal a covenant "that shee would never reveall his secrits" when John and Rebecca felt that the marriage vows were sufficient. Now the court was left imagining just *what* secrets Burroughs tried to hide.

Elizer Keyser told of an unnerving encounter with the confined Burroughs at Beadle's tavern, after which Keyser saw a cluster of glowing balls of lights in his own darkened chamber that very night, surely a "diabolicall apperition." (Elizer was a brother of the long-distracted Hannah Keyser who Mary Warren had mentioned as being not in her right mind.)

Various men spoke of Burroughs's uncanny strength, for rumors told of Burroughs hefting a heavy barrel of molasses from a canoe by himself, which he denied, or holding out a long-barreled gun with one hand like a mere pistol. He tried to explain how he had balanced it, but no one was convinced.

That day the court also examined three other suspects, including Bethia Carter of Woburn, and kept all for future trial. (Elizabeth Procter may have been surprised to see Bethia joining the prisoners, for in her youth the woman had accused Elizabeth's grandmother,

Ann Burt, of bewitching her and testified as much at the resulting
court case. Goody Burt had survived that encounter, so perhaps Elizabeth took a grim comfort in that.) No notes for the examinations of
the other seem to have survived, and most of the reasons why they
were suspected are only conjecture; the surviving paperwork does not
indicate that Goody Carter's daughter Bethia Jr. was arrested as ordered. By the end of the session the suspects also included Sarah
Churchill, who was originally considered an afflicted witness but now
regarded as a confessed witch.

Twenty years old and a refugee from Maine, Sarah Churchill came
from a fairly prominent family, though it was one known for violence
(her grandfather) and fornication (her mother). Sarah was working as
hired help for George Jacobs Sr. over on Cow House River when she
experienced convulsions as if bewitched. Her master was unsympa-
thetic to her flailing. Long known as combative and now beset with
arthritis, old Jacobs called her a "bitch witch" and apparently beat her
with one of the two walking sticks he needed to support himself.
However, she had ceased to have fits—Jacobs's beatings may have
cured them—and the magistrates assumed that her pain had stopped
because she had given in and joined the witches. The afflicted reported her specter tormenting them, and at last, like Mary Warren
and Deliverance Hobbs, she "confessed." Her name, she told the court,
was written in the Devil's book twice, listed with the names of her
master, Jacobs, his son, and his granddaughter.

According to Abigail Williams, old Jacobs had made his granddaughter Margaret and the maid Sarah Churchill put their hands to
the Devil's book along with his own son George Jacobs Jr., his wife,
Sarah, as well as "another woman & her husband viz: Mr. English &
his wife" (Philip and Mary English). At some point Sarah Churchill
also said that Ann Pudeator brought her a book to sign and that Bridget Bishop, "alias Olliver," also tormented her.

Sarah was afflicted again at Ingersoll's the evening of May 9 after
her confession, at which time Mary Walcott identified the specter as
Sarah's master, old George Jacobs, "a man with 2 staves."

The latest suspects were probably kept in the Village's watch house
overnight before being crowded into Ingersoll's cart, which had been

rented for the journey to Boston jail But Sarah Churchill, now that she was understood to be a *repentant* witch and thus a potential witness against her coconspirators, was kept in Salem, her arrival a matter of interest to Mary Warren; here was yet another imprisoned witness whose change of heart was not believed.

At Thomas and Ann Putnam's home around midnight Mercy Lewis reported Jacobs's pursuing specter, carrying his two walking sticks and the Devil's book, beating her because she refused to sign and threatening to kill her that very night because she had witnessed against his maid Sarah that day and persuaded her to confess.

Because of this, Hathorne and Corwin issued an arrest warrant on the following day for George Jacobs Sr. and his granddaughter Margaret Jacobs. They ordered these suspects brought to town for a hearing in Thomas Beadle's tavern, where Burroughs had been confined earlier. Sarah Churchill was taken there as a witness, and when she was returned to the Salem jail she had a distressing story full of contradictions that would give Mary Warren even more to worry over.

Sarah had testified against her master as she was expected to do, accusing him of hurting her despite the fact that the old man insisted on his own innocence. She must also have witnessed against Jacobs's granddaughter Margaret, whose case notes are lost, for Margaret broke down and also confessed that she had indeed joined the witches.

But, as Sarah Churchill tried to explain later, the authorities had pressured her to confess. She had belied herself, she said, because *they* would not believe her. *They* threatened to lock her up with the other accused witches—people she had charged, who were thus bound to be resentful. They had kept at her until she was afraid *not* to confess, *not* to lie in the face of that stony disbelief. If she told Reverend Noyes only once that she had signed the Devil's book, he would believe her. If she told him a hundred times that she had not, *then* he would think that she lied. Mary Warren knew what that was like.

Meanwhile, John Willard's specter was also active, for Jonathan Corwin wrote an arrest warrant for the man at some point that day, May 10, and entrusted it to Constable John Putnam Jr., Annie's uncle. But when Constable Putnam reached Will's Hill, he found Willard was not at home.

Sarah Churchill returned to court on May 11, joining Mercy Lewis, Annie Putnam, Abigail Williams, Elizabeth Hubbard, and Mary Walcott, to continue her accusations against Jacobs and his granddaughter. Margaret Jacobs, having confessed, unlike her aggressive grandfather, accused both Mary Warren *and* Goodwife Alice Parker—Mary Warren's enemy.

In Boston on May 10, the day of the first Jacobs examination, Sarah Osborn, unwell to begin with, died in jail. Her nine weeks and two days of imprisonment, as enumerated by the jailer, left an unpaid bill of £1:3:0. Hers was an unhappy and squalid death hastened by illness, no doubt, yet it was a more merciful escape from the prison than a trip to the gallows would be.

It would take time for news of Goody Osborn's death to filter back to Salem, where, on May 12, Constable John Putnam Jr. reported to Hathorne that suspect John Willard was nowhere to be found. The constable had searched Willard's house over near Will's Hill along with "Severall other houses and places," all to no avail. As far as he could tell from Willard's family and friends, "he was ffleed Salem." (Her kinsman's failure to seize this suspected witch could only have made Ann Putnam even more concerned for herself and her children.)

That same day Magistrates Hathorne and Corwin questioned Mary Warren again in the Salem jail. They had interviewed Abigail Hobbs the day before, finding her as cooperative as Deliverance Hobbs and Susanna Churchill. If Mary had hesitated earlier, had held back from further direct accusations—for neither the various hearing notes or the subsequent indictments indicate her presence in court since her own hearing—she now collapsed in a torrent of confession and accusation while Jonathan Corwin took lengthy notes.

She may have agreed with the charge of witchcraft because of fear or confusion, coming to believe that if the afflicted acted as if her specter were pursuing them, perhaps it was. The magistrates and the ministers, educated gentlemen all, were convinced that this was true. Maybe she believed—or almost believed—it was true, for they said that her actions could give the Devil permission to use her appearance even if she were not aware of it.

Or Mary gave in and agreed to the charge solely to save her skin. A proven witch would be put to death. But a cooperating repentant witch could be considered sufficiently free of Satan to live long enough to testify. So she did as she was expected to do—she confessed and accused her supposed coconspirators. Besides, Goody Parker had been named among the specters, and that was an accusation she could believe. That her own specter was also reported was an inducement to cooperate, to contradict *that* sighting.

Yes, she admitted, she *had* signed the Devil's book, saying, "I did nott know itt [then] butt I know itt now, to be Sure itt was the Devills book in the ffirst place to be Sure I did Sett my hand to the Devills book; I have considered of itt, Since you were here last, & itt was the Devills book, [that] my Master Procter brought to me, & he Tould me if I would Sett my hand to th[a]t book I should be well." So by now she was accusing John Procter as well as Elizabeth.

Mary, like others, seemed to embroider actual innocuous events to fit the magistrates' expectations. She denied hurting the afflicted children with magic and then admitted to using poppets. Her mistress, Elizabeth Procter, had brought her a cloth doll representing either Abigail Williams or Annie Putnam. Her master brought her another poppet representing Abigail Williams. The specters of Goodwives Alice Parker (*that* woman who had killed Mary's mother) and Ann Pudeator had brought her in prison other dolls as well, representing girls such as Mercy Lewis and Mary Walcott. Alice Parker and Ann Pudeator had bragged of the people they had killed, Mary said. Parker had caused the deaths of local men at sea and drowned Goody Orne's son in Salem Harbor, washing him up by his mother's very door. Pudeator poisoned her own husband. While Mary "was thus Confessing," Corwin wrote, "Parker appeared & bitt hir Extreamly on hir armes as she affirmed unto us."

Many witch specters continued to confront her, Mary said, naming other prisoners, ranging from Rebecca Nurse to Dorothy Good, telling how Goody Corey's specter turned into John Procter's on her lap. They paused in the session when Reverends Higginson and Hale arrived in order to observe. As Corwin read his notes aloud to the two ministers, Mary "Imediately ffell into dreadfull ffitts" when he read

Goody Parker's name. The woman's specter had appeared, as did that of Goodwife Ann Pudeator when Hathorne spoke her name.

According to Mary Warren, the Parker specter had not only struck wealthy John Turner unconscious for a time when she knocked him out of a cherry tree in his orchard but also bewitched the power of speech away from Mary's own sister. Yet Parker failed completely in her attempt to bewitch Mr. Corwin's mare to prevent the magistrate from riding to Salem Village. Burroughs likewise failed to hobble Hathorne's horse to thwart his trip to Boston. They were not *that* powerful. They could not bewitch Hathorne, but they could evidently attack Mary, who fell into such severe fits that Hathorne and Corwin issued an arrest warrant for both Pudeator and Parker and ordered Marshall Herrick to bring them in immediately for questioning. (The location is not specified but may have been Beadle's tavern as before.) The afflicted witnesses against them would be Mary Warren and Margaret Jacobs.

When the marshall brought in Alice Parker, Mary English's tenant and neighbor and Bridget Bishop's friend, Mary Warren did not hesitate to accuse her. All the resentment at everything her family had lost—her sister locked in silence and her mother dead—due to this perceived enemy boiled over.

Mary Warren, face to face with Alice Parker, does not doubt her accusation. Not now, not with this *woman. She may only half believe her own confession, but even when she had declared that her fits were part of a distraction, even when she tried to recant, she had no reason to doubt the reality of witches, of malefic magic, of the Devil's malice. Someone could be causing her misery and the afflictions of the other women and girls, and who would want to do such things? Goody Parker is so obvious a threat. Does not the woman go rigid and blank, as though her soul flits elsewhere, invisible to her victims? If anyone is a witch, this woman is for sure, one of the Devil's willing servants.*

But Goodwife Parker denies the charge, denies bragging about murder victims, denies saying anything to Mary, much less threats. "I never spake a word to her in my life."

"You told her also you bewitched her sister, because her father would not mow your grass," says the magistrate.

"I never saw her." After all, Goody Parker's dealings had been with Mary's father.

Does the woman even remember the young girl present somewhere during her dispute with Goodman Warren? Mary is older now, but Mary has not forgotten. She has relived the scene again and again in her mind. Now she raises her hand to strike Parker's lying mouth, but when she tries to step forward she cannot proceed but instead jerks backward, pushed down by something invisible.

While Mary struggles to recover herself, Margaret Jacobs accuses Parker of sending her spirit to Northfields, where old Jacobs's farm is.

Marshall George Herrick reports that when he arrested the prisoner she had said, "[T]hat there were threescore Witches of the Company."

John Louder, who also suspected Bridget Bishop, was there too and says the same.

Goody Parker says she does not remember what number she had said or who had told her about it. But no one believes her, least of all Mary.

All through Goody Parker's examination convulsions thrash Mary, her words are choked off and strangled. She persists and gradually is able to tell her tale—of the sorrows that have eaten into her heart ever since her father's encounter with Parker, of the grief that has become rage. She tells the magistrates how her father had promised to mow Parker's grass crop "if he had time." But he had not had time, so that woman came to his house and threatened him, saying "he had better he had done it." Soon after that, Mary's sister, Elizabeth, fell ill, then Mary's mother. Her mother died, and the sister was left deaf and dumb, imprisoned by silence.

Goodwife Parker stands there, looking astonished and shaking her head as though she knows nothing about this.

But even that was not enough for Parker, Mary continues, speaking now to the prisoner as well as to the magistrates. For Parker's specter pursued Mary still, bringing poppets and a needle, weapons with which to torment the other girls. When Mary refused to torment them, refused to join Parker in the Devil's work, the specter threatened to run the needle through Mary's own heart.

Mary now stares the accused directly in the eye—or tries to—but she cannot meet the witch's gaze but instead falls as though struck. She hears her enemy speaking, calling on God to prove her innocence. "I wish God would open the Earth and swallow me up presently, if one word of this is true."

But although the earth does not open, the magistrates and other onlookers see Mary's reaction as the result of Parker's evil magic being cast then and there, right before them in the court, "dreadfully tormenting" Mary, punishing the girl for standing up to her.

Along with some thirty other witches, Parker took part in the Devil's bloody sacrament at Reverend Parris's pasture, Mary says when she can continue. The woman had boasted of that and of chasing John Louder along Salem Common. And all during this questioning Parker kept sending her own specter directly out of her body to afflict Mary.

Reverend Noyes speaks up to remind the defendant of an earlier time when Goody Parker was ill, when he visited her to inquire about then-current rumors of witchcraft. He had asked "whether she were not guilty," and Goody Parker had answered that "If she was as free from other sins as from witchcrafts she would not ask the Lord mercy." That reply is now taken to be an evasion rather than a reference to sins she did not *commit.*

At this Mary convulses in a "dreadful fit," during which her tongue pulls from her mouth, straining until it turns dark.

This is too much for the defendant, who snaps, "Warrens tongue would be blacker before she died"—black with lies, that is.

The magistrates ask Goody Parker why she afflicts and torments Mary.

"If I do," she answers, "the Lord forgive me."

But the court does not believe Goody Parker's claim of innocence and holds her for trial. Mary Warren can rest assured the witch who destroyed her family will get her just desserts.

(8)

May 12 to 30, 1692

The little nagging doubts have receded further back in Mary Warren's mind, smothered like embers in ash. As she tries to sleep the night after her encounter with the Parker woman, she feels triumphant and terrified at the same time. Now what will happen? Mary has confessed after all, and she is not sure what the law allows for penitent felons, remorseful witches. If she ever gets out of here—the rancid cell, the small barred window, the jail's confinement—then what? No one at the Procter farm will have her back. No one there is about to welcome her. Not now.

She must find somewhere else to work. The magistrates and the other men of authority—did any of their households need a maid? Would any of the women who testified against their neighbors hire her? And if they did, what then? She can see herself aging as she supports other people's families until she is too old and infirm to be worth hiring. She thinks of the older women servants she sees about Salem—a few widows, others unmarried but no longer young, like that odd Soames woman over on the road to Boston. She is never in the meeting house, but then again, she's also a Quaker. People say she comes out only at night. Is that Mary's future? Will her own life stretch out as bleak as that—if she is ever freed?

The alternative is too terrible to face. She moans at the crowding thoughts.

The new prisoners may have spent the night in Salem jail, but right after Alice Parker's May 12 hearing Hathorne wrote a *mittimus*, the order to transfer Parker and Ann Pudeator to Boston along with Giles Corey, George Jacobs Sr., William Hobbs (who, unlike his wife and daughter, had not confessed), Bridget

Bishop, Mary English, Sarah Bishop, with her husband, Edward Jr., Sarah Wildes, and the slave woman Mary Black. (By a slip of the pen Hathorne wrote *Ann Putnam*'s name among the prisoners, noticed his mistake, and wrote "Pudeatter" over Putnam.)

Having testified so thoroughly against the woman she blamed for her mother's death, Mary Warren was in even less of a position to draw back from her confession. On May 13, while Mistress English, Goodwife Bishop, and the others made the long journey south to Boston, Hathorne wrote an arrest warrant for one Abigail Soames, charging her with afflicting Mary Warren. Constable Peter Osgood brought the woman before the magistrates at Thomas Beadle's tavern directly.

Mary, escorted to Beadle's, continued to experience symptoms and, as she passed through the tavern gate, something seemed to bite her. Recent confessor Margaret Jacobs was also present but let Mary take the lead in making accusations.

Once the constable brought in the prisoner, Mary fell "into a dreadful fit," feeling stabbed and "continually Crying out that it was this very Woman tho she knew her not before, only affirmed that she herself in apparition had told her that her name was Soams, and also did affirm that this was the very woman that had afflicted her all this day, and that she met her as she was comeing in att the gate, and bit her Exceedingly."

The guards, searching the prisoner for possible magical weaponry, found concealed in her apron "a great Botching Needle" (a mending needle), which they removed gingerly. Although it was a logical tool of housewifery, Soames nevertheless denied knowing anything about it.

Mary, no longer reacting as if stabbed or pinched, continued to talk, telling them that the woman's apparition had revealed that her name was Abigail Soames, that her brother was cooper John Soames, "that she Lived att Gaskins, and that she had lain Bedrid a year."

The magistrates asked the defendant if John Soames *was* her brother, and Abigail refused to answer—"peremptorily," the scribe noted—"for all was false that Warren said." (Abigail, still single at thirty-seven, did have a brother John who was a cooper. The family were Quakers from Gloucester and had had no end of trouble some fifteen years earlier for flouting public worship, under laws that were now no longer in effect.

Quakers' avoidance of "Orthodox" (i.e., Congregational) religious services, their rejection of a college-educated ministry in favor of personal inspiration from the "Light within," their insistence on a greater equality (male Quakers refused to doff their hats to those in authority, even when indoors), and their cutting criticisms of the status quo had seemed a threat to public peace and community solidarity in uncertain times. The "Light within" was supposed to be God's light, but just how, non-Quakers wondered, could anyone be so sure of the *source* of these spiritual messages? It seemed more like an invitation to communication with lying, devilish spirits, especially if the recipient fell to trembling in his enthusiasm, which gave the Society of Friends the nickname "Quakers," or acting out shocking metaphors, as when Rebecca Nurse's kinswoman appeared naked in public. The authorities had set fines for this behavior, exiled the more outspoken repeaters, and sometimes applied the death penalty to those who returned. (Anglican Virginia, in contrast, whipped and expelled Quakers and continued to do the same again to any who returned.) Massachusetts's draconian policy was not only ineffective but also caught England's attention, which helped lead to the loss of the charter. Ironically, the crown required that Massachusetts grant more civil rights to the local Friends than England then allowed to Friends in England. This happened after one Samuel Shattuck had sailed to England to petition the king for help and had had the satisfaction of bringing the order back to the Massachusetts authorities who had once persecuted him. His son, Salem dyer Samuel Shattuck, was convinced that Bridget Bishop had bewitched his son, revealing that Quakers shared the same views about witchcraft as their Congregational neighbors did.

Back then Abigail and her brother Nathaniel were reprimanded, but John was arrested twice and even whipped. Abigail now worked for Samuel and Provided Gaskill (or Gaskin), a Quaker couple in Salem. Why Mary accused Abigail is not clear. The road from the Procter's farm to Salem Harbor did run past the Gaskill's door, but probably, as with the other defendants, gossip had whispered about Abigail for years, the suspicions common knowledge. Perhaps Mary saw herself in Abigail's situation—alone, unwell, working as hired help in another woman's home, and with precious little to show for it—a fearsome future.

Soames, said Mary, had caused the death of one Southwick, a local man recently dead, as other afflicted girls had likewise reported his ghost. When Abigail heard this accusation she looked directly at Mary, who fell again, racked by convulsions, apparently bitten by an unseen entity. Her reactions were so severe "that the Like was never seen on any of the afflicted," the scribe observed. Soames did it, said Mary when she could speak. And the Soames specter had told her that very day that "she would be the death of her," then stuck two pins into Mary's side for good measure, drawing blood.

The magistrates asked Goodwife Gaskill if Soames really *had* been bedridden as Mary had claimed. Goody Gaskill admitted that, yes, Abigail "had kept her Bed for most parts these thirteen months."

And she went out only at night, Mary continued.

Yes, said Goodwife Gaskill, "that was the Usual time off her goeing abroad."

For three nights, Mary continued, Soames had tormented her, trying to bargain, promising to stop hurting Mary if the girl would in turn promise not to tell anyone how sickly she was—for who would hire a maid too weak to work?—haggling for Mary's silence *and* for a promise to join her among the witches.

But, Mary told the court, she had replied that "she would not keep the Devils Councel."

To that Soames's specter said, "she was not a Devil but she was her God." And the specter appeared three more times with the same claim or to say that "she was as good as a God."

The magistrates were shocked by such a blasphemous notion. "Mary Warren is this true?"

"It is nothing but the truth."

They then asked the defendant *who* was hurting Mary in her fits if not her.

"[I]t was the Enemy hurt her," said Abigail—the Devil hurt her. She tried to explain what she believed was happening, for she herself had once seen apparitions. "I have been . . . myself distracted many a time, and my senses have gone from mee, and I thought I have seen many a Body hurt mee, and might have accused many as wel as she doth. I Really thought I had seen many persons att my Mothers house at Glocester, and they greatly afflicted mee as I thought."

When Abigail had not attended the approved public worship back in 1681, the court record noted, "She hath been in a distracted condition about this two months, and her brother Nathaniel hath been forced to make it his whole employment to look after her."

And now it was Mary who was distracted and now fell in another "dreadful ffit." The magistrates ordered the touch test, in which the defendant must touch her supposed victim to break the spell causing the convulsions. The theory behind the test was that the "the venemous and malignant particles, that were ejected from the eye" of the witch into the victim would flow back into the witch through the touch.

However, the afflicted, at the beginning of the troubles, had been able to interrupt and thereby stop *each other's* convulsions by a touch. "They did in the Assembly mutually Cure each other, even with a Touch of their Hand," Deodat Lawson had noted. But the magistrates appeared to have forgotten this.

Mary Warren "immediately recovered," say the notes. "[T]his Experiment was tryed three times over and the Issue the same." After one of those recoveries the court told Mary to touch Soames. Mary tried "several times" and "with great Earnestness," but she could not get near, falling instead into another "dreadful ffit." The magistrates ordered Soames to take Mary's hand, and as they expected, Mary, "her Eyes then being fast shut," immediately recovered. She had "felt some thing soft in her hand . . . which revived her very heart."

When asked why she could not step close enough to Soames, Mary said that she saw Soames's specter step from the woman's body, "meet her, and thrust her with Violence back again, not suffring her to Come near her."

During Mary's explanation Abigail said more than once that "it was distraction in talking." She even laughed at Mary's stories, but this reaction only caused Mary to fall in another fit.

Was this the result of witchcraft? the magistrates asked Soames. Did she think "there were any Witches in the world?"

But Abigail knew nothing about this. "[I]tt was the Enemy," she said, the Devil, "or some Other wicked person or the Enemy himself that forces persons to afflict her att this tim"—but not herself.

Now Mary passed into a trance, during which, as she related once she regained consciousness, Soames promised "that she would thrust an Awl into her very heart and would kil her this night." Every time the defendant looked at Mary the girl appeared to be hit, "struck so dreadfully on her breast, that she cryed out she was almost killed" and burst into an "abundance of tears."

When the magistrates took her to task for this, Soames, "instead of bewailing itt, Broke forth into Laughter." This only caused Mary to be "afflicted by the wringing of her mouth after a strange, and prodigious manner."

Ordered to look at the struggling Mary, Abigail flatly refused. Ordered to face her victim, Abigail turned toward her—or was made to turn—but "shut her Eyes Close, and would not look on her." Ordered to touch Mary, she did so "and immediately Warren Recovered." At that, Abigail opened her eyes, and Mary, seeing her gaze, fell "into another most dreadful and terrible fit."

"[I]n this manner," the magistrates concluded, "she practised her Witchcrafts severall times before the Court." By now Mary responded to Abigail's every motion. During the questioning Abigail had "put her own foot behind her Other leg," at which Mary's legs clamped together so rigidly "that it was impossible ffor the strongest man there to Untwist them, without Breaking her Leggs, as was seen by many present."

Abigail Soames was held for trial, but Mary's suffering was not over. She said she saw the specters of Rebecca Nurse and one of the Procters (probably Elizabeth) standing before her with Burroughs, who bit her savagely. People could not see the specters, but they could see the tooth marks.

Margaret Jacobs, who had apparently kept to the background during the hearing, began to cry. She too had seen Burroughs's specter just now, she said, and it predicted that her grandfather Jacobs (whom she too had accused) would be hanged.

Abigail Soames and the confessor witnesses were returned to Salem jail, with Mary exhausted and bloodied by her ordeal and Margaret stricken by the Burroughs specter's prophesy, which put into words what she feared in her heart was a logical outcome of her own folly. But she did not yet dare to change her story.

Mary and Margaret seem to be the only afflicted witnesses brought against Abigail Soames. Annie Putnam was home at her father's house on May 13 when Goodwife Elizabeth Hart arrived, having come from Lynn to confront the girl. Although Annie would later say that she had seen but not recognized that woman's specter among the witches, word that she was suspected had obviously reached Goody Hart. Once again Ann and Thomas witnessed their daughter face a supposed witch in person.

Goody Hart identified herself to Annie and asked outright if the girl thought she had ever hurt her. Annie admitted she had not, meaning her specter had not. But Goody Hart was no more successful in her attempt to set the matter right than was Martha Corey or John Willard. Shortly after this encounter the Hart specter began to hurt Annie "most greviously severall times" and hound her to sign the book she brought.

The more that people like the Putnams fought against the enemy, the more supposed witches there seemed to be. Annie was now tormented not only by Elizabeth Hart but also by Thomas Farrar Sr. (old Pharaoh) of Lynn, Elizabeth Coleson of Reading, and Bethia Carter of Woburn as well as several Salem Village folk: George Jacobs Jr., his wife, Rebecca, and her brother Daniel Andrews, old Sarah Buckley, and her widowed daughter Mary Whittredge. These specters had seemingly attacked not only Annie but also Mercy Lewis, Mary Walcott, and Abigail Williams as well as unspecified "others of Salem Village."

Thomas Putnam and Nathaniel Ingersoll entered a complaint against the new witches on Saturday, May 14. Marshall Herrick arrested Elizabeth Hart and old Farrar the following day, a Sabbath. Reading's Constable John Parker, however, made "Diligent Search" for Elizabeth Coleson, but the woman, a granddaughter of the already arrested Lydia Dustin, had heard of her impending arrest in time to flee. "[B]y the best Information," Parker reported on Monday, "shee is att Boston in order to bee shipt ofe and by way of Escape to bee transported to some other Countery."

Likewise Constable Jonathan Putnam, although he had confined Goodwives Buckley and Whittredge at Ingersoll's as ordered, was unable to find either Daniel Andrews or George Jacobs Jr. He made "delegant sarch" of each of their houses, but to no avail. He did arrest Rebecca Jacobs, for her husband had left her behind with the children, who, now with both parents gone, were on their own.

By now, if not earlier, Mercy Lewis was staying with the family of John and Hannah Putnam, the couple whose infant had died so suddenly in April. Although Annie was still afflicted, the maid's absence would spare Ann Putnam considerable turmoil. Nevertheless, she still worried about the four escaped witches, especially Willard, all of whom were responsible, she believed, for the death of her infant Sarah. The devilish threats continued to increase, so much so that neighbors consulted Annie and Mercy and some of the other afflicted girls as to which specters were causing local ailments.

For one thing, Bray Wilkins, patriarch over at Will's Hill, had suffered a painful blockage of urine ever since his trip to Boston for the election festivities, then his grandson Daniel fell ill. On May 12, the day of Parker and Pudeator's examinations and two days after Willard's flight, Mercy Lewis saw various specters hurting the old man—including a specter of Bray's grandson-in-law John Willard. Every gossip knew Bray and Daniel had been at odds with Willard. By May 14, with the real Willard's whereabouts still unknown, young Daniel became mute and refused to eat, spitting whatever anyone tried to spoon-feed him back in their face. After that, Mercy Lewis and Mary Walcott reported Willard's specter, aided by Goodwife Sarah Buckley's specter, attacking Bray and Daniel and even vowing to kill Daniel within two days. The following day, the Sabbath when Goody Hart was arrested, Bray's son Benjamin and neighbor Thomas Fuller Jr. persuaded the Salem magistrates to issue a second arrest warrant for Willard, and that evening Annie reported seeing Willard's specter torturing Daniel's sister Rebecca as well. Annie relayed the specter's threat to kill Daniel with the help of the more powerful Burroughs—a threat the boy doubtless heard, a threat he had already taken to heart.

On May 16 the Wilkins "sent to the french Doctor," as Benjamin Wilkins would state, "but hee sent word againe [that] it was not A naturall Cause but absolutly wichcraft to his Judgment." Then, at some point that day the afflicted girls cried out that Willard was taken, and, as they later learned, that was the hour that Constable John Putnam arrested Willard himself miles away in Lancaster—or at least that was how they remembered it later.

That evening Mercy Lewis and Mary Walcott arrived at Will's Hill, reported the spectral Willard and Buckley torturing Daniel, and predicted that the spirits would soon kill the lad. Annie apparently arrived later and saw the same as she waited among the watchers while Daniel Wilkins died, gasping for breath that would not come, choked, all were sure, by his uncle Willard.

Mrs. Ann Putnam was not the only party concerned about the number of fugitives. Someone sent word to Boston, where John Hathorne and Jonathan Corwin were with the rest of the legislature to welcome the new royal governor. Sir William Phips, a Maine-born, Boston-based shipbuilder and entrepreneur, had made his fortune and received his title by recovering sunken treasure in the Caribbean. As he had brought the newly granted charter, negotiated by Reverend Increase Mather, Massachusetts was once again a legal political entity— or would be once the government was reconfigured to meet English requirements. As one of the earliest actions under the new charter, Hathorne and Corwin, "By order of the Governor and Council," wrote a second arrest warrant for the three suspects still at large, while the Suffolk County Sheriff began a search for Elizabeth Coleson in Boston.

But by May 17 most of the recent suspects were in custody at the Village, packed into the watch-house, including Willard, who had been brought all the way from Lancaster, where he had been found in plain sight, hoeing corn. The afflicted, Annie Putnam presumably among then, fell into such a terrible state at the sight of him that Marshall George Herrick "was forced to pinion" the man to prevent the specter from tormenting them further. Between this commotion and collecting a coroner's jury to examine young Daniel's body, the authorities had to postpone the scheduled hearings by a day.

Thomas Putnam had petitioned with other neighbors for a coroner's jury but did not sign the return as a member; rather, he wrote the account of what the other men discovered:

> [W]e find severall bruised places upon the back of the said corps and the skin broken and many places of the gratest part of his back seemed to be prickt with an instriment about the bigness of a small awll and own [i.e. one] side of his neck and ear seemed to be much bruised to his throat and turning the corps the blood Run out of his nose or mouth or both and his body nott sweld neither did he purge elce whare and to the best of our judgments we cannot but thinke but that he dyed an unnaturall death by sume cruell hands of wicthcraft or diabolicall art as is evident to us both by what we have seen and hard consarning his death.

(Reverend Parris was absent from the Village but would note, "Dan: Wilkins Bewitched to death," in his record of Village deaths.)

In Boston John Hathorne and Jonathan Corwin took their oaths of office as Governor's Councilors (the new name for Assistants) on Monday, the day Daniel Wilkins died. They were in Salem Village Wednesday, May 18, when they presided over the next hearings in the Village meeting house. Their entourage this day included Mary Warren, brought from Salem jail to serve as a witness, along with Annie Putnam, the Sheldon, Lewis, Williams, and Hubbard girls, plus John Indian. Sarah Churchill and Margaret Jacobs were most probably present as well. And although she is not named in the transcripts of the examinations, Mrs. Ann Putnam's name is among the afflicted witnesses in the surviving indictments. Whether she stood among the others or had a bad turn in the audience is not clear. Most of the notes for the day have been lost, but Samuel Parris's summary of Sarah Buckley's questioning and two versions of John Willard's remain, written out from the shorthand he scribbled on the spot.

The afflicted faced the latest defendants with the usual reactions. Sarah Buckley, an elderly Salem Village woman with "scragged teeth," was made to touch the writhing girls to bring them out of their fits. Mary Warren said that when she saw Goody Buckley among a great company of witches the woman tried to make her join them at the Devil's sacrament up in Reverend Parris's pasture. Goody Buckley protested her innocence, but Annie, who had had to be carried in a fit over to the suspect to be healed by a touch on the arm, stated, "I believe in my heart that Sarah Buckly is a wicth," so that view prevailed.

Goody Buckley's widowed daughter Mary Whittredge was also questioned, as was Elizabeth Hart and the disreputable seventy-five-year-old Thomas Farrar Sr. of Lynn, a man too fond of drink and violence. He had once accused Elizabeth Procter's grandmother of bewitching two of his own children.

At first the afflicted did not recognize the next suspect until one of them, probably Elizabeth Hubbard, exclaimed, "[D]on't you know Jacobs the old Witch?" Rebecca Jacobs, unstable to begin with, broke down and confessed not only to witchcraft but also to killing her own child (Mary, who had drowned in a well accidentally seven years past). Her husband, George Jacobs Jr., and her brother Daniel Andrews had fled before they too could be arrested, thus leaving Rebecca to be taken. Daughter Margaret was already in jail, and the other Jacobs children had to fend for themselves until neighbors—most likely Sarah Cloyce's family—took them in.

The afflicted must have reported the specter of folk healer and sometimes witch finder Roger Toothaker, for the magistrates issued a warrant for his arrest as well and likely questioned him along with the others this same day.

All the afflicted except John Indian fell "in most miserable fits" when Willard was led in, torments that repeated if he so much as looked at them. Even so, he appeared cowed before the authorities, who made it plain that his flight was taken as "an acknowledgement of guilt." Nevertheless, they said, "we require you to confesse the truth in this matter."

"I shall, as I hope, I shall be assisted by the Lord of Heaven," Willard babbled. "& for my flying away . . . I was affrighted & I thought by my withdrawing it might be better, I fear not but the Lord in his due time will make me as white as snow."

"What do you say?" a magistrate demanded. "Why do you hurt them, it is you or your appearance?"

"I know nothing of appearance."

But both Mercy Lewis and Elizabeth Hubbard fell at his glance when the court read aloud their statements about recent torments.

Willard, at a loss for words, chewed his lip, at which Mary Warren and Annie Putnam wailed, "[O]h, he bites me."

"Open your mouth, don't bite your lips," the magistrate snapped.

"I will stand with my mouth open, or I will keep it shut, I will stand any how, if you will tell me how." When Annie Putnam's and Susanna Sheldon's statements were read he marveled at the reports of what he had supposedly done to old Bray and young Daniel.

"What do you say to this murdering and bewitching your relations?" asked the magistrate.

"One would think," Willard answered, "that no creature except they belong to hell from their Cradle would be guilty of such things."

When he "offered large talk"—trying to explain his side of the story—the magistrates cut in: "We do not send for you to preach."

Willard might have groveled, but his statements did not fit with his relatives' accounts of his cruelty toward both his animals and his wife. According to Benjamin Wilkins and others, Willard not only beat Margaret but did so hard enough to break the stick he struck her with until she ran away to hide from his fury. "There are a great many lyes told," Willard objected. "I would desire my wife might be called." His reputation, however, was too well known, so it was easy to believe that he had committed murder by magic against several recently deceased locals as well.

As the afflicted witnesses still reacted to Willard's movements, the magistrates proposed the touch test. Annie Putnam volunteered—to the defendant's alarm. "[L]et not that person but another come."

Now even John Indian cried out, "Oh! he cuts me."

When Susanna Sheldon exclaimed that the Devil was whispering in Willard's ear, he protested, "S[i]r I heard nothing nor see nothing."

But the magistrates were not convinced, especially when Susanna tried to approach Willard and seemed repelled. He did take her hand, "with a great deal of do," as Parris noted, but that did not break the spell as it was expected to do, and the girl kept shouting, "O John Willard, John Willard."

When she finally recovered, she explained that "The black man stood between us"—the shadowy form of the Devil—to prevent the touch from working.

"They cannot come near any that are accused," said Willard.

"Why do you say so," said a magistrate, "they could come near Nehemiah Abbot, the children could talk with him." Abbott, as was now well known, had been released for lack of evidence when the afflicted could not positively identify him with one of the specters.

When Mary Warren was the next to convulse, deputies carried her to Willard, who clasped his hand on her arm, at which point her body relaxed.

"Why," Willard demanded, "was it not before so with Susanna Sheldon?"

Constable John Putnam Jr. and various bystanders said that it was because the bystanders had not held his hands still then.

By now most of the afflicted reported the ghosts of Willard's murder victims drifting about the room, calling for vengeance.

"Do you think these are Bewitcht?" the magistrate asked Willard.

"Yes, I really beleive it."

"Well others they have accused it is found true that they are the guilty persons, why should it be false in you?" And just how, they wanted to know, did he send his spirit from his body to attack the witnesses? as Mary Warren and Susanna Sheldon now said he was doing.

"It is not from me, I know nothing of it."

The magistrate reminded him how incriminating his reputation for cruelty and his flight from the law were, stating, "[I]f you can therefore find in your heart to repent it is possible you may obtain mercy & therefore bethink your self."

"S[i]r I cannot confesse that which I do not know."

Willard tried the Lord's Prayer test, but he garbled a line of that familiar prayer, tried again, and again missed. The general belief was that anyone pledged to the Devil's work would be unable to repeat the prayer's desires, especially that God's will be done. The commotions of the afflicted could not have helped his concentration. As Thomas

and Edward Putnam would soon depose, the afflicted were "most greviously tormented as if their bones would have been disjoyned."

"It is a strange thing," he said. "I can say it at another time. I think
I am bewitcht as well as they." He laughed, but no one else did. Nor
did the court consider Willard as beset as the afflicted were.

He missed twice more. "Well this is a strange thing I cannot say it."

And after the fifth time he cried, "Well it is these wicked ones that
do so overcome me."

The afflicted witnesses must have taken particular notice of *that*
remark.

"Do not you see God will not suffer you to pray to him?" asked a
magistrate. "[A]re not you sensible of it?"—perhaps the magistrate
here referred to Proverbs 28:9: "He that turneth away his ear from
hearing the law, even his prayer shall be abomination."

"Why it is a strange thing."

"No it is no strange thing that God will not suffer a wizard to pray
to him," the magistrate replied. "There is also the jury of inquest for
murder that will bear hard against you. Therefore confess. Have you
never wisht harm to your Neighbours?"

"No never since I had a being," Willard responded. But there were
plenty of people present who recalled Willard's temper and his reputation for beating his wife as well as his livestock.

"Well confesse & give glory to God," said the magistrate. "[T]ake
counsell whilst it is offered."

"I desire to take good counsell," said Willard pointedly, "but if it
was the last time I was to speak, I am innocent."

John Willard was held for trial, a relief to Ann Putnam, who was
evidently afflicted during his questioning.

The magistrates then re-opened Mary Esty's questioning. Imprisoned nearly a month, the woman not only insisted on her innocence
but, like her sister Rebecca Nurse, also had strong family support.
Somehow—the papers for this are lost—her family persuaded the
court to reconsider the evidence the afflicted witnesses had given.

This time only Mercy Lewis spoke against Goody Esty; the rest
were no longer sure she really was the same as the reported specter.
And this time the magistrates released Mary Esty, a move that would

bring great relief to her and to her family, give hope to her sister Rebecca Nurse, subdue—if only temporarily—the afflicted witnesses who may have felt a glimmer of doubt about what they said (even while it alarmed Ann Putnam), and reinforce the magistrates' confidence that they were indeed impartial.

Although both Sarah Churchill and Margaret Jacobs were present as witnesses at Willard's hearing, it is possible that neither of them spoke against him, for neither is named in the hearing notes. However, a later list of witnesses says that Churchill and Warren were the ones "that Willard diswaded from confession." Whether the two young women said this was the case or whether only the other afflicted witnesses said that Willard's specter dissuaded them is unclear. However, the fact that Margaret's mother, Rebecca Jacobs, was questioned during this same session, had confessed, and was being held for trial must have prayed on the daughter's conscience. Even if she had not testified against her own mother, her past accusations had endangered her whole family.

The magistrates ordered Willard, Farrar, Toothaker, and Goody Hart removed directly to the Boston jail. They also took a deposition from a new girl, eighteen-year-old Elizabeth Booth, who had already lost both her father and stepfather. She blamed her sufferings on two specters: the absent Daniel Andrews, who brought the Devil's book to her to sign, and Mary Warren. Even though Mary had testified against the day's suspects and convulsed like the rest of the afflicted, Elizabeth evidently did not trust her. On the night before last, said Elizabeth, Mary Warren's specter had appeared at "her bed side and brought a little Baby to this Deponent and told her that she might sett her hand to the Book and not know of it," and if she would not, she said, Andrews would torment her. (Certainly Mary had nearly admitted to touching the book that Procters' specter brought her without realizing what she was about, but the significance of the baby is unexplained.)

In the Salem jail Mary Warren continued to be tormented. Perhaps the visions were nightmares or hallucinations, or perhaps she later embroidered her distress as stories. She had reason to worry whether other afflicted witnesses continued to report her specter among the accused. Burroughs's spirit, Mary later told the authorities, had invaded her cell around this time, blowing a trumpet to summon a meeting of his witches. Mary said she refused to join them in spite of their wheedling assurances that their bloody sacrament was better than wine. She named several suspects already in custody: Abigail Soames, John Procter, Rebecca Nurse, and Goodwives Parker, Pudeator, and Duston.

Ann Putnam now lacked Mercy Lewis's help—not that she had been any help lately, however—cousin Sarah Trask took her place in Thomas Putnam's household. Sarah, fortunately, remained immune to afflictions and convulsions—a relief to Ann, who was shorthanded and feeling the frequent effects of pregnancy and the occasional effect of bewitchment. Even though the witches still tormented Young Annie, she still attended the hearings and visited afflicted neighbors faithfully.

On May 20, two days after the court had freed Goodwife Esty, when John Putnam was busy in Salem town, Samuel Abby showed up at Thomas Putnam's doorstep with a plea from Hannah Putnam for Annie to come over and see what specter still tortured Mercy. So Annie, along with Abigail Williams from the parsonage and accompanied by Sarah Trask, went off to help. Thomas probably followed them later with other concerned neighbors, for Annie did not return until the next morning.

Their news was not encouraging. Stalked by specters of Esty and another woman, the girls rode horseback to the neighbor's house only to find Mercy in convulsions. For hours the specters of Goody Esty, aided by Willard and Mary Whittredge, set upon her. Other visionary girls joined the watchers—Mary Walcott, Elizabeth Hubbard, Abigail Williams—and they reported the same spirits plus John and Elizabeth Procter's daughter Sarah with her aunt Sarah Bassett and elderly widow Susanna Roots. The Esty spirit was the worst, Ann learned, threatening to kill Mercy before midnight in retaliation for the girl's testimony against her. Esty had magically blinded the other witness against seeing her specter before, but Mercy could not blinded.

"Deare lord Receive my soule," Mercy had wailed. "[L]ord let them not kill me quitt." For much of the time she could hardly breathe, let alone speak.

Elizabeth Hubbard showed up at one point, and though all of the afflicted watchers were tormented at intervals, Elizabeth and Mercy "fell into fits by turns, the one being well whilst the other was ill," both complaining of Goody Esty. All of the afflicted appeared choked, but a spectral chain choked Mercy.

When John Putnam returned with Benjamin Hutchinson and Marshall George Herrick, Mercy seemed almost dead of exhaustion. The three men hastened the six or so miles to town to find Hathorne and get a warrant to arrest Goody Esty anew for this latest assault and confine her at Beadle's tavern. Thus, paperwork in hand, the three men headed for Topsfield, racing to capture Esty before the midnight deadline. And so they did, Thomas told Ann, returning to John's house at midnight to find Mercy still alive yet still badly tortured, seizing again and again, resisting the specter that threatened her with a coffin and a corpse's winding sheet while it pushed the Devil's book at her to make her sign allegiance. This kept up all night, with the terrible convulsions continuing until the Salem magistrates, informed of the situation, shackled Esty in irons. This at last subdued the specter, and Mercy grew quiet and slept from exhaustion. When the groggy neighbors finally trailed home at dawn on Saturday, the girl still seemed close to death. She would, however, recover.

Here was more reason for Ann to fear for her own daughter—so far Annie remained healthy when she was not in a fit, and her fits did not last as long—and fear for herself as well as for the next baby.

Thomas took practical measures, going down to town with John Putnam Jr. and entering complaints against the latest batch of suspects: widow Susanna Roots, Elizabeth Procter's daughter Sarah, and Elizabeth's sister-in-law Sarah Bassett.

On Monday Hathorne and Corwin brought Mary Esty to Salem Village from Thomas Beadle's tavern, where she had been kept apart from the other prisoners. Once again she faced the afflicted witnesses, now including Mary Warren, in the meeting house. But this time they were not blinded to the Invisible World. Though Goody Esty was likely still in chains, the afflicted choked so badly that the magistrates could not proceed until well after prayer time. When at last they were able to speak they all accused Goody Esty of causing them "that mischef," and some of them blamed her for stabbing at them with an iron spindle. This time Mary Esty was held for trial for sure.

Annie must have told her mother all of this at day's end as well as about the other specters that tried to overcome them: those of Benjamin Procter, Sarah Pease, and Elizabeth Procter's sister Mary De-Rich. These suspects and the three arrested on Saturday were all questioned and held for trial.

Another woman, Mistress Elizabeth Cary, had been bold enough to travel with her husband Captain Nathaniel Cary all the way from Charlestown to persuade the magistrates of their error in believing Abigail William's report of her specter. The result was no different from the other attempts at confrontation, for Mrs. Cary was arrested straightaway and questioned. But she cowed neither Annie nor John Indian, who had accepted a mug of cider from Captain Cary earlier and shown him his scars. As the afflicted reported Cary's specter making John convulse on the floor, he pulled Mrs. Cary down after him when the magistrates ordered the touch test. In spite of Captain Cary's fury and his wife's tears, she was held for trial.

The following day Magistrates Hathorne and Corwin left for Boston for the legislature's first session under the new charter. Behind them trailed a slower cavalcade of the latest suspects being carted to Boston's jail: Mistress Elizabeth Cary, Abigail Soames and Susanna Roots, John Procter's son Benjamin, Sarah Bassett, Mary DeRich, and Mary Esty.

Mary Warren, left behind in Salem jail, fought off specters. When the convulsions passed and Mary seemed to be in a trance, she was heard conversing with the spirits.

"[W]ho ar the[e] what is your name[?]" asked Mary. "[W]hat totheker[?] Doktr toothekers wiffe[?] I wont i wonte i will not touch the book."

When she came out of her trance she explained that the specters of Goodwives Mary Ireson and Mary Toothaker had tried to make her sign the Devil's book, threatening her with a coffin and a winding sheet—threatening to kill her.

Although the legislature was still sitting in Boston, word of their deliberations trickled back to Salem. One of their first decisions was to appoint Thursday, May 26 as a fast day due to the troubles of the times. Salem Village appears to have hosted the Thursday lecture on this occasion, but afflicted fits interrupted the day throughout.

A flock of specters, including that of Mistress Mary Bradbury, attacked Annie Putnam, Mary Walcott, and Mercy Lewis. Mrs. Mary Marshall from nearby Reading also convulsed, targeted by a specter of her neighbor Goodwife Sarah Rice. (That Mrs. Bradbury would assail Annie would be no surprise to her mother, for Ann and several of her kin had suspected that woman for years.) The afflicted also reported the specters of Goodwives Wilmot Read of Marblehead and Elizabeth Fosdick of Malden. The latter, said Annie, boasted of hurting her uncle Mr. Peter Tufts's slave woman.

The magistrates returned from Boston to Salem by May 28 to a flurry of additional complaints from Villagers Joseph Houlton and John Walcott against even more suspected witches, including John and Elizabeth Procter's fifteen-year-old son, William. The magistrates themselves could report how the new government was reestablishing itself and how, while that slow process proceeded, there was at last an official, if temporary, court of Oyer and Terminer to handle the crowd of cases overwhelming Essex County and spilling into Middlesex and Suffolk as well.

Thomas Putnam, who had served as scribe to write down many statements and complaints—for others as well as for his own family— made out the paperwork for an official complaint against Mrs. Cary, who had been arrested earlier after her visit to the Village. From there she had been taken first to the Boston jail then, after much effort from her husband, transferred to the Cambridge jail in their own county of Middlesex. After her first night there the jailer fastened eight pounds of leg irons on her body to subdue her reported specter. This distressed her so that she fell into "Convulsion Fits." Her husband thought she would die of them, but pleading with authorities to remove them for the sake of her health did nothing to change the order.

Also on May 28 Thomas Putnam wrote a list of the thirteen recently accused suspects along with the corresponding victims of each. He wrote Mary Walcott's name beside each entry and Annie's name by three (though she may be included with "& the rest" afflicted by

Captain Flood). In addition to the suspects named in the complaint—Martha Carrier, Elizabeth Fosdick, Wilmot Read, Sarah Rice, Elizabeth How, John Alden, William Procter, John Flood, Mary and Margaret Toothaker, and Arthur Abbott—he wrote the names of Elizabeth Paine and Mary Warren, who were not in the official complaint. Their victims were listed as Mary Walcott, Abigail Williams, Mercy Lewis, and Ann Putnam (his daughter). Evidently the afflicted still did not fully trust Mary Warren's confession.

Mary continued to act afflicted, however, for Nathaniel Putnam and Joseph Whipple made out a second complaint against Goodwives Elizabeth Fosdick of Malden and Elizabeth Paine of Charlestown for tormenting Mercy Lewis and Mary Warren of Salem Village. They presented the paper to Hathorne and Corwin in Salem on May 30, but for some reason the magistrates did not order arrest warrants yet for either of these suspects. The magistrates did, however, record statements the same day relating to the spectral activities of Bridget Bishop, including one from miller William Stacy.

Philip English's specter was also reportedly active. Susanna Sheldon had stated on May 23 that his and other specters threatened to cut her throat or cut off her legs if she would not sign his book or if she told the magistrates that he had drowned John Rabson. When she resisted, Philip's specter rushed away to Boston, vowing to kill several folk there and to try to kill the governor, "the gretes ininemy he had," within six days "if he wos not tacken up [i.e., arrested]." But the real Philip English's luck ran out, for the law finally found him in Boston on May 30 during a second search of the home of merchant George Hollard, one of his colleagues, where he had hidden all along.

Although the paperwork ordered the prisoner be committed to the marshall of Essex, that office had just been replaced by a sheriff when the government began to be reorganized. George Herrick was now a deputy sheriff under Sheriff George Corwin, Jonathan Corwin's twenty-five-year-old nephew. It took a while for people to get used to the new terms and remember which to write on the official papers.

Sheriff Corwin's duties with the newly established Court of Oyer and Terminer began with an order dated in Boston on May 30 and signed by Deputy Governor William Stoughton and Samuel Sewall.

It ordered him "in their Majesties' Names" to publicize the sitting of that court:

> [U]pon Thursday next the Second of June next at Eight in the morning, for the tryal of all Crimes and Offences done and perpetrated within the sd County, Requiring all persons concerned as prosecutors or Evidences to give their attendance; And to Return Eighteen honest and lawfull men of yor Bailywick to Serve upon the Grand Enquest, and fforty Eight alike honest and lawfull men to Serve upon the Jury of Tryals at the said Court.

The witch trials had begun.

But first the local magistrates had to examine the latest batch of suspects in the Salem Village meeting house on Tuesday, the last day of May.

John Hathorne and Jonathan Corwin brought Mary Warren to the Village along with the rest of their entourage to join Annie Putnam and the other afflicted witnesses: Mary Walcott, Mercy Lewis, Abigail Williams, Elizabeth Hubbard, Elizabeth Booth, Sarah Bibber, and John Indian.

Although his name does not appear on the official documents of this day, a new magistrate, Bartholomew Gedney (father-in-law of George Corwin, the new county sheriff), was evidently present in addition to Hathorne and Corwin. Reverend Parris prepared to take notes as usual, and Stephen Sewall served as the new court clerk. Thomas Newton, the new king's attorney, attended as an observer, for this was still a preliminary hearing. Once the trials began he would represent the government's side of the cases as he had against old Goody Glover in Boston when Sir Edmund Andros was governor—the same Goody Glover who was found guilty of witchcraft and hanged. But for now he watched, as astonished by the goings-on as the other out-of-town gentlemen who came to observe. Reverend Nicholas Noyes of Salem was present and probably offered the opening prayer. Mrs. Ann Putnam was among the onlookers.

Captain John Alden, "Mariner," lived in Boston when in port. Evidently his accusation caused some stir among the authorities, for he frequently served in the defense of Massachusetts, largely as a privateer. His recent expedition to ransom captives, including his own son, from the Baron de Sainte Castine in the Eastward territory had failed, however, and public opinion already thought him more interested in private trade than public defense. In fact, Marbleheaders had nearly rioted a few years earlier when he tried to remove that town's cannon—as ordered—for colony use elsewhere.

The authorities had ignored other suspicions against the better sort before, apparently dismissing them as mistaken before anyone entered a formal complaint.

According to Alden's own account of the matter, after "a company of poor distracted or possessed Creatures or Witches" accused him, the Salem magistrates "sent for" him on May 28, and he was "sent by Mr. Stoughton" to Salem, where he arrived May 31. Perhaps he traveled north from Boston with the group bringing Philip English, but as he still wore his sword, evidently he was not yet under arrest.

Once in the Village meeting house, he regarded the afflicted with contempt. "Wenches . . . ," he later wrote about the girls—Mary Warren and Annie Putnam among them—"who plaid their juggling tricks, falling down, crying out, and staring in Peoples Faces." One of the girls pointed wordlessly at another military man, Captain Hill, when the magistrate asked her who hurt her. The officer standing behind the girl had to tell her which man was Alden. She had never seen the man in the flesh, she explained, but her hesitation made the magistrates order defendant and witnesses out of the dim building into the light of day for a better view. This had happened before with Nathaniel Abbott, who had been released, so Alden may have felt encouraged.

The afflicted circled Alden in the road outside the meeting house, and the same girl—again, not named—pointed at him. "[T]here stands Aldin, a bold fellow with his Hat on before the Judges, he sells Powder and Shot to the Indians and French, and lies with the Indian Squaes, and has Indian Papooses."

At this point Alden was taken into custody, his sword confiscated because the afflicted said his specter menaced them with it. Thomas

Newton then wrote out the arrest warrant for Alden, which Hathorne and Corwin signed. Both Annie Putnam and Mary Warren were listed among his supposed victims.

The magistrates set Alden's case aside for a time while they questioned Elizabeth How of Topsfield. Although her neighbors suspected her of bewitching one of their children to death, the afflicted girls made the greatest impression against her. Annie Putnam and Mary Warren were stuck with pins. They fell at her glance, beginning with Mary Warren, and recovered, though with some difficulty, at her touch. They appeared repelled when they tried to get near the woman and claimed that her specter stepped from her body to belabor them. John Indian and others said her specter bit them.

"I am not able to give account of it," Goody How protested. "I cannot tell, I know not what it is."

But one of her neighbors had seen her specter in the company of Bridget Bishop's specter: "goode ollever of Sallam that hurt william stace of Sallam the millar."

Martha Carrier from Andover was more defiant. She had endured neighborhood suspicions for years, especially after a smallpox outbreak that killed several of her relatives. When Susanna Sheldon said, "[S]he looks upon the black man"—meaning the Devil—Annie Putnam agreed, and Mary Warren cried that something pricked her.

"What black man did you see?" one of the magistrates asked.

Goody Carrier shot back: "I saw no black man but your own presence." (Black hair ran in both the Hathorne and Corwin families.)

Asked if she could look at the accusers and *not* knock them down, she said, "They will dissemble if I look upon them." The screaming and flailing continued to escalate, with pins again pricking Mary Warren. Goody Carrier held to her innocence and insisted she did *not* see the reported ghosts of her supposed murder victims flocking throughout the room. "It is a shamefull thing," she lectured the magistrates, "that you should mind these folks that are out of their wits."

The afflicted fell in such severe seizures that the court not only held her for trial but also carried her out bound hand and foot. At this the afflicted relaxed, able to resume their duties.

Most of the afflicted went into a frenzy at the sight of Wilmot Read, a long-suspected Marblehead woman, and had to be carried to her for touch-test relief, even John Indian.

During the examination, according to Parris's notes, Annie said that although she had often seen the woman's specter hurting the others, it had never hurt her before. Parris's notes did not mention Mary Warren at all, who would later state that, although she believed the woman was a witch, Goody Read had *never* hurt her.

"I cannot tell," said Goody Read when the magistrates asked what she thought ailed the afflicted if *she* were not the cause. "I cannot tell." The most she could say to their relentless questions was, "my opinion is they are in a sad condition."

Captain Alden was more forthright when he was marched back into the meeting house and made to stand on a chair so the witnesses could have a better look at him. Why, he demanded, did they think he would come all the way to Salem Village to hurt people he did not even know? Herrick, meanwhile, held Alden's hand still to prevent any further pinching of the afflicted with magical gestures. When Magistrate Bartholomew Gedney, an old friend and fellow merchant, urged him to confess, Alden replied that confession to these false accusations would only gratify the Devil. He dared anyone to bring any *real* proof against him. Gedney said that, as Alden later remembered, "he had known Aldin many Years, and had been at Sea with him, and always look'd upon him to be an honest Man, but now he did see cause to alter his judgment."

The court told Alden to look at his accusers, at which the afflicted fell at his glance. Alden turned to look meaningfully at Gedney and asked why *he* did not fall over, but Gedney did not answer. Instead the magistrates ordered the afflicted to be carried to Alden for his touch. In exasperation, Alden wondered why Providence allowed "these Creatures to accuse Innocent persons."

Reverend Noyes interrupted him, to lecture, with no little sarcasm, on Alden's reference to the Almighty, who governed the world in peace and order, in contrast to the uproar and disorder surrounding Alden. When he could get a word in, Alden snapped to Gedney that there was "a lying Spiritt" in the girls. "I can assure you that there is not a word of truth in all these say of me."

Deputy Marshall Jacob Manning brought Philip English, who had been passed from the custody of one county to another, before the magistrates. Unfortunately notes for his questioning are lost. Known for his temper, Philip was presumably no more cooperative than was fellow mariner-merchant Alden. Like Alden, he probably called his accusers liars. But like Willard, he had fled and been captured, and the magistrates saw his avoidance of the law as an admission of guilt.

This day other prisoners also facing the court and the noisy afflicted witnesses included Mary Toothaker, wife of jailed folk healer Roger Toothaker, and their nine-year-old daughter, Margaret; Captain John Flood, a militia leader even less successful than Alden; and William Procter, the seventeen-year-old son of John and Elizabeth Procter. Constable John Putnam had brought in the Procter boy.

According to Thomas Putnam's list of those afflicted as of May 28, William Procter's specter had tormented Mary Walcott and Susanna Sheldon "& others of Salem Village." Precisely what Mary Warren, herself still suspected by the other girls, did and said during William's questioning is, unfortunately, lost, as is how William felt toward her and who among his brothers might have dared be in the audience. Although their household had not been without conflict before, they must have been united in resenting her for helping to rupture the family so thoroughly.

The surviving paperwork indicates that William's specter tormented Mary Warren and Elizabeth Hubbard, who most distrusted Mary, presumably during questioning. William refused to confess, and the court then took the unusual move of tying him neck and heels, a military punishment that drew the prisoner's head down toward his bound feet. As John Procter would write,

My Son *William Procter*, when he was examin'd, because he would not confess that he was Guilty, when he was Innocent, they tyed him Neck and Heels till the Blood gushed out at his Nose, and would have kept him so 24 Hours, if one more Merciful then the rest, had not taken pity on him, and caused him to be unbound.

All of those questioned were held for trial, including an Arthur Abbott, who lived "in a by place" near Major Appleton's farm on the border area of Ipswich, Topsfield, and Wenham. Though "Complained of by Many," his sparse case notes suggest that he, like Mary Esty, would be set free in the near future. Unlike her but like Nehemiah Abbot (no relation), he would apparently remain free.

Before the magistrates left the Village Mrs. Ann Putnam submitted a deposition that Thomas had written out for her. In it she related how Rebecca Nurse's specter began to torture her from March 18 onward. Martha Corey's specter was just as bad, nearly tearing Ann to pieces, attacking with "dreadfull tortors and hellish temtations," urging her to sign her soul away "in a litle Red book" with "a black pen." But the tortures Nurse inflicted "no toungu can Express." On March 22, when Nurse had appeared in her shift, "she threatened to tare my soule out of my body blasphemously denying the blessed God and the power of the Lord Jesus Christ to save my soule." Ann was also tormented on March 24, especially during Rebecca's examination, so "dreadfully tortored . . . that The Honoured Majestraits gave my Husband leave to cary me out of the meeting house," allowing her to recover. And that had ended the specters' power to hurt her.

Just having to talk about it again was distressing. As a court official read her words back to her prior to her swearing to them, she became overcome and convulsed—right in front of the magistrates, in front of her daughter. It was Nurse's vengeful specter attacking her—Nurse, her great enemy. Yes, said Annie. It *was* Goody Nurse, and Goody Cloyce and Corey too—all attacking her mother.

Samuel Parris, having taken most of the day's examination notes, added to Ann's deposition. She had not been troubled since Goody Nurse's hearing "untill this 31 May 1692 at the same moment that I was hearing my Evidence read by the honoured Magistrates to take my Oath I was again re-assaulted & tortured by my before mentioned Tormentor Rebekah Nurse."

Francis Nurse, however, was busy gathering signatures on a petition verifying Rebecca's good character. In part it stated, "Acording to our observation her Life and conversation was Acording to hur profesion [of Christianity] and we never had Any cause or grounds to suspect her of Any such thing as she is nowe Acused of."

Thirty-nine neighbors signed, with Israel and Elizabeth Porter (Hathorne's sister), who had visited in March, among the first. Eight Putnams signed, including John and Rebecca Putnam, whose baby had died mysteriously. Daniel Andrews, another of the March visitors, had also signed, but he had already fled some weeks before after being accused himself, so how useful the document would be was in question.

The other prisoners from Salem in Boston's jail would resent Tituba for her confession—Tituba, the catalyst, whose lies had helped get the rest of them in so much trouble. Did any of them empathize with her impossibly difficult situation? Or did they keep their distance, marking out territory in the big common room? Some were chained down and had no choice. Perhaps Tituba associated with the other nonwhite woman in that place, with Grace, a slave under a death sentence for infanticide. In the long, endlessly boring days and sleepless nights Tituba and Grace might have shared stories of their past lives. If so, Tituba would have learned how Grace, working in Boston as the property of the province's treasurer, had born a child—alone, in winter—dragging herself to the backyard privy for privacy. Then, once rid of the burden, she jammed the infant headfirst down the privy hole. That was where someone had found the tiny body. Grace was arrested for murder, tried and convicted. Yet with no charter and the government in limbo, she could not be executed. The local government would not presume so far until they knew what England expected of them. So Grace languished in the Boston prison for years, she and Elizabeth Emerson, a young unmarried white woman from Ipswich who had born twins who were later found dead, sewn in a sack and buried in her parents' garden. Elizabeth told the authorities that they were born dead, but something about the bodies suggested otherwise. She too was found guilty of murder and awaited execution. Now that the government was being re-formed—enough for the courts to try the witchcraft cases—death sentences could be brought against Elizabeth and Grace as well.

The court records do not indicate whether Grace had conceived the child from a consensual act or from rape, nor did it say if she killed the infant as an unwelcome reminder of the rapist who had sired it or killed the child to free it from a life of slavery and humiliation. Perhaps Tituba learned.

More and more suspected witches have been sent from Salem to Boston's jail. Tituba is surprised that so many respectable women are among them—or at least women whom neighbors had once regarded as respectable. Even church members and those women of wealth and prestige were here alongside poverty-stricken Sarah Good. Mistress English has servants who bring changes of clean linen. Others, like Goodwives Nurse, Esty, and How have devoted families who make the long journey to visit. It takes the horses more than half a day to cover the distance from Salem to Boston. Others must hope for the sparse help of strangers.

A few brave folk venture to visit, usually armed with spiritual comforts instead of the practical necessities so desperately needed. Others send a servant to do so, a more convenient way to store up credit in Heaven.

At the least it breaks the monotony to watch them. Tituba notices Sarah Good begging a bit of tobacco from a nervous hired girl who is trying not to look any of the suspects in the eye. Clearly she does not want to be there.

Sarah, already more on edge than usual since the death of her infant, raises her voice to repeat the request, but doing so makes it sound like an order.

The girl panics, snatching a handful of the dirty wood shavings from the floor. "That's Tobacco good enough for you!" she shouts, throwing the filthy remnants into Good's face.

Sarah erupts in an enraged spate of ill words that terrifies the maid even more, sending her running to the guard to be let out.

The suspected witches are a fearful class of prisoner to most of the population, though this prisoner class clearly makes its own distinctions—Tituba and Good apart from Nurse and Esty, all apart from Cary and English. Later, word trickles back that that girl has become as wracked by fits as any in Salem.

Tituba is not surprised. When the mischievous and malicious run free, aren't we all, both high and low, enslaved by other's whims?

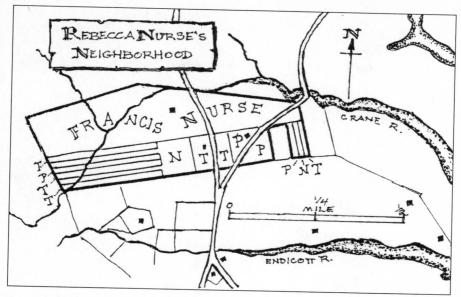

Francis and Rebecca Nurse's Neighborhood. Francis Nurse divided about half of his farm in 1690 and parceled the various lots to his son Samuel Nurse and sons-in-law John Tarbell and Thomas Preston. (Map by the author. *Source:* Perley, "Endicott Lands, Salem in 1700.")

N Samuel Nurse
T John Tarbell
P Thomas Preston

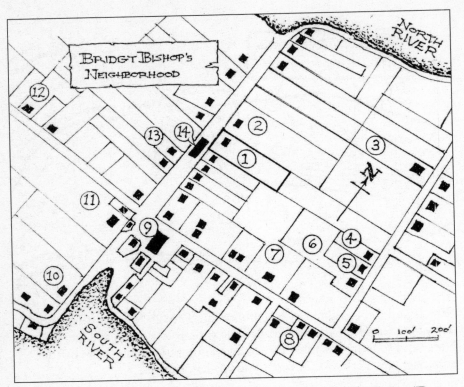

Bridget Bishop's Neighborhood. (Map by the author. *Source:* Perley, "Part of Salem in 1700," Nos. 1, 2, 3, 14, 15, 28.)

1. Edward and Bridget Bishop, the Thomas Oliver estate.
2. Daniel Epps, schoolmaster.
3. Jail.
4. Samuel Beadle, tavern.
5. Robert Gray, said he was tormented by Bridget's specter.
6. John Burton, surgeon, examined Bridget and other suspects for witch marks.
7. Ship Tavern.
8. Samuel Shattuck, said Bridget bewitched his son.
9. Salem Meeting House.
10. Sheriff George Corwin.
11. John Hathorne, magistrate and judge of the Court of Oyer and Terminer.
12. Stephen Sewall, clerk of the Court of Oyer and Terminer.
13. Reverend Nicholas Noyes.
14. Town House, scene of Oyer and Terminer trials.

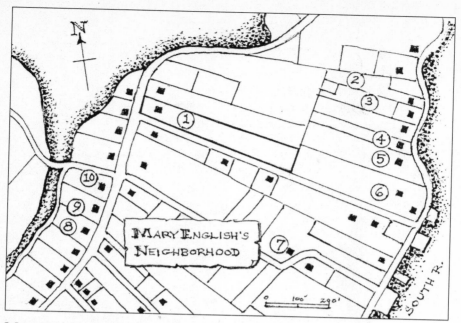

Mary English's Neighborhood. (Map by the author. *Source:* Perley, "Part of Salem," Nos. 21, 23, 22, 23.)

1. "English's Great House," Philip and Mary English.
2. Walter Whitford, fisherman, died 1692.
3. John and Bridget Whitford. John also died 1692. Whitford is presumably the same as Whatford. A distracted Goodwife Whatford said the specters of Bridget Bishop and Alice Parker tormented her.
4. William and Elizabeth Dicer here 1668 to 1685 when William sold the lot to Philip English and moved to Maine. Elizabeth called Eleanor Hollingworth a witch in 1679 (and would herself be accused in 1692).
5. Fisherman John Parker and wife Alice rented this house. Originally owned by William Hollingworth, it passed to his daughter Mary English, and then to Philip English.
6. Blue Anchor Tavern, operated by Eleanor Hollingworth in her home, deeded to her daughter Mary English in 1685, descended to Mary's son John English Jr.
7. In 1735, John Beckett inherited half of the family home and purchased the remainder for himself and his wife Susanna (Mason) Beckett.
8. Rental property owned in 1662 by Eleanor Hollingworth, then by her son William who sold it. A few owners later, Philip English bought it in 1675 and later willed it to his daughter Mary (English) Browne.
9. Rental property purchased in 1674 by Philip English (when the tenants were William and Sarah Buckley and their family, who later moved to Salem Village where Sarah and a daughter were accused of witchcraft in 1692). Philip later willed this property to his daughter Susanna (English) Touzel.
10. Bridget Bishop's widowed husband Edward Bishop, the sawyer, bought this house 1694. John and Susanna Beckett eventually owned it.

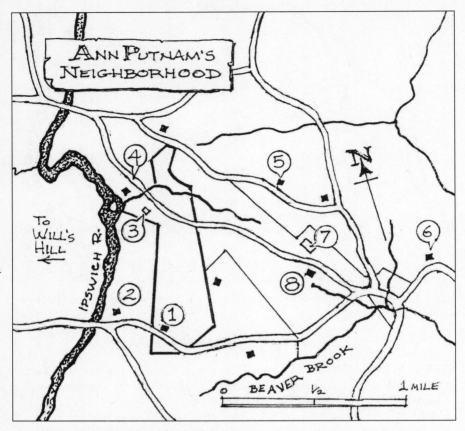

Ann Putnam's Neighborhood. (Map by the author. *Source:* Perley, "Hathorne: Part of Salem Village in 1700. No. 1," and [2]; "The Plains No. 2.")

1. Thomas and Ann Putnam.
2. Constable John Putnam.
3. Location of Thomas and Ann Putnam's 1697 house.
4. Edward Putnam.
5. Eleazer Putnam.
6. Alexander and Sarah Osborn, (she was one of the first three people to be accused).
7. Putnam Burying Ground.
8. Joseph Putnam.

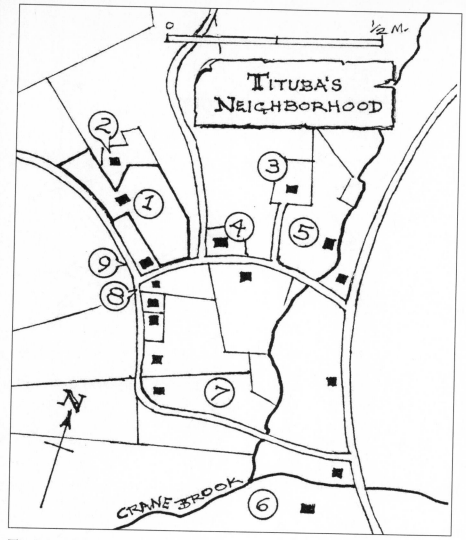

Tituba's Neighborhood. (Map by the author. *Source:* Perley, "Center of Salem Village in 1700"; Trask, *"The Devil Amongst Us."*)

1. Salem Village parsonage, (the Ministry land owned either by the Village or by Reverend Samuel Parris); Tituba lived here.
2. Jonathan Walcott, his afflicted daughter Mary Walcott.
3. Samuel and Mary Sibley (who recommended the "witch-cake" countercharm).
4. Salem Village Meeting House.
5. Reverend James and Mary (Carr) Bailey, (house was rented out after they moved away).
6. Francis and Rebecca Nurse.
7. Widow Sarah Holton.
8. Watch House.
9. Nathaniel Ingersoll's ordinary.

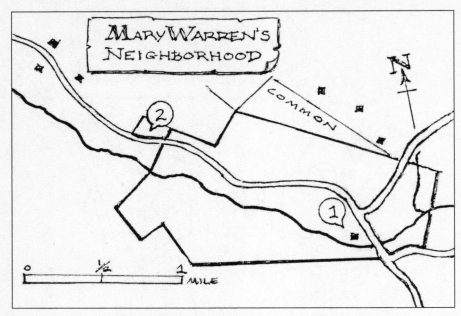

Mary Warren's Neighborhood. (Map by the author. *Source:* Perley, "Groton, Salem in 1700"; Brown, *A Guide to the Salem Witchcraft Hysteria of 1692.* [corrects house location though the present building is probably post-1692], 28, 103-104; Upham, *House of John Procter.*)

1. John Procter's rented farm, "Groton;" Mary Warren lived here.
2. Lot owned by John Procter.

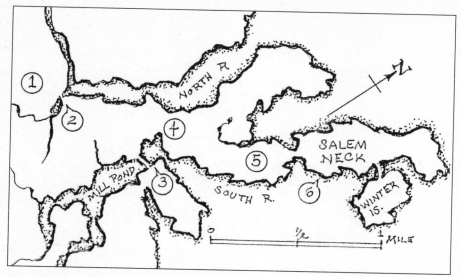

Salem Town. (Map by the author.)

1. Gallows Hill.
2. Town Bridge.
3. Stacey's mill.
4. Bridget Bishop.
5. Mary English.
6. Point of Rocks.

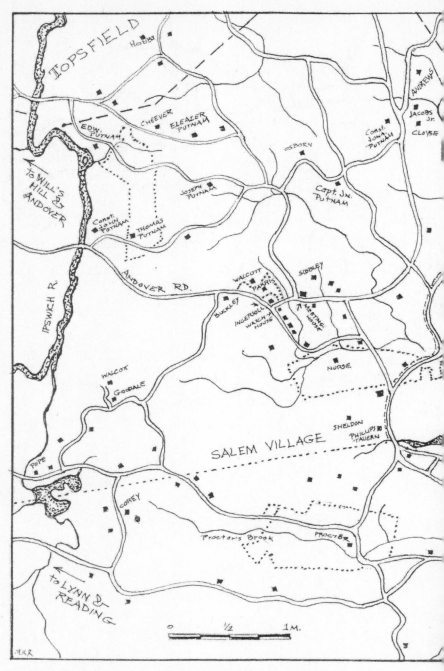

Salem and Vicinity. (Based on Marilynne K. Roach, "A Map of
Salem and Vicinity in 1692." Sassafras Grove Press: Watertown, MA,
1985, 1990.)

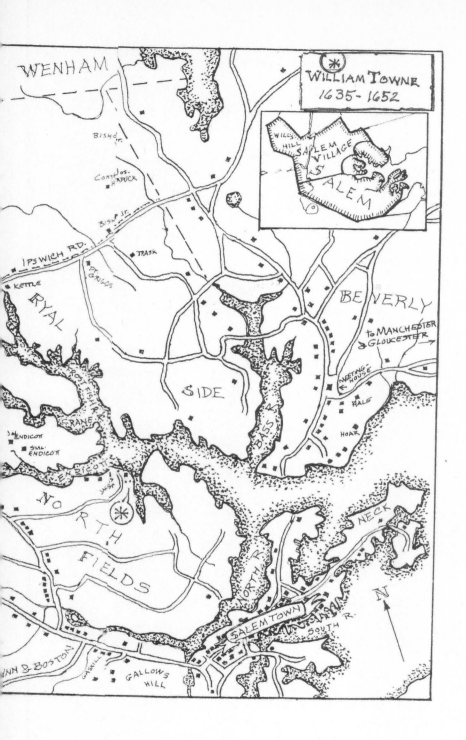

WENHAM

WILLIAM TOWNE
1635-1652

WILLS
HILL
SALEM
VILLAGE
S
SALEM

BISHO Jr.

Con JOS. HARRICK

BISHP Jr.

IPSWICH RD.

TRASK

DT. GRIGGS

KETTLE

RYAL

SIDE

BEVERLY

to MANCHESTER
& GLOUCESTER

MEETING-
HOUSE

HALE

HOAR

ROYAL FISH R.

CRANE

J L ENDICOTT

SML ENDICOTT

ENDICOTT

BASS R.

NORTH

FIELDS

NO
RTH

NECK

NORTH R.

SOUTH R.

N

SALEM TOWN

YNN & BOSTON

CASWLL

GALLOWS
HILL

Three items excavated by Richard Trask from the 1681 Salem Village Parsonage Archaeological Site: part of a blue and gray Rhenish stoneware jug; a green glass wine bottle neck; and a metal plate rim monogrammed SPE (Samuel and Elizabeth Parris). (Photo by Richard B. Trask.)

Salem Village Parsonage Site. The view of the L-shaped house is from the cellar hole marking the lean-to, with the main room (the hall) to the left, and the cellar hole beyond that was under the parlor. Tituba testified how, when she stood in the hall, she could hear the cries of the girls in the parlor. (Photo by the author.)

Rebecca Nurse Homestead, Danvers, Massachusetts. (Photo by Tina Jordan.)

Salem Village Meeting House replica, based on dimensions in the Salem Village records, built on the Nurse Homestead property for the film *Three Sovereigns for Sarah*. (Photo by Tina Jordan.)

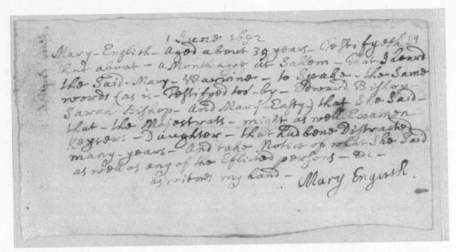

Mary English's statement concerning the unreliability of Mary Warren's testimony, dated June 1, 1692. Mary may have signed this herself, though not all scholars agree. (Essex County Court Archives, Vol. 1:19, deposited with the Peabody Essex Museum. Used courtesy of the Massachusetts Supreme Judicial Court Archives. Image courtesy of University of Virginia's *Salem Witch Trials Documentary Archives*, http://salem.lib. virginia.edu/archives/ecca.html)

Gravestone for Mary English's brother William Hollingworth and their mother Eleanor Hollingworth, Charter Street Burial Ground, Salem, Massachusetts. (Photo by the author.)

Mary Hollingworth's sampler, c. 1665. (Courtesy of the Peabody Essex Museum, Salem, MA.)

John Procter's brass sundial, dated 1644. (Courtesy of the Peabody Essex Museum, Salem, MA.)

Bridget Bishop's name carved into the Witch Trials Memorial, Salem, Massachusetts. (Photo by the author.)

Cloth poppet reportedly found walled into the brickwork of a
first period house in Gloucester, Massachusetts, on loan to the
Witch House/Corwin House, City of Salem. This was
probably meant to be a protective charm, unlike the pin-
studded poppets supposedly found in Bridget Bishop's cellar.
(Photo by the author. Used courtesy of the City of Salem.)

Putnam tomb, Putnam Burying Ground, Danvers, Massachusetts. The unmarked mound in the foreground is the site of the tomb. (Photo by the author.)

Dedication of the Rebecca Nurse Monument on July 30, 1885. (Photo courtesy of Danvers Historical Society.)

(9)
June 1 to 9, 1692

Mistress Mary English, surveying the Boston jail's common room, notices that something is afoot in the bustle of the guards and the tension of the prisoners. Court would sit soon—at last, after years of suspension— though no one quite knows whether or not that is good.

The new justices are men of influence responsible for the public's safety. Yet considering the evidence brought against the accused— against herself—at the hearings, could those men truly discern what had and had not happened? Some of the Salem magistrates are part of the new court, and their acceptance, so far, of what the witnesses say is far from encouraging. The court must be informed of the true situation. The Nurse kindred thinks so too, having collected an impressive number of names on Rebecca's behalf. The justices are reasonable men, aren't they? Usually reasonable, anyhow, even if Hathorne and Corwin get carried away by the noise and fits.

Soon the heavy door rattles open, and the jailer, John Arnold, enters with a document. Certain prisoners, he announces, will be transferred to Salem to stand trial, moved out today—now. The prisoners have been expecting this, yet the moment still sends a shock of fear through the room, with their desire for something to break the monotony warring with trepidation.

Bridget Bishop, the officer calls, Susannah Martin, Rebecca Nurse, Sarah Good, Alice Parker, Tituba, John Willard, John and Elizabeth Procter.

Not yet, *Mary English thinks.* Not this time. *She watches the leave-takings wondering when—and under what circumstances—she will see Philip again. The guards have told her of his arrest.*

Rebecca bids farewell to her sisters Mary Esty and Sarah Cloyce.

The Procters part from son Benjamin, Elizabeth from her sister Mary
DeRich and sister-in-law Sarah Bassett. John murmurs some sort of fa-
therly advice to Benjamin, the words lost in the room's commotion.

No one mentions it, but all know they might never see each other
again in this life.

The jailer's men move among them, unlocking the chains from the
wall, levering the elderly and unsteady from the floor, where they have
sat for so long.

The guards part Sarah Good from her daughter, the mother protesting,
struggling, and the child wailing at this additional loss, frantic to join
her mother but left behind all the same.

The door thuds shut at last, and the bolts clank into place. Dear God,
thinks Mary. What next?

Led, shuffling and clanking into the daylight, into a fresher
breeze of salt air from the harbor after the closed-in fetor of
the common room, hearing the sharp cries of gulls, most of
the prisoners would be hoisted into a cart, John Procter likely insisting
on helping Elizabeth. Tituba, as a repentant witch, was being treated
as a potential witness. Newton had sent orders for her to be kept apart
from the others, so perhaps she rode on a pillion behind one of the
mounted officers. The procession left the stone jail, and as they
headed to the ferry at the north end of Boston's peninsula, they could
probably hear Dorothy Good's muffled wail, the child's cries fading as
the party threaded the narrow streets to the ferry wharf.

Once across the mouths of the Charles and Mystic Rivers, they began the journey through and around the great stretch of marsh that
hummed this time of year with mosquitoes, unless the wind favored
them. Partway though the trip the party encountered another cavalcade heading south, men on horseback with another wagonload of
people—the latest batch of prisoners assigned to Boston. The groups
would pause while the guards conversed, exchanging news and gossip
of the latest suspects, the goings-on in court. From the wagons the
prisoners could eye each other, the Procters recognizing their son
William in the other cart headed for the Boston jail, as he saw his
parents heading for trial and, after that, who knew what.

Philip English was in the cart as well and would reach Boston prison after the long, tiring trip, entering the stone jail where his wife awaited him.

But Mary English did not wait idly. On June 1 she and Mary Esty, with Edward and Sarah Bishop, submitted statements regarding Mary Warren's testimony, determined to tell the court just what sort of "evidence" was being given against them. All four had been present in the Salem jail when Mary Warren explained that her visions had been only distraction—distraction or the Devil's delusions, the four knew. Not accurate in any case. *Certainly* not accurate.

Prisoners could acquire ink, pens, and writing paper from visiting relatives (or servants), or obtain such supplies from the jailer for a fee. The Bishops and Goody Esty appear to have dictated their joint statement about the Warren girl to someone else:

> Aboute three weekes Agoe . . . In Salem Goale . . . wee Heard Mary warrin severall Times say that the Majestrates Might as well Examine Keysars Daughter that had Bin Distracted Many Yeares And take Noatice of what shee said as well as any of the Afflicted persons . . . [Warren said] when I was Aflicted I thought I saw the Apparission of A hundred persons for shee said hir Head was Distempered that shee Could Not tell what shee said . . . [and] when shee was well Againe shee Could Not say that shee saw any of the Apparissions at the Time Aforesaid.

Mistress English was none too sure about these Bishops, what with that raucous, illegal tavern of theirs, not since her desperate cousin—one of the Bishop's long-suffering neighbors—cut her own throat after trying to reason with them. However, she and they agreed about Warren. In any case she was quite capable of writing her own statement. Looping the letters across the paper and signing it at the end, she wrote,

1 June 1692

Mary English Aged about 39 years Testifyeth that about a Month agoe at Sallem That I heard the Said Mary Warrine to Spake the Same

words (as is Testifyed too by Edward Bishop Sarah Bishop And Mary
Easty) that She Said that the Majestrats might as well Examen Keysers
Daughter that had bene Distracted many years And take Notice of
what She Said as well as any of the Eflicted persons &c

    as witnes my hand Mary English

There. The court *had* to listen to that.

One way or another the two papers found their way into the official
files, but just how is a puzzle considering the four were suspected of
adhering to the Prince of Lies.

Prior to this, perhaps Mistress English had been able to secure a
private sleeping room for herself, one of the spaces along the common
dungeon's outside wall, and this would offer not only a measure of privacy but also a small window. This would cost more than the usual
room and board fee charged to the prisoners, but Mary had a good
head for business and a reputation for speaking up. She could well
have been in contact with her staff in Salem. Someone had to be
watching the children, and as later generations had it, her servants
were loyal. Once Philip was with her in Boston as well they could see
about better accommodations. The law, as Mary English would learn,
had searched the home of merchant George Hollard, one of Philip's
Boston colleagues, but they found nothing the first time. What gossip
did not yet know was that Philip had hidden under a pile of dirty
laundry in Hollard's house, a place the constables did *not* examine. But
Philip would join Mary in the Boston jail before the day was out.

That prisoners would be brought to Salem on the first of June was
common knowledge to anyone following events. In Salem Village that
same day Ann Putnam felt attacked once again by the specter of her
enemy, Rebecca Nurse. While the real Goody Nurse circled the
marshes with the other prisoners, the tormenting spirit lit into Ann,
snarling its intention to murder her at last for her defiance and bragging of the local people it had killed. More frightening still were the
ghosts of murdered children that appeared, clamoring for vengeance.

Thomas Putnam wrote an account of his wife's vision to give to
the authorities. The Nurse specter had choked Ann, it said, also
declaring,

that now she was come out of prison she had power to afflet me and that now she would afflect me all this day long and would kil me if she could and she also tould me that she and hir sister Cloyes and Ed Bishops wife [i.e., Sarah, not Bridget] of Salem village had kiled young Jno putnams child because yong Jno putnam had said that it was no wonder they ware wicthes for their mother was so before them and because they could not aveng themselues on him they did kill his child. and Immediatly their did appere to me six childeren in winding sheets which caled me aunt: which did most greviously affright me. and they tould me that they ware my sisters Bakers children of Boston and that gooddy nurs and Mistris Cary of Chalstown and an old deaf woman att Boston had murthered them and charged me to goe and tell thes things to the majestrats or elce they would tare me to peaces for their blood did crie for vengeance.

The ghosts of Ann's sister Mary Bayley and three of her children, all in grave clothes, all accusing Goody Nurse of their murders, soon joined those violent ghosts.

John Hathorne and Jonathan Corwin, preparing for the trials, interviewed some of the confessors—Deliverance Hobbs and her stepdaughter Abigail as well as Mary Warren—while Thomas Newton took notes. After Abigail described the specter of Reverend Burroughs as he threatened to make her join the great witch meetings in Reverend Parris's field, Mary Warren told how Burroughs announced that Devilish witch-sacrament with a trumpet blast and tried to make her join them. This had happened "in prison in Salem about a fortnight agone." Goodwives Nurse Procter, Parker, Pudeator, and Dustin as well as Abigail Soames were in his troupe along with Goodman Procter "& others unknowne." While she deposed, specters of Rebecca Nurse and Philip English invaded the room, with Nurse choking the three women and English running a pin into Mary's hand.

At some point this day Constable John Putnam informed the witnesses against Rebecca Nurse to report to the court by eight o'clock the following day, Thursday, June 2: Abigail Williams, Elizabeth Hubbard, Mary Walcott, Susanna Shelden, Mercy Lewis, Ann Putnam Jr., and Ann Putnam Sr. Constable Putnam also warned Abigail

Williams, Mary Walcott, Susanna Shelden, Mercy Lewis, Ann Putnam Jr., and Nathaniel Putnam to appear in court as witnesses against John Willard at nine o'clock the same morning—but not Elizabeth Hubbard or Mrs. Ann Putnam, for all that she thought he had killed her infant daughter.

Ghosts continued to accost Ann Putnam, as fierce as the witch specters. Two dead neighbors from Will's Hill, Lydia Wilkins and Samuel Fuller, materialized at her bedside the morning of June 2. John Willard had killed them, they told her with savage desperation, aided by Martha Corey and William Hobbs. If she would not tell Mr. Hathorne about this, they would tear her to pieces and appear in the courtroom themselves, they told her. Their murders *must* be made known. "I knew [them] when they were living & it was Exactly thier resemblance & Shape," Ann told Thomas, who recorded this incident as well. The specter of John Willard appeared also to brag of those and other murders, for he had killed seven children in the Village, including "this deponents Child. Sarah 6 weeks old."

One after another the inhabitants of the Invisible World invaded the visible world, terrifying and vengeful. But she had to be brave—as brave as her daughter. She *had* to go on.

Some hours into the morning of June 2, their first full day back in Salem, five of the women were examined for witch-marks (presumably apart from the male prisoners). Nine local matrons and a male surgeon looked them over, hunting for what might be the Devil's marking of his own, something normally hidden under clothing: Bridget Bishop, Sarah Good, Susannah Martin (none of whom would have submitted meekly to this), Alice Parker, Rebecca Nurse, and Elizabeth Procter.

The jury of women gingerly or more roughly fingered the subjects to determine by sight and touch what imperfection—a mole, a scar, a wart—might be natural or might be an old wound where a devil branded a convert to mark possession, just as farmers notched their cattle's ears in patterns of ownership, or might be a sore spot where an imp familiar had suckled bloody nourishment, drawing life and strength from the witch-host in Hellish parody of mother's milk. Such matters were obscure, and the interpretations of such marks subject to debate.

They observed that Susannah Martin's breasts were "very full; the Nibbs [nipples] fresh & starting," odd for an older woman—though not so odd for an uncovered woman if the room were cold. The midwives would have discovered the more ordinary fact that Goody Procter was with child. They especially noticed that she, along with Nurse and Bishop, had, as the surgeon John Barton wrote, "a preternaturall Excresence of flesh between the pudendum and Anus much like to tetts [teats] & not usuall in women, & much unlike to the other three that hath been searched by us." Later Court Clerk Stephen Sewall, added that these excrescences "were in all the three women neer the same place."

Her excrescence, Rebecca Nurse explained, was due to difficult childbirth episodes. The eldest matron, a well-known midwife agreed that the imperfections looked natural, but none of the other women on the jury agreed. The prisoners pulled their clothes back together, and the surgeon went off to examine John Procter and Giles Corey with a jury of men, where they found nothing unusual.

Bridget Bishop, meanwhile, was taken from the prison to face the Grand Jury. Where her husband, daughter, or son-in-law were is open to question. Had anyone visited her in jail? Had anyone brought her a change of clean clothes? Was there anyone who did not believe her to be guilty?

Flanked by guards with staffs of office, preceded by the sheriff, they left the jail and passed through the gate to the lane. Onlookers would not have skipped this opportunity to gawk. The route to the court must have been lined with people, both locals and out-of-towners. From the lane they turned into the main street, making their way past the staring crowd, past the Ship Tavern—she had had trouble with those neighbors before—toward the town square by the pump and the meeting house. It was supposed to be under repair, but the workmen were absent, probably neglecting their job for the prospect of her trial's entertainment. Bridget glanced toward that large building as they approached, just as something inside it made a great bang. The procession paused while men were sent into the meeting house to see what had happened. A board studded with nails, they reported back, had fallen from its place—*just* when the prisoner had looked in that direction—and the board was not particularly near where it had been originally, as if it had been thrown by some invisible presence rather than just come loose and dropped. This left the guards and crowd wondering if some entity had come to rescue one of its own.

But no rescue came, and Bridget was urged around the corner and up the rise to the town house. Two stories high plus a garret, the brick building stood in the middle of the street with Bridget's home to the right and Reverend Nicholas Noyes's to the left. Salem stored fire-fighting equipment in the town house attic, and the local grammar school occupied ground level. (If school was in session, there would be little concentration today. Translating the Latin of Caesar's *Gallic Wars* could not be as gripping as eavesdropping on the war between God and Satan upstairs.) Town meetings and selectmen meetings ordinarily gathered upstairs, as did the Quarterly Court. Now the Court of Oyer and Terminer convened there to try the multitude of witch cases. Bridget's would be the first.

While Bridget was being transferred from the jail, Chief Justice William Stoughton administered "in open Court" the oaths of office to Thomas Newton as their Majesties' attorney general, who promised to "act truly and faithfully on their Majesties behalf, as to Law and Justice doth appertain, without any favour or Affection," and to Stephen Sewall to perform the duties of clerk of the court.

The eighteen grand jury members also needed to take their oaths, for this body would consider all the cases and determine which of them ought to proceed to the trial jury or be dismissed. Unfortunately, their names are lost except for that of the foreman, John Ruck, a Salem town merchant and brother of Reverend Burroughs's late second wife.

Stoughton presumably withdrew after the oaths, for judges did not preside at grand jury sessions, and the officers fetched Bridget Bishop to face the jurors, the attorney general, and her accusers. There may not have been a general audience for this part of the proceedings. Without the judges or onlookers, the grand jury hearings were evidently somewhat more subdued than the hearings had been or the petty jury trials would be.

Various witnesses, if they had not already done so, swore before John Hathorne that their written statements were true. Attorney General Newton had collected the written accounts and the examination notes from Bridget's hearing in order to decide just what evidences he would present to the grand jury and which alleged victims to name in the indictments.

Once Bridget was brought up the staircase to the packed courtroom—all eyes on her, a wave of whispers at her appearance—Newton produced five indictments, of which four remain, for Bridget's supposed torments against Mercy Lewis, Abigail Williams, Mary Walcott, Elizabeth Hubbard, and Ann Putnam Jr. He had prewritten forms ready, a Latin heading dating the document in the fourth year of William and Mary's reign (1692) and phrased in standard legal language, handwritten with blanks left for the names of accused, victim, dates, and other specifics. On number five, for Annie Putnam, Newton wrote in the spaces as follows (here in italics):

Anno Regni Regis et Reginæ Willim et
Mariæ nunc Angliæ &tc Quarto:
Essex ss

The Jurors for our Sovereigne Lord & Lady the King & Queen prsents that *Bridgett Bishop alis Olliver the wife of Edward Bishop of Salem in the County of Essex Sawyer* the *Nyneteenth* Day of *April* in the *ffourth* Year of the Reigne of our Sovereigne Lord & Lady William and Mary By the Grace of God of England Scottland ffrance & Ireland King & Queen Defendrs of the ffaith &tc and divers other Dayes & times as well before as after certaine Detestable Artes called Witchcrafts & Sorceries, Wickedly and felloniously hath used Practised & Exercised at and within the Towneship of Salem, aforesd in upon and agt one *Ann puttnam of Salem Village in the County aforesd singlewoman* by which said wicked Arts the said *Ann puttnam* the *sd Nyneteenth* Day of April in the *ffourth Year* abovesd and divers other Dayes & times as well before as after was & is hurt, tortured, Afflicted Pined Consumed wasted

& Tormented agt the Peace of our said Sovereigne Lord & Lady the King and Queen and against the forme of the Statute in that Case made & Provided.

Below this Newton wrote the names of the witnesses to this charge, listing the same five afflicted people on all the other indictments—Ann Putnam Jr., Mercy Lewis, Mary Walcott, Abigail Williams, Elizabeth Hubbard—all of whom had reported seeing the specters torment each other. There were also the names of three nonafflicted observers who had been present at Bridget's hearing to see the reactions of the five and hear them name the accused—Samuel Parris, Nathaniel Ingersoll, and Thomas Putnam. These men did not claim to have seen the specters.

Back in April Elizabeth Hubbard had said that Goody Oliver (Bridget) had appeared to her wearing only a shift, but most of that paper accused Mary Warren, so it may not have been used against Bridget.

Susanna Sheldon made two rambling statements, one back in mid-May when she seemed to have been targeted by every witch in the region. Bridget's specter tormented her with the book, in company with Giles Corey, Philip and Mary English, and the Devil as a "blak man with a hicrouned hatt" whom the witches worshiped on their knees. The whole crew of them suckled their familiars, even the men. Bridget's imp was "a streked snake [that came] creeping over her shoulder and crep into her bosom." Both Bridget and the Devil told Susanna that Bridget had been a witch for twenty years. Susanna was not asked to swear to any of this, so it was probably set aside.

Susanna's statement, dictated to Thomas Putnam on this same day, involved the ghosts of Thomas Green's dead infant twins, who accused Bridget's specter of murdering them, "seting them into fits wherof they dyed." As dramatic as it was, this statement also was not sworn.

Mary Warren's statement, written down by Thomas Newton, seemed more believable—that Bridget's specter had tormented Mary back on April 19 after Bridget was jailed in Salem. Mary swore to the truth of this in front of John Hathorne and Jonathan Corwin this day, but the statement appears not to have been used against Bridget.

Instead, Newton presented eight or nine depositions from people other than the usual afflicted witnesses: Bridget's neighbors who had suspected her for years, who knew all about the earlier charge against her even though that case had been dismissed. Bridget had to stand and listen to their stories being read—the strange lights, the dying babies, the sick children, the imp, the poppets, and on and on, with the deponents swearing to the truth of their statements. None of the incidents related to the five individuals named in the indictments as her supposed victims. The grand jury listened to all this, deliberated, and decided there was enough suspicion to put her case to trial. Thomas Newton wrote at the bottom of each indictment: *billa vera* (Latin for a true bill), and below that came the signature: "John Rucke fforeman in the name of the Rest."

So now Bridget's case would proceed to the trial jury before the Oyer and Terminer judges. Time between the grand and trial juries might take days or months, but in Bridget's case all occurred on the same day. (How much time she had between the courts is unclear, or whether she faced her jury trial before four o'clock, when she and the five other women were searched again for witch-marks by the same committee of women as before.)

Records for all of the summer's trials are missing. What happened during any of them can be partially reconstructed from standard English court procedure; the surviving depositions; and a summary of how matters went from a critical letter written the following October by Thomas Brattle, a wealthy gentleman and treasurer of Harvard College. In addition, Cotton Mather, asked to compose the official account of the witch trials, provided with copies of the court papers, and, most likely, told anecdotes by Stoughton and the Boston judges, described Bridget's trial and four others in his *Wonders of the Invisible World*.

Once again Bridget was led into the courtroom, this time to face the bench of five or more judges: William Stoughton, Samuel Sewall, and Bartholomew Gedney plus at least two others, probably John Richards of Boston and Nathaniel Saltonstall of Ipswich.

The defendant could challenge selected jurors before she was sworn in, but whether Bridget did so, for all that she could be outspoken, is not recorded. She had no legal council to speak for her, as this was not yet British custom in any criminal case. The justices were to advise if necessary.

The clerk read the indictments, and Bridget, after being asked how she pled to the charges, replied, "Not guilty." Asked how she would be tried, she gave the traditional response that allowed the court to proceed: "By God and by my country." Bridget certainly knew her own innocence, and God knew the truth of things. The court was another matter.

Once Bridget had pled, the afflicted witnesses were brought in. If they had been at all restrained during the grand jury session, now they acted as tormented as usual. To the justices, jurors, and the audience of observers, as Mather reported it, "There was little Occasion to prove the Witchcraft, it being Evident and Notorious to all Beholders." The question was: How to prove the defendant was responsible for it?

"[T]he first thing used, was the Testimony of the Bewitched," according to Mather. Several spoke of the spectral attacks that left them bitten, pinched, and choked; others reported specters which pestered them to sign the witches' book and threatened them if they refused. One of the afflicted told how the defendant's specter snatched her from her spinning wheel and hauled her to the river and nearly drowned her, how it bragged of other folk already killed, how the ghosts of those murder victims materialized to the afflicted and called for vengeance. While Bridget herself thought her accusers were liars or, at best, the Devil's dupes, the court found the actions of the afflicted convincing and were impressed by tales of her alleged victims' ghosts crying, "You Murdered us!"

(Much of this testimony that Mather included obviously refers to Susanna Sheldon's statements, though the documents have no notation that she had sworn to them. Perhaps she spoke in court—the court heard *viva voce* testimony as well as written—or perhaps the clerk sent Mather copies of *all* the paperwork and Mather only assumed it had all been used in the actual trial. In any case the judges must have been aware of the stories circulating about the Bishop specter.)

Nevertheless, as impressive as the reports of specters and ghosts seemed, the court had to be cautious as to their value. The reports were suspicious, but were they true? A charge of any crime required two credible witnesses to the same act or a confession with supporting evidence.

The judges had consulted standard English works: Richard Bernard's *Guide to Grand Jurymen ... in Cases of Witchcraft* (1627), John Gaule's *Select Cases of Conscience Touching Witches and Witchcrafts* (1646), and William Perkins's *Discourse of the Damned Art of Witchcraft* (1608).

These three sources drew a distinction between evidence that was suspicious and evidence that proved a point. As Perkins put it, matters of suspicion "give occasion to Examine, yet they are no sufficient Causes of Convicton." One purpose of all three works was to eliminate "irregular" methods of detecting witches—folk methods and torture.

Swimming a suspected witch or assuming a witch could not weep was mere superstition. It *was* suspicious, however, if a person had a longstanding reputation of being a witch, shared kinship or friendship with a known witch (for the craft could be taught), cursed others (especially if a death or other misfortune followed), had an odd mark possibly made by the Devil, identified another suspect as a fellow witch, and so on.

The best evidence was a full and free confession with some corroborating proof, for, according to Gaule, "*Confessions* without *Fact* may be meer Delusion, and *Fact* without *Confession* may be a meer Accident," or testimony from two credible witnesses to the same act.

But cases involving evil magic left few clues, as with most poisons, and allowed for more circumstantial evidence. Most of the testimony in cases of supposed witchcraft concerned suspicious activity. Most of the witnesses corroborating the cause of various afflictions were themselves afflicted. Others who had observed an afflicted person's torments swore to that person's reactions and statements but did not claim to have seen or experienced what the supposed victim claimed.

The justices had sheaves of notes and depositions from the afflicted and from neighbors, notes from Bridget's April 19 hearing in Salem Village, and paperwork from the 1680 case that had jailed her but was eventually dismissed. Now she listened to it all over again, all the gossiping fears the neighbors had worked themselves into, all the suspicions that ought to have been settled and explained years beforehand.

She stood at the bar, weighted down by iron shackles until her legs ached while the clerk read the notes and depositions and her neighbors stood under oath and related incidents she found preposterous—things that had happened years ago, incidents from the other day.

Deliverance Hobbs, no longer denying her recantation, testified as a repentant witch and appeared tormented by Bridget's specter in court. She said that Bridget threatened her with the book and whipped her with iron rods to make her deny her earlier confession and that Bridget partook of the diabolical sacrament at the great witch-meeting in Salem Village.

The other afflicted witnesses, meanwhile, convulsed as they had before, appearing to be knocked down if she only looked at them, as if her eyes gave a spectral blow. The court made Bridget revive them with a touch, noting that only *her* touch worked.

When the clerk read the hearing notes describing how Bridget's motions affected the afflicted, making them twist about to mirror "some Special Actions of her Body," she shook her head and turned her eyes away. The afflicted followed that motion too, and one of them, commenting on Bridget's supposed lack of compassion, said that the defendant "could not be Troubled to see the Afflicted thus Tormented."

More testimony followed amid all this—old incidents to show intent, character, years of supposed malice. Eighteen-year-old John Cook saw her specter a half dozen years ago grinning at him in his chamber one sunrise before it struck him on the side of his head. Samuel Gray, haunted by her specter fourteen years ago at his bedside in a locked room, felt her trying to put something in his mouth when his "Child in the Cradle gave a great screech out as if it was greatly hurt," whereupon the specter vanished. Thereafter the baby's health declined, and in a few months it died. (Gray had sworn to his story on May 30, but the document lacks the notation "Jurat in Curia," suggesting it may not have been used at the jury trial. However, Cotton Mather saw a copy of it, for he summarized the testimony in his account. Robert Calef, criticizing the trials a few years later, thought that the persistent rumors of Bridget's association with witchcraft all stemmed from "the Accusations of one Samuel Gray").

John and Rebecca Bly described the strange fits visited on the sow they bought from Edward Bishop—Bridget's sow—without her approval. Richard Coman, told how, eight years earlier, her pesky specter stalked him by night, paralyzing him when she appeared in the locked room and began clawing at his throat, pulling him nearly out of bed. Samuel and Sarah Shattuck, twelve years past and already suspicious of her transactions at his dye-works, had encountered not a specter but Bridget herself, whom he blamed for the sudden change in his son, who lost his understanding and continued to be plagued with fits and fancies, a danger to himself and a constant worry to his parents. Doctors deduced witchcraft at work.

Naomi Maule testified in court that Bridget's evil magic had killed her baby. John Louder—that drunken liar—related his visions of imps and spectral hogs after a quarrel with Bridget when her hens scratched up his employer's garden behind the Sun Tavern. At this Bridget protested that she did not even know Louder, but the judges did not believe this, for she and Louder had been neighbors for years and had quarreled more than once. (How did Bridget phrase her objection? Or had she not recognized Louder for some reason? The fearful situation of being tried on a capital charge must have quickly turned anxiety to terror, as it became more and more clear that the court believed only her accusers' tales and did not believe anything she tried to say in her defense.) William Stacy the miller blamed her for miring his cart, told of her specter menacing him at his bedside, of something heaving him against a stone wall one night, and of something causing his infant daughter Priscilla's untimely death.

John Bly returned with his son William to depose about how, when Bridget had hired them to remove a wall in the cellar "of The owld house she formerly Lived in," they found poppets walled up in the cellar—actual poppets made of rags and hogs bristles and studded with headless pins points outward. Whatever she said to this did not impress the court but instead sounded merely like a thin excuse. (Had she known the poppets were there, or had they been walled into the building at its construction before Bridget's occupancy?)

As far as the justices were concerned much of what Bridget said sounded like lies or, at best, contradictions even when making her plea. The apparent witch teat that the jury of matrons found earlier was no help either.

Once all the witnesses had had their say, Bridget's fate was left to the jury. Perhaps she hoped that the jurors would balance the testimony against the obvious fact that the afflicted, when not convulsing, appeared perfectly well, that their health was not physically damaged as the indictments specified. Although Thomas and Ann Putnam would not have agreed, the fact was certainly evident to others present, such as Boston merchant Thomas Brattle, who noted that the afflicted, though taken by "scores of strange fits in a day," were otherwise "hale and hearty."

But Chief Justice Stoughton saw things differently. "[W]hen the chief Judge gave the first Jury their charge," Brattle would write, "he told them, that they were not to mind whether the bodies of the said afflicted were really pined and consumed, as was expressed in the indictment; but whether the said afflicted did not suffer from the accused such afflictions as naturally *tended* to their being pined and consumed, wasted, etc. This, (said he,) is a pining and consuming in the sense of the law."

The jury withdrew to deliberate, leaving Bridget clinging to shreds of hope that the twelve men would realize that whatever they thought of her accusers, they could see that nothing that had been presented proved that *she* had caused any of the troubles. But when they returned, the foreman pronounced the verdict that they had found Bridget Bishop guilty of witchcraft as charged.

It must have been as though the ground dropped out from under her feet, as the complete unreality of the verdict filled her mind along with the cold, opposing knowledge that it was very real indeed, her consciousness nearly overwhelmed with this cold drench of horror.

Bridget was brought back, furious and frightened, to the jail where the other prisoners, waiting to hear what happened, to learn what *they* might expect, could read the verdict in her face.

Word of the trial's outcome spread among the suspects—disheartening news for sure. Given the general attitude toward all the accused, the guilty verdict was not wholly unexpected. Now a sickening dread joined apprehension. Now they knew the justices were accepting the spectral evidence of the afflicted witnesses at face value, accepting the accusers' stories but not accepting any retractions or alterations in interpretation. Now Mary Warren knew not only that testimony like hers could have deadly results but also that her story would be even harder to change.

But there was no time left that day for the court to consider the cases of Rebecca Nurse or John Willard. Witnesses summoned for Rebecca's trial would have to return on the morrow. There was time enough, however, for various people to swear to their depositions. Ann Putnam swore to her statement that John Willard's specter and the ghost of his murder victims—dead neighbors, dead babies—had appeared to her that very day, the tale implicating William Hobbs and Martha Corey as well. Her deposition against Rebecca Nurse enumerated more murdered victims, including Ann's nieces and nephews and "young Jno putnams child" because he had commented on Rebecca and her sisters "that it was no wonder they ware wicthes for their mother was so before them."

Bridget and the other women faced a second search from the matrons at four o'clock, and this time the searchers noted certain changes. They now found Bridget Bishop "in a clear & free state from any preternaturall Excresence." Rebecca Nurse, the report emphasized, now had "only a dry skin nearer to the anus" although it apparently lacked feeling. "& as for Elizabeth Procter which Excresence like a tett red & fresh, not any thing appears, but only a proper procedentia Ani"—which is, according to the Oxford English Dictionary, a "prolapsus or slipping down of the rectum." "& as for Susanna Martine whose breast in the Morning search appeared to us very full; the Nibbs fresh & starting, now at this searching all lancke & pendant"—more as one would expect from an older woman or from one who had given nourishment to greedy imps. The report did not mention Alice Parker or Sarah Good at all.

Due to the old continuing suspicions and her earlier arrest, the court had evidently selected Bridget's case to be the first. The case against Rebecca Nurse would not be as straightforward, as she was a member of the Salem town church and backed by a supportive family and many neighborhood friends. The night before her postponed grand jury trial had to have been nearly as difficult for Rebecca as it was for the condemned Bridget Bishop.

The grand jury for Rebecca Nurse convened on Friday, June 3, with Mrs. Ann Putnam as well as her daughter Annie among the witnesses.

Annie swore that she had seen Rebecca's specter hurt her and the other afflicted girls during the March 24 examination, that it had bitten and pinched since March 13, even though at first "I did not know what hir name was then tho I knew whare she used to sitt in our Meetinghouse."

Thomas Putnam had written the account for his daughter as he had for Elizabeth Hubbard and Mary Walcott about their spectral torments. Both Elizabeth and Mary swore to the statements before the Grand Jury.

Susanna Sheldon, though summoned, is presumably the witness whose name was written as Joanna Childen when she deposed that the ghost of Goodman Harwood accused Rebecca's specter of killing him by pushing him off his cart. She was not asked to swear to the statement, however, so presumably it was not used.

Mrs. Ann Putnam swore to her statements about Rebecca's spectral attacks that had begun in March, how her enemy had tried to argue scripture against her and hurt her so terribly during the March 24 hearing that Thomas had had to carry her bodily from the meeting house.

Abigail Williams swore to her March statements against Rebecca Nurse and Sarah Cloyce—how they had tormented her with that book and how they had participated in the Devil's sacrament.

Various other papers more favorable to Rebecca's case may have been submitted this day, papers her family had gathered. Clement Coldum, when giving Elizabeth Hubbard a ride to the Village, had heard her claim that not only was she not afraid of the Devil but also, he said, "she could discourse with the Devil as well as with me." Who could trust anyone who trusted the Devil so?

Rebecca's daughters Rebecca Preston and Mary Tarbell, countering the search committee's report, also submitted a paper:

we whos nams are under written cane testiefie if cald to it that goodde
nurs have bene trobled with an Infirmity of body for many years which
the Juree of wemen seme to be Afraid it should be something Elce
   Rebcah preson.
   Mary Tarbel

Many neighbors sided with Rebecca. At some point, possibly as
early as her hearing, Israel and Elizabeth Porter (Hathorne's sister)
wrote a statement about their visit to Goody Nurse in March, with
Peter Cloyce and Daniel Andrews describing Rebecca's sincerely surprised reaction to the rumor that she was suspected of witchcraft.

In addition, Francis and his children had gathered a petition of
thirty-nine names—neighbors speaking out on her behalf. Whether
this was submitted or not is in question. Daniel Andrews had signed
it, and he had recently been accused of witchcraft and fled before the
law could reach him. His name thus may not have helped her case, although the Porters had noted Andrews's presence at the March visit
along with Peter Cloyce, who was married to Rebecca's suspected sister Sarah. Judge John Hathorne, thinking himself to be objective,
could well have disregarded his sister's opinion, assuming that the Andrews and Cloyce names verified his view. In any case, Rebecca had
many supporters.

The grand jury considered the offered evidence, the account of
events during Rebecca's hearing, and their own observation of the afflictions before them among the witnesses as well as the four indictments against her. She had, the documents declared, on March 24
(during the initial examination) and at "Divers other Dayes & times
as well before as after certaine detestable Arts called Witchcrafts &
Sorceries wickedly and ffelloniously hath used Practised & Exercised
at and within the Towneship of Salem" against Ann Puttnam Jr., Abigail Williams, Mary Walcott, and Elizabeth Hubbard.

Mangling the Latin, foreman John Ruck signed all four "Bill
Avara." Rebecca Nurse's case would proceed to the trial jury.

While guards took Rebecca back to the jail, her family and friends
still determined to do all they could on her behalf, the witnesses
remained as John Willard faced the grand jury. The report of the

coroner's jury on the mysterious death of young Daniel Wilkins plus testimony about the torments the afflicted witnesses endured at Willard's May 18 hearing seemed to have made up the bulk of the presented evidence. Reverend Samuel Parris, Nathaniel Ingersoll, and Thomas Putnam swore before the grand jury about what they had witnessed. Along with the other afflicted witnesses—including Sarah Bibber, a married woman—Annie Putnam swore to her lengthy statement itemizing Willard's spectral assaults against her and how his specter told her "he had whiped my little sister Sarah to death."

Thomas Newton had seven indictments drawn up against Willard for tormenting seven victims during his May 18 examination. On each document all seven names were listed as witnesses to each other's torments: Mercy Lewis, Abigail Williams, Mary Walcott, Susanna Sheldon, Ann Putnam Sr., Ann Putnam Jr., and Elizabeth Hubbard. (The fifth and sixth indictments are missing but presumably named Mrs. Ann Putnam Sr. and Mary Walcott, for the names are listed in the same order on all seven documents.)

All but one, it seems, were declared *billa vera*. The grand jury rejected Susanna Sheldon's—her testimony tended to be more embellished than any of the others—and this indictment was marked "Ignoramos," with *ignoramus* being Latin for "we don't know." The judges and jurors must have been confident that they were capable of winnowing out the mistaken or false claims from the true in so important a charge.

Newton listed two additional afflicted witnesses against Willard, Sarah Churchill, and Margaret Jacobs, noting that Willard (his specter) had dissuaded them from testifying. Sarah would still be among the confessors months later, but Margaret seemed less and less willing to accuse the suspects.

Brooding on her confession and accusations, Margaret finally marshaled her thoughts and courage and, at some point, recanted her earlier admission of witchcraft. It was all false, she told the magistrates. She was *not* a witch, *none* of her family were witches. She would no longer give the Devil power over her with her lies. The magistrates did not believe her any more than they had believed Mary, Deliverance, and Sarah. Because she was no longer a cooperating witness to the supposed plot, they placed her in close confinement, where she was not allowed to go outside. Regretting her earlier cowardice, Margaret left the relative freedom of the status that Mary still occupied, greatly relieved by her decision.

Mary Warren certainly did not change her story, probably did not dare to by now and possibly half convinced (at least sometimes) of whatever the magistrates thought of her—these men so respected, so diligent in the public's interest, so educated and so wealthy, so unlike herself.

This first session over, the Oyer and Terminer judges presumably returned home to their several towns before the next Sabbath. Even so, Ann Putnam must have felt confident that court was proceeding in the right direction, that although the jury trials of her two greatest enemies—Nurse and Willard—were postponed to a later session, the law was at last working to protect her family.

However, spectral troubles continued to plague Salem. On Saturday, June 4, Annie Putnam, Susanna Shelden, Mary Walcott, Elizabeth Hubbard, Elizabeth Booth, the married woman Sarah Bibber, and Mary Warren witnessed at a hearing for laborer Job Tookey of Beverly. Bartholomew Gedney presided with John Hathorne and Jonathan Corwin as the afflicted girls convulsed, accusing Tookey, declaring that the ghosts of five of his murder victims were present, crying for vengeance. Annie, Susanna, and Mary Warren swore that Tookey himself had boasted that "he had Learneing and could Raise the divele when he pleased." Tookey may have made some kind of rash statement, for one James Darling also swore that he had heard Tookey say "he was not the Devills Servant but the Devill was his."

John Louder, who had testified against Bridget Bishop, swore that Tookey told him he could "freely discourse the Divell as well as he speaking to him." Four other men heard this exchange and backed up Louder's claim.

Nevertheless, Hathorne also jotted the note: "Job Tuckey sayth its not he but the divell in his shape that hurts the people"—which a servant devil, as well as an interfering imp, might do after all.

Evidently the afflicted saw other people's specters. Edward Putnam and Thomas Rayment entered a complaint before Hathorne against

Goodwife Mary Ireson of Lynn for tormenting Putnam's niece Annie, Abigail Williams, Susanna Shelden, Mary Walcott, Elizabeth Booth, and Mary Warren. Mary Warren had claimed that Goody Ireson and Goodwife Mary Toothaker tormented her with the Devil's book: while in a trance-like fit on May 24 she was heard conversing with a specter of Dr. Toothaker's wife that also brought the book and threatened her with a coffin for not signing it.

By ten o'clock, Monday, June 6, the constable of Lynn brought Goodwife Mary Ireson before Gedney, Hathorne, and Corwin at Thomas Beadle's tavern. Merchant Simon Willard prepared to take notes.

The afflicted fell in fits even during the opening prayer, even before the suspect was brought into the room. This time the justices experimented with the afflicted witnesses' ability to identify their attacker when seen in the flesh—perhaps Bridget's assertions that she had never seen certain parties had some effect. As some of Goody Ireson's relatives had accompanied her, the magistrates indicated the suspect's sister and asked the girls if *she* were the same person whose specter tormented them. No, they said, "it was she that had a hood on." That Goody Ireson wore a more eye-catching riding hood was not taken into account.

"Do you not see how you are discovered?" a magistrate asked Goody Ireson. Mary Warren and the other witnesses, meanwhile, fell writhing if Ireson so much as glanced at them. Although all the afflicted identified the specter, only Mary Walcott said that she had seen the woman in person before. Willard's notes name Mary Warren, Susanna Sheldon, Mary Walcott, and Elizabeth Booth among the afflicted but not Annie Putnam or Sarah Bibber, even though they were named in the complaint.

The touch test helped bring them out of their fits, as time consuming as that was. Goody Ireson admitted to having a temper, which perhaps, she said, had left her vulnerable to this misfortune, but she was not guilty of witchcraft—not that sin.

Susanna Sheldon declared that Ireson tried to rip out her throat right there in court for refusing to sign the Devil's book. Goody Ireson stared fixedly at nothing—perhaps in shock, perhaps trying not to look at any of the accusers directly and set off more convulsions. She was looking at the Devil, some of them cried, who was telling her not to confess. The justices and Goody Ireson's own uncle Goodman Fuller "urged her to confess & breake the snare of the devill." She replied that she did not know that she was in it and asked whether "she might be a witch & not know it." The justices said no, she could not. At that she said, the scribe noted, "she could not confess till she had more light."

Goody Ireson was held for trial.

Evidently other specters attacked Mary Warren and Susanna Sheldon that morning, for Gedney, Hathorne, and Corwin issued an arrest warrant for Mistress Ann Dolliver of Gloucester for tormenting them. Constable Peter Osgood brought her before the justices in short order, for the woman, deserted by her husband, was living in Salem with her father, Reverend John Higginson. Her brother John Jr. was a recently appointed magistrate, but he did not preside today.

"[W]here be my accusers," she demanded. "I am not willing to accuse my selfe." Despite her status and local connections, Ann Dolliver was known to be, as her own father had said, "by overbearing melancholy crazed in her understanding." She was at frequent loggerheads with her stepmother and known to ramble about alone over the countryside, staying away at night who knew where. The afflicted said she visited Goodwife Nurse at her home. Mrs. Dolliver explained that she had been there only once when she mistook her way, walking home the long way round from Beverly "becaus she would not goe over with the ferry man"—that "ugly fellow."

Asked if she had seen the Devil, she snapped if the Devil took the shape of a man as reported, "she knew not a spirit from a man in the night," and this left the court to wonder what she did refer to. Mary Warren and some of the others allowed that the defendant was the same woman who had hurt them, for even though she was dressed differently, her face was the same. They also saw the ghost of a dead child form in the courtroom and heard it crying for vengeance because Dolliver, they said, had pressed the life from its body. Now the little victim accused her of its murder and accused her also of trying to kill her own father.

Mrs. Dolliver denied trying to hurt anyone with witchcraft, while the afflicted said she kept "poppits in a secret place that she afflicted with." Eventually she admitted that fourteen years before she had made one or two wax poppets "becaus she thought she was bewitched & she had read in a book that told her that tha[t] was the way to afflict them that had afflicted her." (She, like Goody Sibley, had resorted to countermagic.)

But Mrs. Dolliver would not confess.

On the following day, Tuesday, June 7, Mary Warren witnessed against Job Tookey before Justices Gedney, Hathorne, and Corwin while merchant William Murray took notes.

"Did you not say the other day that yow saw the Devil?" the justices asked.

Tookey answered, "I knew not then what I said."

As before, according to the afflicted, the room crowded with the shifting forms of ghosts: three men, three women, and two children, all murdered by the defendant's image magic. Gamaliel Hawkins, said Mary, died in Barbados when Tookey stabbed a pin through a poppet's heart. Andrew Woodbury, Betty Hewes—the names of his murder victims came pouring out. As the ghost of John Trask's dead child appeared under the magistrates' table, wailing for vengeance, specters of Tookey and a Mr. John Busse attacked Mary. Busse had been reported before at the great witch meeting in Parris's pasture. The real Busse was a sometime preacher and sometime physician who had worked in Wells and Oyster River before those towns were attacked. He had to remove to Boston and was, moreover, a son-in-law of Mary Bradbury, the Salisbury woman that Ann Putnam's family so mistrusted.

Mary Walcott, Susanna Sheldon, and Elizabeth Booth Jr. saw the ghosts as well, and all had to receive Tookey's touch to recover from their convulsions.

The ghosts' testimony bore hard against him, so Tookey remained in jail.

Elizabeth Booth Jr. was a new afflicted witness, called "junior" because, already with child and hastily married at sixteen to George Booth, she was younger than her eighteen-year-old sister-in-law Eliz-

abeth Booth, "singlewoman." She was also a sister of the afflicted Rebecca Wilkins and the late Daniel Wilkins.

On the following day, June 8, Lieutenant Governor and Chief Justice William Stoughton signed the death warrant for Bridget Bishop
and sent it on to Salem, where it would have arrived by the June 9 at
the latest.

Massachusetts laws would remain in force until the legislature
rewrote them in accordance with British laws—or at least those not
"repugnant" to British law, which would only attract more unwelcome
attention and interference. Witchcraft was definitely illegal in England—a capital crime—and something had to be done about the
overcrowded jails.

Sheriff George Corwin and the town fathers, knowing there would
be executions, would have decided on a site for the hangings. In the
past all executions took place in Boston, as all capital crimes were tried
there before the Governor's Assistants in their capacity of an upper
court. As the unprecedented number of witch suspects had made
holding the trials in the Essex County seat of Salem more practical,
the executions would take place there as well.

The exact site is not specified in the remaining papers. Contemporary references place it at a distance from the jail and on a hill.
The height outside the town center where the road bent north to
Salem Village and skirted the hill to head for Boston became known
as Gallows Hill. There, on town-owned common pasture, open and
elevated enough to be seen from the main road as an example to
would-be malefactors, the authorities either built a gallows or used
an existing tree. An oak with strong horizontal branches would be
ideal.

---

*Rebecca Nurse's family persist on her behalf, visit her in the Salem jail,
and seek neighbors willing to speak a good word about her character. The
court never should have indicted her, Francis insists, not on that evidence. But an indictment is not proof, the family remind themselves, and
it is certainly not a verdict.*

Two of Rebecca's daughters, Goodwives Rebecca Preston and Mary Tarbell, are willing to explain their mother's "Infirmity of body" that the women on the search committee thought was suspicious.

Francis and their children know that Rebecca has more friends than does the Bishop woman—a better reputation and a better chance for the truth to be heard. When they visit her in the jail, so crowded now and so squalid in the summer heat, they offer hope—and avoid catching Bridget Bishop's eye.

(10)
June 10 to 30, 1692

Bridget Bishop has passed the days after her trial in a fog of fear and fury. Then the official word arrived: tomorrow, they told her, tomorrow she would hang. The order had arrived from Boston, and everything was ready. If she wished to settle her soul, this was the time to do it.

She does not sleep the night before during the long hours that yet pass more swiftly than she realizes.

Just hearing the foreman's verdict of guilty had made her dizzy, as though the courtroom suddenly became unreal. None of this had anything to do with her, yet she understood the words, knew what they meant, and what they would mean soon enough.

All those neighbors and their stupid fears, so-called witnesses coming out of the woodwork, remembering old slights, magnifying their own unfounded suppositions. Bridget knows she is no witch, but she is helpless to prove it.

Some of the other prisoners try to console her. Others act afraid to be near her, as if bad luck would rub off.

The door opens and the guards come for her. Bridget straightens up, takes a last look at the wretched room and the other prisoners—all eyes on her once again—and walks toward the door.

In the prison yard, out in the fresh air and a breeze from the sea, they unlock and remove her shackles. The unaccustomed lightness feels wonderful, even if it means a step closer to the gallows. The men grasp her elbows and heft her up into a cart, facing her backward. The sheriff—too young for the job, she thinks—is mounted. Lesser officers on foot carry their black staffs of office. They try to look formal and official, but none of them has done this before and some of them look nervous. I am going to die, thinks Bridget, and they look nervous.

Hands tied, she braces herself against the side of the cart, standing so the crowd can see her, can be sure she is gotten rid of. The gate swings open and there are people already swarming the street for a look at her, a glimpse of the witch they fear, staring. The horse starts forward and the cart creaks into motion as the little procession moves from the prison yard into the street. A man with a staff walks ahead to clear the way. Doesn't anyone work, have anything better to do than loiter about to watch her misery? The walking guards, the sheriff on horseback, then onlookers falling in to make a growing tail of gawkers.

Bridget scans the crowd for a friendly face, a sympathetic face, but she cannot find any. Her associates have been arrested also, but where is that husband of hers? She does not want her child to see her like this, but she longs for one last look at her daughter, her granddaughter. Will their kinship be held against them? What sort of future does the child face now, in the eyes of the neighbors as a witch's brat?

The line of march turns into the main street and proceeds slowly the length of the town, southwest down the peninsula, past the meeting house (still under repair but no crashing beams this time), past the town pump, past the homes of her judges Hathorne and Corwin—both men in Boston now with the legislature. Facing backward, she sees the town recede away from her. A familiar couple stand next to their house then join the following crowd. They look satisfied, pleased at what they at least consider justice done. Maule—that was the name—another family with a dead child they blame on her. What of her own dead children? Did they think they were the only family to suffer such a loss? She thinks of her granddaughter again and hopes the child will not see any of what is happening, what is about to happen.

Now and then sharper shrieks pierce the jostle and murmur of the crowd—the afflicted girls are nearby. Naturally they would not miss the chance to see their handiwork.

The cart lurches right (Bridget's left) and begins to head downhill. How far are they taking me? *she wonders. All the staring eyes, jeering mouths—she wishes it would end yet knows that her life will end first. The salt-and-sulfur reek of low tide grows stronger as they head toward the causeway over the bend in the North River, where a stream flowing down the steep hill before them cuts a thin channel of fresh water into the retreating salt tide and becomes lost in the river and the harbor and then the sea beyond. The causeway crosses the marshy swampy ground to midstream, then the cart rumbles over a plank bridge and the road rises again. They had taken her this way before for the hearing in the Village, but this time, with officers shouting orders and the cart horse straining, the procession turns up a path into the common pasture and onto a low ledge above the tidal inlet. The hangman waits there under a tree with his ropes.*

The men get her down from the cart and up onto the rungs of the ladder leaning against the tree. She struggles not to trip on her petticoats. From up those few steps she looks over the sea of faces, the shifting mass of the curious, the excited, the fearful, the vengeful. Beyond them, below the level of the ledge they stand on, the sun glitters on the falling tide, sparkles off the restless, scavenging crabs scouring the mud flats, reflects from the white wings of gulls diving for those crabs, highlights the roofs of the town beyond, and blazes down from the midday, midsummer sky.

Someone steadies her on the ladder while one of the other men ties a cord around her legs, compressing her skirts close. Modesty, *she thinks.* No show here for the lecherous, but no kicking either.

The sheriff is speaking, reading the death warrant that makes what he is about to order legal. The crowd quiets for that:

Whereas Bridgett Bishop alias Oliver the wife of Edward Bishop of Salem . . . at a speciall Court of Oyer and Terminer . . . before William Stoughton Esqr. and his Associates Justices of the said Court was Indicted and arraigned upon five severall Indictments for using, practicing, and exercising . . certain acts of Witchcraft in and upon the bodies of Abigail Williams, Ann Putnam Jun., Mercy Lewis, Mary Walcott and Elizabeth Hubbard of Salem Village, singlewomen, whereby their bodies were hurt, afflicted pined, consumed, wasted and tormented . . .

What utter nonsense, *Bridget thinks.* Those girls are here now and looking anything *but* wasted and consumed.

"In the Name of their Majesties William and Mary now King & Queen over England," the sheriff continues, reading through the order

for him to proceed on this day, "between the hours of eight and twelve[to] *safely conduct the said Bridget Bishop . . . from their Majesties' Gaol in Salem aforesaid to the place of Execution and there cause her to be hanged by the neck until she be dead."*

Then someone else was talking, one of the ministers—Hale from Beverly, who had walked out with the crowd—praying for her soul. The ministers look like crows to her, the lot of them.

A few of the other onlookers seem disgusted by the offered prayer. She recognizes Maule, the trouble-making Quaker, who blames her for his brat's death. He smirks and rolls his eyes at the minister's prayer. Is Shattuck here as well to gloat? Strangled shouts and shrieks punctuate the prayer from one side, where the so-called afflicted huddle together: two young women, the Putnam girl, and that Bibber woman, who is old enough to know better. As Bridget turns to see, one is on the ground rolling in the dust. "Jacobs!" *she hears the girl yelp. It's old Jacobs, clubbing her with one of his walking sticks. The Devil, the other afflicted explain, is present to support old Jacobs's specter.* It must be as arthritic as Jacobs's body. Will they never quit their nonsense? *she wonders. The prayer ends.*

And then something rough drags over her head—the noose. The hangman is on a ladder beside hers. He pulls the rope firmly through the knot and secures it snugly behind her neck. She feels a cold sweat that is more than the slight sea breeze and hears the blood sing in her ears as she tamps down rising panic—she will not give her persecutors the satisfaction. She will not *plead or cry or act the fool. She looks out over the crowd toward the sea, hears the gulls cry as the people hush in anticipation, sees a flash of white wings as the distant birds wheel.*

And then the bag comes down over her face, blots out the world beyond, stifling her breath in the heat. Slight gleams of daylight glare through the rough weave of the sack, which stinks of a barn. A man's voice barks an order, and before she can figure what he just said, her feet jerk out from under her and a terrible pressure slams into her throat and the base of her skull.

And then there is no support, nothing to hold onto or stand on. She strains against the cords that hold her hands useless, tries to kick her feet to find purchase, but there is nothing. Her head feels as if it will explode, and the little light though the sack darkens as darkness rushes toward her, into her. She is vaguely aware she is soiling herself, but pain and desperation overmatches embarrassment or shame. No, she thinks, No. *Her consciousness is one great shout of* NO.

And then, . . . and then . . .

A nd beyond that is only speculation.

Hangmen then still used a slipknot rather than the later, more elaborate "hangman's knot." A quick snap of the neck was rare, so death came by a slower strangulation.

Below the gallows, meanwhile, Thomas Maule directed loud comments at Reverend John Hale, who had prayed for Bridget's soul. Maule declared that if anyone had asked *him* to pray for Bishop, he certainly would *not* pray for her—not for a witch, a malefactor who had forsaken God to join the Devil and thus committed the unforgivable sin. *That* was the sin that scripture said we must *not* pray for. Besides, the woman had killed one of his children with her magic, and he could have testified to that if he had desired. (His wife had testified.) Most of the prisoners were witches as well, Maule continued. (To him, anyone not a Quaker was in the Devil's pocket.)

When the work was finished Deputy Sheriff George Herrick wrote an account at the end of the warrant that Sheriff Corwin then signed, ready to submit to the court:

> June 10th 1692
> According to the Within Written precept I have taken the body of the within named Bridget Bishop out of their Majesties' Goale in Salem and Safely conveyed her to the place provided for her Execution and Caused the said Bridget to be hanged by the neck until she was dead and ~~buried in the place~~ all which was according to the time Within Required and So I make Return by me
> George Corwin Sheriff

The crossed out phrase may indicate someone else claimed the body, although there is no written record of that. Or perhaps, as

Herrick may have written more than the original order had described, he then omitted the part about burial to let the phrasing of the return match the phrasing of the warrant. The custom, after all, was to leave felons' bodies hanging for a time as a warning and then bury them near the gallows they had died on. How long Bridget's body was left hanging is not known.

On June 13 word reached Boston that French and Indian forces had attacked Wells, Maine, Reverend Burroughs's town, on June 10 (the day of Bridget's execution). Governor Phips ordered a detachment of the Essex County regiment to march north and placed an embargo on all Massachusetts ports for as long as French ships prowled the coast. Physical as well as the spectral woes besieged New England.

That the current methods of the witch trials might at least be aggravating the region's trouble must have crossed some people's minds—though presumably not Stoughton's. Governor Phips had requested advice from the Boston-area ministers on how to deal with the spiritual world, and the answer, largely composed by Reverend Cotton Mather, was submitted Wednesday, June 15, the same day the legislature determined that while they were revising their code of Massachusetts laws all the old laws not in contradiction to the new charter or "repugnant" to the laws of England would remain in force.

"The Return of Several Ministers" took note of the serious sufferings of the afflicted and the prudence of the magistrates who had to cope with the complicated matter. Principally it warned against accepting spectral evidence, which was, after all, "received only upon the Devil's Authority." Thus, blind acceptance would "be a Door opened for a long Train of miserable Consequences." They recommended Perkins and the other standard English law books, and they rejected the use of folk tests (like the touch test) as too easily "abused by the Devil's Legerdemains." Most of all they warned that "it is an undoubted and notorious thing, that a Demon may, by God's Permission, appear even to ill purposes, in the Shape of an innocent, yea, and a virtuous Man." Ignoring spectral evidence could end the whole "dreadful Calamity." The court should employ "the speedy and vigorous Prosecution of such as have rendered themselves obnoxious" by using "the Laws of God"—that is, no folk methods—"and the wholesome statutes of the *English* nation."

Justice Nathaniel Saltonstall, "very much dissatisfyed with the proceedings of it," resigned from the Court of Oyer and Terminer at some point, presumably before the next sitting but possibly later.

If Francis and any of the rest of Rebecca's family still attended services in Salem Village, they found no comfort in Reverend Parris's prayers and sermons. If Parris mentioned concern for the suffering, he meant the supposed afflicted. If he mentioned the accused, it was clear that he believed they were guilty. Samuel and Mary Nurse went to the Sabbath meeting occasionally, but she avoided the communion services that he sometimes attended.

People in the village still spoke of Rebecca's specter. On June 18 Jonathan Putnam was taken "very ill," as Reverend Parris noted when he wrote a statement about the incident. The family summoned Mercy Lewis to check what specters might be at work, and the girl, though she was for a time entranced and unable to speak, at last "said she saw Goody Nurse & Goody Carrier holding said Jonathans head."

With reports like *that* still circulating, knowing that Rebecca's trial fast approached and remembering all too well what had happened to Bridget Bishop, the Nurse family put their hope in God's mercy *and* in their own efforts to gather names and statements on her behalf. How much mercy the court might have was yet to be seen.

Ann Putnam, meanwhile, likely found Bridget's hanging a blessing—one witch gone—and worried about that Bradbury woman who gave her kin so much trouble, who was still at large, her specter still reported to be active.

On June 28 the grand jury considered the case of Sarah Good. Someone wrote a list of witnesses, both the presently afflicted, like Annie Putnam, as well as others who had had strange encounters with Good or her specter in the past. One of the names is "Tittube indian," written somewhat indented from the rest. She could have spoken about the spectral torments of February and March, the events she had described at her own March 1 hearing and subsequent confessions. Whether Tituba was actually called to testify or what she actually said is, unfortunately, unknown. Sarah Good was indicted on at least three counts: for tormenting Sarah Bibber beginning May 2 and for tormenting Elizabeth Hubbard and Annie Putnam on March 1.

The court also dealt with a flurry of depositions, mainly against Sarah Good but also one *for* Elizabeth How from her husband as well as a petition from Rebecca Nurse herself.

To the Honourd Court of Oryn and Terminer now sitting In Salem this 28 of June Ano 1692
The humble petission of Rebecca Nurse of Salem Village
Humbley Sheweth

That whareas sum Women did sarch Yor Petissionr At Salem as I did then Conceive for sum supernaturall Marke, And then one of the sd Women which is Known to be, the Moaste Antient skillfull prudent person of them all as to Any such Concerne did Express hir selfe to be of A contrary opinion from the Rest And did then Declare, that shee saw Nothing In or Aboute yor Honors poare pettissioner But what might Arise from A naturall Cause And I then Rendered the said persons a sufficient Knowne Reason as to my selfe of the Moveing Cause Thereof which was by Exceeding Weaknesses decending partly from an overture of Nature And difficult Exigences that hath Befallen me In the Times of my Travells And therefore Yor pettissionr Humbley prayes That yor Honours would be pleased to Admitt of sum other Women to Enquire Into this Great Concerne, those that are Moast Grave wise and skillfull Namely Ms Higginson senr Ms Buckstone Ms Woodbery two of them Being Midwives Ms Porter Together with such others, as may be Choasen on that Account Before I am Brought to my triall All which I hoape yor Honours will take Into yor prudent Consideration And find it Requisite Soe to doe for my Life Lyes Now In yor Hands under God And Being Conscious of My owne Innocency I Humbley Begg that I may have Liberty to manifest it to the wourld partly by the Meanes Abovesaid

And Yor Poare pettissior shall Evermore
pray as In duty Bound &c
                                                Rebecca Nurse

Someone else wrote the paper, but Rebecca inked her mark below her name. However, there is no indication that the court ordered this second examination before her trial on the following day.

On Wednesday, June 29, the grand jury indicted Elizabeth How and Susannah Martin—Annie Putnam witnessed against both of these suspects—while Thomas Putnam swore to his testimony against Goody Martin. The Court of Oyer and Terminer tried three witchcraft cases this day: Sarah Good, Susannah Martin, and Rebecca Nurse.

King's Attorney Thomas Newton listed the evidence offered against Sarah Good, beginning with "Titabe's Confession & Examinacon agt her selfe & Sarah Good abstracted"—so perhaps Tituba was not present in court today nor had been the day before with the grand jury if an abstract from the hearing notes was sufficient. Newton summarized the supposed events of February 28 when Good and the other spectral witches invaded the parsonage "& stopped her Eares in prayer time" as they tried to make Tituba hurt the children. Failing this, "Good with others are very strong & pull her with them to Mr putnams & make her hurt the Children." She also described Good's familiars: a cat, a yellow bird, and "a thing all over hairy."

(Newton's note that "Sarah Good appeared like a wolfe to Hubbard going to proctors & saw it sent by Good to Hubbard" does not clarify whether Tituba said she saw Good send the wolf or whether Elizabeth Hubbard said this. Newton also noted, "Dorothy Goods Charge ag[ains]t her mother Sarah Good That she had three birds one black, one yellow & that these birds hurt the Children & afflicted persons." This deposition is otherwise lost, but Dorothy, still in Boston jail, was not present to testify.)

The "confessions" of Deliverance and Abigail Hobbs that described Good's activities at the witch sacraments were introduced with these women presumably in court, as they would be during Rebecca Nurse's trial. Perhaps Mary Warren was also brought in to recount her jailhouse apparitions, for under "Mary Warrens Confession," Newton wrote, "That Sarah Good is a Witch & brought her the booke to signe to weh she did." The last four words were crossed out as if Mary had insisted that, though threatened, she had *not* signed. However, neither

Mary Warren nor Tituba's name appears in the list of witnesses to the three indictments.

Most of the other testimony against Good came from various folk, including several relatives who had suffered livestock losses after refusing to let her move in with them.

Robert Calef later recounted an incident from this trial that was *not* preserved in the official papers. On recovering from a fit, "one of the afflicted" accused Sarah Good of "stabing her in the breast with a Knife"—breaking the blade in the process. A fragment of knife blade was indeed found in her clothing, the discovery of which caused a stir in one part of the audience. A young man was allowed to come forward to show "a Shaft and part of the Blade" to the court.

The justices could see clearly that the accuser's fragment exactly fit the young man's broken blade. The day before, he explained, he had happened to snap his own knife in two and "cast away the upper part, this afflicted person being then present."

This development must have given Sarah Good a flicker of hope and confounded the accusers. The Nurse family would have reacted very differently from Thomas and Ann Putnam—for a brief time at least. (As the young man did not say he had actually *seen* the afflicted person take the fragment, perhaps the justices preferred to imagine that a witch might have spirited away the piece of blade to use against her accuser.) The court dismissed the young man, then, turning to the accuser, merely warned her "not to tell lyes"—perhaps uncertain whether she had lied or not—and allowed her to continue as a witness. The Putnams could relax at this, whereas Sarah Good and the Nurse family were plunged back into too-familiar dread.

Who was this afflicted person? A badly torn statement from William and Rachel Bradford and William Rayment Jr. questioned Mercy Lewis's honesty by recounting events within the previous two and a half years when Mercy lived in the Bradford household.

Perhaps this was Susanna Sheldon, if she is the deponent whose name was given as Joanna Childen, who had claimed back on June 2 that she had seen the ghost of Sarah Good's dead infant, who had accused her own mother of murdering her and called Sarah a witch.

Good's specter in turn said she had killed the child "becaus that she Could not atend it" and that "she did give it to the divell." This accusation was not used at the trial, so Sarah Good was spared this painful charge at least, though the Sheldon girl would testify against other defendants.

In addition, even more people expressed their low opinion of Sarah Bibber's honesty—neighbors and people who had had the misfortune to have hired Goodman John Bibber and his wife as live-in help: Joseph Fowler, Thomas and Mary Jacobs of Ipswich, Richard Walker, John and Lydia Porter. All agreed the woman was an idle, "double tongued," malicious, lying gossip, "a woman of an unruly turbulent spirit" who "would have strange fitts when shee was crost." The Nurse family would collect a sheaf of statements against Bibber, if they had not already done so.

Meanwhile, the jury found Sarah Good guilty as charged.

Susannah Martin, a combative widow, having faced the grand jury this same day, also faced the trial jury. The documents in her case include statements from the afflicted (written out for them by Thomas Putnam), including Annie Putnam, Mercy Lewis, and Sarah Bibber about her spectral torments during Martin's hearing and at other times; statements from Reverend Parris, Nathaniel Ingersoll, and Thomas Putnam concerning what they saw the afflicted do and say at certain times; and statements from various neighbors in Amesbury who had had unfortunate encounters with her. Evidently Goody Martin spoke her mind in vivid terms during the proceedings, but this only helped convince the court that she was, as Cotton Mather relayed the opinion, "one of the most Impudent, Scurrilous, wicked creatures in the world." Susannah Martin was also found guilty.

During one of the day's trials, according to Robert Calef, one of the afflicted "cried out publickly of Mr. Willard Minister in Boston as afflicting of her." Reverend Samuel Willard, minister of the Second Church where Samuel Sewall was a member, had criticized the court's methods. The justices, however, knew Willard and trusted his character enough to assume the accuser had confused the name. *John* Willard was, after all, under arrest for suspected witchcraft and murder by witchcraft. The court sent her from the room, and word went around that "she was mistaken in the person." Again, Calef did not name the accuser.

As the grand jury had accepted four indictments against Rebecca Nurse—for afflicting Annie Putnam, Mary Walcott, Elizabeth Hubbard, and Abigail Williams—her family had been busy gathering materials to refute these specific charges and to discredit the other accusers.

Rebecca's son and son-in-law, Samuel Nurse and John Tarbell respectively, told how, shortly after her arrest, they had questioned the Putnam women and found that Annie had not been at all sure of the specter's identity until either her mother or the maid named it and how then Ann Putnam and Mercy Lewis each said that the *other* had first made the identification. At the very least this showed uncertainty.

Potter James Kettle recalled a Sabbath in May when he visited Dr. Griggs's house and spoke with Elizabeth Hubbard. "I found her to speack severall untruthes in denying the sabath day and saying she had nat ben to meting that day but had onely bean up to James houlltons. this I can testifie to if called." However, Kettle had also deposed that when he had been at Dr. Griggs's house on May 10 he had witnessed Elizabeth "in severall Fitts," during which "she Cried & held her apron before her face saying that she would not se them"—"Them" being Kettle's two dead children, according to Elizabeth, killed by Sarah Bishop—"& they were by her description much as they were when they ware put in to there Coffins to be buried." The bereaved father must have had second thoughts about Elizabeth's trustworthiness.

Similarly, Joseph Hutchinson of Salem Village described how, when Abigail Williams told him about an encounter with the Devil, "I asked her if shee wos not afraid to see the devell." She replied that at first she had been afraid and had tried to flee, "but now shee wos not afraid but Could talke with him as well as shee Could with mee." To him, this attitude implied too great a familiarity with the Fiend.

William and Rachel Bradford along with William Rayment Jr. submitted a statement about Mercy Lewis's lack of honesty, which may have been intended to defend Rebecca Nurse. Unfortunately, today the paper is badly torn.

Robert Moulton Sr. wrote that while watching the ailing Susanna Sheldon he heard her contradict her own claims about spectral goings-on. He signed his statement, witnessed by Samuel Nurse and Joseph Trumball.

If Susanna Sheldon was the same person as the accuser whose name was written as Joanna Childen, her account of Goodman Harwood's ghost claiming Rebecca Nurse had killed him was *not* used in court.

As none of the papers in favor of Rebecca Nurse were sworn, they do not indicate how or even if the court considered them. Testimony against her came from the afflicted, people who verified the actions and words of the afflicted, as well as neighbor Sarah Holton, who was convinced that Rebecca had had something to do with her husband Benjamin's illness and death after a particularly bitter argument with Rebecca over Holton pigs damaging Nurse crops.

Nathaniel and Hannah Ingersoll said that although Benjamin Holton "died a most violent death" from "fittes like to our poor bewicthed parsons," at the time "we hade no suspition of wicthcraft. amongst us." Even though Thomas Putnam wrote the statement for them, the words offer some ambiguity as to cause of death.

John Putnam Jr. and his wife, Hannah, definitely blamed Rebecca for the "cruell and violent death" of their infant back in April. However, John Putnam Sr. and Rebecca Putnam, testified that although their daughter Rebecca Shepard and son-in-law John Fuller had died "a most violent death . . . wee did Judg then that thay both diead of a malignant fever and had no suspition of wichcraft of aney nether Can wee acues the prisner at the bar of aney such thing."

Francis Nurse had persuaded Thomas Putnam's uncle Nathaniel Putnam Sr. to testify on Rebecca's behalf. Although the document is torn, Nathaniel was clear that "what i have observed of her human frailtys excepted; her life & conversation hath been according to her proffession [of Christainity] & she hath brought up a great family of children & educated them well . . . i have known her differ with her neighbors but i never knew nor heard of any that did accuse of what she is now charged with."

Not all of the testimony was written down, and some of the statements against Rebecca lay in the "confessions" of those who had succumbed to pressure and incriminated themselves, describing Rebecca among their fellow witches.

Facing judges and jurors, Rebecca Nurse pleaded not guilty. Her hearing, however, was not strong. She had heard or heard about the accusations before. She knew that certain neighbors had spoken for her and that many had signed the petition attesting to her good Christian behavior. She could see the afflicted writhing and contorting even when the words reaching her were muffled. She stood at the bar, exposed and tired as people came and went—clerks, officers, witnesses for and against her.

Though she did not notice, from the audience her daughter-in-law Sarah glimpsed the Bibber woman palm some pins from her clothing and then clutch her own knee and cry out that Rebecca's specter had stuck her.

Another group entered the chamber under guard—fellow suspect Deliverance Hobbs and her stepdaughter Abigail Hobbs, that strange girl who ran about the woods at all hours. Why were the guards bringing in other prisoners?

"What?" asked Rebecca. "[D]o these persons give in Evidence against me now?" She asked, stating they "were of our Company."

But the Hobbs women spoke, going on, as far as Rebecca could hear, about the great witch meeting.

The jury withdrew and waiting began. Eventually the men returned to the courtroom, and Foreman Thomas Fisk stood to deliver the verdict. *Not* guilty, he said, and as Rebecca's kindred felt the exhilarating relief at that good news, all of the afflicted in the courtroom shrieked, the startling noise soon followed by more screams from the other afflicted witnesses outside, with the "hideous out-cry" amazing not only the audience but the court officers as well.

So even though she was declared not guilty, Rebecca was not dismissed. Court recessed, with the justices, exiting, in conversation. Clearly many interpreted the painful reaction of the afflicted to have been spectrally induced, however self-defeating it would have been for Rebecca to take such revenge on her accusers at such a time. Then again, it may have been supposed, the devils she allegedly dealt with had their own agenda and had not released their hold on the woman.

Some of the judges thought they might indict Goody Nurse on this latest evidence of torture.

When court resumed, Chief Justice Stoughton informed the jury that although he would not try to "impose" upon them, they might consider the defendant's comment about one of the Hobbs women— a self-confessed witch—as "one of us." The jury, confused and in doubt after the hair-raising shrieks, asked if they might reconsider the verdict. Stoughton agreed, and the jury withdrew again—and again the courtroom waited, tense with apprehension and dread. Rebecca and her family prayed that the jury would be sensible, the afflicted wondered if they would be charged as liars or as tools of the devils, and Thomas and Ann Putnam were aghast that the court might release a witch to rove among them (and Thomas was concerned for his own credibility in the matter).

The jury filed back into the room. Rebecca, standing again at the bar, must have been exhausted physically and emotionally. The foreman said something. So much talk, so many words—they buzzed in her weary ears like so many flies with only a few clear snatches. He said something else, then the jury retreated again. After a time they returned, and Fisk stepped forward. Guilty, he said, guilty of witchcraft. The justices said something, and the guards led her away, back to the jail.

Later, when her family was able to speak with her, they asked why, *why* had she not explained what she had meant when she had the chance, to explain that when she called the Hobbs woman "one of us" she meant one of us *prisoners*. The jury had already found her innocent. And Rebecca realized she had not heard the question, had not known she was offered a chance at life and freedom and thus had thrown away that chance.

But Rebecca's family did not give up. Her daughter-in-law Sarah Nurse had someone write out her description of what one of the afflicted—Sarah Bibber, that turbulent gossip, a grown and married woman—had done during Rebecca's trial:

the testimony of Sarah Nurs aged 28 years or there abouts who testifieth and saith that being in the Court this 29 of June 1692 I sawe goodwife bibber pull out pins out of her Close and held them betwene her fingers and Claspt her hands round her knese and then she Cryed out and said goody Nurs prict her this I can testifie if Calld as witnes my mark

Sarah signed with a rough, S-shaped mark, and the family added the document to a growing sheaf of papers in their mother's favor.

Tituba paces the end of the prison yard by the high fence, feeling a slight breeze from the North River, one of the few advantages of cooperation. The other confessors had such privileges but kept to themselves in little family knots. The summer was growing hotter, and the shaded side of the jail offers small relief. She paces to stay moving and wishes she had something specific to do. Enforced idleness lost its charm after a time, even for such as herself, so long forced to work for others.

Shouts from the street catch her attention. The front gate creaks open, and a bristle of guards escorts Sarah Good back inside the fence. She has been tried, and there is no need to ask about the verdict—the woman looks more furious than usual.

"You!" she shouts, catching sight of Tituba watching. Good struggles against the guard who is trying to steer her toward the jail door. "See what you started?" Sarah rails. "They're taking evidence against you too. Don't think you're safe just because you confessed." The guards finally push her inside, and whatever else she is saying is lost, muffled by the walls.

The other prisoners in the yard stare at Tituba, who wonders again what would be happening now if she had held out against all those questions last March. But denying the charge had not helped Sarah Good, so perhaps nothing would be different for her. She walks away from the others, trying to get some distance between them without beating a retreat. The day drags on with occasional seabirds gliding overhead and the sounds of passersby through the fence.

After more time the gate swings open again and another group enters. Rebecca Nurse this time, also returning from her trial. This older woman does not shout and struggle. She looks exhausted and stunned—a far different appearance, though the verdict must have been the same as Good's.

Out in the lane the woman's family calls to her, offering hope, assuring her that they have not given up yet. One of them sees Tituba and frowns, the confession once again remembered.

Tituba mulls over Sarah Good's news—testimony against her—they still remember that. *Eventually, when the rest are dealt with, the confessors will be tried, and then what? When she is no longer potentially useful,* then *what? She does not like to imagine what will happen.*

A deputy rounds up the prisoners in the yard and herds them back inside the jail. She hears Sarah Good's voice from another room: "One child dead and the other left behind—alone in that prison with witches and pirates, burglars and baby killers." The fierce shout rises to a sob: "Dorothy!" Sarah cries before a guard's voice tells her to shut her mouth.

Tituba has heard that despairing tone before, of a mother calling for her child.

"Dorothy, what will become of you?"

Tituba shivers. What *will* become of such a young child? What will happen to any of us here?

July 1 to 18, 1692

Still shackled, Rebecca Nurse shuffles into the Salem meeting house and pauses, blinking, just inside the door to let her eyes adjust to the dusky interior after the brightness of the midday street. Faces turn to stare at her, as people shift on the benches and in the pews while bolder youths lean over the rails of the galleries above. The familiar high space rises above her to the beams under the ribs of the roof lost in shadows.

As a girl in Yarmouth she had seen a seat in the grand stone church there made from the skull and vertebrae of a whale that had washed up on a nearby shore, a trophy from the sea. To sit in it was to pretend to be Jonah swallowed by the whale. Now, in this distant rustic land, she feels swallowed indeed, consumed by events. Yet she must still trust in God. She knows her own innocence. This fight is not over, Francis and their children have told her. They have names and documents. They will go to the governor himself if they have to and make *him believe the truth. There is still hope, they say.*

The guards urge her forward down the center aisle toward the pulpit. It is Sacrament Sabbath, but the bread and wine will not be offered to her even though she has been a communing member of this church for two decades. So many Sundays she has shared the Lord's Supper here, joining the other full members reaching in a line of the faithful that goes all the way back to the Apostles in a chain of fellowship that honors Christ and his great sacrifice.

But not today.

Not for her.

She has been told the vote was unanimous. The elders had formally asked the voting members—the men—if she ought to be excluded from the Sacrament of the Lord's Supper, from communion—excommuni-

cated. As the civil court had so recently considered her case and found her guilty of witchcraft, of joining the Devil's forces against the Lord's people, then her partaking of the Sacrament would be hypocrisy at best—a sacrilegious lie. People had testified that they saw her not only distributing Satan's sacrament but partaking of it also.

Now here she stands, guards gripping her frail arms to keep her upright, to prevent her escape—as though she could suddenly bolt and run— brought to hear the church's decision pronounced to her face. The younger minister, Reverend Nicholas Noyes, a stout amiable gentleman—but not amiable now—stands ready to deliver the judgment. Today he is all seriousness, as he has been at the hearings and trials. He begins to speak, but most of the words buzz past Rebecca's fading hearing. He recounts her supposed sins, the crimes the court thinks it has proven against her.

The Lord knows my heart, *she thinks.* I know I am not perfect. I have let my temper flare from my control. I have not done everything I might have done and ought to have done. But I have not done *that.* I have not willingly joined the Devil's troop.

Mr. Noyes lists detail after detail, with only the occasional phrase making its way to her hearing.

"For these and many other foul and sinful transgressions . . . pronounce you to be a leprous and unclean person . . . cast you out and cut you off from the enjoyment of all those blessed privileges and ordinances . . . which you have so long abused . . . deprive you of them . . . that you may learn better to prize them by the want of them."

Rebecca's legs ache from standing.

"And for the greater terror and amazing of you," Noyes continues, "deliver you up to Satan . . . you who would not be guided by the council of God . . . for the humbling of your soul, that your spirit may be saved in the day of the Lord Jesus, if it be His blessed will."

No, *she thinks.* I at least tried to follow God's councils.

"As an unclean beast and unfit for the society of God's people . . . pronounce you an excommunicated person from God and His People." At last he finishes talking, and one of the elders steps forward.

She catches some of his words: " . . . depart the congregation as one deprived worthily of all the holy things of God."

At which the guards nudge her to turn and walk back down the aisle and out the door into the glaring daylight as Reverend Noyes leads the congregation in a blessing on the Sacrament that he and the rest of the members will soon share.

Although this deprivation of the Sacrament was the most severe punishment the churches could impose upon an errant member, many who were so cast out—for lying, infidelity, and the like—were later reinstated if they showed sufficient change of heart and habit. But for Rebecca, facing death by hanging if her family could not obtain a reprieve, there would be no such future redemption.

Mary Warren, meanwhile, continued among the afflicted. Day after day she witnessed against suspects and writhed and shrieked in pain when the specters appeared (or seemed to appear). If she doubted her visions now, then she no longer dared to mention it. Perhaps she had come to believe that the afflictions were real—at least some of the time. Consciously or unconsciously she responded to suggestions—other people's suspicions, general gossip, the movements of the accused.

Mary testified with the others on July 2, when Ann Pudeator faced them a second time. This record for this case is spotty. Goody Pudeator had been sent to Boston's jail back in May, but she may have been set free like Abbott, for here she was again—back in Salem, arrested anew, and brought to Beadle's tavern.

There Sarah Churchill, who, like Mary Warren, no longer tried to recant, accused Pudeator of trying to recruit Sarah by offering her the Devil's book to sign. More damning, however—and the possible catalyst for her second arrest—was the death of her neighbor Goodwife Mary Neal (ironically a distant relative of Rebecca Nurse). Jeremiah Neal told how his late wife grew more ill after the defendant, this "ill-carriaged woman," borrowed the mortar they used to mix medicines. Regardless of all the woman's pretensions of neighborly concern, his wife had weakened and died. The many jars of who-knew-what the constable had seen when he fetched Pudeator from her home seemed suspicious. Her answers did not impress the court, and soon enough some of the afflicted began convulsing. Although Annie Putnam, like Sarah Bibber, said she had never seen the woman before that day, she too convulsed until the court, over Pudeator's protests, ordered the suspect to touch the wrists of the afflicted to free them from their seizures. Her touch only temporarily relieved Mary Warren, who continued to be wracked by shuddering seizures.

Mary was present for the questioning of Mrs. Mary Bradbury as well that day, for the old woman had been brought down to the court from Salisbury.

Annie blamed the woman for her family's losses, repeating her father's complaints: "[Mrs] Bradbery or hir Apperance tould me that it was she that made my ffathers sheep to run away till they ware all lost and that she had kiled my ffathers cowe and also kiled that horse he took such delight in."

The suspect's specter assaulted both Mary Warren and Annie, and both said they saw the ghostly form of Annie's dead uncle John Carr drift into the courtroom and heard it accuse Mrs. Bradbury of murdering him. Before the day was out, the specter of a slave woman named Candy tormented Mary and Annie as well.

Back on Friday, July 1—before Rebecca Nurse's excommunication, while her family continued to gather more potentially life-saving documents, and the day the grand jury considered the case of Martha Carrier—two new specters beset Annie Putnam, Mary Warren, and Mary Walcott. Consequently, Thomas Putnam and John Putnam Jr. entered a complaint against "Margret Hawkes Late of Barbados now of Salem and her Negro Woman" before Clerk of the Court Stephen Sewall.

On Monday, July 4, Mistress Hawkes and her slave woman Candy faced not only the magistrates and the three victims listed in the complaint but also Deliverance and Abigail Hobbs.

The identity of these suspects is uncertain. They had evidently not been in Massachusetts for long, but they had been there long enough that Candy could tell what the locals *thought* was happening. She confessed in short order.

"Candy no witch in her country. Candy's mother no witch. Candy no witch, Barbados. This country, mistress give Candy witch."

"Did your mistress make you a witch in this country?" asked one of the magistrates.

"Yes. In this country, mistress give Candy witch." Her mistress, she went on, brought her pen and ink and had her make a mark in a book. *That* action made her a witch.

Magistrates Gedney and Hathorne wanted to know *how* Candy tormented her victims. When she volunteered to show them, they allowed her to go, with a guard, to fetch her poppets from her lodging.

She returned with a handful of odds and ends—rags, grass, a lump of cheese, a knotted handkerchief. Poppets had been described before but not produced in court, and seeing actual poppets sent Mary Warren and the Hobbs women into convulsions. They said they saw the Devil helping Candy and Mrs. Hawkes pinch the rags to cause them pain.

The magistrates decided to experiment on the poppets to see if the objects themselves held a sort of magic or if the suspects were directing the effects. They ordered Candy to untie the knots, but that had no effect and offered no relief to the afflicted. Then they ordered Candy to eat the blade of grass, but again, nothing. The magistrates, forgetting they ought not have anything to do with magic, took the rags into their own hands and burnt one of them. The afflicted shrieked and writhed as if on fire. Unnerved, the magistrates doused the rags in water. Two women—not identified but perhaps the Hobbs—gasped and strangled as if drowning. A third—perhaps Mary Warren—bolted from the building and, with guards trailing behind her, ran headlong for the river.

Rattled by it all, Mrs. Hawkes confessed to witchcraft as well. Both she and her slave were held for trial.

Burdened by the presence of the child growing within her and oppressed by the increasing heat of summer, Mistress Ann Putnam had the satisfaction of knowing that at least *one* of the witches would soon no longer be a problem. The near acquittal of Goody Nurse must have unsettled her as much as it had frightened the afflicted witnesses, but the justices had, as the Putnams saw it, corrected that error. Not that Rebecca's family seemed to accept the verdict, as definite as it now appeared to be.

While Annie and the others continued to speak out against the suspects and endure their torments, Ann had the additional pleasure of
knowing that her family's long-time adversary Mary Bradbury was
also under arrest. The woman could protest and claim innocence, but
Annie and the Warren girl had reported the ghost of Ann's own dead
brother—John Carr, draped in a winding sheet, up from his restless
grave to name his murderer—appearing in the courtroom. The next
day Rebecca Nurse's excommunication followed. Ann would think this
was most appropriate for one who had lied all these years about her
devotion to good and her reverence for God, as Ann believed, yet all
the while plotted to bring it down, to let the Devil's rule prevail even
here in New England, the new Zion. Although Ann, as she saw it, felt
other witches still prowled and persecuted the innocent, she could feel
some comfort in the thought that the Nurse harpy would be soon
turned off, unable to hurt any more of them. Her child would surely
be born when the world was safer. Surely the Putnams would prevail.

But Rebecca Nurse's family saw the matter *very* differently. Knowing their mother's innocence and still trusting in the power of reason,
they increased their efforts to save her. Francis Nurse already had a
petition from three dozen neighbors that attested to Rebecca's good
character:

> We have knowne her for many years and Acording to our observation
> her Life and conversation was Acording to hur profession [of being a
> Christian] and we never had Any cause or grounds to suspect her of
> Any such thing as she is nowe Acused of.

True, one of the thirty-six signers was Daniel Andrews, now a fugitive from a witchcraft charge. The family may not have risked using
this petition before, or they may have hoped any one name might be
overlooked. Perhaps the governor would not notice that detail.

Now on Monday, July 4, the day after Rebecca's excommunication,
while the local magistrates dealt with the unruly examinations of Mrs.
Hawkes and Candy, the Nurse family collected statements and copies
of court papers to support their case with an emphasis on clarifying
the association of Rebecca with the Hobbs woman as "one of us."

Clerk of the Court of Oyer and Terminer Stephen Sewall provided a sheaf of twenty copies and penned this comment on the sheet containing Rebecca's indictment for tormenting Annie Putnam:

In this Tryall are Twenty papers besides this Judgment & these were in this Tryall as well as other Tryalls of the Same Nature Severall Evidences viva voce which were not written & so I can give no Copies of them Some for & Some against the parties Some of the Confessors did alsoe Mention this & other persons in their Severall declaracions which being promised & Considered the sd 20 papers herewith fild is the whole Tryall attest Steph Sewall Clerk

　　Copy of the above wrote on the Judgmt wch I Gave out to the Nurses

Francis then approached Thomas Fisk, the jury foreman for Rebecca's trial, for a statement:

I Thomas Fisk, the Subscriber hereof, being one of them that were of the Jury the last week at Salem-Court, upon the Tryal of Rebecka Nurse, &c. being desired by some of the Relations to give a Reason why the Jury brought her in Guilty, after her Verdict not Guilty; I do hereby give my Reasons to be as follows, viz.

　　When the Verdict not Guilty was, the honoured Court was pleased to object against it, saying to them, that they think they let slip the words, which the Prisoner at the Bar spake against her self, which were spoken in reply to Goodwife Hobbs and her Daughter, who had been faulty in setting their hands to the Devils Book, as they have confessed formerly; the words were "What do these persons give in Evidence against me now, they used to come among us." After the honoured Court had manifested their dissatisfaction of the Verdict, several of the Jury declared themselves desirous to go out again, and thereupon the honoured Court gave leave; but when we came to consider of the Case, I could not tell how to take her words, as an Evidence against her, till she had a further opportunity to put her Sense upon them, if she would take it; and then going into Court, I mentioned the words aforesaid, which by one of the Court were affirmed to have been spoken by her, she being then at the Bar, but made no reply, nor interpretation of them; whereupon these words were to me a principal Evidence against her.

Thomas Fisk

Rebecca herself dictated a statement to clear up the misunderstanding:

These presents do humbly shew, to the honoured Court and Jury, that I being informed, that the Jury brought me in Guilty, upon my saying that Goodwife Hobbs and her Daughter were of our Company; but I intended no otherways, then as they were Prisoners with us, and therefore did then, and yet do judge them not legal Evidence against their fellow Prisoners. And I being something hard of hearing, and full of grief, none informing me how the Court took up my words, and therefore had not opportunity to declare what I intended, when I said they were of our Company.

Rebecka Nurse.

The packet probably also included the statement from two of Rebecca's daughters, Rebecca Preston and Mary Tarbell, offering to testify about the supposed witch-mark. This impressive collection of all the testimonials in Rebecca's favor, the petition, the juror's explanation that matched Rebecca's own—surely the governor would see reason.

As Rebecca's statement was dated July 4, the family must have taken the papers to Boston soon afterward. The legislature recessed on July 5 until October, but Phips was still in town to meet with his Council of Assistants (which included John Hathorne and Jonathan Corwin, who were also justices of the Court of Oyer and Terminer). Fortunately Phips had not yet returned to the frontier to oversee defenses. There was no point in approaching the lieutenant governor, William Stoughton, the rigid chief justice on the court that had found Rebecca guilty and, therefore, was unlikely to change his mind. July 6 was Harvard's commencement, a day when everyone and his uncle seemed to crowd into Cambridge for the ceremonies and festivities. On July 7 Phips commissioned Anthony Checkley as the new King's attorney to replace Thomas Newton, now secretary of New Hampshire. (Newton's leaving appears to be for professional advancement rather than for any disagreement with the court's method of dealing with spectral evidence.) Then, on July 8, Phips announced that he would soon return to Maine.

So the Nurse kin, led by Francis, presented their petition and paperwork on Rebecca's behalf for the governor to consider during the first week of July before his return to the frontier war.

William Phips had grown up at the edge of English settlement in Maine, apprenticed as a ship carpenter, progressed to owning and captaining his own trading vessels, and, full of ambition, moved to Boston, where he married another Maine native, Mary Spencer, who, some hinted, taught him to read. Phips gambled on a sunken treasure expedition that failed, narrowly escaped mutiny from his piratical crew, got backing from King Charles II himself, failed once more, started a third expedition backed by various London merchants, and then finally succeeded beyond expectation. London balladeers made songs about his triumph, and the new king, James II (whose treasury was enriched by the crown's share of the recovered treasure) knighted the New Englander. Now *Sir* William Phips, he was nevertheless more at home among seafaring men and soldiers than he was with politicians. His working relationship with William Stoughton was decidedly uneasy.

The preponderance of favorable documents along with whatever they were able to say in person to Phips at last convinced the governor that the second verdict *was* based on faulty information. Phips issued a reprieve, and the Nurse family, enormously relieved after months of worry and days of desperation, returned home from Boston in triumph.

But as soon as this reversal was known—or at the moment Phips signed the order, as the afflicted later claimed—the interested parties panicked. Certainly, the startling news threatened Ann and Annie Putnam, as their testimony had branded Rebecca as their great enemy. Fear of a freed witch returning to exact revenge and that their own testimony was now in doubt must have terrified them. As the accused so well knew, not being believed held deadly consequences. Even if they were fully convinced, as they may have been, that what they said was true, a warning voice in the back of the head must have sounded. Repercussions that could befall them—from neighbors; from the courts; from God Himself, who despised liars, considering them heirs of the Devil, Prince of Lies. To them the Nurse woman *had* to be guilty; the Putnams' fears *had* to be real and based on reality.

All of the afflicted witnesses fell into seizures severe enough that "some Salem Gentlemen" hastened to Phips and persuaded him to rescind the order.

It took most of a day to reach Boston. Who were those unnamed "Salem Gentlemen?" Thomas Putnam and his supporters seem likely candidates as do the local magistrates sitting on the Court of Oyer and Terminer who had ordered the second session after the original guilty verdict. As representatives for Salem in the General Court, Hathorne and Corwin would be in Boston. As Assistants, they would have the governor's ear. Perhaps Thomas Putnam—if it were he—contacted them once he hastened to Boston, and they arranged an interview with Governor Phips, no doubt letting him know their strong views on what was occurring.

Did Rebecca ever go free? Even for a short time to see her loved ones in her own home? Or did the second order arrive so quickly that it dashed all hope of that before the jailer could release her? So close, so close—and still that door slammed shut.

On Tuesday, July 12, Stoughton signed another death warrant:

To George Corwine Gent. High Sheriff of the County of Essex Greeting

Whereas Sarah Good Wife of William Good of Salem Villiage Rebecka Nurse wife of Francis Nurse of Salem Villiage Susanna Martin of Amesbury Widow Elizabeth How wife of James How of Ipswich Sarah Wild Wife of John Wild of Topsfield all of the County of Essex in thier Majesties' Province of the Massachusets Bay in New England Att A Court of Oyer & Terminer held . . . On the 29th day of June last were Severaly Arraigned On Severall Indictments for the horrible Crime of Witchcraft by them practised & Comitted On Severall persons . . . they were Each of them found & brought in Guilty by the

Jury that passed On them according to thier respective Indictments
and Sentence of death did then pass upon them as the Law directs . . .

[Sheriff George Corwin was therefore commanded] in thier
Majesties' Names . . . upon Tuesday Next being the 19th day of . . . July
between the houres of Eight & twelve in the forenoon the Same day
you Safely conduct the sd Sarah Good Rebecka Nurse Susanna Martin
Elizabeth How & Sarah Wild from thier Majesties' Goal in Salem
aforesd to the place of Execucion & There Cause them & Every of them
to be hanged by the Necks untill they be dead . . . Given under my hand
& Seale at Boston the 12th day of July in the fourth yeare of the Reign
of Our Soveraign Lord & Lady Wm & Mary King & Queen &c

Anno Dom. 1692 Wm Stoughton

Learning that the death warrant had been formally issued would
have eased only some of Ann Putnam's anxieties, for the plague of
witches had now spread to Andover. The conspiracy was growing, despite her family's valiant efforts.

A rider leading another horse arrived in Ann's dooryard one day
around this time to respectfully ask Mr. Putnam whether he would allow his daughter to use her spectral sight to reveal who tormented the
wife of his master, Joseph Ballard, a constable in Andover. Might the
girls do for Andover what they had done at Will's Hill?

So Annie and Mercy Lewis rode off to Andover. They later returned to recount how tortured the feverish Goodwife Elizabeth Ballard was and who she said she saw lurking at her bedside.

The girls saw specters too: of elderly Ann Foster, her daughter and
granddaughter, as well as Mary Bradbury, whose material body was
locked in Salem jail. The latter was no surprise to Ann or most of her
Carr relatives; Bradbury's specter had been going after Timothy Swan
in Andover for some weeks already along with specters of old Ann
Foster and her kin.

On this spectral evidence and for Goody Ballard's sake, Ann Foster
was under arrest and in Salem Village for questioning by Friday, July 15.

For this session local justice John Higginson Jr. joined Gedney,
Hathorne, and Corwin on the bench. Higginson, son and namesake

of Salem's senior minister, was also brother to Ann Dolliver, who was currently jailed on suspicion of witchcraft. If any suspects hoped that Higginson's presence would change the other justices' minds, they would be disappointed.

Elizabeth Hubbard and Mary Walcott were especially tortured during this hearing, and Goody Foster confessed, verifying the accusers' fears to the court. The old woman described how the Devil had come to her six months earlier as a strange, big-eyed bird that "came white & vanished away black." It promised prosperity, which the Devil never delivered, and she had had the gift "of striking the aflicted downe wth her eye ever since." But it was Martha Carrier who persuaded her to hurt *these* afflicted people.

Over the next few days she claimed her devilish service was six years, then two—but still blamed Goody Carrier. The witches' purpose in afflicting the Village folk was part of their plan "to set up the Divills Kingdome," she said, and then signed her confession with a mark. Her story kept changing, but because she did not try to deny her confession, the magistrates believed her.

But her confession did not prevent her relatives' specters from assaulting the languishing Goody Ballard as well as Timothy Swan. Swan, from a large, raucous family farming in Haverhill across the Merrimack from Andover, was found guilty of siring Elizabeth Emerson's first child, the infant she said was the result of rape, though the court did not believe that part of the story. This was the same Elizabeth Emerson presently in Boston prison awaiting execution for the infanticide of the twins she bore a few years later.

Francis Nurse has not attended Sabbath services in Salem Village for months now. Not only was the twitching of the afflicted distracting, but their yelping also drowned out the prayers and sermons—which may have been a blessing, because, when they did shut up, Reverend Parris was bound to be gabbling claptrap that made the suspects seem guilty of witchcraft. Even Rebecca. Even my *Rebecca, he thinks.*

All that and those furtive sidelong glances from his neighbors when they thought he didn't notice—it was only a matter of time before all the

Nurses are accused. It is simpler to keep heading north to Topsfield come Sunday. Then they can be with their kin, the families of Rebecca's accused imprisoned sisters. And Topsfield's minister, Reverend Capen, was willing to believe the accusations might be mistaken.

That man still has his wits about him.

Francis is profoundly tired but cannot sleep.

If he sleeps, then he dreams, and he has woken too many times as he reaches across the bed and finds . . . emptiness. Rebecca has been imprisoned for months, and yet encountering her palpable absence still frightens him. All those petitioners, all those papers, all the trips to Boston—and still this emptiness gnaws at him. Sometimes he feels as though his heart has been ripped out.

And then he thinks, As God sees fit.

The rest of the diminished household are quiet behind their bedcurtains, but Francis needs air even if it is night. He steps outside the front door and away from the quiet house into the sweltering night.

There—over the fields he and his sons have worked so long to own and cultivate—rising in the constellation of Aquarius floats the full moon. Capped by an icy white crescent, most of it is shadowed by a rust color, like dried blood, nearly eclipsed.

Francis sees this with a farmer's eye.

This cosmic "miracle" is not unexpected, having been forecast in the year's almanac. When he first read about it the previous winter it seemed a wonder. Now, it seems an omen—even if it is natural. He watches the moon in the vast stillness. He listens to the dry rustle of his corn—the fields need rain but no rain falls—and the shrill song of night insects.

He turns back into the house and locks the door.

A little light flickers from the hearth. He finds the Bible box and reaches in for Tully's Almanac. *Leaning close to the hearth's embers, he finds the pages for July 17 and on eclipses.*

Considering its placement in the sky, this total eclipse of the moon "may presage the Death of Aged persons, as well as persons of Quality."

Or presage the deaths of God's own saints, *he thinks.*

He grips the almanac. On Tuesday next his wife of forty-four years will hang.

July 19 to 31, 1692

Ann and Thomas Putnam wait by the roadside west of Salem's Town Bridge for the procession to arrive. She holds her husband's arm. Annie and the servant Mercy, quiet and composed—for now at least—sit on the grass in the shade of the wagon. A few other families from the Village have gathered at the base of the hill. Where is the sense in going all the way into town—events will come to them.

Except for the occasional burst of nervous laughter, conversations are subdued. Ann can hear the ripping sound as their horse tears at the grass and weeds within his reach. Some of the other men greet Tom, hailing him respectfully—as they ought, considering all the work he has done for the community and how many of their lazy carcasses he has employed.

Workmen near the base of the hill bend under the already hot sun and dig. The sharp shush *of their iron spades cut the shallow earth and make muffled thuds when a blade hits rock. Bedrock lies close under the surface of this hill and shoulders out of the dry grass. The men must dig a larger grave for this execution than they did for Bridget Bishop, now half forgotten. The diggers sweat, but imbibing at the tavern seems hours distant.*

Today five will hang.

The oppressive day grows hotter. The hangman, pipe clenched in his teeth and a line of smoke trailing him, arrives with his ropes and sets about arranging them on the gallows.

Eventually, from the distance, Ann and the rest of those waiting hear a crowd approaching from town. The diggers hurry to finish their work.

On the far side of the tidal inlet a churning clot of people on foot and on horseback heaves into view as it follows a cart near the head of the procession. The crowd's murmur increases as the parade advances down the slope until the mass of people and horses narrows to cross the causeway and clump across the bridge. For a solemn occasion the crowd nevertheless sounds nearly festive at the prospect of what will happen. The workmen scramble from the completed grave and drift aside, as there is no profit in being recognized. The sheriff and his men urge their mounts up the steep turn-off from road to rocky pasture, and the cart's wheels screech on the sharp slope. This official part of the procession arranges itself along the level ground as the followers vie for a view of the gallows. The crowd seems more edgy, the officers more wary, than they had been at the Bishop hanging, for a rumor is circulating throughout the region that the Devil himself will attempt to rescue his own.

Thomas lifts Ann down from the wagon and they walk up the slope to find a vantage point. Annie and the maid move off to stand with the other afflicted witnesses, as is their right. The prisoners' cart lurches toward the gallows, and there, among the other condemned Ann sees the Nurse woman, that self-righteous hag, brought to earthly justice at last, though not yet before the final judgment of God.

Rebecca Nurse, Ann's idea of a supposedly powerful sorceress, droops against the side of the cart. She prays silently, as she has been praying through much of the restless night past. Not far from the more eager folk, her family stands grimly with the kindred of the other women to be hanged: Susannah Martin, Sarah Good, Sarah Wildes, and Elizabeth How.

The deputies support the shackled women, stiff from the jolting ride, down from the cart. Rebecca looks around to see where her children are— to look once more on Francis. She picks them out at the margin of the seething mass and thinks she recognizes some of How's family as well.

Does Sarah Good have anyone here? *she wonders.* And what will happen to young Dorothy, discarded in Boston jail? That father of hers seems of no more help to the child than he's been to his wife.

The sheriff reads out the warrant for the execution of the five. A minister or two step forward to offer prayers, for hope that these souls of the condemned be not utterly lost. The soon-to-be executed make their own defiant statements, praying that God will reveal their innocence.

Some listeners snort in derision.

The long confinement and blistering summer heat have weakened nRebecca. Nevertheless, when it is her turn, she is resolved to face the

Almighty with a clear conscience. This means dying in a spirit of Christian charity, offering forgiveness toward one's enemies rather than exiting this life in a fury of resentment. Her voice falters, but she is equally determined to speak the truth about herself and prays that God will prove to these people that she has never *allied herself to Satan.*

Reverend Noyes begins talking again. Rebecca hears only some of his words as he raises his voice to urge Sarah Good to confess for the good of her soul.

Exasperated at Good's stubborn refusal, Noyes declares, "You are a witch. You know *you are a witch."*

Good cuts off whatever he might say next. "You are a liar!" she shouts. "I am no more a witch than you are a wizard."

The onlookers gasp. Someone titters at such futile boldness. "And if you take away my life, God will give you blood to drink!" She speaks loud enough that even Rebecca hears. The afflicted who are present hear it too and raise a commotion.

Ann Putnam is aghast at Sarah's impudence. She recognizes the Scriptural reference of God's vengeance from the Book of Revelation: *"For they shed the blood of the saints, and prophets, and therefore hast thou given them blood to drink." She knows Reverend Noyes also recognizes the verse, for he makes* Revelation *the subject of much scholarly study and many sermons. Saints and prophets, indeed!*

But the defiance of the damned changes nothing.

The executions proceed: Good and Martin are proud and resisting, Nurse, Wildes, and How submit with humble dignity. The relatives witness it all as if memorizing the deed, storing the details like ammunition for future confrontations. The afflicted utter cries of relief as, one after another, each hooded body swings free from the ladder and the crowd mutters their reaction.

The Putnam kin present feel relief at each death—one less threat, one less rival. And they note, with satisfaction, that the Devil did not arrive to save any of Satan's handmaids. Bitch-witches, old George Jacobs had called his accusers, but now see who triumphs.

Finally—it is over.

The edge of the crowd frays and scatters.

The relatives linger. By custom the bodies must dangle where they are for a certain time as warnings, but the day is hot, and the now-empty mortal shells will need to be buried soon.

Mrs. Ann Putnam breathes deeply, but despite the heat, she leans against Thomas and wraps her shawl closer, a thin protection for herself and the child inside her.

Now Nurse's soul is safely locked in Hell, *Ann thinks.* At least she can't harm this child. *Ann has counted back the months and estimated that this baby was conceived when all this trouble began. Nor has it ended—five witches this time, the prisons full, yet more still free to pursue their wicked plans.*

What will become of my child?

Annie, who has been standing with the other afflicted, comes over to her parents. It is time to go home.

Francis and his family do not leave. They wait for the workmen to bring the bodies down from the gallows and bury them in the shallow grave dug earlier. Determined to give Rebecca a proper burial at least, they wait in stony silence to claim her body.

A strong family tradition would relate that Rebecca's family collected her body by night, disinterred it in some accounts, and brought it home. When historian and former Salem mayor Charles Upham recreated the scene in 1867, he speculated that they brought her body "tenderly in their arms along the silent roads and by-ways" to the Nurse farm. Other tellers have them carry the body to a small boat on the stream leading to the North River, row downstream under cover of darkness into the estuary and north to the mouth of Crane Brook, then work their way upstream to their own land. In both versions they buried Rebecca's body, but it would need to be washed first and then wrapped in a winding sheet. The farm, over the generations, maintained a small family burial ground across the fields to the west of the house and barn, not far from Crane Brook.

But would they need to do all this in secrecy?

Supposed witches and other felons were not barred from burial in consecrated ground, for Puritan burial grounds were not consecrated in the first place. Burying a felon by the place of execution was traditional in England and New England, but if families removed a body, then that was one less task for the county to pay for. The land route would have been the simpler, more direct method of bringing her broken body home.

Another part of the family lore was that Caleb Buffum helped remove the body. Buffum lived across the Town Bridge from the ledges, within sight of the hangings and was, moreover, related through marriage to Rebecca's aunts. In some versions he helped secret the body to a waiting boat or helped dig the body from the shallow common grave or even provided a coffin, for he was a carpenter as well as a farmer.

On the same day as the executions of the five women, Constable Joseph Ballard entered his formal complaint against Mary Lacey of Andover and her daughter Mary Jr. (daughter and granddaughter of confessor Goody Foster). They had tormented his wife Elizabeth Ballard, who had been "this Severall monthes Sorely aflicted & visited wth Strange pains and pressures & remains So to this day which I verily beleive is Occasioned by Witchcraft." He presented this in Salem to magistrates Bartholomew Gedney, John Hathorne, Jonathan Corwin, and John Higginson Jr., and this time he posted a bond of £100 to prove his intention to prosecute. (Such a bond was required by law, yet only one other witch complaint this year, entered before local Ipswich authorities, had so far included this detail. Either Ballard, as a constable, expected to post bond, or Higginson, as a new member of the magistrates, reminded the others of the requirement. The magistrates thereafter would apply this part of the law's requirements.) Hathorne signed for all.

The law arrested Goodwife Mary Lacey of Andover—old Goody Foster's daughter—for tormenting Goodwife Ballard and brought her, but not her daughter, to Salem for questioning by Gedney, Hathorne, Corwin, and Higginson. Mercy Lewis and Elizabeth Hubbard were especially tormented during this hearing, and soon enough Mary Lacey too confessed to attending the great witch meeting in the Village. However, she said that although her mother, who had already confessed, also attended, she was not a part of it. Her mother only "stood at a distance off and did not partake at that meeting" of the Devil's sacrament.

Hathorne then issued the arrest warrant for Mary Lacey Jr. for tormenting Goodwife Ballard, again signing for the other three. He added a note to the arresting officer: "You are likewise required to Search diligently in the house & aboute it for popetts &c."

Abundant, if disordered, notes for the daughter's questioning, which began the following day, survive. Mary Warren was definitely among the afflicted witnesses on July 21, when all three generations faced the magistrates. Ann Foster had already confessed to placing her mark in the Devil's book and, perhaps unaware of her daughter's earlier assertion, today described the great witch meeting in Salem Village while trying not to implicate her daughter, much like the way Mary Lacey had tried to direct the court's attention away from her mother Goody Foster. However, both had separately confessed.

"Oh, Mother! We have forsaken Jesus Christ," Goody Lacey wailed. "And the devil hath got hold of us. How shall we get cleare of this evil one?"

When Goody Foster murmured something to herself, the afflicted said she was talking with the Devil.

"I was praying to the Lord," she protested.

"What Lord?" asked a magistrate.

"To God."

"What God do witches pray to?"

"I cannot tell, the Lord help me."

The two older women were taken from the room, and the granddaughter was brought in. As far as the four magistrates could see, Mary Lacey Jr.'s presence alone was enough to trigger violent seizures in Mary Warren.

"How dare you come in here, and bring the Devil with you, to afflict these poor creatures?" one of them scolded.

"I know nothing of it," the girl protested. But when her touch revived Mary Warren, Mary Lacey exclaimed, "Where is my mother that made me a witch and I knew it not?"

In the past her mother, exasperated with her wayward daughter, had frequently exclaimed "devil take you" in their arguments. Now perhaps this expression had come terrifyingly true.

The magistrates told her to look upon Warren "in a friendly way" so as not to hurt her. Mary Lacey tried, but Mary Warren fell at her glance anyway, so Lacey began to confess. The words tumbled out in a torrent.

The Devil had appeared to her as a horse and as "a round Gray thing" a week ago or a year ago. He promised her "happy days" and "better times" and (blasphemously) that "I should want nothing in this world & tht I should obtain glory wth him." However, "He bid me not to be afraid of any thing, and he would not bring me out; but he has proved a liar from the beginning."

The Devil was hurting Warren now, but she herself could squeeze things to hurt folk: Warren, Timothy Swan, Mrs. Ballard, the child of James Fry. Sometime the sons of Martha Carrier helped her. The Carrier boys' specters were in the room now, having received the power to hurt from their mother. (Martha Carrier had been the first arrested in Andover, even before Annie Putnam and Mercy Lewis were called in.) Mary Warren fought off all the specters in her seizures.

At one point, Higginson noted, Mary Warren saw the specter of "a Young man" on the table "& was Just then herself afflicted And this Mary Lacey said she saw Young Carrier Sitt upon Warrens Stomack." Mary Lacey Jr. had much to say about the spectral depredations of Richard and Andrew Carrier and how their mother, Martha, had threatened her own family into joining Satan's side—Martha whom the Devil had promised would be "Queen of Hell." Once Mary Lacey Jr. confessed enough, she could take Mary Warren's hand safely, both girls weeping, with Lacey begging forgiveness for hurting the other.

The magistrates brought back Goodwives Foster and Lacey so they could question all three generations together, and the session descended into a turmoil of accusations, admission, and confessions— both daughters now blaming their mothers, all three accusing others of being in the Devil's snare. "Here is a Poor Miserable Child," one of the magistrates observed, "a Wretched Mothr & Granmother."

"[O] Mothr," the granddaughter wailed, "Why did You give Me to the Divell. . . . [you] Have often wished that the Divel Would ffetch Me away alive O My hart will break within me . . . O lord Comfort

Me and bring out all that are witches." And to her grandmother: "O Granmother why did you Give Me to the Divel . . . doe not You deny it you have bin a verry bad Woeman in Your time I must Needs Say."

Even in her fits Mary Warren would have heard the Lacey girl berate her mother and grandmother, this girl so at odds with her family that she had even run away from home the year before to hide out with neighbors. Mary Warren, however, had lost her own mother to a fever that had been brought on, she was sure, by the malice of a witch. What did she think when faced with a young woman about her own age, a confessed witch with no apparent loyalty to her own mother? Mary Warren is described as suffering severe seizures during the questioning, convulsing until the blood ran from her mouth. What might have the Lacey clashes triggered? How much was self-punishment for her own persistent accusations? If Mary Warren had known before that she had experienced spells of distraction, how much had she managed to convince herself was real since then? So many respected and educated gentlemen were *convinced* that the Devil was behind the current troubles. Who was *she* to counter that?

As the three suspects described how they signed the Devil's membership list, "Mary Warren then had a fitt and Cried out Upon Richd Carrier."

With the brothers repeatedly implicated for this torture, the four magistrates issued an arrest warrant for Richard and Andrew Carrier, "Sons of Thomas Carier of Andivor Husbandman."

The Foster and Lacey women were committed to the Salem jail, and the court was left with a strong suspicion that here was a whole family in thrall to the Devil.

The following day, Friday, July 22, eighteen-year-old Richard and sixteen-year-old Andrew Carrier were in the custody of Andover constable Joseph Ballard, whose wife still pined in her fevers. Ballard brought them to Thomas Beadle's tavern in Salem for questioning by the same four magistrates.

At first the Carrier brothers "returned Negative Answers to all" the magistrates' questions, while Mary Lacey Jr. spun elaborate tales of how she and they went about torturing people at the Devil's behest and while the afflicted said they saw the Devil and Martha Carrier among other specters, all of whom were preventing the boys' confessions.

As the details accumulated, all of the afflicted "were Grevously tormented," especially "Mary Warrin in a bad ffitt & blood Runing out of her Mouth." Andrew Carrier caused that, said Mary Lacey Jr. Andrew uncharacteristically "Stammered & Stuttered Excedinly in Speaking," but nonetheless, he denied it all.

Consequently, as the court's notes have it, "Richd and Andrew were Carried out to another Chambber—And there feet & hands bound a Little while." As John Procter would soon write, the court "tyed them Neck and Heels till the Blood was ready to come out of their Noses," a rare form of punishment for civilians. Returned to the court, the brothers confessed. With Mary Lacey Jr., they described the witch meetings in detail, their means of inflicting pain, their many victims, and their Devilish baptisms. The magistrates noted that Andrew no longer stammered, speaking plainly as he ordinarily did. At one point Mary Warren spoke up to say his specter told her that "the Divel baptized him wthin this Month at Shawshin Riuer, the Divel put his head into the Wattr."

The five new confessors implicated other suspects, Burroughs especially, plus Rebecca Nurse and the four other women recently hanged. *Those* five had all declared themselves to be innocent, but the dead cannot defend themselves. Now, as far as the court was concerned, the confessions of these Andover suspects annulled the earlier claims.

They also implicated Goodwife Martha Emerson (Martha Carrier's niece and Roger Toothaker's daughter), who was arrested on the same day and examined on the next.

On Saturday, July 23, John Procter, speaking for other prisoners as well, addressed a letter to several Boston ministers:

[Due to] the Enmity of our Accusers and our Judges, and Jury, whom nothing but our Innocent Blood will serve their turn, having Condemned us already before our Tryals, being so much incensed and enraged against us by the Devil . . . [they humbly asked the] Reverend

Gentlemen [to present] this our Humble Petition to his Excellency [the governor], That if it be possible our Innocent Blood may be spared, which undoubtedly otherwise will be shed, if the Lord doth not mercifully step in. The Magistrates, Ministers, Jewries [i.e., juries] and all the People in general, being so much inraged and incensed against us by the Delusions of the Devil, which we can term no other, by reason we know in our own Consciences, we are all Innocent Persons.

He referred to the five recent confessors from Andover and their accusations, "which we know to be Lies," and to some of the petitioners as attending the Devil's Sacrament when they were in fact locked in "close Prison." Two of those five were Carrier's sons who "confessed" only after enduring the torture of being tied neck and heels. Procter's own son William had been so bound, released not by a false confession but by a jailer's mercy.

"They have already undone us in our Estates, [and now they want] our Innocent bloods."

Therefore, the petitioners begged that their trials be moved from Salem to Boston or, if not, that other magistrates be put in charge of their cases or at least that some of the ministers attend their trials and do what they can to save them.

Whatever the Boston ministers may have done in response, if anything at all, did nothing to change the venue or the court's methods. Governor Phips was frequently absent, overseeing frontier defenses Eastward in Maine, leaving the lieutenant governor in charge: William Stoughton, chief justice of the Court of Oyer and Terminer.

Meanwhile, on the same day, July 23, Richard Carrier and Mary Lacey Jr. joined Mary Warren to testify against Goodwife Martha Emerson. Again, Mary Warren's convulsions seemed the most severe among the afflicted. She fell into "a long dumb fitt" but was able to communicate by raising her hand to second a neighbor's tale of his being hag-ridden by Emerson's specter—forced by the witch to serve as her steed in the night.

After denying the charge, Goody Emerson reluctantly confessed, hoping to save her own life, for she was not only Roger Toothaker's daughter but, like Goody Sibley, had also actually attempted countermagic in the past and the court knew it. Confession and becoming a cooperating witness could at least earn a reprieve. Her hesitation, she said, was due to the threats from her aunt Carrier and Goody Green of Haverhill, who "took her by the throat & . . . would not lett her confess."

But despite the accusations from Mary Warren, Mary Lacey Sr. and Jr., and Richard Carrier, Goody Emerson had second thoughts about the spiritual consequences of her lie. "[A]fter ward," said the court's notes, "she denyed all & sd what she had sd was in hopes to have favour & now she could not deny god that had keept her from that sin."

"[T]hough he slay me," she told the court later, "I will trust in him."

Though what good the recantation might do before the earthly courts was another matter.

But the Lacey and Carrier confessions did not save Elizabeth Ballard, for the woman died of her fever on July 27.

So witches were still about and still dangerous. Annie and Mercy tirelessly continued their sessions in Andover, identifying the nest of witches there. The suspects initially denied their guilt and involvement, but neither the girls nor the public were fooled. From the stories Annie brought home, even some of the women's *husbands* believed their wives had joined the Devil. And in the face of such certainty, most of the women confessed.

Yet, Ann knew, others persisted in their claims of innocence. Mary Bradbury, for all that the Carrs and the Putnams could say about her and despite the Lacey woman's witnessing Bradbury's baptism by the Devil at the falls, refused to confess.

The day after Goody Ballard's death, Thomas Bradbury addressed a petition to the court:

July the 28: 1692
Concerning my beloved wife Mary Bradbury . . . wee have been maried fifty five yeare and shee hath bin a loveing & faithfull wife to mee, unto this day . . . wonderfull laborious dilligent & industryous in her place & imployment, about the bringing up o[u]r family . . . eleven childeren of o[u]r owne & fower grand-children . . . Shee being now very aged & weake, & greived under her affliction may not bee able to speake much

for her selfe, not being so free of Speach as some others may bee I hope
her life and conversation hath been such amongst her neighbours, as
gives a better & more reall Testimoney of her, then can bee exprest by
words

   own'd by mee Tho: Bradbury

By July 22 Thomas Bradbury had managed to gather well over one
hundred names on a petition supporting his wife's character as a good
Christian and a helpful neighbor. Like Francis Nurse, Bradbury was
not about to cease in his efforts for his wife. This would not have comforted the Putnams, though they well knew that in the end Francis
Nurse's efforts had come to nothing.

Meanwhile ordinary legal matters went forward. Simon Willard,
who occasionally took notes for the court, helped appraise the estate
of the late Thomas Oliver, Bridget Bishop's second husband. With
the widow's life interest in the property now expired upon her death—
by hanging—the land and chattels would now be distributed among
the Oliver heirs. The inventory was brief and itemized only what
Oliver had owned at the time of his death thirteen years before: an
acre "with the old house that was late upon it," about ten acres in
North Fields (since sold), and "a little table and a chest."

By now Mistress Mary English had at least moved to better quarters. After Philip was brought to the Boston jail back on June 1, he
and Mary moved into a room in the prisonkeeper John Arnold's
house, a prerogative for gentlefolk who could pay the extra fees. This
was still confining and a far more humble accommodation than their
own grand mansion, but it was more likely to be away from pickpock-
ets, prostitutes, and—they hoped—fleas.

Family lore noted that they were even allowed to move about the
town by day at least to attend religious services—if accompanied by
an armed guard, whose salary they also paid. They had one of their
daughters brought from Salem, six-year-old Susanna, to live with
them in the jailer's house, and they found places for the other children
to board in Boston. Philip's friend George Hollard funded their im-
mediate expenses and provided their meals.

The news from Salem was not encouraging, and their status seemed less and less likely a protection against the court's methods. News from Boston, however, offered some small hope: three Frenchmen cut through the window bars of the cell they shared during the night of July 25–26 and successfully vanished.

So it was possible.

With Candy now in the Salem jail, Tituba has someone in a similar sit-uation with whom to talk. As the New England summer swelters, they reminisce of Barbados—the long hot months, the abundance of flowers, the prevalent fevers.

There is a fever here in Massachusetts as well, and people die of it.

Candy asks about winters in this northern place. It is hard to imagine now, but Tituba does her best to describe the bone-chilling winds, the strangeness of snow, how it can pile up against the houses and persist into the spring in melting drifts. And the cold—the master complains all the time about the need for firewood.

The two women walk the prison yard, pacing the fence line, hearing snatches of conversation in the street outside, catching fugitive glimpses of seabirds gliding above the nearby North River, seldom catching a cooler breeze that makes its way over the high board fence.

They make small talk together and also listen to what news they can glean from the conversations of guards and visitors.

Near the end of July they begin to hear of prisoners escaping—not from this jail, but three from Boston and another from Cambridge.

Tituba remembers Boston's stone prison, remembers the little rooms along the outside wall of the central common area. Some men—not witch suspects, she hears, but rather a suspected pirate and some Canadian cap-tives—had removed the bars from a small window and disappeared into the night. The law had not caught them yet. And in Cambridge Mistress Cary—she who John Indian had accused in Salem Village—had van-ished as well. Her husband had something to do with it—money chang-ing hands most likely. He was arrested for that, but once released on bail, he too vanished.

So it could be done, *Tituba thinks, if* you had the money, *if* you had someone to help.

Tituba doubts that will happen for her. Would John Indian even try *something like that, even if he could? And where could she go and not be immediately suspected—if not recognized?*

Still, knowing it could happen is satisfying.

For now, she will have to wait and see.

So Tituba waits.

August 1 to 11, 1692

Mary Warren faces John and Elizabeth Procter once again across the courtroom, one after the other, as she had back at the end of June before the grand jury and now again before the trial jury and the panel of judges.

As the clerk reads the indictment, Mary hears only snatches of the now-familiar form.

John Procter of Salem . . . husbandman . . . certaine Detestable Arts called witchcrafts and Sorceries wickedly and ffelloniously hath Used, Practised and Excercised Upon and against one Mary Warren of Salem . . . Singlewoman by which said wicked arts the said Mary Warren . . . was and is Tortured, Afflicted, Pined Consumed wasted and Tormented . . .

She hears her name and her master's name, and she remembers signing the paper as a witness to the acts—she and the Walcott girl.

Now the court presents depositions, and each time the clerk reads one, Mary and the other afflicted witnesses are shaken and twisted, gripped by something invisible.

Goodman Procter glares at her. Other people testify—she is not the only one—but he fixes her with an expression of utter disgust. Months ago he beat her to her senses, and she can tell he longs to do so again, to clout her beside her head and take a switch to her back. But he cannot reach her and can only clench his fists at his side and clench his jaw to shut in words that will not help his case. Mary feels the force of his stare. That thought alone grips her, and she moans and twists in her seat. The other afflicted pick up on her motions, and the court has to wait once

again for the turmoil to subside. Then Procter looks even more contemp-
tuous. Mary turns away.

Once, she had wondered what it would be like to be married to him,
to receive kind glances from him at least. Now he regards her as he would
something on the bottom of his boot.

The clerk reads her depositions. Yes, she said that. Yes, yes, it is all true.
That is what he said. That is what he did. Yes, she swears to it. She has
thought of those incidents often, mulled them over during the long nights
in her cell. They must be true. Clearly, Procter does not believe it. He
scorns her stories—fancies, lies. But the magistrates, the judges—they be-
lieve her. The other afflicted witnesses believe her. So it must be true. She
can see in her mind's eye what she has described. That must have been
the way it happened—it had to be. Therefore, it is not that Procter fails
to believe the reality of her torments but that he is angered that his mis-
deeds are revealed. That must be it.

Mary does not desire Goodman Procter now, but his wife, when it is
her turn to face the court, stares at Mary with fierce hatred. Goody Proc-
ter is visibly with child. How many months have passed since the Proc-
ters' arrest? Sometimes it seems as if life has been like this forever.

Darkness closes in again as Mary's body twitches and then flails help-
lessly. She tastes blood in the back of her throat and tries not to think of
what Sarah Good shouted at Reverend Noyes—of blood in the mouth of
the unmerciful, of liars.

She is not a liar.

Surely she is not.

John Procter, in the Salem jail preparing for his trial, had made out
a will on August 2, leaving his land and goods to his several children, even though he had deeded all of it to them and to Elizabeth
in 1689.

Styling himself as a yeoman, he left the land to his two eldest sons,
Benjamin, who was in jail, and John Jr., who, as executors, were to distribute the remaining goods equally among the rest of his children.
Elizabeth was nowhere mentioned. Either he despaired of her chances
with the court or they had quarreled. In the usual manner of wills he

bequeathed his soul to God and desired that his executors deliver "My Body unto Decent Buriale at the Discretion of my Executor[s]."

After someone read the text aloud Procter signed and sealed the document. Three men witnessed the reading and signing and then added their own names to the will: John's brother Joseph, Philip Fowler, and Thomas Chote.

A few days later Procter added a paragraph. He now desired "If any of my children be taken away that their assigns be divided amongst [the remaining children]"—taken away under arrest, that is, and condemned to death as he was.

Only the day before, the grand jury had finished considering evidence against Elizabeth Procter, Mary Esty, and George Jacobs Sr. Mary Warren affirmed that Jacobs's specter had beaten her with his staff and beaten Annie Putnam and Mary Walcott as well. She was not asked to sign as witness on the other indictments, however, and the grand jury actually rejected as *ignoramus* the indictment against old Jacobs for tormenting the Putnam maid Mercy Lewis.

Jacobs went before the trial jury the same day. Sarah Churchill, no longer trying to deny the truth of her recantation, testified against her old master. His granddaughter Margaret held to her recantation and did not testify against her grandfather.

Jacobs's neighbor John DeRich, Elizabeth Procter's sixteen-year-old nephew, testified that the old man's specter had tormented him along with specters of the Englishes, the Procters, and the Procter children. This very day, he went on, the shining angel appeared to him, bringing the ghost of Mary Warren's mother, who "told him that goodwife Parker & Oliver did Kill her"—Alice Parker and her crony Bridget Bishop.

John Willard was tried the same day. The grand jury had already rejected the indictment against him for tormenting Susanna Sheldon but returned six more *billa vera*, including those for Annie Putnam and—presumably, as two are lost—Mistress Ann Putnam.

The court found both George Jacobs and John Willard guilty of witchcraft.

When John Procter came to trial on August 5 other afflicted girls reported his specter, but Mary Warren's testimony and, even more so, her fits and convulsions seemed to count most against her former master.

Yet not all the testimony was entirely negative. James Holton of Salem Village verified that although some of the afflicted had said that Procter caused certain pains he had suffered and that his pain stopped when the girls said the specter turned on them, he did not claim to have seen the man's specter himself. Less ambiguous and more positive, Holton's name was also among the twenty Salem-area neighbors who signed a petition vouching for both John and Elizabeth Procter:

> We whose names ar under written havinge several yeares knowne John Procter and his wife do testefy. that we never heard or understood that they were ever suspected to be guilty of the crime now charged upon them and several of us being their neare neighbours do testefy that to our aprehension they lived christian life in their famely and were ever ready to helpe such as stood in need of their helpe.

In addition, thirty-two people of Ipswich, where John had grown up and still had family, signed another petition for him. Referring to the Old Testament story of the witch of Endor, who supposedly summoned the ghost of the prophet Samuel, they pointed out—as others had done that year, to no avail—"the Abuse [the Devil] Does the famous Samuell, In Disquieting his Silent Dust, by Shaddowing his venerable Person in Answer to the Charmes of witch Craft." But yet again, this caution against the acceptance of spectral evidence at face value went unheeded.

The court found John Procter guilty as charged.

Elizabeth Procter had argued in the past with the local physician. John Indian and a few hired men reported her specter, sometimes in company with Rebecca Nurse's. Besides Mary Warren, Annie Putnam and the rest of the afflicted females claimed that her specter had hurt them.

Countering this, along with the petition for her and John, was Daniel Eliot's account of some of the girls' jests. "[T]hey must have some sport," one of them had said. But Arthur Abbott testified about something alarming—the paperwork is gone—that he claimed to have seen in the Procter household.

Elizabeth Procter was found guilty of witchcraft. Because she was with child, however, and the child was presumably not yet corrupted by its *parents'* devilish lessons, the mother's execution was postponed until after she could give birth.

As the trials proceeded, Salem filled with even more spectators, "a Vast Concourse," as Cotton Mather put it, arriving from Boston to attend Reverend George Burroughs's trial on August 5. They would have brought word of the recent apocalyptic earthquake that had swamped the harbor town of Port Royal in Jamaica, drowning seventeen hundred people on both land and ships in port. Many New England merchants had trading contacts there. Their world seemed besieged from all sides.

Mrs. Ann Putnam, more and more encumbered by the child to come, had much to do at home during Thomas's frequent absences on court business that hot dry summer—dealing with the younger children and a new hired girl and keeping an eye on the hired men left to care for the crops. Regardless, she was evidently a witness the day before against John Willard, the murderer of her baby Sarah, whipped to death by spectral means. And now here was Burroughs brought to justice, the Putnams' enemy. She had never liked the man and would hardly have missed George Burroughs's trial for the world.

Reverend Burroughs's trial promised to be the most sensational thus far. That a minister, even one not yet ordained to any particular church, would join the Devil's troop, would turn against all he presumably stood for—that was terrifying to imagine.

As usual the afflicted—from Mercy Lewis, who had worked for the Burroughs's family in Maine, to confessing witches like Abigail Hobbs, who had been a neighbor in Maine, and Ann Foster, who feared his specter might kill her in revenge for her accusations—testified against Burroughs. The afflicted appear to have been brought into the courtroom one at a time, for only one was present when she paused, "cast into Horror," she said, by the sight of ghosts: Burroughs's two dead wives "crying for Vengeance" against their murderous husband, accusing him to his face.

Assuming the others knew nothing of this turn of events, the court brought the other afflicted witnesses into the room one by one, but each reported the same fearsome apparitions.

Burroughs was appalled but insisted he could see nothing of the sort.

The afflicted's testimony took tedious time as the girls and women convulsed, unable in their fits to say anything. During one such pause Chief Justice Stoughton asked Burroughs who he thought prevented these witnesses from speaking.

Burroughs answered that he thought it was the Devil who caused their fits.

"How comes the Devil so loathe to have any testimony born against *you*?" asked Stoughton.

Burroughs had no answer to such a question.

The ghosts, the tortures, the biting specter, the repeated pestering threats with the Devil's book and the offered bribes—witnesses and confessors presented all these stories to a packed courtroom as well as how Burroughs appeared as leader of the witches, how he presided over the great meeting in Salem Village and promised better times for those who joined the Devil's side as he worked to replace the Kingdom of God with the Kingdom of Satan.

Other witnesses spoke of Burroughs's rough treatment of his late wives (though not all the offered testimony seems to have been used at the trial), of his apparently uncanny ability to know more about what happened when he was not present (or not *visibly* present), of his unexpected strength for such a little man that he could manage a long-barreled fowling piece one-handed or lift full molasses barrels from a canoe with no trouble (he had always been strong for his size).

Tales that he could lift that long gun with merely one finger inserted in the barrel were, however, disregarded, as were the stories of the ghosts—though everyone seemed to accept the truth of them. Whatever answers Burroughs made to all these allegations seemed, to the court, thin excuses at best, inconsistent and contradictory. He spoke up to challenge juror selection, but nothing he said helped, certainly not his opinion of some of the witnesses' reputations. Finally he presented a paper to the jury explaining that contracting with the Devil or sending imps to harm others at a distance was impossible. The judges recognized the statement as a passage copied from Thomas Ady's book *A Candle in the Dark*. Ady was a skeptical Englishman who argued that people's foolish imagination caused the problems blamed on witchcraft. When the judges noted the source, however, Burroughs denied copying the words, as the court understood his protest, and said that "a gentleman" gave him the piece. But his phrasing now seemed like a lie about its source. To the court, his whole defense sounded like "Contradictions, and Falsehoods," and neither they nor Mrs. Ann Putnam, whose daughter was named as victim in one of Burroughs's four indictments, were swayed by his "Reflecting upon the Reputation of some of the witnesses."

In any case the jury found George Burroughs guilty.

When the foreman pronounced this verdict Burroughs said that he could see why the judges and jury condemned him with "so many positive witnesses against him," as Reverend John Hale remembered it, "But said, he dyed by false Witnesses."

If this was sarcasm, it was lost on such as Ann Putnam. But the statement bothered Reverend Hale enough that he later visited one of the confessing witnesses in prison, someone such as Abigail Hobbs or old Ann Foster.

I seriously spake to one that witnessed (of his Exhorting at the Witch Meeting at the Village) saying to her; You are one that did bring this man to Death, if you have charged any thing upon him that is not true, recal it before it be too late, while he is alive. She answered me, she had nothing to charge herself with, upon that account.

If Mary Warren witnessed this exchange, it may have smothered any lingering doubts she had of her own claims.

Reverend Increase Mather, having traveled up from Boston to observe the trial, may also have taken the opportunity, as he would again later, to question some of the confessors in the jail. "More than one or two of those now in Prison," he later wrote, "have freely, and credibly acknowledged their Communion and Familiarity with the Spirits of Darkness, and have also declared unto me the Time and Occasion, with the particular occurrences of their Hellish Obligations and Abominations."

Mrs. Ann Putnam showed no doubts of that sort of testimony, not with her family so busy for the cause, as she saw it, of right. Thomas was often in Salem town working with the magistrates or over in Andover with Annie. Sometimes the afflicted families in Andover sent people with horses to accommodate her daughter and Mercy. Not that these trips were without danger, however. Annie fell from her horse once and said that one of the witches had pulled her off. The Putnams saw Andover as infested by witches—whole families of them gone over to Satan, like weeds among God's wheat, blighting the crop. But Ann could take comfort in the thought that those witches had lost the advantage of surprise now that their plans were known.

And that Bradbury woman was also revealed for what she was, as far as Ann was concerned. Yet, like Goody Nurse, Bradbury had her supporters, some no doubt deluded, others probably collaborators. That husband of hers had collected a long list of names on a petition, just as the Nurse family had. Even a gentleman in Salisbury had written to question the court's methods, to question the judges' wisdom in believing the accusations. But the conclusion would no doubt end the same as the Nurse case had.

Ann prayed fervently that it would.

Rebecca Nurse's still-grieving family faced similar fears far differently motivated from Ann's. If witchcraft was thought to run in families, as in Andover, what did the neighbors think of *them*?

But this legitimate concern for their own welfare did not keep them from trying to help their kin, the two aunts, Sarah Cloyce and Mary Esty, who were currently jailed.

Still, most of the family no longer felt comfortable—or safe—attending services at the Village meeting house. What were services now but Parris's offensive views and the afflicted's interruptions? They fully expected to be accused—if not now, then soon enough. So they mostly attended services elsewhere, probably in Topsfield, as Reverend Capen had not assumed that the accused were necessarily guilty.

Thinking "it our most safe and peaceable way to withdraw," they avoided their neighbors. But they did not give up resisting but rather only waited for an opportunity to do something that might help.

More suspects came in from Andover on August 11—some of Martha Carrier's younger children, and a daughter and granddaughter of Andover's senior minister. (But then again, Reverend Francis Dane was also Martha Carrier's uncle, no less.) The children had confessed in Andover at their initial questioning the previous day, though the local magistrate Dudley Bradstreet had his doubts about the whole matter, "being," as he said, "unadvisedly entered upon [a] service I am wholly unfit for." Annie Putnam and Mercy Lewis did not doubt, and the Salem magistrates accepted the confessions readily. Now two Andover girls witnessed among the afflicted: Martha Sprague and Sarah Phelps—local girls, not just the Salem Village experts.

The Carrier children, aged eight and ten, confessed even more about their witchly activities, about how their own mother had recruited them to the Devil's cause. Betty Johnson was twenty-two, but as her grandfather Reverend Dane would say, she was "but Simplish at the best." She, like others, had also formed the hope that the court would spare confessors rather than merely postpone their cases, as was the reality. "I feare the common speech that was frequently spread among us, of their liberty, if they would confesse," Reverend Dane would soon write, was what tempted many into false confessions.

Unlike her niece, Goodwife Abigail Faulkner refused to lie, stating, "I know nothing of it." Perhaps, she said, "it is the devill dos it in my shape." But she would not confess, not even when her niece urged her to do so "for the creddit of her Town."

Goody Faulkner's gaze and the fact that she nervously twisted a handkerchief as she spoke set off convulsions among the afflicted. Mary Warren's fits were so severe that she ended up under the table as if dragged, but Goody Faulkner's touch broke the cycle and relieved the girl, though doing so brought no relief to Goody Faulkner.

Mary English sits by the window of their small room in the jailer's house to catch the daylight. She knots the silk in her needle with a deft twist of one index finger and draws the strand through the strip of hooped linen in her lap. She has obtained, along with clean clothes, something to embroider with, although there is less and less contact with their servants in Salem now, and Philip's friend Mr. Hollard provides their meals.

"Now watch, Susanna," she says to the six-year-old girl beside her. But her father's pacing back and forth across the cramped space distracts the child. He acts like a caged wolf even though they do get to walk about the town from time to time as long as they pay for the guard who accompanies them.

"Watch."

Outside, the street sounds of Boston compete with conversations in the prison yard and the clamor of gulls.

Mary slides the needle back through the cloth. "See? This is called a running stitch." She repeats the design. "Now you try."

Philip, muttering curses in French, progresses to fuller complaints about the courts. "The fools, to believe the lying wenches who accuse me, who accuse both of us of witchcraft! Fools and liars to accuse and more fools to believe them!"

His harangue, not the first since their arrival here, is making the girl uneasy and offers no comfort to Mary either, but there is no use in asking him to calm down.

"Stitch them closer next time. Try again."

Philip moves on, with his voice becoming more defiant, to his disgust over the new governor. He had never liked Phips, even before their arrests. "Sir Edmund was the better governor," he fumes. "But no, these imbeciles would have a local man regardless of whether he could govern. That Phips—practically a pirate—may do well enough on a quarter deck, but can he lead gentlemen? Not bloody likely." Philip has learned to curse in English as well.

Everyone knows he dislikes Governor Phips. One of the so-called afflicted girls, they have heard, reported Philip's specter hurrying off from Salem to Boston to deal with "his great enemy the governor." Philip never did hide his emotions, *Mary thinks.*

"All that misguided hope placed in this new governor," Phillip goes on. "All this talk of a change and see what they get. The lout couldn't even read until he was over twenty!"

Mary has heard that too. Taught by his wife, people say. Philip English and William Phips certainly do not socialize, but their wives are clearly of equal rank and do. She has heard the rumors that some prisoners have escaped. It had to be possible.

Mary makes a few more running stitches as examples and hands the hoop to Susanna. "Practice," she says.

(14)
August 12 to 31, 1692

The remaining Procter brothers, mucking out the cow yard, hear the creaking wagon before they see it. If this is a customer, then they can use the business, though supplies are low and, with their stepmother in jail, there is no one to brew more beer. John Procter Jr., at twenty-three, is the eldest remaining son. He squints down the sloping road under the sun's glare.

Too much dust for just one cart, *he thinks,* men on horseback too. *The younger half-siblings are in the house—or are supposed to be. Three-year-old Abigail darts outside, asking,* "Papa? Is it Papa come home?"

Her brother Samuel follows, trying to exert his six-year-old authority. They tussle as the other children watch from the doorway.

The cavalcade is closer now, and John discerns a bristle of black staffs. No, this is not their father returning. This is the law—again. Hot from the day and his work a moment before, John realizes he is drenched in cold sweat.

Dear God, who are they arresting now?

Part of him wants to run away. Part of him wants to fight back.

Instead, he stands by the gate.

Abby breaks away and stumbles toward the road.

John clamps a hand on her shoulder as she tries to pass and calls to his other sister: "Mary, get them back in the house. Now."

I should have sent them to our older married sister, *he thinks.* I should have insisted she take them in.

The procession turns into the farmyard. A gentleman at the fore halts his mount and surveys the area. His men fan out. Sheriff Corwin, only a few years older than John, holds the reins in one hand and rests the other lightly on the polished hilt of his sword.

"John Procter Junior?"

Clutching the dung fork in one hand and restraining the struggling child with the other, John is all too aware how his grimy work clothes and the cow shit on his boots undermines any attempt at dignity. Even so, he draws himself up, trying to act as he feels their absent father would. "I am."

Abigail begins to cry: "Mama? Did they bring Mama back?"

Finally Mary scoops up the child and carries her away. Sheriff Corwin produces a paper from his pocket and reads it through, but something about it is different. John hears the name of their father and the names of the monarchs but no name for the accused.

"What?" It is not another an arrest warrant. Nearly dizzy with relief, he cannot hear what the sheriff says next. Corwin looks annoyed and repeats himself.

"Take the felons' goods into custody. I trust no one will interfere with my men."

"Goods?" What is he talking about?

Corwin nods to his deputies, who split into groups and head for the barn and the house.

"Wait! What goods do you mean?"

Some of the men start herding the cows from the nearby pasture and, to judge from the squealing, try to drive the pigs from their pen.

Thank heaven some swine are loose in the wood lot.

Abby's wail from the house sends John running inside. The deputies— one looks almost apologetic, one sneering—haul boxes and sacks of supplies from the root cellar.

"You're frightening the children," says John, but the men keep working, piling the Procters' supplies and possessions into the center of the room. Someone clumps across the floor above.

One of the deputies rolls a sloshing barrel from its corner—the last of the beer supply.

"Get rid of it," one of the men orders. "And I don't mean drink it."

They heave the barrel over, sending the beer foaming onto the hearth, then begin packing brass and iron kitchen gear. Everything else—anything of value—vanishes into sacks.

"Wait!" says Mary. "That's our dinner."

The sneering deputy doesn't reply but instead lifts the pot from its hook and slops its contents onto the small cook fire beneath. The thin broth hisses as it quenches the frail flame and sends a small twist of smoke up from the wet ashes.

"What are we supposed to live on?" John demands. "When do we get any of this back?"

Corwin still sits upon his horse, directing the operation from on high and, thus, keeping his hands clean. John Procter seethes and dares to do nothing, as his relief at not being arrested turns to anger. It seems to take hours, but eventually the procession forms again. The loaded wagons creak forward back down the road toward town, followed by a ragged drove of cattle lowing their unease at the change of routine. The pigs give more trouble, but they too are prodded along with the rest.

Dear Lord, what will happen next?

John slumps against the sundial's post and watches the thieves recede.

How have they missed taking the brass sundial? *he wonders.* First their father and his wife are taken, then Benjamin and William, then Sarah. *We should be grateful no one was arrested this time, but still— what* are *we to live on?*

His younger brothers and sisters are watching him, waiting to be told what to do. He straightens up. "Mary, see what's left in the house. Thorndike, come with me. We must find the rest of the cows—and hide them."

Confiscations, as the Procters had endured, were a new twist on the treatment of convicted felons, a part of English common law not used before in Massachusetts Bay but used now in the government's efforts not to violate the charter's repugnancy clause. The idea was to remove a convicted felon's material possessions and store them so as to prevent the felon's family and other supporters from disposing of them before sums due to the Crown (or the Crown's provincial government) could be paid. After that, the deceased felon's heirs could be provided for. However, with the escalating number of prisoners being jailed that summer, at least some of the goods were being used to feed them or sold to pay for the court's many expenses.

The result was even greater resentment among both the families of the accused and the population at large.

John's sons could, in visits to the jail, have told him the discouraging news—how the sheriff and his men had arrived not to arrest any more of the family this time, a fear foremost in their minds, but instead to take forfeited goods. (Possibly Mary Warren would have overheard or been told what had passed, what her fancies and distractions had caused.) In whispered fury the sons would have told their father the details during a prison visit. The law had "left nothing in the House for the support of the Children," as they would later report.

The cattle, as they had learned, were either sold at half the price they were worth or slaughtered, with the meat salted for the West India trade. The government had no place to keep livestock, so selling was the only solution. The Procters would be lucky to get the money equivalent back, but the cattle and other possessions were gone for good.

Mary Warren, preparing to leave the jail with the rest of the afflicted to witness the latest hangings on August 19, could not help overhearing her former master arguing with someone—the sheriff, perhaps, and Reverend Noyes.

He was not ready to die, John Procter's voice carried down the corridor. He needed more time to settle his soul.

Reverend Noyes's voice carried even more clearly. Because Procter would not confess to what was so obvious, what the court had proven, how could he presume to be able to put his soul to rights under those circumstances?

Procter objected. At least pray with him now, he asked.

But Noyes refused, unwilling to waste compassion on the obviously guilty—what was the point?

Mary could not stop listening. The other prisoners stayed quiet, straining to hear.

They had already heard that Margaret Jacobs, once a confessor-accuser but since recanted, had asked to see Reverend Burroughs the day before to acknowledge personally that she had given "altogether false and untrue" evidence against him, as well as her grandfather George Jacobs and John Willard, and to ask for his forgiveness. Burroughs not only forgave Margaret but also prayed with her. (She may have apologized to her grandfather as well, for he had a line added to his recent will, leaving her £10 in silver.) But neither Mary Warren nor the other confessors were willing to change their stories.

Now Martha Carrier made her farewells to her children. But the youngest of them at least, their shrill voices verging on tears and then dissolving into weeping, begged their mother to confess, to choose life and stay with them. One of them lamented that their own mother had dedicated them to the Devil, but the mother's impatient harried tones interrupted all of this. Words were hardly distinguishable, the emotions too raw to miss.

So sad, Mary thought, then corrected herself. Her own mother had been taken by witches, bewitched to death, and where was the pity then?

Finally, the five felons were boosted into the waiting cart. The procession assembled, and the gate creaked open. The usual crowd was out there, more along the street—more all told than for any of the previous executions. An influx of gentlemen, including several out-of-town ministers from Boston and elsewhere, had come in to witness the end of their erstwhile colleague, George Burroughs.

Mary trudged on among the afflicted, down the road to the Town Bridge, over the creek that entered the river bend in its little marsh, and up on to the ledges above the tidal pool. The crowd jostled its way onto the more level land, leaving a space around the gallows. The proceedings began as the other executions had, but this time the prisoners in the cart had more to say and turned to one of the visiting ministers, Cotton Mather from Boston—Mary heard the crowd murmur his name—to ask him to pray with them. Unlike Noyes, Mather agreed, and together the five felons and the minister addressed the Lord. They prayed for God to identify the true witches among them; to forgive their accusers, the judges, and the juries for finding them guilty; and to forgive all their sins—their actual sins. The prisoners also repeated their claim of innocence and prayed "that their blood might be the last innocent blood shed upon that account." Procter and Willard appeared unaccountably dignified and collected. Even old Jacobs seemed to impress some in the crowd. From what Mary had heard, he rarely forgave a slight ordinarily.

But none of this was ordinary despite that it happened so often now.

Reverend George Burroughs had more to add once he stood on the ladder, teetering a little, for his hands were tied behind him. He also offered a prayer, addressed as much to the onlookers as to God, again declaring his innocence. More people in the crowd murmured to hear it, especially when Burroughs ended with the Lord's Prayer—word perfect. The magistrates had allowed the recitation of this so-familiar prayer as a test for the accused, even though that was a folk test, not a proper use of Scripture. Everyone knew it, but several accused had slipped on the lines, mangling the meaning. Willard certainly had. And a witch sworn to Satan's cause would hardly express the sentiments of that prayer perfectly. "May *Thy* will be done, on earth as it is in Heaven." *God*'s will, Burroughs emphasized—not necessarily man's will.

Although more people reacted to this delivery, some even moved to tears, and restlessness rippled through the throng, no one stepped forward to do anything about it—yet.

"The Devil whispered the lines to Burroughs," some among the afflicted said. "He could not speak so well otherwise."

The hangman kicked the ladder away.

Burroughs dropped and slowly died.

The crowd muttered, and their tone was angrier than it was before. Mary couldn't see over their heads, and too many of the people were looking *her* way, toward the afflicted. She caught snatches of conversation discontent that the law had hanged a minister, one who prayed so well, a man ordained of God. Were they going to hit someone?

Reverend Mather spoke out over the rising din from his horseback vantage point. She heard most of what he said: *not* ordained (that was true) folk tests could not be trusted (yet the court used the touch test—did Reverend Mather know that?) nor outward appearances, for even the Devil had disguised himself as an Angel of Light to deceive. Mary knew that a shining angel-like personage had been reported among the specters. What did *that* mean?

The crowd pulled back, objections dwindled, and the threat of riot subsided. The hangings continued—the whole messy, reeking process of wringing a soul from its body. When the last corpse stopped swinging, the crowd began to pull away. They moved back down the ledge to the road, while the deputies began to dispose of the bodies—to a waiting grave, to waiting relatives. The day was hotter than ever, and nothing seemed to have been settled.

Thomas Brattle, treasurer of Harvard College, was one of the gentlemen who attended the executions of August 19. The conduct of the condemned impressed him, especially that of "Proctor and Willard, whose whole management of themselves, from the Goal to the Gallows, and whilst at the Gallows, was very affecting and melting to the hearts of some considerable Spectatours." He could not forget their prayer "that their blood might be the last innocent blood shed."

Oddly, Brattle did not mention Reverend Burroughs, whose last words from the ladder would be reported by Robert Calef, his claim of innocence phrased "with such Solemn and Serious Expressions, as were to the Admiration of all present; his Prayer (which he concluded by repeating the Lord's Prayer), was so well worded, and uttered with such composedness, and such (at least seeming) fervency of Spirit, as was very affecting, and drew Tears from many (so that it seemed to some, that the Spectators would hinder the Execution)."

In Boston, meanwhile, Philip and Mary English planned an escape, or at least Mary did—family lore would have much to say on the matter—for the outcome of the trials was not in the least encouraging. Philip's £4,000 bond allowed the couple visitors and some restricted movement about town, especially to attend religious services. The oldest of Boston's three Congregational churches, the First Church, was closest, its meeting house halfway between the jail and the town house, where the legislature met. Reverend Joshua Moody was one of the two ministers there, and one August Sabbath, according to the family story, he invited Philip and Mary to attend. On that occasion he delivered a sermon on the text Matthew 10:23: "And when they persecute you in this citie, flee into another," the minister announced from the pulpit. Moody himself had been hounded by the royal governor of New Hampshire, who insisted that Moody conduct the more ceremonial Church of England services that were against the minister's Congregational principles, then forbad him to deliver any sermons at all. Moody had no intention of conforming to the Episcopal practices so many had left England to avoid, so he relocated to Massachusetts. (Boston had a Church of England congregation, but no one *had* to be a part of it—or a member of any of the churches there, for that matter.)

After the service Moody and Reverend Samuel Willard of the nearby Third Church visited the Englishes in their rented quarters. Some of the Oyer and Terminer judges attended Willard's church, but he himself had warned, in a series of sermons, that the Devil raged against Christians without the help of recruited witches. Although the judges in his congregation seem to have ignored it, his stance prompted "unkindness, abuse, and reproach from many men" and may have led to him being accused around the time of Rebecca Nurse's trial. Fortunately the court informed that accuser that she was mistaken. (Samuel may have been a distant relation of the condemned John Willard of Salem Village, who was not as lucky.)

Now, according to later family lore, the two ministers spoke more directly to the Englishes.

Had they taken note of his sermon? Moody asked.

Philip replied that he had, but what exactly did Moody mean?

Their lives were in danger, said the minister bluntly, and they should do everything they could to escape. "Many have suffered," he told them.

"God will not permit them to touch me," Philip insisted. (Family tradition wholly ignored Phillip's earlier escape and his month hiding in Boston, burrowed, when necessary, under a pile of dirty laundry.)

The same anecdote had Mary speak sense to him. "Do you not think that they, who have suffered already, are innocent?"

Philip agreed reluctantly.

"Why then, may we not suffer also?" asked Mary. "Take Mr. Moody's advice."

The ministers declared that if Phillip would not try to save them both, they would take his wife to safety themselves. They had made arrangements already with the jailer, with various "worthy persons" of Boston, even, some would say, with the governor himself.

And escape they did, for both Philip and Mary English were established in New York by early October.

The story has a few variants as it passed from generation to generation as well as several problems and contradictions.

In one version Philip escaped alone on horseback, with the horse's iron shoes nailed on backward to confuse trackers (the same story also applied to Captain John Alden).

More often the couple are said to have used a coach provided by Boston sympathizers or New York merchants, with Mary in the coach, Philip on horseback outside, or both in the coach with their eldest daughter, Mary, Susanna having been sent to boarding school.

One variant had the coach waiting outside South Meeting House (Reverend Willard's Third Church) during services. When the Englishes left the building under guard, friends jostled between the couple and the guards, crowded the latter back inside, and somehow locked the doors to allow Philip and Mary to get a good enough head start.

Another story had a "conveyance" meet them by the prison door at midnight and spirit them to New York along with letters of introduction to the governor there, some from Phips himself, while officials turned a blind eye to the departure.

A midday escape would attract too much attention, reversed horse shoes seem fanciful at best (a sure way to lame the steed), and the only known coach in all of Massachusetts belonged to the governor's lady. (Philip owned a carriage of some sort, but that was in Salem, inaccessible.)

Although Mary, Lady Phips, was sympathetic to the prisoners, the coach would only draw attention to itself. Moreover, roads outside Boston were not yet suited to such a vehicle. Boston itself was still a peninsula, with the road south connected to the mainland through a guarded gate and over a narrow neck flooded by the month's highest tides. A ferry ran north to Charlestown, itself built on another peninsula, with another ferry going to Winnisimmet and the road to Salem over the wide marshes. All of these choices were exposed to view even without a coach involved.

That Moody and Willard would help engineer an escape, however, is quite plausible. Reverend Willard's son John had already helped

Captain Cary secret Mistress Cary away from the Cambridge jail and into hiding.

The couple did not take any of their children with them into exile. The eldest daughter, Mary, stayed in the household of Philip's business associate George Hollard, and Susanna, who had lived with her parents in the jailer's house, stayed with the family of the absent Captain Alden. The sons must have been provided for elsewhere, but on this, tradition was silent.

Philip had contacts with merchants in New York as well as in Boston. He was not however, on good terms with Governor Phips, "his great enemy," as one of the afflicted girls said. Mary English, despite her husband's politics, was of similar rank with Lady Phips, who, like her husband, had grown up in Maine but was far better educated. Mary English is remembered as determined to escape. Mary Phips would be rumored to have aided a woman prisoner to escape.

The governor and his wife were named William and Mary—just like the monarchs. Legal documents tended to begin by invoking the names of the king and queen. How closely did the guards read the repetitious official documents transferring prisoners anyway? Mary Phips wrote and signed a warrant to discharge one of the imprisoned women, and one of the jailers accepted the document. Thus, the prisoner found her freedom and the jailer lost his job. Despite her rank, Lady Phips had committed an act that would be illegal even if witchcraft were not involved. So soon she too was rumored to be a witch.

When historian Thomas Hutchinson heard the tale a generation later he did not believe it until the former jailer showed him a copy of the warrant and told him the whole story. However, Hutchinson's account of the incident referred to the prisoner as a "poor woman"—which could apply to Mary English only if he meant "unfortunate"—and did not mention Philip's presence at all. Certainly, Mary Phips herself was called a witch around this time, but no one leveled formal charges against her.

Concerning the English family, a descendant wrote, "It is a tradition in this family that several of the Boston clergy espoused the cause of Mr. and Mrs. English when confined in jail there; that Cotton Mather, who was a great friend of Mrs. E[nglish]," said, that though she was accused, "he did not believe her to be guilty; that her accusers evidently believed her to be so, but that Satan was most probably deceiving them into that belief."

Certainly by now, as the accusers named more suspects of higher rank, the magistrates and justices tended to assume the charges were mistaken at best, particularly if they knew the suspects, trusting their own opinions of their peer's reputations—Judge Corwin's mother-in-law, Mistress Margaret Thatcher, for one.

The law knew where the various fugitives had gone. No one tried to extradite them back to Massachusetts but rather kept an embarrassed silence. They called for no hue and cry as they had when a privateer and some prisoners of war escaped from Boston jail in July that same summer.

Some years earlier Reverend Increase Mather had donned an uncharacteristic cloak and wig to leave his house unidentified in order to sail for England and negotiate the new charter in spite of Governor Andros's displeasure. The Englishes may well have done the same, taking a sea route to New York by using Philip's maritime contacts: quietly leaving their lodging in the jailer's house, aided by coins and a blind eye even if not the forged warrant, and dressed, perhaps, in a more rustic manner than usual, they slipped away to the wharves and into a small craft that took them to a larger vessel that was waiting for the turn of the tide.

Philip later estimated he had run up £50 in expenses during their nine weeks in Boston, not all of it yet paid. (In contrast, Salem Village allotted Reverend Samuel Parris £60 a *year*, when they paid him at all. Because neither Philip nor Mary had been tried, he assumed that his posted £4,000 bond would protect his possessions from confiscation. He was mistaken.

Edward Bishop brushes the sawdust from his knees and then stretches, hands clasped over his head, trying to unknot his shoulders.

I'm getting too old for this, *he thinks as he sits in a scrap of shade.*

A group of younger workmen has collected off to one side, tackling their noon meal in a larger pool of shade.

Edward shades his eyes with one hand and looks down the road toward a familiar figure approaching through the heat: his stepdaughter Christian Mason, who has one arm hooked through a basket and her child Susanna clutching the other. "It's fish today," she says when she reaches the woodyard. Setting down the basket, she lifts out a napkin-wrapped bundle and a stoneware bottle. Edward accepts the package and opens the napkin across his knees to reveal a slice of cold fish pie in an indestructible rye crust.

"Good," he says, chewing.

No bones anyway, *he thinks.*

Christian rests in the thin shade while he eats, keeping an eye on her daughter, who is occupied with a handful of smooth pebbles.

"So do you hear from that husband of yours?" *he asks.*

"Still at sea or coasting along off Maine," *she says.*

"Does he ever think of moving back there?"

"Not safe," *she says. No, not with the Indians and French attacking so often, but then again, Salem hasn't proved safe either.*

Edward is grateful for his stepdaughter doing for him—cooking, washing his shirts, all the chores and necessities he has no time and little skill for. He is so starkly aware now that he is a widower.

"Grandpa?" *Susanna pipes, but her mother shushes her.*

"Don't bother your grandfather. I told you."

"But he'll know."

"Susanna." *Christian looks reproachful, frowning at the child, who in turn looks defiant, and just then Edward sees Bridget in both their faces, mother and daughter. It takes his breath away.*

"Ask me what?"

"A child's silliness. You shouldn't be bothered."

But it is too late. Susanna blurts out, "Polly won't play with me anymore."

"Who?"

Christian sighs. "A neighbor's child. They don't want their children playing with Susanna anymore."

"They say Grandma is a witch. Is that true?"

"Of course not," *says Edward. He wishes he were certain.* "Just ignore them."

Susanna accepts this advice. "Good," she says, then adds, "When is Grandma coming home?"

Her mother looks as if she might cry. "Be quiet! What did I tell you?" Christian slaps the girl. "Just stop it! We don't talk about that."

Susanna cries for real but softly, burying her face in her petticoat.

"Time for work," says Edward. He stands up and hands back the napkin.

Christian takes the basket. Mother and child head back slowly along the sun-baked street.

The other workmen watch but say nothing.

September 1692

Mary Warren, if she still doubts her fits as mere distractions, shows no sign of hesitation about Alice Parker. Not this woman, whose quarrels had killed her mother and deafened her sister. In her mind's eye she sees her mother trying to get a word in edgewise during Parker's rant against Mary's father, sees the baleful look of disgust that Parker shoots back while never stopping her own harangue, sees her mother ill and fading, growing weaker and weaker until she can no longer rise from bed, tossing and feverish, with her hands picking at the sheets and her mouth moving with words she is too weak to say aloud until at last all movement stops.

It is a wonder that Mary does not catch the illness, but the little sister is not so lucky, smoldering with fever as well but living through it to wake muffled in perpetual silence. No, Mary does not doubt Parker's malice nor where she got her power to harm.

Later, just thinking about that day as she sits in the jail with Abigail Hobbs, Sarah Churchill, and the other confessors, Mary expects the witch's spite to find her. The woman is elsewhere in the building, after all—not that distance matters much with magic, certainly not for those who can separate soul from body at will. She shudders at the thought, and the shudder becomes a spasm until Mary convulses, bent in half, gasping for breath.

The other prisoners stare and wonder who is after Mary now.

On the first of the month more suspects arrived from Andover to Salem for additional questioning: the young sons of other defendants, more of Reverend Dane's family, and most of the Wardwell family—Samuel and Sarah Wardwell, their nineteen-year-old daughter Mercy, and her elder half-sister Sarah Hawks. (Only the youngest of the Wardwell children were left behind to fend for themselves, with neighbors wary of taking them in.) All of the new prisoners confessed to the charges when faced with the writhing crowd of bewitched witnesses, the afflicted from Salem, including Mary Warren, and girls from Andover.

Samuel was known as a fortune-teller and had made no secret of it, telling neighbors—especially if they asked—who would marry whom, how many children they would have, and who would be injured by illness or mischance. Moreover, he claimed he could make straying cattle come to him—no easy task. Although he began by insisting on his innocence, he admitted his fortune-telling *might* have encouraged the Devil's attention and ended by confessing. According to the record "He used to be much discontented that he could get no more work done, and that he had been foolishly Led along with telling of fortunes, which sometymes came to pass, He used also when any creature came into his field to bid the devil take it, And it may be the devil took advantage of him by that." He said he had signed the Devil's contract on the promise "that he should never want for any thing," and for the last fortnight he had tormented the neighbors with his magic. Martha Sprague of Andover and Mary Warren were most afflicted during his examination.

His stepdaughter Sarah Hawks had turned a sieve to tell the future, and all the family admitted a dangerous discontent that let the Devil in. Samuel himself, as a confessor, soon joined the afflicted to accuse other suspects.

During the commotions that ensued the following day, September 2, when Andover widow Mary Parker (no relation to Alice Parker), faced the grand jury. Mary Warren convulsed alarmingly and had to be dragged, flailing, "haveing a pin run through her hand and blood runeing out of her mouth," to the defendant for a healing touch. Warren then identified the woman as the same whose specter she had seen at an earlier hearing, perched on a beam above the court in Salem Village.

On Saturday, September 3, Ann Putnam likely saw her daughter Annie off with Elizabeth Hubbard and the other visionary girls, escorted the sixteen or so miles to Gloucester, this time to help Goodwife Eleanor Babson and Mistress Mary Sargent, the magistrate's wife, grown women of respectable families. Annie returned with the news that two more culprits had been identified—or rather their identity verified, as the afflicted women already had a good idea who tormented them.

Consequently, Goodwives Margaret Prince and Elizabeth Dicer were in Salem on Monday to face the magistrates and the throng of convulsing witnesses. These included Mary Warren, Elizabeth Hubbard (struck dumb as the Prince woman's specter had foretold back in Gloucester), sisters Elizabeth and Alice Booth with their sister-in-law Elizabeth Booth (now four months gone with child two months after she had married their brother George), and several confessors from Andover, including Mary Lacey Jr., some of confessor Mary Bridges's daughters, and Samuel Wardwell.

Thirteen years earlier Elizabeth Dicer, when she lived in Salem, called Mary English's mother "a black-mouthed witch and a thief" and been fined for the slander. Now *she* was the suspected witch. Thus, accusing one's neighbor did not make one immune to other neighbors' suspicions.

When Goodwife Mary Taylor was arrested with other Reading women on the Sabbath, accused mainly by her neighbor, the widowed Mrs. Mary Marshall, Goody Taylor commented, "who ever lived to se it would finde Mrs Marshals cace like Mary Warins." Evidently, Mary's attempt to define her fits as distractions was fairly well known, the news being common knowledge in Reading, which was about twelve miles west of Salem. "There was a hott pott now," Goody Taylor continued, " & a hottr pott preparing for her here after."

Now, in court, Mary Warren fell at Goody Taylor's glance and required the suspect's touch to revive. Warren had to have heard the statement repeated and heard the defendant's explanation that "by the hotter pott," she meant "that if Mrs Marshall wronged her hell would be prepared for her"—another reminder of what happened to liars and false witnesses.

Samuel Wardwell's brother-in-law William Hooper had died August 8, not long after quarreling with Goody Taylor. Hooper's house burned shortly afterward, with the body inside prior to the funeral. Wardwell blamed Taylor for causing both the death and the fire, badgering her in court as he stood among the afflicted witnesses—though he himself was not afflicted—and briefly assuming the role of hectoring magistrate. (British courtroom procedure at that time allowed more audience participation than would later be thought wise.) Goody Taylor, like so many from Andover, confessed.

Wardwell was equally aggressive against two other Reading women accused of causing Hooper's death: Goodwives Jane Lilly and Mary Coleson. According to Mary Warren, Goody Lilly sometimes visited the Procter's house—fellow witches all—but Lilly "denied that ever she had had any conferrance with Procter or his wife" or had anything to do with Hooper's death. Despite the convulsing afflicted all about her, neighbors' accusations, and Wardwell's bullying, Jane Lilly declared that "if she confessed any thing of this she shoud deny the truth & wrong her own soul." By now fewer of the accused had the fortitude to stand firm in their own innocence.

Dorcas Hoar, a widow from Beverly whose family had pilfered from their neighbors, including Reverend Hale, for years, was tried and found guilty in Salem on Tuesday, September 6. The trial of Ann Pudeator, the grand jury having indicted her for afflicting Mary Warren during the July hearing, began the same day around noon—the witnesses were summoned for twelve o'clock—and continued into the following day.

Alice Parker, already questioned at her May 12 hearing, was examined anew late on September 6. (The reason for this is not at all clear, as she had already been jailed. Perhaps, like Pudeator, she may have been released and arrested a second time, as Mary Esty certainly had been. Such a development would have stunned Mary Warren.)

Parker's specter was also reportedly active, for Annie Putnam would testify the following day that Parker's specter hurt Mary Warren and the rest of the afflicted "last night in the Court." Sarah Bibber, Mary

Walcott, and Elizabeth Hubbard were present as well, choked and
squeezed by that spirit. But Mary Warren was its particular victim,
and Goody Bibber said that she saw Mary struggle as Parker's vengeful specter "did choke sdd Warin the last night & griped her abo[u]t
the waste."

Fellow confessors Sarah Churchill and Abigail Hobbs also said they
witnessed this attack. Abigail added that "she has seen. Alice Parker
afflict Mary Warin when sd Warin was at prison. [A]lso I have seen
her afflict An Putnam by choking of them."

Thomas Putnam wrote a statement for himself and William Murray, who also took occasional notes for the court, that they had witnessed the torments of Mary Warren, Mary Walcott, and others on
September 6 during Alice Parker's examination and that the men believed that the defendant really did strike the afflicted with her glance
and recover them by her touch on that occasion and "has often hurt
the above said parsons by acts of wicthcraf."

When the grand jury indicted Alice Parker on September 7 for tormenting Mary Walcott and Mary Warren, the latest spectral attacks
counted for more than the similar assaults in May, so the clerk adjusted the date on the documents from May 12 to September 6:

The Juriors for our Sovr Lord and Lady the King and Queen doe
p[re]sent That Allice Parker Wife of John Parker of Salem In the
County of Essex aforsaid ffisherman, the ~~Twelfth~~ sixt day of ~~May~~ Sep-
tember . . . [has practiced] Certaine detestable Arts called Witchcraft
and Sorceries Wickedly Mallitiously & felloniously . . . against one
Mary Warren of Salem Aforesaid Single Woman by which said
Wicked Acts the said Mary Warren . . . was and is Tortured Aflicted
Consumed Wasted Pined and Tormented.

In June, when the jury of matrons examined several of the accused
women for witch-marks, they reported nothing unusual on Goody
Parker. Now, three months later, several people had their suspicions
about her. John Westgate had sworn a statement before John
Hathorne on June 2 and swore to it again before the grand jury September 7. According to Westgate Goody Parker had stormed into

Samuel Beadle's tavern looking for her husband one evening eight years earlier.

> [she] scolded att and called her husband all to nought, whereupon I . . . tooke her husbands part telling of her itt was an unbeseeming thing for her to come after him to the taverne and raile after thatt rate wth thatt she came up to me and call'd me rogue and bid me mind my owne busines and told me I had better have said nothing.

On his way home that night a fierce black hog pursued him, frightening even his dog, (yet never caught Westgate for all that he had to crawl along a fence-line to get his bearings). Because of his dog's panicked reaction, the hog, he supposed, "was Either the Divell or some Evell thing not a Reall hog"—either Goody Parker in spectral disguise or some imp she had sent.

John Bullock and Martha Dutch testified about the January incident, when Goody Parker was found unconscious, seemingly dead in the snow. She never responded while Bullock carried her home over his shoulder, not even when he dropped her, and not while the neighbors helped put her to bed. But afterward, said Bullock, "She rises up & laughs in o[u]r faces." Moreover, this wasn't the only time she was discovered in this condition. Even though such spells were known to have natural causes, hers now seemed all the more suspicious under the circumstances.

Widow Martha Dutch remarked on Goody Parker's gloomy foreknowledge of who would or would not survive sea voyages. Two years previously, as they had watched a returning vessel tack into Salem Harbor, Goody Dutch had remarked, "[Wha]t a great mercy itt was for to see Them Come home well and Through mercy . . . my husband had gone & Came home well many Times & I . . . did hope he would Come whome This voyage well alls[o]."

To which Goody Parker answered, "[N]o Never more in This world."

And that was exactly what happened, Goody Dutch testified, "for he died abroad as I sertinly heare."

Quaker Samuel Shattuck, who had already testified against Bridget Bishop for bewitching his son, blamed Alice Parker for worsening the boy's condition back in 1684:

[Young Sam, already] Supposed to have bin under an ill hand for Severall years before was taken in a Strange & unuceall [i.e., unusual] maner as if his vitalls would have broak out his breast boane drawn up to gather to the uper part of his brest his neck & Eys drawne Soe much aside as if they would never Come to right againe he lay in So Strange a maner tht the Docter & others did beleive he was bewitched.

This happened shortly after Goody Parker had visited, feigning concern.

Shattuck had already tried folk magic against Bridget Bishop—with no reproach from the magistrates that this was imprudent—and he did so again against Alice Parker. Actually, he said, it was "some of the visitors" who cut a lock of the boy's hair to boil (in order to harm the witch who sent the pain), but this made the child shriek. They next put the hair in a skillet over the fire, but as soon as their backs were turned the hair was thrown out into the empty room. So they put it to boil again, and Goody Parker appeared at the door as if drawn to the place. She had a thin story about coming to sell some chickens, but that tale unraveled over the next few days into contradictions, evasions, and lies.

Finally, Goody Parker and her husband both went to Shattuck's house, where she demanded to know if he had accused her of bewitching his child. "I told her I did belive She had."

"[Y]ow are a wicked man," she retorted. "The lord avenge me of you. The lord bring vengance upon you for this wrong."

Then she stormed into the sickroom and shouted at Shattuck's wife, Naomi, calling her "a wicked woman" for saying such things about her. "I hope I Shall See the downfall of you," she shouted before she left "in a great anger."

In court, when not convulsing, Mary Warren had a great deal to say about the defendant.

Mary Warren upon oath affirms to the Jury of Inquest that she hath seen Alice Parker afflict Mary Walcot, Elizabeth Hubbard, Ann Putnam, & Goodwife Vibber the last night by choking them & squeezing them. Said Parker has afflicted me, has brought me the book to sign to. She brought me a poppit & a needle & threatened to stab me if I would not stick the needle into the poppit. & she did run the needle a little way into me. Said Parker said she was a cause of the death of Thomas Wastgate [John Westgate's brother] and crew that was foundered in the sea. She was also a cause of the death of Goodwife Ormes her son that was drowned before their door and was a cause of the death of John Serlese his Barbadian boy. She was the cause also of Michael Chapman's Death in Boston Harbour. she also told me she bewiched my mother & was a caus of her death also that she bewiched my sister Eliz tht is both deaf & dumb.

The grand jury pronounced Parker's indictment *billa vera* (a true bill), a case with enough evidence to proceeded to a jury trial before the Court of Oyer and Terminer.

Ann Pudeator, for tormenting Mary Warren on July 2, was likewise held.

On September 8 William Procter, his father recently hanged as a witch and his mother waiting under a death sentence, faced the grand jury, charged with sending spectral torments against Elizabeth Hubbard and Mary Warren during his May 31 hearing back in Salem Village. Most of his paperwork is lost, so precisely what evidence Anthony Checkley presented to the grand jurors is a matter of guesswork, but something was different about his case, for this time the grand jury pronounced *both* indictments *ignoramus*. William would *not* be tried as a witch. Once he paid his jail bill—if he could—he would be free to go home.

His mother, if she heard the news in time, would have been relieved that at least her son was spared. But the result must have shaken Mary Warren and Elizabeth Hubbard, staggered that the court doubted their testimony. If there were doubt here, what else would be called into question? If the authorities would not believe their assertions, what then? William's specter attacked the girls afresh, they said, and would continue to do so in the ensuing days. What else could they expect from the son of two convicted witches?

The court tried Rebecca Nurse's sister Mary Esty and Mary Bradbury on September 9, and both, to Ann Putnam's relief, were found guilty despite their supporters. Mary Esty and her sister Sarah Cloyce had petitioned the court to allow witnesses to testify on oath on their behalf—Reverend Joseph Capen of Topsfield for one. But the only surviving record in the sisters' favor is a statement from prison keeper John Arnold and his wife that while the two women were jailed in Boston "thare daportmont wose varey s[o]bere and civell."

Sarah Cloyce was supposed to come before the grand jury on this same day, but she did not. Sarah's widowed sister-in-law Mary Towne and her four children had been summoned to testify but tried to avoid appearing. On September 7 Mary Towne wrote,

> [W]e are in a straing Condicion and most of us can scars git [out] of our beads we are so wake and not abell to Ried at all as for my dafter Rebaka she hath straing ffits somtimes she is knoked downe of a sodin and that espachaly If hur ant Easty be but named.

Widow Towne evidently thought better of including the remark about her daughter's fits at the sound of Aunt Esty's name and drew a line through that phrase—but did not obliterate it. On the following day the court issued another order for Mary and Rebecca Towne to appear against Mary Esty on September 9, and on that day the niece Rebecca seemed to be tormented by Sarah Cloyce.

Also on September 9 Giles Corey, the litigious and cantankerous farmer whose testimony helped condemn his wife and who now stood accused of the same crime, refused to cooperate with the court. He pleaded not guilty but would not consent to the trial, to speak the phrase that would allow it, partly from principle and partly, it is assumed, in an attempt to prevent property seizures. Even if he feared his land would be lost—and, in fact, no one's land would be confiscated—everyone knew what had happened at the Procter farm and the English mansion. For now his stubbornness postponed his trial.

Considering the expense of jail bills and the Procter family's losses, William Procter probably never left jail after the grand jury dismissed his case. Now, facing John Hathorne and other local magistrates on September 17, he endured a second hearing for tormenting the usual afflicted victims, but Mary Warren and Elizabeth Hubbard especially.

He denied the charge, but when he looked at Mary Warren, his family's former servant, she collapsed as if struck. His touch restored her, allowing her to say, "that Wm Proctor had almost murdered her to death this day by pains in all her bones and Inwards also." His specter, she added, also afflicted the others.

All of the afflicted fell at his glance and revived at his reluctant touch: Mary Warren, Annie Putnam and Mary Walcott ("in dreadfull fitts"), Elizabeth Hubbard, sisters Elizabeth and Alice Booth, Sarah Churchill, and a new girl, Mary Pickworth. "Elizabeth Booth said she saw him twist and pinch poppets this very day," whereas Hubbard and Walcott claimed that he made them promise not to tell the court what he was up to.

Yet again William Procter was held for future trial.

Giles Corey, even with friends trying to convince him that refusing to cooperate could be suicidal, continued to stand mute. After three refusals over as many days the court turned to a technique newly available to them from English law—pressing. He would be placed on his back under boards with heavy weights stacked on top until he either relented or was crushed. Giles still would not agree, and the torture was scheduled for September 19. If Massachusetts law had to conform to English law, then they would threaten the man with pressing to force him to plea.

Mrs. Ann Putnam, who was growing close to her time, may have depended even more on Thomas and Annie for news from the courts. It would not do to risk the babe, now that it was so truly quickened, by such proximity to the evil of the Devil's witches. Such baleful proximity could mark an infant even before birth. Day after day the courts questioned defendants, heard witnesses relate their testimony, marshaled evidence—much of *that* observed right before their eyes in the convulsions and pain of the bewitched. And day after day the defendants were found guilty, thus removing, in Ann's mind, another enemy, another source of harm.

Mary Esty, sister to Rebecca Nurse, had been found guilty, which was no surprise to Ann, who knew the authorities had located witch-marks on the woman, and was sentenced to hang. Goody Esty submitted a second petition to the court after the guilty verdict was pronounced:

[B]eing condemned to die . . . [the woman had written, or had some-one write for her, and] knowing my own Innocencye Blised be the lord for it and seeing plainly the wiles and subtility of my accusers by my selfe can not but Judg charitably of others that are going the same way of my selfe if the Lord stepps not mightily in . . . I Petition to your ho-nours not for my own life for I know I must die and my apointed time is sett but the Lord he knowes it is that if it be possible no more Inno-centt blood may be shed which undoubtidly cannot be Avoydd In the way and course you goe in I Question not but your honours does to the uttmost of your Powers in the discovery and detecting of witchcraft and witches and would not be gulty of Innocent blood for the world but by my own Innocencye I know you are in the wrong way . . . I would humbly begg of you that your honours would be plesed to ex-amine theis Aflicted Persons strictly and keepe them apart some time and likewise to try some of these confesing wichis I being confident there is severall of them has belyed themselve[s] and others as will ap-peare if not in this wo[l]rd I am sure in the world to come whither I am now agoing. [T]he Lord above who is the searcher of all heart[s] knowes that as I shall answer it att the Tribunall seat that I know not the least thinge of witchcraft therfore I cannot I dare not belye my own soule

But neither the court—nor the Putnams—changed their minds.

Mistress Mary Bradbury, a thorn to so many of the Carr family, was likewise found guilty and condemned September 9, the same day as Esty. "I am wholly inocent of any such wickedness," she had declared. Over one hundred of her neighbors had signed a petition attesting to her good behavior, including Ann Putnam's kin William and Elizabeth Carr, a circumstance that could only make Ann wonder how some people could be so deceived. But, as Ann saw it, the magistrates' perception had weighed all that against the obvious evidence unfolding before their eyes in the sufferings of the afflicted, and the woman was condemned with the rest. Even more disconcerting to Ann would be the appalling news soon after that Mrs. Bradbury had disappeared from the jail.

Where was she? Was she heading for distant parts to hide in another jurisdiction? Or was she lurking nearby, unseen, waiting to take revenge on those who opposed her?

She was gone, simply gone, spirited out of the jail by . . . what? Spirits? The Devil?

By bribery, more likely. Gold could buy anything, it seemed. Ann, counting herself a reasonable woman, could understand the venality of men. So the Putnams could not let down their guard in this righteous, necessary cause. Ann could not relax yet.

Other prisoners escaped as well. By mid-September John Alden managed to flee the Boston jail, first to his family in Plymouth County, so descendants would say, then further to the province of New York, following Mrs. Cary and the Englishes.

With Giles Corey still stubbornly uncooperative, the Putnams learn, the court has ordered him subjected to peine forte et dure *to make him agree to be tried—to be pressed to death if he would not answer how he would be tried. The evening before this happens witch-specters yet again assail Annie Putnam.*

At the end of the torture Annie seems to be listening to some other entity. It is the ghost of a man in a winding sheet, the girl says. Corey killed him—"Pressing him to Death with his Feet"—and then the old man sold his soul to the Devil to escape the murder charge.

Ann and Thomas remember the death and the ensuing trial. It is quite true that Corey was tried for the murder of his hired man Jacob Goodall, a neighbor's slow-witted son ("almost a Natural Fool" in Thomas's opinion, for the man had been born that way), and it was true that Corey had beaten the man severely. Yet no one had mentioned this during the trials, and it happened well before Annie's birth.

Annie relays the ghost's message: It must be done to him as he has done to me.

This is indeed significant. Thomas composes a letter to Judge Samuel Sewall relating the vision and what he remembers of the old court case. "[I]t cost him a great deal of Mony to get off," in addition to collaborating with the Devil, Thomas writes. He forgets—or prefers to forget— that Corey beat Jacob with a stout staff rather than his feet and that as other impatient people had struck the man as well from time to time, the coroner's jury's opinion was inconclusive. Joining with the Devil makes more sense. This way the Putnams need not feel sorrow for Corey or guilt for themselves when he faces the morrow's torture.

Rebecca Nurse's family, meanwhile, continued their lives, journeying to Topsfield for Sabbath services, avoiding the neighbors. Francis, a widower now, had begun to lose her months before in March, when she was first taken away. The house may have seemed empty then, but since her death a profound absence pervaded it—the silence when a voice should answer and cannot, her familiar footsteps gone along with the little disregarded sounds of everyday life as she went about her tasks—all ended, leaving a hollowness in life itself. Absence filled the house, the farm, the world—but not his heart, for all its wounds, or his resolve.

Her sisters still needed help, and her good name *must* be cleared. The Lord knew her true worth, of that Francis was certain, but the world and her neighbors who inhabited it must be made to understand the truth of what had happened, the travesty of justice and the treachery of men and young girls who cared not whether the blood they shed was guilty or innocent.

With Giles Corey still stubbornly uncooperative, the court ordered the *peine forte et dure*. He remained silent and died under the torture on September 19. Because Giles still owed jail fees, Sheriff Corwin and his men went to the Corey farm to seize goods in payment. Giles's daughter Elizabeth Moulton and her husband, John, who had already gone to months of trouble and expense providing for both Giles and Martha in prison, scraped together £11:6:0 to prevent this. In the rush, the "personal Estate" Martha had been caring for as inheritance for her son Thomas Rich was lost as well.

Yet again the procession formed on September 22, yet again a crowd of spectators gathered near the prison's gate to see the condemned led out. Mary Warren joined the little knot of afflicted witnesses. Behind them two more of the recently condemned remained, their deaths postponed. Dorcas Hoar confessed at last, after so many protestations of innocence, *after* she was found guilty and pleaded for time to settle her soul before she died and faced God's judgment. Unlike John Procter's plea for time, however, hers was granted—the confession seeming, to the court, like honesty. Abigail Faulkner also stayed behind until her next child was born—she and Elizabeth Procter having at least that in common. Old Mrs. Bradbury was absent from the procession as well; the sheriff and deputies kept an embarrassed silence about that.

Even so, the cart held eight today: Martha Corey, Mary Esty, Alice Parker, Mary Parker, Ann Pudeator, Wilmot Read, Margaret Scott, and Samuel Wardwell, who, after confessing at his hearing and accusing others in court, had, at his own trial, repudiated his confession when he saw that it would not save him. Of the ten more condemned prisoners, nine waited behind for another session of executions.

The weather was cooler now, with the fall colors in the leaves hastened by a dry summer as the drought continued.

Down the road they passed, kicking up dust that gritted the eyes and dried the breath as it coated yellowing roadside weeds and scarlet vines, ghost-like, beneath a skin of dust. The crowd turned downhill to the causeway in the marsh, bunching up as the way narrowed at the bridge over the stream. The prisoners and officers preceded the rest, and as the loaded cart turned up the further hill, its wheels became stuck in the soft earth. Some of the afflicted and others took up the cry that the Devil was trying to hold back the cart. Mary Warren joined in, but for all of Satan's boasted power, the delay was only temporary. The deputies heaved against the cart, the wheels soon lurched free, and the procession continued on up to the gallows.

The condemned, given their chance to speak last words, remained calm and solemn. Two in particular impressed Robert Calef. As he later reported the incidents:

> Mary Esty, Sister also to Rebecca Nurse, when she took her last farewell of her Husband, Children and Friends, was, as is reported by them present, as Serious, Religious, Distinct, and Affectionate as could well be exprest, drawing Tears from the Eyes of almost all present.

Martha Corey, Gospel woman to the last, "concluded her Life with an Eminent Prayer upon the Ladder."

Samuel Wardwell, who had had so much to say about his own fortune-telling abilities in the past and even more when he blamed other suspects of committing witchcraft, was, according to Calef, less successful.

> At Execution while he was speaking to the People, protesting his Innocency, the Executioner being at the same time smoaking Tobacco, the smoake coming in his Face, interrupted his Discourse, those Accusers said, the Devil hindered him with the smoake.

But if he were the only one silenced, then even Alice Parker, Mary Warren's enemy, made an appropriate statement.

Hands and feet tied, one by one they were turned off the ladder, and one by one they died with the usual painful messy contortions. Then there was nothing left but to let the workmen bury the dead, with the corpses hanging there long enough to warn and deter other evildoers.

As Mary and the rest began to turn back toward town and relatives of some of the dead waited at the edges to claim their kin home for burial, Reverend Noyes regarded the eight bodies swaying at rope's end from the gallows and commented, "What a sad thing it is to see Eight Firebrands of Hell hanging there."

Before the afternoon was out, clouds gathered and began to rain on the parched dry land. Then it rained harder. People could hope that the long summer's drought had ended, but there was still the next court sitting to contemplate. What the courts might do was even more uncertain than New England's weather.

Tituba thinks she hears a light rain pattering outside on dust too dry to absorb it yet. She is preoccupied, however, with the knowledge that eight more are dead, hanged like the rest. But not Giles Corey, who refused to cooperate and was pressed to death. Tituba shudders at the thought. The jail had been quieter that day, after old Corey was taken out and not brought back. Some of the deputies working that detail returned ashen and haggard, as though they had been sick. Tituba had overheard some of what they said.

"But that stubborn old man kept refusing to cooperate. He even said, 'More weight,' as if he was directing the job."

"Oh, how do you know what he said? I hear you were puking your guts out."

"That was later . . . and you didn't hear his ribs crack."

A third guard chimed in as the voices receded down the corridor: "I hear that after Corey finally died the sheriff had to poke the man's tongue back into his mouth with the tip of his cane."

The prisoners kept an appalled silence. Would the court order pressing for any of the others? No one knew.

Martha Corey, widowed by this nastiness, had long before dismissed Tituba, Good, and Osborn as "idle slothful persons," easy prey for prowling devils. But Tituba has to admit that she admires how the woman faced her death. By all report, she had said her piece from the gallows, another one of her public prayers that shocked the men so. And the week before that, Reverend Parris and the deacons from the Salem Village Church had arrived at the jail to excommunicate Goody Corey—her, the Gospel woman herself. Tituba heard only snatches from down the hallway and overheard more from jail yard gossip. Goody Corey had refused Reverend Parris's prayers, boldly and right to his face—not that that stopped him—and talked back to his comments, something Tituba had never dared to do. Yes, she has to admire the woman for that.

Mistress Bradbury's escape is likewise encouraging, though Tituba, as she hears the rain increase, does not imagine anyone is working to help her break out. She thought she heard some furtive noises that night, of people moving around, the grate of a key in a lock, hushed voices and the shuffle of an old woman too long in chains. Looking back, Tituba thinks that the escape must explain those sounds—as well as the angry voices the following morning.

Outside, rain drips from the eves.

Not so encouraging is Samuel Wardwell's swift trial and condemnation. He confessed as Tituba has. He accused others also and was far more vigorous about it than she ever was. Yet he was not kept alive as a future witness but instead put before the grand jury within days when he gave up the pretense, admitted his innocence, and was tried and condemned. Now he is dead, hanged with the latest batch of eight.

How does this affect her own future? Tituba can only guess.

The sound of the rain increases to a hiss, and a damp breeze wanders through the small window.

(16)

October 1692

Mary English, shivering in the sea wind, draws her cloak closer about her.

Her new maid is busy watching the boats maneuver among the wharves and a larger ship tacking along the channel. It seems strange to look south into the harbor instead of east, but New York City lies at the southern tip of Manhattan Island. The buildings are different too—Dutch architecture and Dutch speech instead of English for the most part. Her maid's native Dutch is more fluent than her English. Sometimes it is a trial to communicate with her new servants. Mary is used to the French she heard in the streets of Salem and at home, but here there are more tongues and peoples. It is a good enough place, though, and they have found helpful people, but it is not home. Philip is more comfortable here than Mary is—her husband has traveled so much and so far, so this is hardly surprising. Mary finds herself comparing everything to Salem—the harbor, the houses. Salem is deadly to them as things stand, but she is homesick and Philip's talk of locating here permanently vexes her.

She calls to her maid, and they begin the walk home from the market. As the wind picks up she feels a tightening in her chest, fumbles for the handkerchief in her pocket, and presses it to her mouth to muffle a cough—and another cough. On the flight south or here in this alien city she has caught something she cannot shake.

Philip is home before them, full of fresh air and news from the marketplace.

"Finally!" he says in a triumphant tone. "The fools in Massachusetts are admitting doubts, consulting New York ministers for their advice in handling the witch accusations." Philip knows how the accusers ought to have been treated from the beginning. "Liars all of them," he has said of-

ten enough. "Fools. Maybe someone will listen this time," though he has his doubts about Will Stoughton. "That obstinate cochon *never changes his mind."*

He goes on about this and about how the province of New York is the place in which he should have settled years ago. The news is hopeful, but it makes Mary all the more homesick. Although New York was unlikely to prosecute witch suspicions, the politics here can be savage: the leaders in the government that took over after Andros's fall were drawn and quartered as traitors when the new royal governor arrived.

And the children—how are they faring? Sooner or later the witch scare has to end, but will Philip let her return? She longs to be in her own home among her own things, though many of their goods were confiscated after their escape became known. She thinks of her girlhood sampler. Where is it now? Things like that are not just possessions, earthly goods as opposed to treasures in Heaven. They hold her history and maintain ties to her past, to her mother.

Philip has lived in so many places—it isn't the same for him. He does not long to see Salem again, the light on the sea, the blue and distant islands, the long back of Marblehead across the harbor, beyond the bristle of Salem's masts and spars—home.

The September hangings marked a turning point in the witch trials. Enough people harboring uncertainty had joined those who opposed the trials that officials allowed a month's pause until the next session on November 2 so the legislature might convene in Boston to rewrite the laws of Massachusetts. This created a breathing space as well as an excuse to pull back. It gave the Nurse family time to plan and hope.

But not everyone thought the court had been mistaken.

Neighbors in Lynn, Boston, Reading, and Gloucester still feared—and accused—their neighbors. A girl in Andover thought a certain dog was an imp, so someone shot the creature dead. Another dog acting strangely in Salem Village was thought to be the *victim* of witchcraft, ridden by the specter of John Bradstreet (the Andover magistrate's brother), but someone killed this animal anyway. Critics of the court's methods remarked acidly that this was the only afflicted victim who was punished; clearly they thought the human afflicted needed punishment. Mary Warren must have heard this view expressed, must have seen disapproving glares directed at her, which now replaced the approval that had encouraged her deadly antics all summer. Nevertheless, for the time being both Dudley and John Bradstreet as well as John's wife fled to New Hampshire.

At some point the afflicted in Salem named a gentleman in Boston who, instead of fleeing, immediately informed his accusers that they were liable to an expensive lawsuit if they continued. The accusers backed down, abruptly and conveniently unsure of their identification.

Another unidentified Boston man "of no small note," convinced that his ailing child was bewitched, brought the child all the way to Salem for spectral diagnosis and received the names of two Boston-area women whom he already suspected: Mrs. Mary Obinson and Mrs. Elizabeth Cary. Yet when he returned home and made his complaint before Boston magistrates, they refused to have any part of it; Mrs. Cary was in New York by then anyway, but Mrs. Obinson, a quarrelsome woman in a turbulent marriage, was spared arrest.

Reverend Increase Mather gave the man a severe dressing-down. Was there not a God in Boston, Mather snapped, that he felt he had to go to the Devil in Salem for advice? Mather had recently finished writing a lengthy essay, *Cases of Conscience*, that marshaled the reasons why spectral evidence should *not* be used in court. Increase made it clear that he believed in the reality of witches but did not trust the court's present methods of discerning them. Spectral evidence, he argued, had its source in the Devil and therefore could not be trusted. On October 3 his son Cotton Mather had read the piece to the monthly meeting of Boston-area ministers in Cambridge for its first public presentation.

Suspects were still being arrested, however, for on the same day as the reading of *Cases of Conscience*, Sarah Cole of Lynn faced the Salem magistrates, her very presence sending Mary Warren into the usual fits. Mary recounted the names of other suspects' specters consorting with the defendant, but Sarah Cole was convinced that specters besieged *her*, blaming her own sister-in-law. The most self-incriminating information she admitted now was, when she was a girl, using a Venus Glass and egg "to see what trade their sweethearts would be of"—folk magic that some of the afflicted girls had tried themselves.

By October 6 the court had already begun releasing prisoners on bail, beginning with the children and young people from Andover—even Mary Lacey, who had accused her own mother and grandmother. Bail was high, far higher than Reverend Parris's £60 yearly salary—when he was paid, as he had not been—and would be forfeited if the defendants were not produced for trial when called. Neighborhood men joined forces to assemble the required sums: £500 sterling each for Mary Lacey Jr. and John Sawdey; somewhat less for five others, including Martha Carrier's daughter Sarah. At least twelve more would be released before the year ended.

Other prisoners managed to break jail instead, although escapees were subject to fines. On October 7, the day after the Andover releases, Sheriff George Corwin nearly confiscated the goods and chattels belonging to fugitives Edward and Sarah Bishop, but their son Samuel managed to borrow and pay the £10 fine, for which he received a receipt.

Boston Merchant Thomas Brattle, like Increase Mather, also composed his thoughts on why the court's present methods could not be trusted, mentioning the people who had escaped to New York and the government's reluctance to recapture them. His argument, dated October 8, circulated in manuscript.

Reverend Samuel Willard, who had been accused back in June—an accusation the court dismissed as an error—and who had helped Philip and Mary English escape, also wrote about the folly of accepting spectral evidence. This appeared in an anonymous pamphlet, though everyone seemed to know who was responsible for it.

At the same time Cotton Mather completed his account of the trials as requested by Lieutenant Governor William Stoughton, who perhaps hoped to fortify the public's wavering support for the court that he led as chief justice. Stoughton called Cotton's work an "Elaborate and most seasonable Discourse" in his letter authorizing its publication.

Although Cotton had previously warned against embracing spectral evidence, he accepted the court's assurance that far more than that had been used to convict the defendants. This stance resulted in some uncomfortable feelings between himself and his father, though the two apparently came to agree that the two books presented dual aspects of this problem. Gossip concluded that the Mathers were at loggerheads, and historians have argued over the matter ever since.

Stoughton's introductory letter referred to him "still Labouring and Proceeding in the Trial of the persons Accused and Convicted for Witchcraft," but when Cotton's book appeared around October 12, many people assumed the Court of Oyer and Terminer was canceled, though no official word confirmed that assumption.

On October 12 Captain Nathaniel Cary set out for New York to join, or rejoin, his wife with the encouraging news as nine men from Andover petitioned the legislature on behalf of their imprisoned wives, daughters, neighbors. Omitting the fact that, for a time, some of them had doubted their own wives' innocence, the men noted that the approaching winter cold and scanty food not only added to the prisoners' sufferings but might also prove deadly if prolonged. Therefore, might at least the repentant suspects "be released to their families to be cared for until the court sent for them?"

A second Andover petition on October 18 emphasized that several of the prisoners were church members with blameless reputations who were now "accused of witchcraft, by some distempered persons in these parts." Furthermore, "we know not who can think himself safe, if the Accusations of children and others who are under a Diabolicall influence shall be received against persons of good fame." Both documents complained of the burdensome court and jail fees that families had to shoulder.

Now and then the prisoners had visitors—relatives bringing food and clothing—if they were lucky—concerned friends and charitable neighbors coming to offer comfort as well as gawkers and the idly curious.

Then, possibly on October 19, two gentlemen from Boston, Reverend Increase Mather and Thomas Brattle, entered the Salem jail to speak with the prisoners. Both had criticized the court's methods and now came to speak directly with the accused. Mather was prepared to take notes. He had spoken with some of the prisoners earlier, when they had held to their self-damning confessions.

Now several Andover women were eager to recant their earlier stories.

Her confession, Mrs. Mary Osgood explained, "was wholly false," the product of "the violent urging and unreasonable pressings that were used toward her." None of it had happened.

Why then, Mather asked, had she provided such specific details about signing the Devil's book, undergoing the Devil's baptism, and the like? Because, she explained, the magistrates had dismissed her denials, insisting instead that she *had* done these things, that they knew when she had done them, and so she must tell them. So she had desperately searched her memory for likely occasions when it *might* have happened and, little by little, concocted enough of a detailed account that the magistrates might accept.

Other women told how they were "frighted into" false confession, hounded until "at last they did say even any thing that was desired of them." They wept with anguish, "enough to affect the hardest heart;" wrote Mather, and they especially lamented that they had accused others, people they never even suspected.

Goodwife Mary Tyler's own brother-in-law had broken her down with his badgering, his main argument being "that God would not suffer so many good men to be in such an errour about it." Now she knew that "she was guilty of a great sin in belying of herself, and desired to mourn for it as long as she lived."

The gentlemen were impressed and convinced by the woman's words and by the way she spoke them "with such affection, sorrow, relenting, grief, and mourning, as that it exceeds any pen for to describe and express the same." But other, younger confessors, despite the sympathetic audience, may have held to their confessions, including Sarah Churchill and some of Mary Bridges's daughters who lacked their mother's resolve.

As Goodwife Rebecca Eames told Mather and Brattle, even her principal accusers, Mary Lacey and Abigail Hobbs, who had taunted and spat at her during her examination until she confessed, had admitted that they knew nothing against her, "Nothing but the Divells delusions."

Unfortunately, the surviving notes say nothing about what Mary Warren might have said.

The legislature, besides considering the recent petitions, faced the problem of what some would call "white witchcraft." By October 25 the House passed a new act specifically forbidding both the practitioner and the client from engaging in fortune-telling and juggling (meaning sleight of hand) in order to reveal a person's future or the whereabouts of lost or stolen items, as such information could come only from evil spirits. "By useing such unlawfull Arts some have been drawn to the horrid sin of Witchcraft to the high displeasure of Allmighty God and theire own destruction." Anyone harboring "any Books of Conjuration, witchcraft Judgling or the like" was to bring those dangerous volumes to the local justice of the peace for public burning.

Anyone committing such attempts at magic would be "publickly & severely whipt" or be fined not more than £20 for a first offense. A second offence would result in the offender standing "upon the Gallows, w[i]th a Paper on his or her breast signifying the Crime, and be whipt as aforesaid, and Imprisoned during the Pleasure of the Court."

Anyone who consulted a fortune-teller or the like, just observed or even heard of such goings-on and did not report it to the justice of the peace, or concealed anyone who possessed "such unlawfull Books" would be fined £5 or be publicly whipped for the first offense and suffer "double punishment" for a second.

The House sent the bill up to the Council for their approval. As word of this proposed new law circulated, many must have recalled the fortune-telling by egg and glass that some of the afflicted girls had tried (and the results) or Mistress Mary Sibley's witch-cake charm. Rebecca Nurse's family certainly noticed how this law undermined the validity of the questions put to the supposedly bewitched girls in their fits. If devils deluded or conspired with the "afflicted," then questioning the girls was tantamount to questioning those devils.

On the following day the legislature proposed a public fast day for the province, wherein the populace would pray for guidance to understand why God had allowed Satan to cause such havoc among them, and, as Judge Samuel Sewall understood it, to understand how best to proceed in the tangled matter of suspected witches. The bill summarized the government's view of the problem by noting that the Devil had prevailed to the extent that "severall persons have been Seduced, and drawn away into that horrid and most Detestable sin of Witchcraft." Therefore, to prevent the spread of these "Satanicall Delutions," the government had formed a special court of Oyer and Terminer composed of "Certaine Gentlemen of the Council . . . persons of known Integrity, faithfullness and . . . Sufficiency who have Strenuously Endeavoured to Discharge their Duty to the utmost of their Power, for the finding out & Exterpation of that Diabollicall Evill so much prevaileing amongst us" for the punishment of the guilty and for "cleaning the Reputation, & persons of the Inocent."

However, "Notwithstanding the Indefatigable Endeavours of those Worthy Gentlemen, with Others, to Suppress that Crying Enormity," they found "the most Astonishing Augmentation and Increase of the Number of Persons Accused, by those Afflicted," that many of these suspects were "persons of good Conversation Godliness and honesty." And complicating this at the same time, "severall persons have Come and Accused themselves before Authority, and by many Circumstances, confessed themselves Guilty of that most abominable Wickedness; with divers Other Strang & unaccountable Occurrances of this Nature through the Rage and malice of Satan, greatly threatning the utter Ruine, and Distruction of this poor Country."

Therefore, they ought to ask for "Divine Assistance" in finding "the Right way, that those That are guilty may be found Out, and brought to Condigne [i.e., deserved] punishment, the Inocent may be Cleared, and our feares and troubles Removed." They also suggested that a "Convocation of the Elders may be Called who with the Honble Council and Other persons" would prayfully "make Inspection into these Intricaces . . . in this Difficult Case."

The bill passed thirty-three to twenty-nine, and most members of the Court of Oyer and Terminer considered themselves dismissed, even though the bill did not specifically say so.

But clearly the bill's view of the crisis did not match that of Rebecca Nurse's kin or the people in exile, particularly as it absolved only the integrity and faithfulness of the magistrates and not the unjustly executed. The court had done precious little toward "cleaning the Reputation, & persons of the Inocent."

Ann Putnam watches her husband go off toward the fields with the hired men trailing behind. Now that he is home more often, maybe those men will get some actual work done. All summer it was anyone's guess whether the day's tasks would be completed. With Thomas so often busy at the court, the men took advantage of their master's absence. She would send young Tommy out with weak beer for the men to wash down their noon meal, and the boy would return to say he had found the tools but not the men; they had gone off to Salem to gawk at the courts. A farm needed its master's eye—and the well-placed toe of his boot, it would seem—to prosper.

Thomas has sacrificed so much this last summer, *she thinks,* risking his livelihood to fight against the spectral threats. *Due to just the Bradbury specter, Thomas has lost his sheep, a cow, and his favorite horse.*

She turns back from the door and draws it shut. Mornings are frosty now, and some places have seen light snow. Although she is relieved that the long hot spell has ended, she has not felt comfortable in months. Her back hurts, her head aches, her ankles are swollen, and she cannot get out of her own way. The child's bulk is oppressive even in cooler weather, and she tries to push that ungrateful thought from her mind.

She heaves open the lid of a chest and again checks her supply of childbed linen: strips to use as swaddling bands, towels to clean herself and the child. She has brewed crocks of beer, now stored in the lean-to for the midwife and the neighbor women who will attend the birth. She hopes that the cakes, resting under a towel, will not grow stale before the baby arrives.

So much can go wrong at the time of any birth. Both the mother and the child—and even both together—can die. And these deaths, however sad, are natural. But in addition there is the matter of witches. At least Goody Nurse is out of the way, safely tucked into Hell, as far as Ann is concerned. And that sister of hers, the Esty woman, is dead as well. The third sister still waits in jail. Might she mean to seek revenge?

Annie still testifies, still identifies the witch specters when asked. Alarmingly, fewer people appreciate the girl's efforts now.

Worse, the children of some Andover witches are being released on bail—their freedom purchased.

Money could buy anything, *she thinks.*

The last Sabbath Reverend Parris had preached, in part, on reconcil-iation, referring to the "jars & differences" among friends. But the next trials will begin early in November, and hopefully more enemies of God (and of the Putnams) will hang. Besides, *she thinks,* is it even possible to reconcile with neighbors who harbor witches?

Worrying over this and her other burden, Ann feels a sensation that turns into a stab. She flinches and another stab strikes. Not a witch's spec-tral torment—this is the baby, her baby, at this vulnerable time.

"Get your father," she tells Tommy. "Tell him to fetch the midwife."

She thinks again of lost Sarah writhing in her arms, convulsing until she died. But the witches will not have this child.

No, they will not.

Ann Putnam gave birth to Abigail, her eighth child, on October 27, a time of gathering storm. The next day brought torrents of rain and the month's highest tides, which washed away coastal roads and drenched Chief Justice *cum* Lieutenant Governor William Stoughton as he made his way over Boston's narrow Neck road from Dorchester to attend the General Court. Other travelers, not as lucky, actually drowned in this storm.

That afternoon, having sent a servant back over the flooding Neck to fetch him dry clothing from home, Stoughton asked the governor and council once again if the Court of Oyer and Terminer should sit the following week as scheduled, for many in Boston already assumed the session would not take place. Phips's answer was a "great silence" that most took to mean the court would *not* sit.

Such an ambiguous nonanswer was not enough. Stoughton was ab-sent the following day, October 29, when James Russell, an assistant who had observed the April examinations of Elizabeth Procter and Sarah Cloyce, asked outright if the temporary Court of Oyer and

Terminer would stand or fall. This time Phips spoke plainly: "It must fall."

On the same day the House passed a list defining thirteen capital crimes, including witchcraft: "If any man or woman be a witch, that is, hath or consulteth with a familiar spirit, they shall be put to death." This was the usual definition of witchcraft and entirely consistent with English legal precedent.

On the next Sabbath, October 30, Reverend Samuel Parris brought out the church's silver baptismal bowl. Over the water, in the shallow, wide-rimmed vessel, two men, both church members, offered their infant children for baptism. Thomas Putnam, holding three-day-old Abigail, presented her to God and the congregation—a living child, a symbol of renewal and hope. But Jonathan Tarbell also brought his son Jonathan, born late the last February, only weeks before his beloved grandmother Rebecca Nurse was arrested for witchcraft.

The Nurse kin had lately avoided their Salem Village neighbors, and none of them trusted Parris anymore. Seeing Tarbell with the child must have surprised more than a few in the congregation. What his relatives thought of his appearance in the meeting house is another question; the awkward tension can well be imagined.

Tituba watches the people come and go in the jail—guards changing shifts, prisoners being taken out and back to the exercise yard, prisoners' relatives to visit. With no court sessions this month, activity has slacked off, tensions lessened—but only a little, for the time being. Candy joins her to pace the yard inside the fence. A brief snow has already fallen earlier in the month, to Candy's astonishment. Now she huddles her shawl closer and shivers when the breeze kicks up, bringing with it the sulfurous scent of low tide from North River. Tituba imagines the slim cut of the channel in the wider muddy width, which she cannot see from the jail.

At the beginning of the month some of the children from Andover were released on bail. No one expected that. And more children have been freed since then. She has heard the guards gossiping about this, and the sums sound unbelievable—more than seven years worth of her master's salary for only a few children. Can that be true? And how did anyone manage to pay it? The only thing she knows for certain is that no one is going to offer that much money for her freedom, not even to buy her outright.

Even though those young prisoners were let go, other, adult suspects decided to take what chances they could to escape. Edward and Sarah Bishop, the couple with the unlicensed tavern, had left somehow. Their freedom did not preclude their impoverishment, though. The sheriff and his deputies had marched off the day after the first children were released to confiscate cattle and other goods from Bishop's farm.

Despite the unexpected releases the next set of sessions scheduled to be-gin in November loom heavier and heavier as time draws on. Life in the jail drags intolerably, yet the remaining time before scheduled tri-als—considering how they always came out—speeds alarmingly closer and closer, the respite dwindling alarmingly quickly as the month reaches its conclusion. The people already condemned to death but not yet hanged have an even worse time of it—how many days until their last? Not everyone in Massachusetts agrees with the courts, what with the way evidence has been presented and regarded. Tituba wonders if the justices will listen to those tempering voices?

Not until the very end of the month does word come that the Court of Oyer and Terminer has been canceled, postponed indefinitely until En-gland sends advice. How long will that take?

Tituba and Candy resume their walk, making one more circuit of the small, open space for the thousandth time.

(17)
𝔑ovember to 𝔇ecember 1692

Mistress Ann Putnam cradles the infant in her arms and watches her sleep. Dreaming of milk, though she has lately nursed, little Abigail makes nuzzling motions with her lips. So tiny and perfect and alive—yet so vulnerable still. Even after seven other births, Ann sees that the little life is amazing—God's work. Ann hugs the baby close as if to hide the child from vengeful eyes, but this makes the baby whine and protest, so she relaxes her hold.

The day is darkening already, with winter drawing close. She expects Thomas and Annie to return at any moment but startles anyway at the sound of voices and the thump of hoof-fall in the door yard. Tommy throws the door open, announcing, "Father is home!" Slamming the door once more, he rushes out in a gust of cold air and the acrid scent of dry fallen oak leaves that swirl on the floor in his wake. He is eager to help his father rub down the mare, and Ann hears their voices receding toward the stable.

Annie enters, looking chilled and more subdued than usual after such journeys.

"Did it go well?" Ann asks.

"Yes."

But her mother hears a hesitation in her voice, so she presses, "What happened?"

Annie saw the specters and so did Mercy. Four witches, all arrested—the same neighbors the dying woman suspected. Annie does not think Mrs. Fisk will survive even if there is an arrest. The doctor does not think she will either, though the family tries to hope and intends to enter a complaint before the magistrates.

Thomas stamps in, bringing more cold air. His wife instinctively draws her baby closer. As he warms himself at the hearth, he completes the story, providing details Annie didn't want to impart. When they approached Gloucester by the Ipswich Bridge, their party encountered an old woman. No, he doesn't know who she was, but by her scowl and the fact that they were on a life-saving mission at the behest of a dying woman's kin, and not for the first time—which should have been obvious, given local knowledge—he does not doubt that she was a witch as well. The withering look she gave them sent the girls, Annie included, into fits. They flinched and convulsed, their pain obvious, but there was no sign of concern from that old baggage. No, she just glared at them, in contempt of their pain. And then she kept on walking.

"But that was not the worst of it," Thomas continues, tugging off his boots by the fire. The other people present, the Gloucester folk who had escorted them as well as a few bystanders—not one of them did anything to help. No one apprehended the woman, much less lifted a finger to help the girls.

Ann shudders, and her shudders rock the sleeping Abigail in her aching arms.

How could people become so blind to the danger? Considering the current lapse in the trials, it all seemed odd . . . more than odd—threatening. And with so many people's views of the matter changing, shifting like so many weathervanes, as if merely being tired of hearing about a problem made it go away.

Although two of the Towne sisters were hanged and—God willing—are no longer a threat, as Ann cannot but hope, one remains while the ghost of the second, Mary Esty, has been reported exhorting a girl in Beverly. And wasn't there a girl in Boston equally beset?

To Ann, it is obvious the witches are still out there, still crowding the jails and others still running free despite these latest arrests. This was not over. No it was not.

What were people thinking of? Were they thinking at all?

Although the most recent Gloucester suspects were soon under arrest, the Herrick girl in Beverly changed her story about the specters that threatened her. One was the ghost of Mary Esty, whereas the tormentor looked like Mrs. Hale, the minister's wife. But Mrs. Hale's likeness was false, the girl said to Reverend Gerrish of Wenham and Reverend Hale himself on November 13. The apparition was a devilish disguise to deceive the girl and to incriminate an innocent woman. That was what Goody Esty's ghost wanted the Herrick girl to know. This revelation appalled Hale, not only because the initial report placed his wife in danger but also because it meant that *any* of the year's reported specters could have been false as well—and probably were. He had had doubts before, but they had not been strong enough to fully change his opinions.

What might Rebecca Nurse's family and the late Mary Esty's kin have thought of Hale's epiphany? Hale and others now wondered: Was Goodwife Esty, that good woman, not satisfied with presenting the petitions before her death to help the other prisoners, now working from the next world to expose the Devil's lies? Or was this the girl's face-saving excuse when not enough people believed her fits were real? In any case, the growing public doubt was encouraging.

By December even some of the prisoners were encouraged enough to petition for release on bail, including Abigail Faulkner, who had already been found guilty of the charges and condemned to death once her baby was born.

Three days later, on December 6, eight Andover men likewise petitioned, describing the prison conditions that "Exposed [their wives and daughters] to great sufferrings, which daily Encrease by reason of the winter comeing on." They had hoped for a general jail delivery, on bail at least, "but since that hath been so long deferred, and we are very sensible of the Extream danger the Prisoners are in of perishing, if they are not speedily released."

In a plea for themselves and for "thre or foure men" also imprisoned, another petition from ten women in the Ipswich jail also described prison conditions. With the trials evidently suspended for the winter, they asked that they might be released on bail until spring. "We are not in this unwilling nor afrayd to abide the tryall," they wrote, but hoped for the law's compassionate consideration "of our suffering condicion in the present state we are in, being like to perish with cold in lying longer in prison in this cold season of the yeare, some of us being aged either about or nere fourscore some though younger yet being with Child, and one giving suck to a child not ten weekes old yet, and all of us weake and infirme at the best, and one fettered with irons this halfe yeare and allmost distroyed with soe long an Imprisonment."

Samuel Ray of Salem Village posted bail in Salem on December 10 so young Dorothy Good could be brought home from the Boston jail, where she had been left chained and terrified for so long. But her father, William, now found her impossible to manage, and years later he would remark that she had "little or no reason to govern herself."

No one petitioned for Tituba's release.

And what might the Putnams have thought? The number of people discharged on bail until their trials, high though the sums were, could not have reassured them.

On December 14 the legislature passed a new law defining witchcraft, an offense already listed in October's list of capital crimes. This "Act against Conjuration, Witchcraft and dealing with evil and wicked Spirits," like the law it replaced, said nothing about signing with the Devil. However, rather than relying on common knowledge of these matters, the new language specified details of potential infractions. Anyone who conjured or invoked evil spirits, then entertained, employed, or rewarded them in any way, who dug up a corpse or any part of a corpse to use for magical purposes, or who used *any* of these means to lame or to waste, pine, and consume anyone else in any way would be executed, along with any of their accomplices, as felons.

However, if any person used *lesser* magical means—less than trying to kill another person, such as using spells to discover precious ores or buried treasure; find lost items; lure another person's love; waste or destroy another person's property, including livestock; or hurt someone bodily without killing them—then that malefactor would be imprisoned for a year. And once every quarter during that year the prisoner would be paraded out to stand for six hours in the pillory at the county seat wearing a placard pinned to the chest inscribed with a description of the crime in capital letters.

A *second* such offence would merit death.

(The legislature had by now forbidden the hated confiscations, even though they were still legal under British law. Because of this discrepancy, the witchcraft law made no mention of preserving the dowry of a male witch's widow after his execution. Due to this oversight, the Privy Council would reject the *whole* witchcraft law in 1695. Thereafter, wishing to have no more to do with the whole distressing matter, Massachusetts would have no laws against witchcraft. England's last witchcraft prosecution, in contrast, occurred in 1944.)

The Superior Court's regular sitting for Essex County had passed, winter was closing in, and the mass of cases still needed sorting out. Governor Phips had written to London in October for advice in dealing with the press of witch cases. But waiting for the Privy Council to act plus the time required for letters to travel across the ocean and back created more difficulties for the crowd of prisoners awaiting trial. Not all of them could afford the high bails the court set, and not all of these could survive the frigid winter, for the jails were not meant to house people for long periods, even given the £16 worth of bedding, blankets, and clothes the legislature ordered for the poorer prisoners in Boston.

On December 16 the legislature passed "An Act for Enabling the Justices of the Superiour Court to hold a Court of Assize and General Goale delivery within the County of Essex upon Tuesday the third of January next." (This would be a sitting of the Superior Court at a special time in order to empty the jails by trying the prisoners within them.)

Four days later the governor and council finally acted upon the request for the public fast that had been pending since October. This document added other troubles besides just the witch trials and omitted dwelling on the "Indefatigable Endeavours of those Worthy Gentlemen [of the court], with Others, to Suppress that Crying Enormity" of witchcraft and how those efforts had instead led to "the most Astonishing Augmentation and Increase of the Number of Persons Accused, by those Afflicted"—the less said about that the better.

Now the fast was to consider "The Various Awful Judgments of God continued upon the *English* Nation, and the Dispersions thereof in Their Majesties several Plantations, by War, Sickness, Earthquakes, and other Desolating Calamities; more especially, by permit-ing Witchcrafts and Evil Angels to Rage amongst his People: All which Loudly Call to Deep Humiliation and Earnest Application to Heaven as the best Expedient for Deliverance."

Therefore, December 29, a Thursday lecture day, was ordered "to be Kept as a Day of Solemn PRAYER with FASTING" in the various towns, and "Exhorting both Ministers and People fervently to Implore Heavens Blessings upon Their Majesties, their Three Kingdoms and Plantations Abroad, and upon the whole Protestant Interest; That a Spirit of Reformation may be Powred [i.e., poured] down from on High, and Gods Anger Diverted, That Divine Conduct may be vouch-safed to all the English Governments, and Success attend their Affairs."

And, they added, "all Servile Labour on said Day is hereby Forbiden."

With the temporary Court of Oyer and Terminer dissolved and new trials pending, the legislature selected members of the new Supe-rior Court on December 22. As before, the justices were John Richards, Wait-Still Winthrop, Samuel Sewall, and, this time, Thomas Danforth, who had earlier expressed reservations about the way the trials were handled. William Stoughton was once more cho-sen to be chief justice. The new clerk of the court, Jonathan Ellatson, sent an order to the Essex County towns to select jurors and grand ju-rors for the next session scheduled for Salem beginning on January 3.

The year moved to its close with congregations observing the public fast by reflecting on the tangle that beset the province. Kin of the peo-ple already hanged contemplated the belated public and legal change of mind—or at least the admission of doubt. People who still feared a real presence of witches wondered how to separate the possibly inno-cent from the surely guilty. Some of the witnesses who had testified earlier perhaps considered how to justify what the summer before had summoned in them. The prisoners, as familiar as they now were to the damp and the cold as well as the indifference to their suffering, still cautiously hoped the new trials would be different in tone—and outcome.

John Alden evidently hoped so, for he had been back in Boston by about mid-December, bringing messages from the parents (one hopes) of young Susanna English, who had been living with Mrs. Alden since the jail break, and to Mary English Jr., who was boarding with the Hollards. On the last day of the year, when Stoughton ordered the transfer of various prisoners from the Cambridge to the Salem jail prior to trial, two of Alden's shopkeeper friends, Nathaniel Williams and Samuel Checkley, posted a £200 bond for his good behavior. This they did in front of Boston magistrate Jonathan Richards, who had been one of the Oyer and Terminer judges and who was now a member of the newly formed Superior Court.

The trials would resume in three days.

The year 1692 ends with absences: people gone, property gone, families broken.

Philip English's wharf stands idle by his stripped warehouses, all lacking their customary bustle, while his impounded ships swing at the end of their moorings in the harbor with only a skeleton crew to keep watch. English's Great House echoes under the step of the few remaining servants tending the nearly empty rooms.

In Bridget Bishop's home her red bodice lies folded away in a chest among musk and lavender to repel moths. Ordinarily such a garment would be passed to the next generation, refashioned if necessary, but never wasted. But this bodice, having identified her spirit to the court, is too unlucky to wear—far too unlucky for a daughter or granddaughter to risk flaunting—so it remains unused and out of sight.

Further inland the Procter farm is unaccustomedly quiet for lack of livestock. The diminished family—master and mistress and siblings gone—move about their chores, a wary eye always on the road, to tend the few cows and pigs and hens left them.

Upcountry on the Nurse farm, beyond the house and barn, down across the fields, Rebecca's grave has had time to green over, the earth no longer as raw as grief. While her family continue their lives, keeping apart from the rest of the Village, falling snow blankets her grave, concealing the disturbed earth and obscuring the evidence of what the family will never forget.

January to May 1693

Blowing on stiff fingers, Reverend Samuel Parris continues writing a draft of his next Sacrament sermon.

"The Author & Institute of this holy Supper is our Blessed Saviour, our Lord Jesus, who is both the Nourisher, & the nourishment"—Parris dips his quill in the inkwell, which has not yet frozen—*"Hence learn we that this great & holy ordinance is not to be slighted or neglected."* Because Christ Himself invites us to it, *"we ought not to disdain, slight, or neglect it."*

But, *he thinks, rubbing his hands together to try to warm them,* the Nurse kin will probably slight the ceremony again. *He hardly saw any of them now, except for Tarbell at the baptism.* That *was a surprise. Apparently, old Francis still clings stubbornly to his wife's innocence. How the man could have been so blind to what was going on in his own house is difficult to believe. (Although Satan's deceits are continuously inventive, Parris has to admit, hiding evil in unexpected places. He thinks of Tituba, the invading serpent amid his own family.)*

Parris stands stiffly and moves to the study window just to stir his blood. He sees John Indian down in the barnyard, ax in hand, heading for the scanty woodpile. His man no longer suffers fits as he had the summer before, so at least John is capable of getting work done. Parris has had to hire a maid to take over Tituba's tasks, money he can ill afford, especially with the slave's jail bills mounting ever higher. What he will do about her *in the future, he does not yet know.*

Nearly a year, a whole year *since this miserable business began—and what? Some of Satan's recruits have been dealt with, but others remain—and many of* those *have confessed. That it all began in his own household is a thorn and a mortification. His critics overlook the fact that the courts subsequently* proved *the guilt of those who were tried.*

It is not just *my* opinion.

Months have passed since he or any of his household attended any court proceeding. Whereas most of the fractious community had once stood against common enemies, Salem Village is now more divided than ever. Moreover, he has yet to be paid, with no resolution of that in sight either.

Parris edges his chair closer to the meager hearth fire and flips open his Bible. His eye falls on random scripture: "Verily I say unto you, in as muche as ye have done it unto one of the least of these my brethren, ye have done it to me." Unto Christ, that is. An uncomfortable verse followed by the exhortation: "Depart from me ye cursed, unto everlasting fyre which is prepared for the devil and his angels"—the accursed in that passage being guilty of sins of omission, of doing nothing when they had a chance to do good. But there is always the difficulty of discerning who is blessed and who is cursed, of how to tell what is really in a person's heart.

He turns again to his sermon and takes up the quill. He should not have to urge church members to participate in the central ceremony of membership, this privilege of Christians that Christ Himself granted, even if some members still make earthly quarrels a stumbling block. "Believers," he writes, "you are not to slight this call of him who has instituted & appointed this holy Ordinance."

Working downstairs by the hall's hearth would be warmer, but—a muffled thump and moan rise from below—concentrating would be harder there. Fits still trouble Abigail sometimes, and that is only one of his problems.

Just see what Tituba's continuing malignancy cause.

That cursed woman!

As the year began, Salem, which included Salem Village, chose the required jurors, including Job Swinnerton, one of the people who had signed the petition on behalf of Rebecca Nurse. Other Essex County jurors included Rebecca's nephew, Ensign Jacob Towne of Topsfield, and two Marblehead men, Richard Read (brother-in-law of the late Wilmot Read) and William Beale (who was still certain that Philip English's specter had haunted him after a business deal turned sour). Beverly chose Robert Cue, stepfather of the formerly afflicted Mary Herrick.

Court met in Salem's town house, cold this time even with the windows shut, so unlike the sweltering press of the long summer before. The first day was concerned with one probate case and swearing in jurors. Swinnerton and Read were sworn as part of the grand jury, with Robert Payne of Ipswich, a former minister with past ties to Maine as the foreman.

The second day, Wednesday, January 4, inaugurated the next round of witch trials.

Again, as in the summer past, a batch of prisoners was taken from the jail and, stepping over snow and slush and huddling together against the wind, led around the streets to the town house. Those left behind could only hope that matters would be different during this session—a modest hope, frail as it was. News that spectral evidence was no longer acceptable had to have reached the prisoners.

The day's defendants returned to the jail with news that *this* grand jury had dismissed *all* of the day's cases but four for lack of evidence, with *ignoramus* (we do not know) written at the end of each indictment. And the four—two sets of mothers and daughters—were all found not guilty even though two of them had confessed earlier: Margaret Jacobs, her recantation believed at last, with her mother, Rebecca Jacobs, known to be distracted, and old Sarah Buckley with her widowed daughter Mary Whittredge, neither of whom had confessed. Now all of them were to be free or at least free as soon as their rising jail bills could be paid. On the third day the grand jury dismissed even more cases, and only two people stood trial, Job Tookey and Hannah Tyler, both found not guilty.

On Friday more were declared *ignoramus*, including Candy, the Barbadian slave, and Elizabeth Procter's son William. Only Mary Tyler was tried, and she too was found not guilty. At this the court broke for the Sabbath.

Mary Warren had been absent from the constant round of hearings and trials. Now back in court, she reacted as before to the movements of the accused, but the justices and even the audience failed to respond with approval or sympathy. Under such conditions it is likely that the spasms no longer felt the same—a different reality or not real at all. Because spectral evidence was not to be accepted, regardless of the actual cause of the convulsions, the court viewed them as either physical ills or the Devil's deceptions.

Mary might wonder if she were like the girl in Beverly who had been duped into believing a disguised devil was actually the minister's wife—until Mary Esty's ghost set her straight. Had Mary Warren herself believed the Devil all along? Far back, months before, she had thought her afflictions were distractions, but the court refused to believe her then, had suspected *her* when she tried to deny it, until she thought she must have been truly bewitched after all. Her master and mistress had not believed her afflictions, not for a moment. Now Goodman Procter was dead and his wife under a death sentence.

When questioned, the most she could safely attest to was that the defendant looked like the specter she *thought* she saw. And in this manner, acceptance of Stoughton's unrelenting judgment continued to crumble.

Court resumed in Salem Tuesday, January 10, minus Wait-Still Winthrop. The grand jury sent Sarah Wardwell, widow of the executed Samuel, and her two daughters to the trial jury, which declared the young women not guilty but found the widowed Goodwife Wardwell guilty as charged. She, her daughters, and her late husband had confessed to witchcraft, and all recanted their self-damning stories, but for some reason the trial jury did not believe Sarah.

Now the mood of the returning prisoners was far more subdued, with hope sharply qualified if not extinguished. Something had changed over the Sabbath break. Perhaps Wait-Still Winthrop, now absent, had been a moderating presence. Perhaps the afflicted girls seemed more believable to the court this time.

On the following day Reverend Dane's niece Elizabeth Johnson Jr. was tried and also found guilty.

That evening Mercy Lewis suffered afflictions, plagued, she claimed, by several specters. Elizabeth Johnson Jr. was one; the Englishes both also pressed their diabolical demands, especially Mary, who pushed the Devil's book at her to sign.

Had the Englishes returned as Alden had? Philip and Mary were likely both present on Thursday, January 12, to face the grand jury unless, unlike any of the others, their cases were handled *in absentia*. Mercy Lewis swore to her account of the previous night's torture and said, "Mrs English s[ai]d she might bring the Book now she thought ever one of them would bee Cleared." The girl recoiled as if struck on the breast and gagged as if choked. Specters were hitting her, she said, English and his wife and old Pharaoh—Thomas Farrar, whose case would be declared *ignoramus* today. They were *there* in the room, right in front of the grand jury, threatening to strangle her!

William Beale, part of the jury pool, also swore to his visions of Philip English after a disagreement with the man and during Beale's bout of smallpox.

But the grand jury recognized all this testimony as deriving from spectral evidence and thus discounted it. The surviving indictments are for Mary English tormenting Elizabeth Hubbard on April 22 among other times and for Philip English tormenting Mary Walcott and Elizabeth Booth, "singlewoman," on May 31 and other times. *All* of these charges were dismissed as *ignoramus*. Yet the grand jury sent five Andover women to trial, and of these, Mary Post was found guilty.

On Friday more prisoners, suspects who would still be alive to face a later court, were freed on bail, and suspects already cleared were freed on payment of fees. Fathers and husbands banded together with concerned neighbors to post the £100 bonds (somehow able to cover sums much more than some ministers' £60 yearly salary).

Perhaps Rebecca Nurse's family attended the legal proceedings for her sister Sarah Cloyce, who was brought down from the Ipswich jail to face another grand jury on January 13. They would have joined her husband, Peter Cloyce, who stood by her, frequently visiting the Ipswich jail.

The grand jury may have considered the statement from Boston jailer John Arnold and his wife, Mary, that, while Sarah Cloyce and her sister Mary Esty were in their care, both women behaved in a "sobere and civell" manner.

The grand jury certainly saw the indictments against Goodwife Cloyce for tormenting her niece Rebecca Towne on September 9 and

for spectrally assaulting Mary Walcott and Abigail Williams on April
11 at the first hearing. (Oddly no indictment survives for tormenting
Annie Putnam on that same April day.) For some reason, perhaps the
change in public opinion, her grand jury hearing in September had
been continued or postponed.

They weighed the accounts along with whatever actions afflicted
witnesses who were present in court may have exhibited, if any—and
disregarded them all. Foreman Robert Payne wrote *ignoramus* on each
document. Sarah was free to go as soon as her jail and court expenses
were paid. The family must have settled her bill quickly, for Peter removed them both to Boston, away from her accusers, as soon as he
could.

Mary Lacey Jr., her grandmother dead in jail of illness a month ago
and her mother found guilty and awaiting execution, returned to fulfill
the condition of her own October release. As she had been a confessor
and energetic accuser, the grand jury passed her case along to the trial
jury despite her later recantation. She pled not guilty to the charges—
of signing the Devil's book and of tormenting Timothy Swan—and
once again the jury passed a verdict of not guilty. And that was the
last of the Essex County trials until the next Superior Court, which
would reconvene in May.

Stoughton, however, signed a death warrant for the three found
guilty in the January session: widow Sarah Wardwell and the two
young women (described by one of the trials' critics as "senseless and
ignorant creatures"). Then, relentlessly methodical, he added the
names of the others found guilty in the earlier trials: Mary Bradbury
(if they could find her, for she was still in hiding), Abigail Hobbs,
Dorcas Hoar (her month's reprieve to settle her soul long over), Mary
Lacey Sr., Abigail Faulkner Sr., and widow Elizabeth Procter. The
hangings were apparently scheduled for February 1, the same day that
the Superior Court's next session would begin in Charlestown for
Middlesex County. In the meantime workmen dug graves in the frost-
hard ground near the gallows site.

Goodwives Faulkner and Procter, both with child, might find their
deaths delayed, but Elizabeth was nearer her time, and before the day

scheduled for the next execution, the pangs of birth gripped her and she delivered her latest child in the Salem prison on January 27.

Unlike Mistress Ann Putnam, Elizabeth Procter lacked the traditional groaning cakes and groaning beer to treat her helpers. She lacked the childbed linens and the family cradle to receive this child. Instead, she struggled on an earth floor covered with (not necessarily clean) straw. Perhaps the other women prisoners clustered round to help, if their chains did not prevent such movement. Perhaps one of them was a midwife, or perhaps the law sent for a midwife to attend her. In any case Elizabeth survived and named the child John after his father, even though he had a half-brother already named John—little help, though, that one had been. Nothing now prevented Elizabeth's death sentence from being carried out. Goodwife Faulkner had not yet given birth, but Elizabeth could now be included with the next group of prisoners destined to die.

Mary Warren, probably kept apart with the other confessors, would have heard the commotion attending the birth and the news that Elizabeth had survived her travail. Mary's reaction—whether satisfaction at Goody Procter's impending peril or remorse for her own part in it—is, like so much of history, lost.

Prisoners from Middlesex County towns found themselves removed from Salem's jail and carted away to stand eventual trial in Charlestown. The condemned prisoners left behind could only pray and try to settle their souls to face death and God's own more merciful judgment. Outside, a driving snow fell the week of January 22, and the next week it melted in a thaw.

Then, on the day they were to be hauled to the gallows, or the day before, the condemned learned that Governor Phips had countermanded Stoughton's orders and reprieved them; they would *not* hang—or at least they would not hang that day or anytime soon. Their futures were still uncertain, but their relief must have been profound.

More surprising news arrived later when they learned that the reprieves had stunned Chief Justice Stoughton. News that he had lost his temper in court and stormed off the bench to confront the governor in a blazing row would have spread as swiftly as gossip could gallop. Mary Warren and Ann Putnam would have found this development alarming—what did it mean for them? The Nurse family and other Towne relatives would have been not only relieved but most likely gleeful as well—at last justified, though admittedly after so much innocent blood had been spilled.

In Stoughton's absence this court found *no one* guilty of witchcraft.

On Monday, February 7, Rebecca's son Samuel Nurse received a visit from a church committee: Reverend Samuel Parris, deacons Nathaniel Ingersoll and Edward Putnam, Nathaniel Putnam, John Putnam Sr., and old Bray Wilkins. For months now, the committee explained, Goodman Nurse, along with three others, had been absent from public worship in the Village Church. He was a member, after all, a fully communing member, and yet he had been absent even from the Lord's Supper. The brethren had chosen the committee to speak privately with him and the other absentees. (Allowing a person speak their side of a question before taking an infraction to the rest of the membership was general church policy.) Samuel Nurse made no explanation but agreed to a meeting the following afternoon at the parsonage.

The committee left to take their message to Samuel's brother-in-law, John Tarbell and to Thomas Wilkins, Bray's son. The fourth absent church member was Peter Cloyce, but he and his wife, Sarah, were now living in Boston. Someone, probably the Nurse kin, must have sent word to him about the committee's visit, and the three local dissenters presumably discussed this new development. The more they thought about it, the angrier they became.

They had been absent from the weekly services in the Village Church—for the most part, that is, as Tarbell had had his son baptized in October. They *had* avoided even the Sacrament of communion, but their intent was not to slight the meaning of the ceremony, much less disregard the great sacrifice that Christ had made for them, as epitomized by the service. No, their quarrel was with their neighbors and, especially, with the minister—as the committee ought to have known. Ever since people had begun accusing Rebecca—their mother, mother-in-law, neighbor—and the minister not only did nothing to stop it but actually believed and encouraged the accusations, they had been too apprehensive of being accused themselves to attend services in the Village. They ceased taking communion in the Village Church in order to avoid sharing the bread and wine with neighbors intent on sending innocent women—their mother and aunts—to their deaths. They would not accept the bread and wine from the person who ought to have calmed the panic and exposed such error but instead, for his own reasons, chose to inflame the conflagration.

Tarbell, Nurse, and Wilkins arrived at Parris's home the next day two hours early for the appointment. The minister agreed to speak with them anyway, if they wished, one at a time, in his study before the rest of the committee arrived. Tarbell went first, following Parris up the stairs while the others waited below. If Parris thought he could offer advice to a troubled soul or divide and conquer the opposition piecemeal, he found himself mistaken. Tarbell pounced and would not let his minister get a word in edgewise. The wait downstairs must have been uncomfortable for Parris's family, as Tarbell's angry voice would have pervaded the parsonage.

After an hour the two men—neither could have looked happy—descended the stairs, and Samuel Nurse headed for Parris's study for his say. He had the same complaints as his brother-in-law. (All three of them did, according to Parris's account of the meetings.) Anger stoked by a summer of fear and frustration boiled over as Nurse unburdened himself of what he had been too cautious to say for so many months. He accused Parris of idolatry for asking the afflicted what they saw, for believing wholeheartedly in what they said, for believing those dubious messages from the Invisible World. And then for giving his oath in court, *swearing* that the invisible specters of specific people knocked down the girls and claiming that the defendants' touch then healed them—all actions that contradicted the precepts of the faith and Biblical scholarship he himself professed. If it had not been for Parris, he said, getting to the heart of the matter, his mother might never have been hanged, might still be alive. But she had been—thanks to Parris's unfounded and unjustified persecution. And because Parris had yet to admit his grave error, when wiser men than he had done so, then Nurse could not—*would* not—join him in worship.

The most Parris had opportunity to reply was that he did not yet see any reason to change his views, which, as he saw it, were confirmed by "known and ancient experience frequent in such cases." If they were going to quarrel, then they must allow him to present his side of the matter.

Before Wilkins could have a turn, the rest of the church committee arrived. At that the three fell silent, and when Parris formally asked them to state why they had withdrawn from "religious communication," giving them the chance to air their complaints before their fellows, they would not say and, despite prodding from Parris, asked only for another meeting and time to consider the committee's demands.

The next day Peter Cloyce showed up at the parsonage to make the same complaints and received the same answers as the others. All four appeared unannounced a short while later, this time bringing William Way, a member of the congregation but not a fully communing church member. If the four were bringing a witness to a formal grievance, then they needed two or three *full* church members. Parris informed them that he intended to follow the letter of the procedure for such problems, and this was *not* the procedure.

Cloyce did not stay in the Village for the February 16 meeting, but the other three did attend. On that occasion Samuel Nurse read a paper wherein they claimed to have proceeded in an orderly manner to protest "the burden of great grievances by reason of some unwarrantable actings of Mr. Parris," but they felt that they were being prevented from stating their complaints, and if that continued, then they would have to air the problem to the whole church, not just this committee. Reluctantly, they allowed Parris to copy their statement and pleaded ignorance of the procedure, but they did not publicly state the grievances they had poured forth in Parris's study. (Parris did not present these damning complaints to the committee either, though he recorded them in his church record.)

Whether Parris's niece Abigail Williams was still ill, still afflicted, when these tense meetings occurred in the parsonage is unclear. She may have been the unnamed girl who, after seeing a coffin when attempting forbidden fortune-telling, died young. Presumably Betty Parris and her younger sister Susanna and brother Thomas were well. Was John Indian still a member of the household, and did the family have another servant, free or enslaved, to replace Tituba? If physical illness still besieged Abigail, then Parris would have been understandably less inclined to alter his view of witchcraft and his role in the recent purge—reasons besides pride as well as the terrible admission of being as mistaken as he had been and at such cost to the community that he was charged to shepherd. After all, at least three supposedly afflicted people had died recently in Andover: old Ralph Farnum on January 8; young Timothy Swan, so often tormented by Mary Bradbury's specter, on February 2; and fourteen-year-old Rose Foster on February 25.

The meetings would drag on into the spring, while at the same time the rates committee refused, as they had for two years so far, to collect Parris's salary. Francis Nurse no longer served on that committee, but his son-in-law John Tarbell did and defiantly paid the fine the Quarterly Court imposed on the committee for neglecting its duties. Nurse, Tarbell, and Wilkins kept changing the terms for the meetings they asked for and also consulted with sympathetic neighbors, witnesses who were not full members of the church. This in effect omitted the interchurch stage of their complaints and treated the matter as one concerning the death of Rebecca as well as her sister and the other dead and all the misery the trials had created. If their absence from the Sacrament was broached, they explained the neglect as being due to the inappropriateness of accepting so important a symbol from the blood-tainted hands of one they blamed for their mother's death by hanging. Perhaps their reluctance to speak their minds before the church committee indicated a lack of preparedness, an awareness that their explosions of temper in Parris's study were spontaneous, releases of pent-up rage that their confounding predicament fueled. They aimed their resentment at Parris, an outsider to the Village who had been precariously placed in the community from the onset, rather than at the neighbors who had accused and testified against Rebecca, people with whom they still had to live. A minister could move away (despite the ordination that was intended to make the association with a congregation permanent), but the likes of Thomas Putnam's family they could not get rid of. In the case of Parris they could argue for his removal.

And they did—vigorously.

Philip English probably returned to Salem in January to face the grand jury, though this is not entirely clear. On March 2, 1693, he penned a letter to Governor Phips (his "great enemy"), demanding his confiscated goods be returned. Phips ordered Sheriff Corwin to make an inventory of all that was taken, but by April 26 this task had not yet been done, so Phips sent another strongly worded letter.

If Mary English returned with her husband, she could at least visit her daughters in Boston: Susanna staying with the Aldens, Mary with the Hollard family, who had concealed her father before his arrest. The mansion, by family tradition, would hardly have been ready for them right away, for the law and covetous locals had stripped the place. Some neighbors may have salvaged items to keep safe and then return; others were merely light-fingered. According to family lore even the family portraits were gone.

Philip's warehouses were empty, his livestock driven away to be sold or consumed, and his ships impounded unless they had been at sea and the crew warned to steer clear from home port. "My Estate was Seised & Squandred away to a great Value & much of my provision used to Subsist the numerous Company of prisoners." He was sure the bobtailed cow in Sheriff Corwin's yard was *his* bobtailed cow. He set about seeing to repairs and itemizing his losses: lumber and hardware, textiles and molasses, cod and cordage from the warehouses, even the three gross of thimbles from the shop in the house. In addition, he had spent a good £50 for proper room and board in Boston and put up a bond of £1,400 to be allowed some freedom of movement there. That bond was forfeit upon his escape, but he wanted it back along with all of his property—*all of it!*

Meanwhile, Edward Bishop, widowed by Bridget's execution and evidently still living in the house he had built on the Oliver property, remarried March 9, 1693, to widow Elizabeth Cash of Beverly.

The Superior Court convened in Boston on April 25 for Suffolk County. Stoughton presided once again with Justices Thomas Danforth, Samuel Sewall, and John Richards. The court considered the infanticide cases of Grace, the slave who had given birth alone years earlier and then thrust her newborn down her master's privy, and Elizabeth Emerson, whose twin bastards were found buried in her parents' garden two years past. Both had been found guilty during the interim government; now Stoughton pronounced the death sentence against them, and their years of waiting in prison ended June 8, 1693, when they were hanged in Boston.

John Arnold, the Boston jailer, who had attested to the good conduct of Sarah Cloyce and Mary Esty, successfully contested an earlier ruling against him for "allowing" certain prisoners to escape the summer before—suspected burglars and pirates. (The awkwardness of the escaped witch suspects was not mentioned.)

John Alden, freed on bail, made his appearance for the witchcraft charge. This time no one appeared to speak against him, so the court cleared his case by proclamation. Again, the court chose to ignore the jail break and his fugitive months out of the province. (In contrast, a September Essex County court had fined John Shepard of Rowley a stiff £30 plus costs, the total reduced to £5, for twice helping his sister-in-law Mary Green escape from the Ipswich jail, where she was being held on a witchcraft charge.)

Mary Watkins, a girl from Milton (south of Boston and far from Salem), also appeared. She had accused her mistress of witchcraft and then, finding no sympathy for her claims, accused herself and attempted a botched suicide before her own arrest. All this only confused the grand jury, whose members asked many questions of the justices and of Mary. After deliberation they pronounced the indictment *ignoramus*. The court disagreed—presumably meaning *Stoughton* disagreed—and requested the jury to reconsider. They did, but the verdict was the same. However, enough doubt remained that Stoughton required Mary to find sureties for her future good behavior and to appear at the next sitting for Suffolk. But she lacked the means, and as none of her family obliged, she would petition to be sold as a bondservant to settle the bill.

The Superior Court's next sitting was for Essex County and took place in Ipswich on May 9, with Justices Danforth, Richards, and Sewall presiding. Stoughton, perhaps due to the outcome of the Suffolk sitting and as a protest to Phips undercutting his judicial authority, was again absent.

Over the next three days the grand jury heard the cases of several Andover and Boxford suspects. On May 9 they brought in Tituba, the first to confess, the first to describe a conspiracy of witches, the first to incite—admittedly under duress—the madness among the whites. Her indictment was for covenanting with the Devil and signing his book, but the grand jury recognized that all of the evidence against her was spectral evidence and dismissed her case as *ignoramus*. They would declare all of the cases in this session *ignoramus*.

Tituba stands in the Ipswich meeting house facing the grand jury and wondering if she will have to face the Superior Court justices as well. It is May 9, the first day of the scheduled spring sitting for Essex County. She has never faced those justices before, but she has heard about them, especially Chief Justice William Stoughton. But he is not here, and she hopes that is a good sign.

She and a cartload of other prisoners have been herded from the Salem jail and carted over the bumpy road to Ipswich, taken from the confines of the prison yard to at least smell the fresh air, to see the green of the season, to be someplace other than the jail. Regardless of whatever awaits them, the trip is a welcome change.

She hears the clerk read her indictment:

Jurors for our Sovereign Lord & lady the King & Queen present That Tittapa an Indian Woman servant to Mr. Samuel Parris of Salem Village . . . upon or about the latter end of the year 1691 In the Towne of Salem Village . . . wickedly maliciously & feloniously A Covenant with the Devil did make & Signed the Devil's Book . . . by which wicked Covenanting with the Devil She the Said Tittapa is become A detestable Witch . . .

Will she hold to her confession, the story that lit such a blaze of panic? Her master, the unforgiving Reverend Parris, frowning and harried, had already confronted her. Her jail bills were adding up, and he was expected to pay them. But he would not consent to do this if she altered her original story, her incriminating confession—for that would be to admit he had been mistaken all along. She could stay in jail indefinitely as far as he was concerned—or until someone else bought her to satisfy the outstanding debt.

She thinks of that now, thinks of her own original explanation—not the confession spurred by terror and beatings, but her earlier protests—that she had nothing to do with hurting the girls she loved, that she knew nothing about the Devil's designs. That had been the truth, and yet no one believed it. So in her desperate straits she had spun a story and had answered their absurd questions the way she thought they expected her to do.

I did what you asked, she thinks. I obeyed as you expect a slave to obey.

But now, before the grand jury, she has to calculate.

What do these gentlemen expect now?

The jurors have papers before them. Her earlier confession must be among them.

"Is this true?" the foreman asks.

If she holds to the lie, Master Parris will pay her bill and she will be released. But released to what? Will he accept her back into his household after all that has happened—she, a woman he thinks is a confessed witch? To live in peace and trust in the same house with the children he thought she menaced? What exactly does he believe about her? She can wait for some unknown party to decide to buy her. Or Parris may pay her fees and then sell her away to be rid of her. If she holds to her confession now, then will she be tried for the witchcraft she did not commit? And then what? The rope? The shallow grave?

But at last she addresses the grand jury, the court, the legal proceedings confronting her:

"No," says Tituba. "None of it is true."

PART THREE
Afterword

Rebecca Nurse

REBECCA NURSE's family, focusing all their rage and resentment on Reverend Samuel Parris, continued to pursue the minister. He called them the dissenting brethren: Samuel Nurse and his brother-in-law Jonathan Tarbell, their neighbor Thomas Wilkins, and occasionally Nurse's brother-in-law Peter Cloyce, who now lived in Framingham.

The dissenters insisted that a council chosen from *other* churches hear their complaint, argued over which churches and which delegates, demanded copies of their opponents' statements, and refused to specify their own complaints. "They said," Parris recorded in October 1693, "their offence was against Mr. Parris and not the Church." But a month later "They openly charged the whole Church as a nest of deceivers."

They hounded Parris through the summer and fall of 1694 and then into the winter. At one November church meeting that only Tarbell attended, Reverend Parris read aloud an apology.

Taken by surprise, Tarbell blurted, "[T]hat if half so much had been said formerly, it had never come to this."

But it was not enough now.

Samuel Nurse, Tarbell, and Wilkins all attended another, public meeting—that is, with not just full church members—a week later, this time armed with a list of complaints and finally stating what they had shouted at Parris in his study nearly two years earlier. After some reluctance the dissenters handed Parris their statement.

They had not attended public services of prayer and preaching, Parris read aloud, because the racket made by persons "under diabolical power and delusions" prevented their hearing what was said, and they feared being accused themselves, as better people than they—meaning Rebecca—*were* accused, nor did they like the tone of Parris's sermons. Neither did they participate in the Lord's Supper because "we esteem ourselves justly aggrieved and offended with the officer who doth administer."

Parris then read his own statement again, the same that Tarbell had heard the week before. The minister admitted that it was "a sore rebuke, and humbling providence" that the calamity had begun in his own family, that his household included both accusers and accused, and that his servants—Tituba and John Indian—had worked "to raise spirits . . . in no better than a diabolical way" for which "God has been righteously spitting in my face." Although he did not pretend to understand the mysteries of that year, he now realized that the Devil *could* counterfeit the specter of an innocent person, that asking the afflicted who hurt them was "to Satan's great advantage," that he no longer accepted the self-incriminating confessions, and that "through weakness or sore exercise," he may have "unadvisedly expressed" himself in public statements.

Therefore, he beseeched God's pardon and asked forgiveness of the dissenting brethren "of every offence in this or other affairs, wherein you see or conceive I have erred and offended," and he asked that all parties seek to resolve the current strife, which only served the Devil's ends.

Parris's admission did not satisfy the dissenters. They still wanted a council of other churches to hear the matter, which stalemated in a series of ill-natured meetings. Finally a council of ten laymen and seven ministers convened at Salem Village in April 1695. The ministers included moderator Increase Mather, who had written *Cases of Conscience* and interviewed the "confessors," Samuel Willard, who had helped Philip and Mary English escape, and Cotton Mather, who had cautioned Judge Richards against accepting spectral evidence but had also trusted that the judges knew what they were doing. This council determined that even though Parris had taken "sundry unwarrantable and uncomfortable steps" in that "dark time of confusion," he was now "brought into a better sense of things, [and] so fully expressed it, that a Christian charity may and should receive satisfaction therewith." Although they hoped the offended brethren would accept Parris's apology, they advised the rest of the Salem Village Church to show more compassion to the dissenters, "considering the extreme trials and troubles" they had endured "in such a heart-breaking day." If "the remembrance of the disasters that have happened" were too much for the dissenters, the church might vote to allow them to transfer their membership to another church. Likewise, if Village "distempers" continued, there would be no shame if Parris left for another post. But "if they continue to devour one another," then God might be provoked to abandon them to all the desolations of a people that sin away the mercies of the gospel."

Francis Nurse, now in his seventies, passed the responsibility of the home farm to his sons and sons-in-law. He divided the remaining land among his eight children equally, with the daughters' portions deeded to their husbands' names. He had already conveyed parcels to his sons and sons-in-law as they married, and he gave them the rest now rather than after his death on condition they pay his debts and provide him with at least £14 a year (35 shillings from each). He signed the document on December 4, 1694.

Meanwhile, the Nurse family were not about to be reconciled with Parris. In March 1695 eighty-four Villagers petitioned the mediating council. As it was impossible for Parris to continue effectively, they asked the council to advise him to leave the Village or allow them to call another, second minister.

The monthly meeting of area ministers in Cambridge considered this in May and concluded that Parris should leave. But their advice resulted in a petition from 105 of Parris's supporters, who wanted him to stay, "For we have had three ministers removed already, and by every removal our differences have been rather aggravated."

At some point Parris's opponents circulated an unsigned paper, giving a clear Scriptural condemnation of Parris's actions in 1692 by citing Leviticus 20:6:

And the soul that turneth after such as have familiar spirits, and after wizards, to go a-whoring after them, I will set my face against that soul, and will cut him off from among his people.

During these wrangles Francis Nurse died November 22, 1695, "age 77," as Parris noted in his records. With the Nurse sons and sons-in-law sharing the expenses, his body was placed in the family burying ground with Rebecca's.

Reverend Parris relinquished the pulpit in 1696 but remained in the parsonage, attempting to collect his back pay. Suits and countersuits followed, as rates committees, sometimes including both Thomas and Joseph Putnam, balked at payment.

On January 14, 1697, Massachusetts observed a public fast to acknowledge several recent calamities, ranging from war with the French to crop failures and the witch trials. These sad events seemed a punishment for some communal sin that needed righting. Therefore, the people, by the day of fasting and prayer, sought to apologize before God and man and to ponder on "whatever mistakes, on either hand, have been fallen into, either by the body of this people, or any orders of men referring to the late tragedy raised amongst us by Satan and his instruments, through the awful judgment of God." In Boston Samuel Sewall, former Oyer and Terminer judge, not only composed the bill but also stood during the fast service when his minister Reverend Willard read Sewall's own statement, which took a more personal blame for the miseries of 1692.

Samuel Nurse and John Tarbell were on the later rates committee when the matter went to arbitration in July 1697. They were *not* legally or morally bound to pay Parris, they argued, because of the requirement that ministers were to be "orthodox and blameless," whereas Parris had not only preached "dangerous errors" and "scandalous immoralities" but also committed perjury when he swore that certain persons, such as Rebecca, cast spectral magic against the supposed afflicted. He not only *believed* the Devil's accusations but actually *promoted* them, showing "his partiality therein in stilling the accusations of some, and at the same time vigilantly promoting others." They submitted this on behalf of themselves, other like-minded Villagers, and those "taken off by an untimely death"—such as Rebecca.

The arbiters, two of them former witch trial judges Samuel Sewall and Wait-Still Winthrop, determined that the Village nevertheless owed Parris £79:9:6. This time the Village *did* pay Parris, who, in September 1697, signed over a quitclaim to the parsonage house and land. He left the Village soon after.

The three dissenters did not return to communion right away, though they seem to have attended the next minister's sermons. That their only quarrel was with Parris, however, was never true. Young Reverend Joseph Green persuaded the voting church members to show Wilkins, Tarbell, and Nurse that they held no grudges against them, "that whatever articles they had drawn up against the brethren formerly, they now looked upon them as nothing, but let them fall to the ground, being willing that they should be buried forever"—or as buried as any grudges could be in the Village.

Jonathan Tarbell, Thomas Wilkins, and their wives plus Samuel Nurse's wife, Mary, all joined with the rest of the full members in taking communion on February 5, 1699, "which," Green wrote, "is a matter of thankfulness." (Samuel Nurse was *not* named among the day's communicants.)

Yet neither Samuel nor the other dissenters objected to Reverend Green's rearrangement of the meeting house seating, even though it placed John Tarbell with John Putnam, Thomas Wilkins with John Putnam's sons James and John, and Samuel Nurse with Thomas Putnam. Samuel's wife, Mary, now sat beside Ann Putnam and Sarah Houlton, both of whom had accused Rebecca, and placed Rebecca's widowed daughter Rebecca Preston with widow Deliverance Walcott, the step-mother of the once-afflicted Mary Walcott.

The following spring the Nurse heirs, with a stake in their parent's homestead, finished paying for the farm. Samuel Nurse and other surviving sons and sons-in-law traveled to Boston, made the last payment, and received the discharge on April 25, 1699. The land for which they and Francis had worked for so many years was theirs, free and clear at last.

But Rebecca's family still wanted their mother exonerated. Petitions to clear the names of the condemned began in 1700. In 1703 several members of Rebecca's family—Isaac Esty Sr. and Jr., Samuel and John Nurse, John Tarbell, and Peter Cloyce—joined with "severall of the Inhabitants of Andover, Salem village & Topsfield" to petition the legislature on behalf of Rebecca Nurse, Mary Esty, Abigail Faulkner Sr., Mary Parker, John Procter, Elizabeth Procter, Elizabeth How, Samuel Wardwell, and Sarah Wardwell:

Your Petitioners being dissatisfyed and grieved, that (besides what the aforesaid condemned persons have Sufferred in their persons and Estates) their Names are Exposed to Infamy and reproach, while their Tryall & condemnation stands upon Publick Record. We therefore humbly Pray this Honored Court, that Something may be Publickly done to take off Infamy from the Names and memory of those who have Suffered as aforesaid, that none of their Surviving Relations, nor their Posterity may Suffer reproach upon that account.

The legislature considered all this, and in May 1703 ordered that the attainders of Abigail Faulkner, Sarah Wardwell, and Elizabeth Procter to be "reversed repealed . . . and made Null and Void." The other names remained unprotected.

Three years later Reverend Green made a surprising proposal to Samuel Nurse. Annie Putnam, now grown, had applied to join the Village Church. To do so she first needed to confess former faults—in her case the great error of accusing Rebecca Nurse. How Green put the question is not recorded, but Samuel agreed not to oppose the woman's acceptance.

That same year the government also came to a decision about the witch trials:

Ordered, That a Bill be drawn up for Preventing the like Procedure for the future, and that no Spectre Evidence may hereafter be accounted valid, or Sufficient to take away the life, or good name, of any Person or Persons within this Province, and that the Infamy, and Reproach, cast on the names and Posterity of the sd accused, and Condemned Persons may in Some measure be Rolled away.

Nevertheless, by May 1709 people who had been arrested but not tried and condemned, as well as the families of those hanged, submitted petitions for restitution of their "Damnified . . . Estates." The "sorrowfull and Distrest Supliants" included Samuel Nurse, Isaac Esty, and their kin. Consequently, a committee of five, including Stephen Sewall, former Oyer and Terminer clerk, met at Salem in 1710 to consider the requests.

Isaac Esty, age "about 82 years," wrote of caring for his imprisoned wife Mary, Rebecca's sister. Before her execution "my wife was near upon 5 months imprisoned all which time I provided maintenance for her at my own cost & charge went constantly twice a week to provide for her what she needed." Three weeks of those five months she was in the Boston prison, "& I was constrained to be at the charge of transporting her to & fro." He estimated his expenses "in time & mony" worth £20 "besides my trouble & sorrow of heart in being deprived of her after such a manner which this world can never make me any compensation for."

Samuel Nurse enumerated the damage done to Rebecca Nurse's family:

1. They had paid all of her prison expenses for four months, while she was incarcerated in Salem and in Boston.
2. They spent considerable time journeying to Boston and Salem and elsewhere gathering testimony in their mother's favor.
3. "And altho we produced plentifull testimony that my honoured and Dear Mother had led a blameless life from her youth up— yet she was condemned and executed upon such Evidence as is now Generally thought to be Insufficient, which may be seen in the court record of her tryall."
4. Because of the guilty verdict, "her name and the name of her Posterity lyes under reproach the removeing of which reproach is the principal thing wherein we desire restitution."
5. They cannot express their "loss of such a Mother in such a way" or know "how to compute our charge." This they left to the committee.

Samuel Nurse, "In the name of my brethren," signed the document and added, "Altho fourty pounds would not repair my loss and dammage in my Estate, yet I shall be Satisfyd if [we] may be allowed, five and twenty pounds. Provided the Attainder be taken off."

On October 17, 1711, Governor Joseph Dudley, long a political opponent of the late William Phips, signed "An Act to Reverse the Attainders of George Burroughs and others for Witch-craft." In 1692,

the document began, "Several Towns within this Province were Infested with a horrible Witchcraft or Possession of devils," to combat
which the government instituted "a Special Court of Oyer and Terminer." The act listed twenty-two individuals this court "severally Indicted convicted and attainted of Witchcraft, and some of them put
to death, others lying still under the like Sentence of the said Court,
and liable to have Executed upon them." (The court had actually condemned twenty-eight people, but not everyone's name had appeared
in the petitions.)

The act blamed "The Influence and Energy of the Evil Spirits . . .
upon those who were the principal Accusers and Witnesses," which
was so great that when it caused "a Prosecution . . . of persons of
known and good Reputation," the government put a stop to the trials
"until their Majesty's pleasure should be known." (The implied timing
ignores the early accusation of Rebecca, a woman of "known and good
Reputation.)

The late Queen Mary's advice, which actually arrived after the
worst of the witch scare was over, graciously approved the court's "care
and Circumspection" and "requir[ed] that in all proceedings ag[ains]t
persons Accused for Witchcraft, or being possessed by the devil, the
greatest Moderation and all due Circumspection be used, So far as the
same may be without Impediment to the Ordinary Course of Justice."

To this the legislature added that "Any Law Usage or Custom to
the contrary notwithstanding . . . no Sheriffe, Constable Goaler or
other Officer shall be Liable to any prosecution in the Law for any
thing they then Legally did in the Execution of their Respective
Offices."

Rather than casting any blame on the judiciary or the legislature,
the act put all the responsibility on the accusers, for "Some of the principal Accusers and Witnesses in those dark and Severe prosecutions
have since discovered themselves to be persons of profligate and vicious Conversation." Therefore,

Upon the humble Petition and Suit of several of the sd persons and of
the Children of others of them whose Parents were Executed,

Be it Declared and Enacted by his Excellency the Governor's Council and Representatives in General Court assembled and by the Authority of the same That the several Convictions Judgements and Attainders against the said George Burroughs, John Procter, George Jacob, John Willard, Giles Core and [Martha] Core, Rebeccah Nurse, Sarah Good, Elisabeth How, Mary Easty, Sarah Wild, Abigail Hobbs, Samuel Wardell, Mary Parker, Martha Carrier, Abigail Falkner, Anne Foster, Rebecca Eames, Mary Post, Mary Lacey, Mary Bradbury and Dorcas Hoar and every of them Be and hereby are Reversed made and declared to be Null and void to all Intents, Constructions and purposes wh[atsoever], as if no such Convictions, Judgments or Attainders had ever [been] had or given. And that no penalties or fforfeitures of Goods or Chattels be by the said Judgments and Attainders or either of them had or Incurr'd.

Once news of this development spread, dozens of interested parties, including Samuel Nurse and his kinsmen, requested copies of the document.

The reparations committee allotted the sums of £20 for Mary Esty to her husband, Isaac Esty, and £25 for Rebecca Nurse to her son Samuel Nurse. When the committee paid in the spring of 1712, Samuel distributed the £25 among the family.

Likewise, the First Church of Salem voted to restore the membership of Rebecca Nurse, as well as Giles Corey, reversing the earlier excommunication, "that it may no longer be a reproach to her memory, and an occasion of grief to her children."

Samuel Nurse continued to live on and work the family farm, which was passed upon his death in 1716 to his son Samuel. His descendants sold the farm in 1886 to a branch of the Putnam family that had also descended from Rebecca. Her descendants continued to keep Rebecca's memory green, her innocence a byword, and, in 1875, to plan a more public memorial. They commissioned a monument of polished Quincy and Rockport granite. One side of the monument bore a poem composed especially for it by John Greenleaf Whittier:

O Christian martyr, who for Truth could die
When all about thee owned the hideous lie,
The world redeemed from Superstition's sway
Is breathing freer for thy sake today.

The other side's inscriptions acknowledged that forty neighbors had petitioned for her and included some of Rebecca's own words:

I am innocent and God will clear my innocency.

This they dedicated July 30, 1885. After a service at Danvers First Church (which had begun as the Salem Village Church, Salem Village having become the independent town of Danvers around 1758), which six hundred or more of Rebecca's descendants from across the nation attended, four hundred of them walked to the homestead burying ground for a ceremony and a group photograph.

"It is believed," the *Danvers Mirror* reported, "that this is the first service of the kind ever rendered to any person (certainly in this country) who was put to death for alleged witchcraft."

Once ownership passed out of the family in 1908, the Rebecca Nurse Memorial Association acquired the farm, restored the house, and opened the place to the public. Reduced in size and surrounded by growing suburbia, the homestead, house, and remaining fields passed into the protection of other preservation organizations. Rebecca Nurse's memory—and innocence—remain duly honored.

Bridget Bishop

BRIDGET BISHOP's third husband, Edward Bishop, is largely absent from the surviving court papers, named only occasionally as a way of identifying his wife. Even then, she was often called Goody Oliver or Goody Bishop alias Oliver. Bishop still owned the house he had built on Thomas Oliver's land, the home from which Bridget had been arrested.

Over a year after Bridget's death, probate judge Bartholomew Gedney, a member of the former Court of Oyer and Terminer, ordered an inventory of the Oliver estate that, as of August 1693, appraised the land at £20 and "the house which stands on the said land" at £9. Gedney granted administration to Oliver's grandson Job Hilliard, a Charlestown shoemaker, on condition he pay certain sums within the year to the Oliver heirs, including £9 to Bridget's daughter Christian Mason plus £9 to "Edward Bishop for his disbursement on the house."

If Christian Mason was still alive as of the payment order, which was dated August 11, 1693, she did not live long, for her husband, Thomas, remarried on November 1, 1693, to widow Abigail Greenslett, widow of Thomas Greenslett, one of hanged Ann Pudeator's sons.

Hilliard paid Bishop his £9 by April 12, 1694, when Bishop signed his X to signify that he had been compensated for his "Charges In building a house on land belonging to the Estate of Thomas Oliver." On that same day the court appointed Bishop guardian of granddaughter Susanna Mason, on whose behalf he took control of the £9 originally granted to the child's deceased mother. The following July Bishop paid £10 toward the £16 purchase price of a house and land owned by one Matthew Butman, land that bordered some of Philip English's property and was not far from English's Great House. With Bishop moved from the Oliver property, appraised at £29, Hilliard sold it the following January to shoemaker Benjamin Ropes for £65.

With both her father, Thomas Mason, and stepmother, Abigail, associated with families of the accused and with no one stepping forward to clear Bridget's name, we can only speculate how much of her grandmother's story Susanna heard, to be preserved and passed down among her own descendants.

Unlike the Nurse family, neither Edward Bishop nor Thomas Mason petitioned for redress along with the other families whose relatives had been condemned, neither to clear Bridget's name nor to recoup court and jail expenses. Perhaps they had not contributed to her prison room and board. Maybe Edward distanced himself as much as he could from his former wife and her difficult history of witch accusations.

Susanna married shipwright John Becket in September 1711 (a month before the witch suspects' attainders were reversed—but not Bridget's). The Beckets lived near his shipyard, in the same neighborhood as Edward Bishop and Philip English.

Ten years later, when John and Susanna Becket sold their share in her father's estate, she was called a daughter of Thomas and Abigail Mason. This, however, was a common way of referring to the stepmother-stepdaughter relationship and gives no hint as to how the family regarded Bridget's memory. Susanna herself lived on until at least 1769. As John and Susanna Becket came to own Edward Bishop's new home, she evidently remained on good terms with her stepgrandfather.

One of Susanna's daughters, Susanna Babbidge (Bridget's great-granddaughter), supported herself and her family for half a century by teaching reading and sewing to young children after being widowed at the age of thirty-one. She outlived all of her seven children, reared several of her grandchildren, and kept her wits and the ability to knit stockings until her death at the age of ninety in 1804. "Her natural faculties were superiour," according to her minister, William Bentley, who memorialized her as "cheerful, of strong memory, & agreeable in all companies . . . an uncommon example of firmness, strength of mind, & of exemplary piety. The number of children she has educated is very great & the public esteem in which she is held is very sincere." Likely more agreeable than Bridget, Mrs. Babbidge appears to have shared her traits of "firmness [and], strength of mind." Although Salem generally knew who Bridget's descendants were, Susanna Babbidge apparently never discussed her great-grandmother with Bentley.

At some point early on, the county court filed Bridget's paperwork with documents relating to *Sarah* Bishop, both being referred to in the texts as Goodwife or Goody Bishop. Consequently, Bridget's red bodice and red petticoat became associated with Edward and Sarah Bishop's unlicensed tavern, thereby leading later generations to picture Bridget as a raucous barkeeper flouting Puritan conventions. Her identity was not clarified until 1981, and she was not officially exonerated until 2001.

𝔐𝔞𝔯𝔶 𝔈𝔫𝔤𝔩𝔦𝔰𝔥

MARY ENGLISH, homesick for Salem, persuaded Philip against relocating to New York permanently. In Salem they found their fine mansion stripped of its contents, supposedly with only a servant's bed left in the house. Mary returned "to find her house plundered, and the lowest indignities offered to her property of every name; her enclosures destroyed and a wanton waste made of her dearest concerns." Certainly a great deal was lost—confiscated by the sheriff or appropriated by neighbors. Family lore would believe more possessions were lost than Philip included in his detailed but admittedly incomplete list of items when he petitioned for restitution. Nevertheless, business papers from Eleanor Hollingworth's time and other pre-1692 documents survived. Mary's girlhood sampler remained in the family, possibly overlooked as being of inconsequential worth, but the bobtailed cow was *definitely* penned in Sheriff Corwin's yard.

Philip's demands for a full account of what Corwin had confiscated continued to go unanswered, despite Governor Phip's orders. While waiting, Philip set about repairing the house, possibly installing a secret room in the large garret, for one was discovered there generations later. Once the mansion was habitable, they brought their children home.

Despite his losses Philip nevertheless remained among the top 4 percent of Salem's taxpayers in 1694. He had been in the top 1 percent before the witch panic and soon regained that status.

Philip must have felt some satisfaction that Governor Phips, his political enemy, was ordered to London to explain himself and died there of influenza in February 1694. The enquiry was for his handling of the defense against French raiders and noncooperation with customs tax officials. (The witch trials were *not* part of London's concern.) But with Phips out of the way, Lieutenant Governor William Stoughton—former Oyer and Terminer chief justice—was in charge.

Mary gave birth to another son, Ebenezer, on April 21, 1694, but the boy does not seem to have lived long. Family tradition remembered

Mary as dying that same year from consumption caught during her sufferings in 1692. However, she was still alive in June 1695, when "Mr. Philip English and Mary his wife," as administrators of her Uncle Richard Hollingworth's estate, brought suit against John Cromwell. Mary and Philip were still suing her Uncle Richard's debtors on December 31, 1695, when they lost a case against Richard Read (or Rea), were ordered to pay £1:7:10 in costs, and appealed the decision.

In order to rebuild his own business Philip sued numerous parties, but most especially George Corwin; he had Corwin arrested for debt on February 26, 1696. The former sheriff, not a well man, could not post the necessary bail, though presumably someone else did so for him.

At a March 31, 1696, sitting of the Quarterly Court at Ipswich both Philip and Mary English were named in their successful suit against Richard Read, who appealed. This court also considered the case of English v. Corwin, with Joseph Neal representing the ailing Corwin, and decided that, as Corwin had been following orders in 1692, the confiscations were legal (rather than personal) and "the plaintiff is non-suited."

But Philip was not through with George Corwin. He appealed to the Superior Court, but Corwin died at home on April 12, at the age of only thirty. Unable to drag his enemy to court, Philip apparently resorted—or threatened to resort—to the folk custom of impounding a debtor's body until the bereaved family paid the debt. Such schemes were never legal but nonetheless happened in England and elsewhere from time to time, resulting in midnight funerals to avoid losing a body to creditors. Stories about Philip's action ranged from his seizing the body and galloping off with it on horseback to only threatening to do so, prompting Corwin's bereaved family to bury the body in the cellar of his own house until matters settled. Philip's granddaughter related a version of the anecdote in 1793: "the body of Curwin the Sheriff was taken from the funeral procession & detained several days in a Cellar of the deceased's House for a . . . debt & . . . plate, linen, &c. were delivered up" to pay it.

Besides the linen and plate the English family would keep as trophies, the late Captain Corwin's estate, once the widow died, delivered

£44:00:6 worth of miscellaneous goods to Philip on December 28, 1704.

Sometime after their 1696 lawsuit, Mary died, before Philip's marriage to widow Sarah Ingersoll on September 20, 1698. Mary was probably buried in Burial Point, but no stone survives, and Salem's vital records have no notice of her death.

At least one of her daughters was educated in Boston. Along with other young gentlewomen, Susanna attended Mistress Mary Turfrey's boarding school, where her lessons included needlework. There she embroidered a two-foot-by-three-foot apron embellished with a crewel-work vase of flowers and birds worked in gold thread, far more decorative than her mother's sampler of practical stitches. She would marry Jerseyman John Touzel, one of her father's business associates, in 1700. By then Philip was not only back in the top 1 percent of Salem taxpayers but had also been elected to serve Salem in the House of Representatives.

Nine years later he joined with twenty-one others, including Nurse and Procter kin, to petition the government to help those "Blasted in our Reputations and Estates" by the witch trials. When the General Court moved to pay restitutions in 1710, Philip submitted a long list of items taken from his warehouses and his home—over £1,100 worth. He concluded by asserting,

> The foregoing is a true Account of what I had seized tacking away Lost and Embazeld whilst I was a prisoner in the Yeare 1692 & whilst on my flight for my Life besides a Considerable quantity of household goods & other things which I Cannot Exactly give a pertickolar Acc[ount] off for all which I Never Resived any other or further satisfacon for them then sixty Pounds 3s payd Me by the Administrators of George Corwine Late sherife deses'd.

And he did not neglect to mention the bobtailed cow.

The legislature had set aside only so much for restitution payments, and the other families, who had less to begin with, lost far more proportionately than Philip had. They refused his petition, yet Philip persisted, and in 1717 the government offered £200.

Once an Episcopal congregation formed St. Michael's Church in Marblehead, Philip sailed across Salem Harbor to attend services there until he helped found St. Peter's parish in Salem. In 1722 his temper flared into not only a denunciation of the late Reverend Noyes as the murderer of Rebecca Nurse and John Procter but also a declaration that the Salem Church was the "Devil's church." Sued for slander, he pled not guilty but again lost his temper, launching "vile" and "abusive language" against both the church and the justices he faced. A night in jail convinced him to apologize. However, the same thing happened again in 1724. His wife, Sarah, died around that time, his business was declining, and his family realized that Philip had become "clouded in mind." In 1727 Philip granted son-in-law John Touzel power of attorney to enact his business matters and went to live with him and Susanna, paying them twenty shillings a week for room, board, and washing (far more than the two shillings and six pence of the basic jail charge).

But his mind continued to dim, with his "estate greatly wasted and daily wasting," according to his son Philip Jr., even with Touzel handling the finances. The Salem selectmen granted guardianship of Philip English in 1732 to his friend Mr. Thomas Manning of Ipswich and to son Philip English, "innholder."

Matters came to a head again "when Mr Touzel turned Father out of doors," as son Philip complained when he had to take in the difficult old man. Philip lived with Philip Jr. until he died on March 10, 1736.

Philip's mind may have been clouded, but he never forgot a grudge. During his last years—if not on his deathbed—when urged to forgive his enemies before he faced the next life, Philip reluctantly agreed, then added at one instance, "But if I get well, I'll be *damned* if I forgive him!"

Philip's body was buried on March 15, 1736, in St. Peter's churchyard on land the family had donated. The church bell tolled his passing. Unfortunately, no stone remains to mark the spot.

The family was then left to settle his estate and, now that the widower was deceased, Mary's estate as well. Philip's outstanding debts triggered a flurry of lawsuits, including one from the family of George

Hollard, who had not only hidden him in 1692 but also provided for him and Mary while they lived in the Boston jailer's house as well as cared for their daughter Mary when they fled to New York.

Philip's daughter Susanna Touzel made sworn statements about these episodes but, "by reason of Sickness & bodily Infirmity," was unable to travel to Boston or even to the Probate Court's sittings in Salem. As Francis Ghatman "Churgion" wrote, "she hath an ulcerous bone in her legg and by [that] reason it is much inflamed." Both she and her husband, John, soon died, leaving three minor children.

Susanna seems to have passed the Corwin spoils to *her* daughter Susanna, who married John Hathorne, a grandson of Judge John Hathorne. When elderly, Widow Hathorne regaled her minister William Bentley with the family stories, showing him the Corwin silver along with the sampler worked so long before by her grandmother. Mary English, Bentley noted on May 6, 1783, "had the best education of her times. Wrote with great ease & has left a specimen of her needlework in her infancy, or Youth. It is about 2 feet by 9 inches, like a sampler. It concludes with an Alphabet & her name, in the usual form. The figures are diversified with great ease & proportion, & there are all the stitches known to be then in use, & an endless variety of figures in right lines, after no example of nature."

After Widow Susanna (Touzel) Hathorne died in 1802, Bentley helped appraise the family possessions in the old English Mansion, marveling that this was probably "the last time the remains of the first generation were to be seen together in any town of Massachusetts. The singular pride of this family has rendered them tenacious of the lands & of the moveables of their ancestors, & a more curious sight was not to be seen in America."

Ownership of the mansion was divided among the heirs, with the "spoils" from Corwin passing to Mary's great-granddaughter Susanna (Hathorne) Ingersoll and later to her only surviving child, Susanna. (Another branch of the family kept Mary's acrostic poem. In 1859 it belonged to "a lady of Boston, one of her descendants.") Like her parents, this Susanna Ingersoll lived in the former Turner Mansion, later remembered as the House of the Seven Gables after her cousin Nathaniel Hawthorne depicted a similar house in his novel of that name. She also came into possession of the whole of the English Mansion, now run down—a tavern in the basement, roof ornaments lost, and facade gables replaced by rows of small attic dormers. When workmen demolished it in 1833, they discovered the secret garret room.

Susanna Ingersoll, who never married, adopted the cook's son Horace Connolly and, on her death in 1868, left her estate to him. Although he was then the Episcopal rector of St. Mark's in Boston, he undertook several other careers in his lifetime with little success, eventually losing his inheritance—the prized family silver, including the pieces from Corwin, melted for scrap—before dying in poverty.

The sampler, however, survived. Connolly may have sold it to someone more concerned with preserving artifacts of Salem's past. When Salem antiquarian George Curwen died in 1900, he willed a large part of his collection to Salem's Essex Institute—including Mary English's sampler. Curwen is a variant spelling of the name Corwin, and George Rea Curwen was descended from Judge Jonathan Corwin of the witchcraft court. The piece remains in the collection of the Peabody Essex Museum, the Essex Institute's successor, an example of history's ironies.

Ann Putnam Sr.

O nce the trials wound down, ANN PUTNAM receded into obscurity, with hints about her life tied to the recorded activities of her husband, her fortunes rising and falling with his.

Thomas had to make up for the losses on his farm incurred during the growing seasons of 1692, when he spent so much time absent, in town on court business—the £5 the court paid him in December 1693 for his writing duties would not go far. He certainly paid close attention to the Village's problems with the rates committee, which still refused to collect the taxes needed both to pay Reverend Parris and to mend the meeting house, which had received such hard use by the crowds during the witch hearings. Thomas's half-brother Joseph Putnam was on that committee along with once-suspected Daniel Andrews and Rebecca Nurse's husband Francis.

The next rates committee was no help either, as it included Rebecca Nurse's sons-in-law Thomas Preston and John Tarbell and Nurse in-law James Smith. When the Village sued this committee for dereliction of duty, Tarbell and Preston each defiantly paid the forty shilling fine plus twelve shillings six pence court costs. And *still* the rates remained uncollected.

Ann, meanwhile, was with child again and gave birth to a daughter on December 26, 1693. They named her Sarah, the same as the child who had died painfully some years before, whose death Ann had blamed on the malice of witches.

Thomas served throughout 1694 on the committee trying to get a written deed and bills of sale for the parsonage house and land—that Parris thought he already owned—from their donors Hutchinson, Holton, and Ingersoll. In addition, the Village remained nervously alert upon news of Indian attacks at Groton in Massachusetts, then further off in Maine and New Hampshire, then suddenly as close as Haverhill. On the day before an assault on Spruce Creek in August, eight-month-old Sarah died—another sorrow. Ann could not blame Rebecca now. If Goody Nurse truly *had* been a witch, then she could not reach them from Hell. If she had never been a witch after all, then that fact may have opened a distressing line of thought.

The following winter Thomas's widowed stepmother, Mrs. Mary Putnam, who shared her husband's last homestead with Thomas's half-brother Joseph and his family, began to fail in health. "I thought she was not a woman long for this world," Dr. William Griggs would testify, "by the disease that was upon her." He did not specify what disease, but he was not so quick to diagnose "an evil hand." In fact, reputable doctors no longer diagnosed the Invisible World as a cause for illness. As time passed, Mary Putnam suffered fits of unconsciousness that "stupified her understanding and memory." She was sometimes lucid and sometimes unable to recognize even the familiar people around her.

Mary Putnam signed and dated her will on January 28, 1695, then died on March 17, after suffering days and nights of reoccurring fits. With Widow Putnam dead, the estate of Thomas Putnam Sr. could now be settled.

Thomas Jr., meanwhile, continued to be plagued by the dissenters' commotions, the stubborn rates committee, the petitions to remove Parris, and the counterpetitions from those who wanted Parris to remain. In May 1695 Thomas and 105 other Villagers—many of them his relatives—petitioned to retain Parris. Fifty-one women signed, but Ann's name was absent. She gave birth to a son, Seth, the day before and would have been recovering from the effort, though her husband could have signed for her. Although Parris would baptize Seth, the omission suggests a possible change of mind. Did Ann regret her former adherence to the minister's views in 1692? Without Rebecca Nurse to blame and fear, might she now doubt her own actions and, by extension, the true state of her soul?

Spring also brought details of Mary Putnam's will, including the disturbing news that Israel Porter had steadied—or controlled—her hand while she signed it. "To my husband Putnam's children" she left small amounts: five shillings to Thomas Putnam, five to Edward, five to Deliverance Walcott, and ten each to Elizabeth Bailey and Prudence Wayman. "Unto all which I have done something already according to my ability and might, and would have done more but that some of my husband's children and relations have brought upon me inconvenient and unnecessary charges and disbursements at several times."

Everything else she gave to her son Joseph.

Furious, Thomas and Edward and brother-in-law Jonathan Walcott petitioned the probate court in June not to accept the will before they could contest it and to require the executor—half-brother Joseph—to take an inventory of their late father's estate. The widow had had *no* right to dispose of Putnam property beyond what her husband—their father—had specified in *his* will.

A week later, on June 10 (the anniversary of Bridget Bishop's death), Thomas Putnam journeyed to Salem town, where he "accidentally"—as he claimed—found Joseph preparing to have his mother's will probated that very day. Thomas immediately dashed off another petition to Probate Judge Bartholomew Gedney, protesting Joseph's move and asking for time to clarify the state of Mary Putnam's mind when she signed: "For it seemith very hard for flesh and blood to bear, for those who know not what an oath means in a word to swear away three or four hundred pounds from the right owners thereof, when the law also requires credible witnesses in so weighty [an] affair." He signed his name and that of his kinsmen.

Gedney evidently complied, for several depositions survive from people who visited Mrs. Putnam during her last illness and found her state of mind varying from ordinary to dazed. The evidence that scuttled the stepson Thomas's claim may have been that of Rebecca Nurse's son-in-law Thomas Preston: Thomas Putnam himself had commented in February that Mrs. Putnam was a very sick woman, unlikely to recover due to the many fits but that he thought she was then as clear minded as she ever was.

So Thomas and Ann were further impoverished, left with five shillings when they expected to have £300 to £400, whereas half-brother Joseph inherited the bulk of their father's estate.

In April 1696 the male church members met in Thomas and Ann's home. There Parris announced his intent to leave, and no one persuaded him to stay.

The year stumbled on while Indians attacked nearby towns and Thomas's prospects faded. He sold "about eight acres of upland, swamp and meadowland" bordering the Ipswich River in Topsfield to a group of Boxford and Topsfield men, joint owners of a new mill. Both he and Ann signed the document on June 4, 1696, and so let that land pass to outsiders, some of them Rebecca Nurse's kinsmen.

In January of the following winter Massachusetts held the public fast largely to apologize for the witch trials. Unfortunately, how that service proceeded in Salem Village—with Ann and Annie and the other once-afflicted folk present in the congregation, Thomas who had been so busy writing the testimony, and Parris sitting among the rest as a private inhabitant while someone else substituted in the pulpit—passed unrecorded.

Thomas, meanwhile, taking stock of his finances, collected a quantity of old lumber and reused it to build a smaller house in the north part of his farm on a road leading to his brother Edward's place. He sold their fine home on the Andover road to the weaver Samuel Braybrook in June 1697 along with the land immediately about the house, but he retained 160 acres of his farm. Ann now had to pack her possessions and move her children to this smaller, lesser home and make the best of it.

Throughout the remainder of the summer the mediators, including Samuel Sewall and Wait Winthrop, considered the Village quarrel with Parris. Finally acting on their advice, the Village paid Parris, who returned the parsonage deed. Once he moved away with the remains of his family—his wife having died in July 1696—the Village voted to ask young Joseph Green to be their minister.

Green was ordained nearly a year later, on November 10, 1698, and ten days later performed his first baptisms: four children, all Putnam kin. Thomas Putnam presented the first two, daughters Experience and Susanna. Thomas apparently made no protest over Green's obliging him and Ann to share benches with Samuel and Mary Nurse.

In the spring, not long after the Nurse kin made the last payment on the family farm, illness crept into Thomas and Ann Putnam's family. The children—or most of them—seem to have survived, but whatever malady seized Thomas overcame him, carrying him off at last on April 25, 1699.

Ann herself was also struck, becoming weaker from whatever the illness was. She must have been aware at some point that she was dying, yet she was unable to blame the misfortune on Rebecca Nurse. In her last days she had time to wonder again about the state of her soul, whether she was really elect or not, whether she had despoiled her hopes of Heaven with her accusations of Rebecca Nurse and the others, whether she had, however unwittingly, furthered the Devil's work. Two weeks after her husband's death, on June 8, Ann also died, age thirty-seven.

The sparse inventory of Thomas's estate amounted to £437:9:0, not counting the debts. It took little space to record the livestock and less to list the furniture. Yet for all his losses, Thomas had retained his "cane with a silver head and ferule," a gentleman's walking stick appraised at £1:15:0.

Annie, the eldest, was nineteen and, by family tradition, assumed care of her siblings. In time the minors chose various uncles as guardians, and the farm seems to have been rented out to others, at least until the sons were old enough to work it.

Eight years later Annie, now twenty-seven, conferred with Reverend Green about joining the church. By this time the requirements for full admission had relaxed to being a strong heartfelt desire for the sacraments and a generally good Christian life rather than a conviction that one was elect. The assumption was that mortals could not really know such a thing. But she and the Village—and God—knew of the chaos and deaths to which Annie had contributed in 1692, how she had furthered the Devil's work.

Reverend Green counseled her, drafted her confession, and consulted with Samuel Nurse, who was still trying clear his mother's name. And Samuel, to Annie's relief, did not object. Green wrote the text of her confession in the church record book, and to this Annie signed, one evening at the parsonage, her whole name—Ann Putnam—not just the mark she had scrawled on some of the witch trial documents.

The next day, August 25, 1706, young Ann rose to stand at her place in the meeting house while Reverend Green read her confession aloud to the seated congregation:

I desire to be humbled before god for that sad and humbling providence that befell my father's family in the year about '92: that I, then being in my childhood, should, by such a providence of God, be made an instrument for the accusing of several persons of a grievous crime, whereby their lives were taken away from them, whom I now have just grounds and good reason to believe they were innocent persons: and that it was a great delusion of Satan that deceived me in that sad time, whereby I Justly fear, I have been instrumental, with others, though ignorantly and unwittingly, to bring upon myself and this land the guilt of innocent blood: though what was said or done by me against any person I can truly and uprightly say, before god and man, I did it not out of any anger, malice, or ill-will to any person, for I had no such thing against one of them; but what I did was ignorantly, being deluded by Satan. And particularly, as I was a chief instrument of accusing

Goodwife Nurse and her two sisters, I desire to lie in the dust, and to be humbled for it, in that I was a cause, with others, of so sad a calamity to them and their families; for which cause I desire to lie in the dust, and earnestly beg forgiveness of God, and from all those unto whom I have given just cause of sorrow and offence, whose relations were taken away or accused.

"She acknowledged it," Green wrote, the members accepted her into communion, and Green read the statement of faith to which Ann had pledged.

She lived nine more years, making her will on May 20, 1715, when she was in uncertain health, and dying aged about thirty-six sometime before her will was probated in June 1716. By tradition she was the last to be buried in the family plot, a raised mound in the family burying ground on land held by her Uncle Joseph. No individual stones seem to have marked the site, and the mound sank over the centuries, obliterating the memorial—but not the history in which the family had played such a dangerous and deadly role.

Tituba

In May 1693 TITUBA found her case dismissed by the grand jury sitting at Ipswich for lack of evidence. "Ignoramus," foreman Robert Payne wrote on the indictment, but her jail bills still needed to be paid, and Reverend Parris refused to do this. So she was taken back to the Salem jail, her relative freedom still elusive, though without the threat of hanging.

If she had admitted to being a witch, thus justifying his actions throughout 1692, Parris might have paid the bill, according to what Tituba later said. But having an admitted witch in his household— even a supposedly repentant witch—would hardly be safe for his reputation. In any case he would likely have sold her to someone else. As it was, she would now be sold to whoever paid the bill, and that sum increased the longer she stayed.

At some point during 1693 Salem jailor William Dounton submitted to the county court a list of unpaid fees for several prisoners' diet and a reminder that his own salary had been only partially paid for the last nine years. Several entries were crossed out, apparently bills no longer outstanding, and the court refused reimbursement of this messy account. Dounton submitted a neater copy dated December 1693 that omitted the crossed-out entries.

Heading the list in the first copy was the following:

~~for tetabe Indan A whole year and 1 month.~~

The sum is illegible. In 1692 she was in Salem jail from March 1 through 7, then removed to Boston jail, where she was held until June 1, when she was moved back to Salem. Boston jailer John Arnold listed her bill, covering both room and board, as

Tituba an Indian Woman from the
7th of March <u>1691/2</u> to the 1st of June
12 Weekes 2 Dayes at 2/6   1//10//8

Not counting her time in Boston, this places her in the Salem jail until July or early August 1693.

But who purchased her from Dounton?

None of the parties who paid the outstanding bills were included in the list. Whoever it was evidently lived in the general area. Salem was a shire town, and people traveled there from other communities to attend court or to trade at the markets. Robert Calef seems to have known where Tituba was when he compiled his book *More Wonders of the Invisible World,* his scathing commentary of the trials, in 1697. "She was," he wrote, "Committed to Prison, and lay there till Sold for her Fees. The account she *since* gives of it is, that her Master did beat her and otherwise abuse her, to make her confess and accuse (such as he call'd) her Sister Witches, and that whatsoever she said by way of confessing or accusing others, was the effect of such usage."

From Calef's account it is clear that Tituba related the information to him or to others *after* being sold for her fees. Her position being even more precarious than others of "witch lineage," she was possibly sold and resold. After Calef's mention she disappears from the records.

As generations passed, Tituba would be referred to in print as a "half-breed" (half Indian and half African), then as African or Negro, dismissed in either case as an ignorant savage practicing pagan rites, even though the only magic she certainly participated in was the English witch-cake charm at the suggestion of a *white* neighbor. That her white contemporaries *always* referred to her as Indian, in contrast to other slaves they consistently called Negro, led to Elaine Breslaw's study of the woman's possible origin in South America. Peter Hoffer, however, concluded that Tituba was a Yoruba name, and therefore, the Salem Village woman *was* African, though there are other possible origins for her name.

If the debate over Tituba's origin remains undecided, at least, having shed the "savage" stereotype, her memory can be that of not just a slave but also a *survivor*, a woman in a dangerous situation with no one to speak for her, a woman who, in her efforts to endure, managed to turn her accusers' fears back upon themselves.

Mary Warren

MARY WARREN was, like Tituba, among those in William Dounton's first list of unpaid fees, though the amount of the bill is illegible:

~~Mary waren 6 months diet~~

As the crossed-out notation was not included in the clean list submitted to the December court, someone must have paid her debt before then. She was questioned by the magistrates for the first time on April 19, 1692, was listed in a Salem prison census in May 1692, and was still among the afflicted the following January. The recorded debt was for food only, not the room fee, so the surviving bill alone does not explain her whereabouts or how her bills were paid.

Her former mistress and object of her scorn, Elizabeth Procter, saved from the noose by the delay her pregnancy caused, returned to the Procter farm to the relief of her own children and to the resentment of her stepchildren. In May 1696 she had to petition the General Court for help. Instead of being granted the usual widow's third of her late husband's estate, she found herself cut out of John's will entirely:

> [I]n that sad time of darknes before my said husband was executed, it is evident sombody had Contrived a will and brought it to him to signe wherin his wholl estat is disposed of not having Regard to a contract in wrighting mad[e] with me before mariag with him. [Now the stepchildren] will not suffer me to have one peny of the Estat nither upon the acount of my husbands Contract with me before mariage nor yet upon the acount of the dowr which as I humbly conceive doth belong or ought to belong to me by the law for thay say that I am dead in the law.

With the guilty verdict and the death sentence passed upon her, she was, as far as the stepchildren interpreted the law, as good as dead, and the dead have no property rights. Probate Judge Bartholomew Gedney thought otherwise and, on April 19, 1697, considered her "absolutely pardoned" of the witch charge and, therefore, "alive in the law, whereby to Recover her Right of Dowry." He so informed the estate's executors, but Benjamin Procter and John Procter Jr. had already divided the estate among John Sr.'s children, with no mention of the widow.

The petition of 1703, asking the legislature to clear the names of several of those once found guilty of witchcraft, included the cases of John *and* Elizabeth Procter. The result, the following year, reversed the attainder for Elizabeth so that she was "reinstated in their just Credit and reputation."

In 1711, when Governor Joseph Dudley signed the order for restitution, he allotted £150 to the cases of "John Procter (and wife)." By then Elizabeth had married Daniel Richards of Lynn, for she is noted in the compensation list of February 1712 as John Procter's "widow, alias Richards." Although stepsons John and Thorndike seem to have collected most of the sums on behalf of their siblings, Elizabeth Richards "alias Procter" signed another list with an X, indicating she had collected something.

But what happened to Mary Warren?

Once the majority of the population ceased to accept the claims of the afflicted, sentiment turned against them, and many of these who were formerly eager to believe were willing to suspect the worst. The Reversal of Attainder blamed the afflicted: "Some of the principal Accusers and Witnesses in those dark and Severe prosecutions have since discovered themselves to be persons of profligate and vicious Conversation."

In his criticism of the trials and their handling, Robert Calef had only contempt for the "several Wenches in Boston, etc. who pretended to be Afflicted, and accused several" as well as for "the generality of those Accusers [who] may have since convinc'd the Ministers by their vicious courses that they might err in extending too much Charity to them." He also called the afflicted "Vile Varlets as not only were known before, but have been further apparent since by their Manifest Lives, Whordoms, Incest, etc." Writing in 1697, Calef did not specifically explain his charges or to whom each charge applied. Females perceived as overly forward have often been assumed to be sexually corrupt as well, regardless of whether any evidence supported those claims.

But the subsequent histories of a few of the young accusers seemed to support Calef's views, however biased they might have been. In their later lives some were fined for fornication, and another was excommunicated from her church for adultery, another gave birth out of wedlock—not as uncommon an occurrence as one might think in a Puritan society—and one was even cast out of town as "a person of evil fame."

Others moved away or simply married, possibly seldom or never speaking of the terrible year and the parts they played in it. Changing their names upon marriage helped to conceal their earlier histories if they distanced themselves from local gossip to other towns.

In any case the December 1693 jail bill is the last known surviving historical scrap that mentions Mary Warren, once so prevalent in court transcripts. If she, like Tituba, had not been part of the witch trials, their presence in the world might never have been preserved at all. Where Mary went, how long she lived, whether her father and her deafened sister still lived—none of that is known. The trail of her life evaporates like frost in sunlight, as insubstantial as a phantom.

CODA &

ACKNOWLEDGMENTS

Salem is a tourist destination now. The maritime trades, so important to Philip English, flowered in the heady days of the China trade and then moved to deeper water ports. The manufacturing that replaced this, in turn, faltered, and tourism filled the void.

To be fair, tourists themselves preceded tourism as an industry once transportation became more accessible. As early as 1892 sightseers descended from the trains, wanting to know the whereabouts of Nathaniel Hawthorne's birthplace and the spot where the "witches" were hanged.

In Salem individuals and institutions now wrestle with overlapping and often conflicting approaches to the witch trials. The historical approach tries to find and present in context the facts of what actually happened. The commercial tries to make a living answering tourists' demands and may or may not strive for accuracy. Another approach is to try to ignore the topic, leaving its presentation in the hands of others.

October's month-long Haunted Happenings draws throngs of tourists and other merrymakers, rendering the drawbacks of this potential conflict all too clear when the carnival atmosphere—sausage vendors, fog machines, blaring music, and strolling zombies—intrudes on the Witch Trial Memorial (intended for quiet contemplation) and the adjacent Burial Ground, with its vulnerable stones.

The memory of the actual people involved in the original tragedy of 1692 can become lost, replaced by stereotypes, or disregarded. They deserve to be acknowledged.

* * *

The living deserve acknowledgement and thanks as well. To the many who have helped me with this book: Michael Dorr, my agent, who suggested the topic and shepherded the manuscript into a presentable state; Elizabeth Bouvier, archivist for the Supreme Judicial Court of Massachusetts, who provided me with digital dockets at a vital point; the staffs of the Massachusetts Archives in Dorchester, the New England Historic Genealogical Society library in Boston, and the South Essex Registry of Deeds in Salem; Irene Axelrod of the Phillips Library of the Peabody Essex Museum in Salem; Jeanne Gamble of Historic New England and Professor Robert Saint-George, who aided my search for some still-elusive poppets; fellow witch trial researchers Margo Burns, Bernard Rosenthal, Richard Trask, and Ben Ray; Tina Jordan, Stacy Tilney, and Alison D'Amario of the Salem Witch Museum over the years, for no end of encouragement and practical help; ditto for Elizabeth Peterson, director of the Witch House/Corwin House site in Salem; Ben Schafer for having the faith to take on the book; Christine Marra and her crew for leading the Luddite through the unfamiliar territory of computer editing at a brisk trot; Gerard McMahon, for vital Internet assistance; and my mother, Priscilla Roach, for her continuing patience.

NOTES

PART ONE: INTRODUCTIONS

Rebecca Nurse

Great Yarmouth: Lupson, *Saint Nicholas Church* 1–8, 49–50, 60, 68–69, 70–71; "Where I Live, Norfolk"; "Plan of Great Yarmouth."

Rebecca's family: Davis, *Massachusetts and Maine Families*, "Towne," 3: 485–491, 504–507, "Blessing," 1: 193–199; Hoover, *Towne Family*, 1–3.

East Anglia: R. Thompson, *Mobility and Migration*, 17–23.

Book of Sports: "Book of Sports," Britania.com.

Townes in Salem: Hoover, *Towne Family*, 1; Perley, "Northfields No. 3," 190, and map opp. 187.

Skerry: Perley, *The History of Salem*, 1: 433; Bentley, *Diary*, 2: 45.

Francis Nurse: EQC, 1: 16; OED, 10: 99 "tray."

Margaret Jones: Hale, *A Modest Enquiry*, 17.

Quakers: Perley, *The History of Salem*, 2: 270.

Porter-Nurse suit: EQC, 1: 363.

Francis's health: EQC, 1: 428.

Rebecca's health: Docs, 340, 31.

Joanna Towne and Reverend Gilbert: EQC, 4: 249, 369–370; Rapaport, "Turbulent Topsfield."

Rebecca joins church: Salem Church. *Church Records*, 127.

SV parish status: Roach, *The Salem Witch Trials*, xxvii.

Clungen: EQC, 5: 430–431, 419–420; Perley, *The History of Salem*, 3: 32.

Goodale: EQC, 6: 190–191

Nurse Farm: Perley, "Endicott Lands," maps opp. 361 and 379; 361–362, 379–382; C. Upham, *Salem Witchcraft*, 53–55; *Suffolk Deeds*: 12: 10–11; Perley, "The Nurse House," 3. C. Upham (53) says that when Francis Nurse purchased the farm in 1678 he had lived about forty years "near Skerry's" on the North River in Salem Town near the Beverly ferry. Francis's inclusion in the 1676 coroner's jury [EQC, 6: 190–191] shows that he was already living in the same neighborhood as what would become his farm. Upham, as usual, gave no source for the statement.

Towne will: Essex, *Probate*, 2: 358.

Hadlock-Nurse agreement: EQC-VT, 57–63–1–57–65–4.

Bridget Bishop

Playfer, Wasselbee, Oliver, Bishop, and Mason: Anderson, "Bridget"; D. Greene, "Bridget Bishop."

Thomas and Mary Oliver: EQC, 1: 160, 173, 112, 182–183, 3: 116; Salem. *Vital Records*, 2: 112.

Marriage to Oliver: EQC, 4: 90–91, 6: 386–387.

Suspicions: Docs, 230 (Gray), 231 (Stacy).

Oliver probate: Oliver, Essex Probate Docket 20009; Essex, County of. *The Probate Records of Essex County, Massachusetts*, 3: 319; EQC 7: 237–238; Perley, "Northfield No. 1," 18, and map opp. 173.

1679 witchcraft case: EQC, 7: 329–330 (Juan is "Wonn, John Ingerson's Negro").

Shattuck: Doc, 279.

Sale to Epps: Perley, "Salem, No. 14," 34.

Goody Whatford: C. Mather, *Wonders*, 249.

Marriage to Edward Bishop and new house: D. Greene, "Bridget Bishop," 131; Essex, *Probate*, 303: 184; Essex Deeds 10: 112; Perley, "Salem No. 14," 35–36; Doc, 280.

More suspicions: C. Mather, *Wonders*, 249; Docs, 280 (Bly), 278 (Louder); Perley, "Salem, No. 14," 23–25.

Alice Parker: Doc, 573.

Mill brass case: EQC–VT, 47–80–4, 47–83–1.

Clothing: Docs, 282, 23; Textiles, British History Online.

Mary English

Hollingworths and kin: GM, 3: 472–477 (Hunter), 3: 380–84 (Hollingsworth); Barclay, "Notes," 77–84; Mahler, "The English Origin," 241–244; Cheever, "A Sketch," 159; Perley, "Salem, No. 20," 114–115, 120–121.

Mary (Hollingworth) English: Bentley, *Diary*, 2: 24; Richter and Peabody, *Painted*, 8–9; Fairbanks and Trent, *New England Begins*, #420 in vol. 3: 403–404. Mary gave her age as thirty-nine in 1692 and was supposed to be forty-two in 1694.

William Hollingworth property: Perley, *The History of Salem*, 3: 88–89; Perley "Salem, No. 21," 164, 167–168; Essex, *Probate*, 3: 191–192.

Eleanor Hollingworth: Perley, *The History of Salem*, 2: 82–83; EQC, 4: 174, 230–231 (struck unconscious).

Eleanor's business transactions and Blue Anchor: Perley, *The History of Salem*, 3: 88–89; Salem, *Vital Records*, 3: 44; Essex Deeds 2: 121, 3: 160–161, 6: 42.

William Hollingworth Sr.'s probate: Essex, *Probate*, 3: 191–193; EQC, 7: 319–320.

Philip English: Cheever, "A Sketch," 176; Bailyn, *New England Merchants*, 144–145; Perley, *The History of Salem*, 3: 252; Belknap, "Philip English," 41.

Essex French: Konig, "A New Look"; Massachusetts Archives 81: 128, 131–132.

English children: Salem, *Vital Records*, 1: 282.

Dicer slander suit: EQC, 7: 238; Perley, *The History of Salem* 3: 90; Perley, "Salem, No. 21," 164, 166.

Salem First Church: Salem, *Church Records*, 152; Cheever, "A Sketch," 164; EQC, 7: 402–403.

Philip English as tax collector: Salem, *Town Records* 3: 141, 151; Konig, "A New Look," 172–173, 176–177.

Philip English buys Dicer's property: Perley, "Salem, No. 21," 166–167.

English's Great House: Bentley, *Diary*, 1: 247–248, 2: 23–26; Perley, "Salem, No. 21," 164, 168–169; Browne, "Youthful Recollections," 49: 198.

William Hollingworth Jr: EQC, 9: 393–396, 441, 448–449; EQC–VT, 48–32–1, 48–104–2.

Philip's possible illegitimate offspring: Hawthorne, *American Notebooks*, 74–75; EQC, 1: 250; Doc, 975.

Eleanor Hollingworth probate: Salem, *Vital Records* 5: 337; EQC–VT, 49–52–1.

Christian Trask: Doc, 189.

Ann Putnam

Carr family: GM, 2: 1724.

Carr's ferry: EQC, 1: 38–39.

Murderous servant: EQC, 1: 97, 2: 2, 243–246.

Drowning: *Records of the Court of Assistants*, 3: 63–66.

James Carr and widow Maverick: Doc, 598; Jackson, *Physicians*, 33–34.

Bradbury: GM, 1: 375–381

John Carr vs. Mary Bradbury: Doc, 572.

Salem Village begins: Boyer and Nissenbaum, *Salem-Village Witchcraft*, 229–234; Roach, *Salem Witch Trials*, xxvi–xxvii.

Bailey family: Bailey, *Bailey Genealogy*, 157, 160–161.

Bailey's house: Perley, "Center of Salem Village," 231–232.

Salem Village Meeting House: Ibid., 227–228.

Putnam genealogy: Perley, *History of Salem*, 2: 109–111.

Putnam houses: Perley, "Hathorne," map opp. 332, 336, 341–342.

Reverend Bailey controversies: Boyer and Nissenbaum, *Salem-Village Witchcraft*, 242–248.

Mary Bradbury and blue boar: Doc, 599.

Salem Village's status: Boyer and Nissenbaum, *Salem-Village Witchcraft*, 249–253.

Land deeded to Reverend Bailey: Ibid., 256.

George Burroughs: Salem Village, "A Book of Record," November 25, 1680; Doc, 126; Roach, *Salem Witch Trials*, xxix–xxx; N. Thompson, "Hannah Fisher."

New Salem Village parsonage: Trask, *"The Devil Amongst Us."*

Topsfield dispute: Boyer and Nissenbaum, *Salem-Village Witchcraft*, 236–237.

George Carr illness and probate: EQC, 8: 348–356; EQC–VT, 38–19–1–38–39–4, 39–6–2–39–13–1, 39–17–43, 39–84–2; Jackson, *Physicians*, 38.

Ellenwood annulment: EQC, 8: 386.

Thomas Putnam Sr. will: Boyer and Nissenbaum, *Salem-Village Witchcraft*, 206–207.

Reverend Burroughs's debt and arrest: EQC, 9: 30–32, 47–49.

Deodat Lawson invited: Roach, *Salem Witch Trials*, xxxi.

Thomas Putnam Sr. deeds land to son Thomas: Boyer and Nissenbaum, *Salem-Village Witchcraft*, 205–206.

Thomas Putnam Sr.'s codicil and will: Ibid., 211–213, 206–207.

Reverend Lawson matter mediated: Salem Village, "A Book of Record," 14: 68–72, February 18, 1686/7; Roach, *Salem Witch Trials*, xxxii–xxxiv.

Thomas Putnam transcribes records: Salem Village, "A Book of Record," 14:74, April 7, 1687.

Samuel Parris arrives: Roach, *Salem Witch Trials*, xxxiv–xxxvii; Salem Village, "A Book of Record," 14: 76–78, October 10, 1689, ibid., 67–72, February 16 and 18, 1686/87.

Goody Glover witch case: C. Mather, *Memorable*, 103–105.

Revolt against Andros: Roach, *Salem Witch Trials*, xxxvi.

Parris ordained and Salem Village Church forms: Boyer and Nissenbaum, *Salem-Village Witchcraft*, 208–209.

Ann Putnam joins Salem Village Church: Ibid., 274.

Elizabeth Carr probate: EQC-VT, 51-4-1; Chamberlain, *Notorious*, 141.

Tituba

Tituba: Breslaw, *Tituba*, 3–62, 207n13, 14; Equiano, *Interesting Narrative*, 58–61; Ramsay, *Essay*, 93; Beckford, *Remarks*, 47, 15, 63, 41–44, 13; C. Mather, *Angel*, 228; Hoffer, *Devil's Disciples*, 205–210; C. Mather, *Diary*, 1: 22.

Parris: Breslaw, *Tituba*, 22; Roach, "That Child Betty Parris," 2–4; Gragg, *Quest*, 13–16.

Parris's slaves: Parris, "Records," 20; Hale, *Modest Enquiry*, 23; Breslaw, *Tituba*, 24–25; (Goodwin case) C. Mather, *Memorable*, 99–131.

Barbados witch: Handler, "Archaeological Evidence'" 176–180.

Salem Village controversies: Salem Village, "A Book of Record"; also see selections of Village and church records in Boyer and Nissenbaum, *Salem-Village Witchcraft*.

Fear of slave revolt: EQC–VT, 49–57–8; 49–58–1, 49–56–1, 2, 49–57–2, 49–58–1.

Slaves and servants: R. Thompson, *Sex in Middlesex*, 159; L. Greene, *The Negro*, 73–90, 16–17.

Mary Warren

Warren: Perley, "Rial Side," 55; Perley, *The History of Salem*, 1: 303, 2: 301.

Parker vs. Warren: Perley, "Salem, No. 21," 166 (Perley says Alice Parker's maiden name was Hollingworth but gives no source); Docs, 144, 585, 662.

Procter family: L. Procter, *John Procter*, 6–14; GM, 1: 190–195, 501–504.

Procter farm: Perley, "Groton," 258–261, map 257.

Procter tavern: EQC, 3: 377, 7: 135–136, 4: 268, 374.

Higginson and Noyes: Phillips, *Elegy*, 2; Dunton, *Letters*, 177, 255; N. Noyes, "Elegy," 6.

Procter family life: Docs, 956, 80; Perley, *The History of Salem*, 3: 1.

Procter deeds: Essex Deeds, 8: 338–341 (deed #123); Perley, "Groton," 267, map opp. 257 (Perley misplaces the house location).

PART TWO

Chapter 1: January 1692

Salem Village Sermon: Doc, 6; Parris, *Sermon Notebook*, 179–180, 183–185 (parts of the morning and afternoon sermons quoted here; spelling and so forth standardized here as in the other fictionalized sections).

Higginson and Noyes: Phillips, *Elegy*, 2; Dunton, *Letters*, 177, 255; N. Noyes, "Elegy," 6.

Salem Village and Salem town: Tully, *Almanac*, "January Hath 31 Dayes," v; H. B., *Boston Almanac*, "January Hath 31 Dayes," 3; Sewall, *Diary*, 1: 286, January 12, 1692; Salem Village, "A Book of Record," 14: 85–86, January 8, 1692; Salem, *Vital Records*, 3: 256.

Alice Parker: Doc, 573.

Afflictions and theories thereon: Doc, 6; Caporal, "Ergotism"; Hutchinson, *History*, 1: 47; C. Upham, *Salem Witchcraft*, 318; Rosenthal, *Salem Story*, 10–31.

Folk Magic: Thomas, *Religion*, 212–251; Hale, *Modest Enquiry*, 132–136; Hansen, *Witchcraft*, 30–31, 149–150; Norton, *Devil's Snare*, 23–24, 336n32, 31; Docs, 562 (Rebecca Johnson), 631, 632 (Wardwell), 556–557, (Dorcas Hoar), 166 (Roger Toothaker); Kittredge, *Witchcraft*, 196, 198–199.

Ergot: Caporal, "Ergotism."

Hysteria: Hansen, *Witchcraft*.

Parris's problems: Boyer and Nissenbaum, *Salem-Village Witchcraft*, 276–277, 357.

York massacre: C. Mather, *Decennium*, 230–231; Hammond, "Diary," 160.

Chapter 2: February 1692

Philip English's pew: Salem, *Town Records*, 3: 259.

Sarah Good begging: Docs, 3, 5.

Parris' sermon: Parris, *Sermon Notebook*, 186, 190, 193 (morning and afternoon sermons combined).

Hannah Putnam's travail: Parris, "Records," 15; Doc, 267; Eben Putnam, *History*, 1: 72–73; Ulrich, *Goodwives*, 126–131.

Other births: Parris, "Records," 14.

Afflictions at the parsonage begins: Hale, *Modest Enquiry*, 23; Calef, *More Wonders*, 342.

Witch-cake: Hale, *Modest Enquiry*, 23–25; Calef, *More Wonders*, 342; Lawson, *Brief*, 162; Thomas, *Religion*, 437–438, 543–544; Boyer and Nissenbaum, *Salem-Village Witchcraft*, 278–279.

Rebecca Nurse and fits: Docs, 27, 31, 23.

Putnam afflictions begin: Ibid., 3–4, 13, 9.

Betty Hubbard's errand: Ibid., 345.

Good accused: Ibid., 3–4, 13, 9.

Tempests: Hammond, "Diary," 160; Sewall, *Diary*, 1: 288, February 28, 1692; Ludlum, *Country Journal*, 15, 70.

First complaints entered: Docs, 1–2.

Specters at the Putnam's: Ibid., 345.
Tituba suspected: Ibid., 6; Calef, *More Wonders*, 343.

Chapter 3: March 1 to Mid-March 1692
March 1 hearings: Docs, 3–5 (Good), 3–5 (Osborne), 3–6 (Tituba).
Elizabeth Emerson: Ulrich, *Goodwives*, 196–201.
Sarah Good at Herrick's: Doc, 337.
Salem jail: Perley, *The History of Salem*, 3: 174.
Tituba's March 2 questioning: Doc, 6.
Tituba's status: Docs, 4, 6, 345.
Tituba's wounds: Hale, *Modest Enquiry*, 26–27; Calef, *More Wonders*, 343.
March 3 questioning: Docs, 4, 862, 868; Lawson, *Brief*, 148.
Dorothy Good specter: Doc, 26.
March 5: Ibid., 4; Hale, *Modest Enquiry*, 27.
Boston Jail: Doc, 612; Roach, *Salem Witch Trials*, 35.
Salem town meeting: Salem, *Town Records* 3: 265.
Martha Corey: Doc, 53, 18; Roach, *Salem Witch Trials*, 37; Essex Deeds 13: 208.
Rebecca Nurse and Elizabeth Procter specters: Doc, 35, 53.
Martha Corey confronts Annie Putnam: Ibid., 21.
Mary Warren and the specter: Ibid., 145.
Rebecca Nurse's illness: Ibid., 28.
Convulsions: Hansen, *Witchcraft at Salem*, 1–2. The presence of hysterical symptoms among the afflicted in 1692 is one of the main topics of Hansen's book, although there is disagreement about how many of the afflictions were truly unconscious reactions.
Martha Corey confronts Mary Warren: Doc, 145.
Mary Warren's vision of John Procter: Ibid. Mary Warren later described the beginning of her fits in a confused and, no doubt, embellished account:

> the first night I was Taken I saw as I thought the Apparition of Goody Cory and Catched att itt as I thought and Caught my master in my lap 'tho I did nott See my master in that place att that Time, upon Wch my master Said itt is noe body but I itt is my shaddow that you see, butt my master was nott befor mee as I Could descerne, but Catching att the Apparition that Looked like Goody Cory I Caught hold of my master and pulled him downe into my Lap; upon Wch he Said I see there is noe heed to any of your Talkings, for you are all possest With the Devill for itt is nothing butt my shape.

Procter beats Mary Warren: Ibid., 501.

Chapter 4: March 18 to 31, 1692
Ann Putnam tormented by Rebecca Nurse's specter: Doc, 30.
Other afflicted women: Lawson, *Brief*, 155.
Complaint vs. Martha Corey: Doc, 15; Lawson, *Brief*, 60.
Martha Corey at Lawson's sermon: Lawson, *Brief*, 40.
Ann Putnam reads the Bible: Ibid., 158 (King James edition).

Annie Putnam's vision of Corey and Nurse specters: Ibid., 156.

Martha Corey hearing: Doc, 16; Lawson, *Brief,* 154–157.

Nurse specter vs. Ann Putnam: Doc, 30.

Friends visit Rebecca Nurse: Ibid., 31.

Reverend Lawson observes Ann Putnam's fits: Lawson, *Brief,* 157–158, 162; Doc, 30.

Reverend Noyes and Revelation: Phillips, *Elegy,* 5.

Arrests of Rebecca Nurse and Dorothy Good: Docs, 22–23; Lawson, *Brief,* 159.

Mary Warren attends hearing: Doc, 501.

Rebecca Nurse hearing: Ibid., 23, 28, 30; Lawson, *Brief,* 158–160.

Dorothy Good: Lawson, *Brief,* 159–160.

Lawson's lecture: Lawson, *Christ's Fidelity,* 64–106 (quotes), 76, 79, 100, 80, 102–103.

John Procter fetches Mary Warren: Docs, 501, 145.

Nurse specter vs. Annie Putnam: Ibid., 32.

March 27 Salem Village service: Lawson, *Brief,* 101 (he mistakes the date, however); Parris, *Sermon Notebook,* 194–198 (quotes), 194–198; Doc, 342; Salem Village church records in Boyer and Nissenbaum, *Salem-Village Witchcraft,* 278–279 (Mary Sibley and witch-cake).

Nurse kin question accusers: Docs, 35 (Putnams), 498, 500.

Mercy Lewis's doubts: Ibid., 499.

Procters and Mary Warren's fits: Ibid., 78, 80, 145.

Public Fast: Ibid., 49, 244, 133; Lawson, *Brief,* 160–161.

Hollingworth suit: EQC, 7:238.

Chapter 5: April 1 to 19, 1692

Note for prayers: Docs, 75, 78.

Mercy Lewis's angelic vision: Ibid., 49; Lawson, *Brief,* 160–161.

Dissemble: Doc, 75; OED, 2nd ed., 4: 835–836.

Procters displeased with Mary Warren: Ibid., 78.

Complaint vs. Elizabeth Procter and Sarah Cloyce: Ibid., 46.

Spectral sightings: Ibid., 61.

Mercy Lewis's uncertainty and visions: Ibid., 48–49; Lawson, *Brief,* 160–161.

Procter arrest: Doc, 46.

Sarah Cloyce and Elizabeth Procter hearings: Ibid., 49.

Mary Warren accused: Ibid., 49.

John Procter hearing: Ibid., 61.

Prisoners to Boston jail: Ibid., 47, 65, 612.

John and Hannah Putnam's baby dies: Ibid., 362; Eben Putnam, *History,* 1: 56–57; Parris, "Records," 21.

Complaint against Mary Warren, Bridget Bishop, and so forth: Doc, 42.

Mary Warren hearing: Ibid., 75, 699.

Chapter 6: April 19 to 30, 1692

Bridget Bishop hearing: Docs, 63–64 (combination of notes by Ezekiel Cheever and Samuel Parris).

Mary Warren hearing continued: Ibid., 75, 699.

Giles Corey specter and Mary Warren questioned in Salem jail April 19 and 20: Ibid., 78.

John Procter vs. Giles Corey suit: EQC, 7: 89–91.

Burroughs specter vs. Annie Putnam: Doc, 457; Lawson, *Brief*, 148. Lawson noted that an unnamed suspect examined before March 19 had said that Burroughs killed Lawson's wife and child. At that point only Tituba was confessing.

Thomas Putnam's letter and complaint vs. Mary Esty, Mary English, and so forth: Docs, 82, 79.

Mary Warren questioned April 21: Ibid., 80.

Arrests of Mary English: Ibid., 79; Cheever, "A Sketch," 163–164; Bentley, *Diary*, 2: 23; EQC, 7: 238.

Christian Trask and Sarah Bishop: Doc, 189; Mahler, "English Origin," 243; Perley, *The History of Salem*, 1: 94–98; Savage, *Genealogical Dictionary*, 4: 624–626

Witch meeting in Parris's pasture: Roach, *Salem Witch Trials*, 88–89.

Dorcas Hobbs hearing: Doc, 89.

William Hobbs hearing: Ibid., 90.

Nehemiah Abbott hearing: Ibid., 83.

Mary Esty hearing: Ibid., 86.

Mary Black hearing: Ibid., 84.

Sarah Wildes hearing: Ibid., 90.

Mary English hearing: Cheever, "A Sketch," 163.

John Willard and Annie Putnam: Docs, 185, 486, 488, 185. Doc, 185, clearly says Willard confronted Annie May 25. As the first arrest warrant would be issued May 10 around the time he fled (Doc, 132), this confrontation may have occurred April 25 unless it happened closer to the complaint, May 2 or 5, perhaps.

Baby Sarah's ghost: Doc, 185. So far genealogists have not found evidence of a first wife for John Willard.

Philip English suspected and familiars: Cheever, "A Sketch," 163; Docs, 163–164, 202.

Complaints against Philip English, and so forth: Docs, 96–97.

Philip English escapes: Ibid., 99.

Boston jail repairs: Ibid., 612, 841.

John Indian and Edward Bishop: Calef, *More Wonders*, 351, 348.

Chapter 7: May 1 to 12, 1692

Deliverance Hobbs confession, Mary Warren's statement: Docs, 116, 95, 262–263.

Election and Fast order: Ibid., 488; Love, *The Fast*, 481, 220.

Philip English's second arrest warrant: Doc, 117.

George Burroughs extradited: Ibid., 99, 97.

Wilkins family ailments: Ibid., 488, 184.

May 2 hearings: Ibid., 96, 98, 102 (Dorcas Hoar), 104–105 (Susanna Martin); 1 Samuel 28.

Prisoners to Boston: Docs, 97–99, 100, 114.

Burroughs specter vs. Mercy Lewis: Ibid., 124.

May 8 torments: Ibid., 119–118.

Parris's sermon: Parris, *Sermon Notebook*, 199.

Reading and Woburn Complaints: Doc, 119.

"Old Pharaoh": Ibid., 157.

Burroughs specter and ghosts: Ibid., 124 (vs. Mercy Lewis), 125 (vs. Annie Putnam).

Mercy Lewis's vision: Ibid., 124; C. Mather, *Wonders*, 217; Matthew 4:1–11; Luke 4:1–13.

George Burroughs examination: Docs, 120–130; C. Mather, *Wonders*, 216–217.

Other suspects: Doc, 215 (Dustin, also Dastin); EQC, 4: 207–209 (Goody Burt).

Sarah Churchill: Docs, 133–134, 258; S. Noyes, Libby, and Davis, *Genealogical*, 142, 98–99.

Prisoners moved to Boston: Doc, 862, 612.

George Jacobs specter vs. Mercy Lewis: Ibid., 134.

George and Margaret Jacobs arrests: Ibid., 131.

Sarah Churchill accuses the Jacobs: Ibid., 133, 261.

John Willard arrest warrant: Ibid., 132.

Sarah Churchill vs. the Jacobs continued: Ibid., 133, 145.

Sarah Osborn dies: Ibid., 612, 841.

Mary Warren questioned: Ibid., 145, 120 (Abigail Hobbs), 699 (other confessors).

Alice Parker and Ann Pudeator warrants: Ibid., 143.

Alice Parker hearing: Ibid., 144–145.

Chapter 8: May 12 to 30, 1692

Mittimus: Docs, 146, 612, 841, 216. Their Boston jail bills begin on May 12, even though the trip to Boston took the better part of a day. A prison census, Doc, 216, says they were sent May 13, which makes better sense.

Abigail Soames's arrest: Ibid., 147.

Abigail Soames hearing: Ibid., 150; Swan, "Bedevilment," 158; EQC, 7: 420, 8: 147, 237, 372, 8: 237; Perley, "Part of Salem, No. 8," 98.

Touch test: Brattle, "Letter," 171; Lawson, *Brief*, 162.

Elizabeth Hart confronts Annie Putnam: Doc, 158.

More arrests: Ibid., 151–154.

Daniel Andrews and George Jacob Jr. escape: Ibid.

May 12, Mercy Lewis reports specters hurting Bray Wilkins: Ibid., 184.

Second arrest warrant for John Willard: Ibid., 156.

Annie Putnam reports John Willard's specter tormenting Rebecca Wilkins: Ibid., 185.

John Willard arrested: Calef, *More Wonders*, 361.

Daniel Wilkins dies: Doc, 165.

Search for Elizabeth Coleson: Ibid., 161.

Governor Phips arrives: Sewall, *Diary*, 1: 291, May 14, 1692.

May 17, coroner's jury on Daniel Wilkins: Doc, 165, 162; Parris, "Records," 21.

Governor's Council sworn: Massachusetts Archives, "Council Records," 165–168.

May 18 hearings: Docs, 296–300, 168, 173–174.

Sarah Buckley hearing: Ibid., 168, 170.

Mary Whittredge hearing: Roach, *Salem Witch Trials*, 131.

Rebecca Jacobs hearing: Calef, *More Wonders*, 371; Doc, 172; D. Greene, "George Jacobs," 73.

Roger Toothaker: Doc, 166.

John Willard hearing: Ibid., 173–174 (dialogue combined, emphasis added), 177 (re-afflicted).

Mary Esty: Ibid., 206 (evidence vs. Mary Esty had come from Annie Putnam, Mary Walcott, Mercy Lewis, Elizabeth Hubbard, and John Indian).

Margaret Jacobs and Sarah Churchill: Ibid., 295, 172, 512, 753; Calef, *More Wonders*, 364–366.

Prisoners transferred to Boston: Doc, 186.

Elizabeth Booth vs. Mary Warren: Ibid., 167.

Specters vs. Mary Warren: Ibid., 255.

May 20, Mercy Lewis's afflictions, Mary Esty re-arrested and so forth: Ibid., 204–205, 187, 601, 191–192, 197.

Sarah Procter and Sarah Bassett accused: Ibid., 195.

Mary Esty's second hearing: Ibid., 601.

Hearings of Benjamin Procter, Sarah Pease, and Mary DeRich: Ibid., 198–201.

Elizabeth Cary: Ibid., 203.

Prisoners transferred to Boston: Ibid., 212.

Mary Warren vs. Mary Ireson and Mary Toothaker: Ibid., 305.

Fast Day scheduled: Ibid., 219; Massachusetts Archives, "Council Records," 170; Love, *The Fast*, 481, 260.

May 26 spectral attacks: Docs, 219, 229.

William Procter and others accused: Ibid., 221.

Court of Oyer and Terminer established: Ibid., 220.

Mrs. Cary: Ibid., 224, 203.

List of suspects and victims: Ibid., 221–222.

Elizabeth Fosdick and Elizabeth Paine, second complaint: Ibid., 221, 229.

Spectral activities: Ibid., 230 (Bridget Bishop), 202 (Philip English).

Philip English arrested: Ibid., 117, 976.

Office of sheriff: Massachusetts Archives, "Council Records," 173–177.

Oyer and Terminer order: Doc, 232.

May 31, afflicted witnesses: Ibid., 233, 241–242.

Bartholomew Gedney: Ibid., 234. Alden's statement has Gedney present, although only Hathorne and Corwin signed the warrants.

Thomas Newton: Ibid., 253; Roach, *Salem Witch Trials*, 144.

Mrs. Ann Putnam present: Doc, 30.

John Alden hearing: Ibid., 233–234; Roach, *Salem Witch Trials*, 10, 51, 97, 149.

Elizabeth How hearing: Docs 241, 243 (Bridget Oliver).

Martha Carrier hearing: Ibid., 235.

Wilmot Read hearing: Ibid., 247, 251.

Alden again: Ibid., 234.

Philip English hearing: Ibid., 117.

William Procter: Ibid., 226, 222, 581–582, 433.

Arthur Abbott: Ibid., 222.

Ann Putnam deposes vs. Rebecca Nurse: Ibid., 30.

Petition for Rebecca Nurse: Ibid., 254, 151–152 (Daniel Andrews).

Elizabeth Emerson and Grace: SCJ, 1: 52; Ulrich, *Goodwives*, 196–201.
Sarah Good and servant girl: C. Mather, "A Brand Pluck'd Out," 259–260.

Chapter 9: June 1 to 9, 1692
Transfer of prisoners: Docs, 253 (Tituba), 512, 841 (Procters).
Esty-Bishop statement: Ibid., 262.
Mary English statement: Ibid., 263.
Boston jail: Roach, *Salem Witch Trials*, 213.
Philip English's hiding place: Doc, 876.
Nurse specter vs. Ann Putnam June 1: Ibid., 267.
Mary Warren and others questioned June 2: Ibid., 255.
Witnesses vs. Rebecca Nurse and John Willard: Ibid., 259–260.
Ghosts attack Ann Putnam June 2: Ibid., 269.
Magistrates question Abigail and Deliverance Hobbs and Mary Warren: Ibid., 255.
Ann Putnam and ghosts: Ibid., 269.
Women suspects examined for witch-marks: Ibid., 271 (and notes), 340.
Men suspects examined for witch-marks: Ibid., 272.
Bridget Bishop before grand jury: Ibid., 264; C. Mather, *Wonders*, 299; Perley, "Salem, No. 14," 20–37, and "Salem, No. 1," 172–173; Roach, *Salem Witch Trials*, 229; Trask, "Legal," 50–51.
Bridget Bishop's indictments: Docs, 273–276.
Testimony not used against Bridget Bishop: Ibid., 76 (Hubbard), 164, 283 (Sheldon), 258 (Mary Warren).
Bridget Bishop before trial jury: C. Mather, *Wonders*, 223–229.
Thomas Brattle's letter: Brattle, "Letter," 174–175.
Acceptable evidence: C. Mather, *Wonders*, 216n1, 304n5; Roach, *Salem Witch Trials*, xxii.
Evidence vs. Bridget Bishop:

> Hobbs: C. Mather, *Wonders*, 224; Docs, 95, 116.
> Afflicted in court: C. Mather, *Wonders*, 223–224.
> Cook: Doc, 277; C. Mather, *Wonders*, 224.
> Gray: Doc, 230 (and note), C. Mather, *Wonders*, 224; Calef, *More Wonders*, 356.
> J and R Bly: Doc, 281, C. Mather, *Wonders*, 225.
> Coman: Doc, 282, C. Mather, *Wonders*, 225.
> Shattucks: Doc, 279, C. Mather, *Wonders*, 225–226.
> Maule: Hale, *Modest Enquiry*, 156.
> Louder: Doc, 278, C. Mather, *Wonders*, 226–227.
> Stacy: Doc, 231, C. Mather, *Wonders*, 227–228.
> J and W Bly: Doc, 280, C. Mather, *Wonders*, 228.

Stoughton and Brattle on afflictions: Brattle, "Letter," 187–188.
Ann Putnam depositions: Docs, 269, 267.
Second witch-mark search: Ibid., 271.
Evidence vs. Rebecca Nurse: Ibid., 291 (Ann Putnam Jr.), 290 (Elizabeth Hubbard), 292 (Mary Walcott), Sheldon/Chibbun (289), 30 (Ann Putnam Sr.), 244 (Abigail Williams).

Evidence in favor of Rebecca Nurse: Ibid., 293 (Clement Coldum), 294 (Goodwives Preston and Tarbell), 31 (Porter, Cloyce, Andrews), 254 (petition).
Indictments vs. Rebecca Nurse: Ibid., 285–288.
John Willard before the grand jury: Ibid., 176 (coroner's jury's report), 301 (Parris, Ingersoll, Thomas Putnam).
Indictments vs. John Willard: Ibid., 296–298 (Sheldon), 299–300 (and note).
Sarah Churchill and Margaret Jacobs do not testify: Ibid., 295.
Margaret Jacobs' recantation: Ibid., 512, 753; Calef, *More Wonders*, 364–365; D. Greene, "George Jacobs," 67–69.
Job Tookey hearing: Docs, 306–307 (Louder).
Mary Ireson accused: Ibid., 303, 305.
Mary Ireson hearing: Ibid., 304, 310.
Ann Dolliver hearing: Ibid., 308–309; Roach, *Salem Witch Trials*, 164.
Tookey's second examination: Doc, 312; Roach, *Salem Witch Trials*, 268.
Elizabeth Booth Jr.: D. Greene, "Bray Wilkins," 105–106.
Death Warrant: Doc, 313.
Hanging site: Roach, *Gallows and Graves*, 7–9.

Chapter 10: June 10 to 30, 1692
Execution of Bridget Bishop: Doc, 313, 408.
Thomas Maule and Reverend Hale: Ibid., 313; Hale, *Modest Enquiry*, 156; Matthew 12:31, 32; Roach, *Salem Witch Trials*, 167–168; Tully, *Almanac*, "June Hath 30 Dayes," xiv. Regarding unforgivable sin (Geneva Bible translation in Weigle, *New Testament Octapla*): "Wherefore I say unto you, everie sinne and blasphmie (against) the holie Gost shall be forgiven unto men. And whosoever shal speake a worde against the Sonne of man, it shalbe forgiven him: but whosoever shal speake against the holie Gost, it shal not be forgiven him, neteher in this world nor in the worlde to come."
Disposal of Bridget Bishop's body: Doc, 313 (and notes).
Wells attack: Massachusetts Archives, "General Court Records," 226; Massachusetts Archives, "Council Records," 178.
Phips consults the ministers: Massachusetts Archives, "General Court Records," 227–228; Boyer and Nissenbaum, *Salem-Village Wtchcraft*, 117–118; Levin, *What Happened*, 110–111.
Nathaniel Saltonstall resigns: Brattle, "Letter," 84.
Nurse family and Salem Village: Boyer and Nissenbaum, *Salem-Village Witchcraft*, 279, 296–297.
Nurse specter vs. Jonathan Putnam: Doc, 360.
Sarah Good before the grand jury: Ibid., 329 (Tituba).
Indictments vs. Sarah Good: Ibid., 330–332.
Statement for Elizabeth How: Ibid., 341.
Rebecca Nurse's petition: Ibid., 340.
Indictments of June 29: Ibid., 347–348 (Elizabeth How); 349–350 (Susannah Martin); 348, 350, 111 (Putnam testimony).

Sarah Good's trial: Ibid., 345, 352–353, 369 (Bradford and Rayment), 326, 364–365, 367 (Sheldon/Chibbun), 364–365, 367 (statements vs. Sarah Bibber); Calef, *More Wonders*, 357–358 (knife episode).

Susannah Martin's trial: Docs, 106, 108–111, 139–142, 159–160, 193, 311, 351, and others; C. Mather, *Wonders*, 236.

Reverend Samuel Willard accused: Calef, *More Wonders*, 360; Haefeli, "Dutch New York," 303.

Rebecca Nurse's Indictments: Docs, 285–288.

Defense for Rebecca Nurse: Ibid., 35 (Samuel Nurse and John Tarbell), 368 (James Kettle), 371 (Joseph Hutchinson), 369 (William and Rachel Bradford and William Rayment Jr.), 370 (Robert Moulton Sr.).

Statements for and against Rebecca Nurse: Ibid., 289 (Sheldon/Chibbun), 358 (Sarah Houlton), 359 (Nathaniel and Hannah Ingersoll), 362 (John Jr. and Hannah Putnam), 372 (John Sr. and Rebecca Putnam), 373 (Nathaniel Putnam Sr.), 285 (other).

Rebecca Nurse's jury trial: Ibid., 366, 416; Calef, *More Wonders*, 358–359.

Rebecca Nurse's comment: The quotation here combines two versions of her comment: Calef, *More Wonders*, 358, has "What? Do you bring her? She is one of us." And in Rebecca's own statement in Doc, 416, "and upon my saying that Goodwife Hobbs and her Daughter were of our Company . . ."

Sarah Nurse's statement: Doc, 366.

Chapter 11: July 1 to 18, 1692

Rebecca Nurse July 3 excommunication: Salem Church, *Records*, 172, 127 (combined); Lupson, *Saint Nicholas Church*, 68–69. Noyes's remarks are based on Robert Keayne's notes for Mistress Ann Hibbens's 1640 excommunication from Boston's First Church, in Demos, *Remarkable Providences*, 279–281.

Ann Pudeator July 2 hearing: Doc, 399; Perley, *The History of Salem*, 2: 39, 122 (Neal).

Mary Bradbury hearing: Docs, 572, 587–589.

Margaret Hawkes and Candy hearing: Docs, 763–764, 395, 414; Hale, *Modest Enquiry*, 80–81.

Nurse family gathers support: Docs, 254 (petition), 285 (Stephen Sewall's statement), 416 (Thomas Fisk statement, see also Calef, *More Wonders*, 358), 417 (Rebecca Nurse's statement, see also Calef, *More Wonders*, 358–359), 294 (Rebecca Preston and Mary Tarbell statement).

Phips and Council: Massachusetts Archives, "Council Records," 180–184.

Commencement: Roach, *Salem Witch Trials*, 194–195.

Anthony Checkley: Massachusetts Archives, 40: 264.

Sir William Phips: Roach, *Salem Witch Trials*, xxxix–xl.

Rebecca Nurse reprieve: Calef, *More Wonders*, 359.

Nurse and others death warrants: Doc, 418.

Invitation to Andover: Brattle, "Letter," 180; Calef, *More Wonders*, 371–372; Docs, 425 (Foster specter), 427 (Bradbury specter).

Ann Foster hearing and confession: Docs, 615–616, 419; Hale, *Modest Enquiry*, 30

Foster specter vs Timothy Swan: Doc, 822; Roach, *Salem Witch Trials*, 175.

Francis Nurse and eclipse: Boyer and Nissenbaum, *Salem-Village Witchcraft*, 296–297; Docs, 596. Tully, *Almanac*, [xiv] "June," 6–7, ("Of the Eclipses") says "*may presage the Death of Aged persons, as well [as] persons of Quality.*"

Chapter 12: July 19 to 31, 1692

Hanging of Rebecca Nurse and others: Doc, 418; Calef, *More Wonders*, 367, 358 (Sarah Good); C. Mather, *Diary*, 1: 142; C. Mather, "A Brand Pluck'd Out," 269. Noyes's remark is paraphrased from Calef's statement: "Mr. Noyes . . . told her she was a Witch, and she knew she was a Witch." Sarah Good's retort is given as: "You are a lyer; I am no more a Witch than you are a Wizard, and if you take away my Life, God will give you Blood to drink." Her folk reference is based on the verse in Revelation 16:6 (see Weigle, *New Testament Octapla* for the Geneva Bible translation), in which the Angel of the Waters empties a vial upon the rivers and the fountains (springs) turning the earth's waters to blood: "For they shed the blood of the Saintes, and Prophetes, and therefore hast thou given them blood to drinke for they are worthie [i.e., deserving of the punishment]."

Burials: C. Upham, *Salem Witchcraft*, 514; Roach, *Salem Witch Trials*, 202; Roach, *Gallows and Graves*, 7–9, 14–17.

Complaint vs. Mary Lacey Sr. and Jr.: Doc, 421 (and note).

Mary Lacey Sr. hearing: Ibid., 426, 424.

Mary Lacey Jr. arrested: Ibid., 422.

Foster and Laceys questioned: Ibid., 424–426. Some quotations are combined from two versions of notes, such as: "[W]e have forsaken Jesus christ And the devil hath got hold of us. how shall we get cleare of this evil one?" Doc 426, and "Oh, mother! how do you do? We have left Christ, and the Devil hath gat hold of us. How shall I get rid of this evil one? I desire God to break my rocky heart that I may get the victory this time," Doc, 424.

Richard and Andrew Carrier arrested: Ibid., 625, 423.

Carrier brothers questioned: Ibid., 423, 425, 428–430; John Procter in Calef, *More Wonders*, 363.

Effect of the Andover confessions: C. Mather, *Diary*, 1: 142.

Martha Emerson arrest: Doc, 427.

John Procter's letter: Calef, *More Wonders*, 362–364 (and notes), addressed to Reverends [Increase] Mather, Allen, Moody, Willard, and Bailey.

Martha Emerson hearing: Doc, 432.

Elizabeth Ballard dies: Savage, *Genealogical Dictionary*, 1: 108.

Husbands accuse wives: Docs, 24 (Giles Corey), 745 (Andover kin).

Thomas and Mary Bradbury: Ibid., 625, 597, 439, 431 (petition).

Thomas Oliver probate: Essex Probate Docket #20009, July 30, 1692 inventory.

Philip and Mary English in jail: Roach, *Salem Witch Trials*, 213; Bentley, *Diary* 2: 24–25; Docs, 975–976.

Jail breaks: Roach, *Salem Witch Trials*, 213; Calef, *More Wonders*, 352; Brattle, "Letter," 178.

Chapter 13: August 1 to 11, 1692

John and Elizabeth Procter's trials: Docs, 310, 389 (grand jury June 31; trial jury August 5).

John Procter's will: J. Procter, "Estate of John Procter Sr. of Salem"; Essex Deeds, 8: 338–341, #123.

George Jacobs Sr.'s trial: Docs, 479 (and note), 480–481; D. Greene, "George Jacobs," 67–66.

John Willard's trial: Docs, 295, 297–300 (and note).

Pro-Procter statements: Ibid., 503, 495–496.

Statements for and against Elizabeth Procter: Ibid., 382, 500, 708; Calef, *More Wonders*, 360.

Jamaica earthquake: Roach, *Salem Witch* Trials, 225.

Putnam baby's death: Doc, 185.

George Burroughs's trial: Ibid., 699; C. Mather, *Wonders*, 215–222; Docs, 446, 452–455; Calef, *More Wonders*, 301; Hale, *Modest Enquiry*, 34–35; I. Mather, *Cases*, 70.

Annie Putnam pulled from horse: Doc., 507.

Pro-Bradbury statements: C. Upham, *Salem Witchcraft*, 697–705 (letter); Doc, 431 (petition).

Nurse family: Doc, 596; petition in Boyer and Nissenbaum, *Salem-Village Witchcraft*, 296, from Salem Village Church Records, November 26, 1694.

Andover suspects: Doc, 503 (and notes), 504, 506 (Carrier children), 745 (Reverend Dane on Betty Johnson); 507 (Abigail Johnson).

Philip and Mary English in jailer's house: Doc, 975–976.

Chapter 14: August 12 to 31, 1692

Procter confiscations: Calef, *More Wonders*, 361; C. Upham, *Salem Witchcraft*, 600 (Upham says some of the older Procter children were at the Ipswich farm but gives no source. However, someone had to be living on the Salem Village farm to provide details of the confiscations); Brown, "Forfeitures," 85–111.

August 19, Procter and Noyes: Calef, *More Wonders*, 364.

Margaret Jacobs: Calef, *More Wonders*, 354–356; C. Upham, *Salem Witchcraft*, 531, 533; D. Greene, "George Jacobs," 67–69.

Martha Carrier: C. Mather, *Wonders*, 74; Roach, *Salem Witch Trials*, 242.

Cotton Mather's prayers: Brattle, "Letter," 177.

George Burroughs: Calef, *More Wonders*, 360–361.

Thomas Brattle: Brattle, "Letter," 177.

Reverend George Burroughs: Calef, *More Wonders*, 360–361.

Philip and Mary English: Doc, 902. August 21 was the Sunday before the next trials.

Reverend Joshua Moody: Sibley, *Biographical Sketches*, 1: 367–380. The Geneva translation of Reverend Moody's text is cited, a more modern version is: "They that are persecuted in one city, let them flee to another."

Reverend Samuel Willard: Brattle, "Letter," 186–187; Willard, *Some Miscellany Observations*; Calef, *More Wonders*, 360; Haefeli, "Dutch New York," 303.

Moody and Willard persuade Philip English to escape: Bentley, *Diary,* 2: 24–25; Cheever, "A Sketch," 164–165. The last also quotes a letter from Bentley to Alden, MHC, 1st ser., 10: 65–66. Dialogue here is combined from Bentley's *Diary* and the account of Cheever, a descendant.

Philip and Mary English reach New York: Brattle, "Letter," 178; Haefeli, "Dutch New York," 306.

English family lore about the escape: Cheever, "A Sketch," 164, 166; Bentley, *Diary,* 2: 25; LeBeau, "Philip English," 35n17.

Reverend Willard's son John helps Mrs. Cary escape: Massachusetts Archives, "Middlesex County Court Records," 158.

English daughters: Docs, 975–976; Bentley, *Diary,* 2: 25.

Mary English and Mary Phips: Hutchinson, *History,* 2: 46; Baker and Reid, *New England Knight,* 147–149.

Accusations ignored: Brattle, "Letter," 177 (Margaret Thatcher); Cheever, "A Sketch," 164 (Mary English).

Extraditions ignored: Brattle, "Letter," 177–178; Roach, *Salem Witch Trials,* 313.

Increase Mather: Murdock, *Increase Mather,* 185–189.

Philip English's expenses: Doc, 902–903, 976.

Chapter 15: September 1692

Mary Warren's mother's death: Doc, 567.

Samuel Wardwell hearing: Ibid., 537–539, 628, 632.

Sarah Hawks hearing: Ibid., 535.

Mary Warren fits, Mary Parker before the grand jury: Ibid., 540.

Gloucester suspects: Ibid., 541; Calef, *More Wonders,* 373. Calef places this in October but seems to confuse this incident with another in November, when four were accused.

Margaret Prince and Elizabeth Dicer: Doc, 545; Roach, *Salem Witch Trials,* 268 (Booth), 249 (Post); D. Greene, "Bray Wilkins," part 2, 105–106; EQC, 7: 238 (Dicer).

Mary Taylor: Doc, 546; Pope and Hooper, *Hooper Genealogy,* 1–7; Roach, *Salem Witch Trials,* 231–232.

Jane Lilly and Mary Coleson: Doc, 544.

Dorcas Hoar: Ibid., 550, 557–561, 568.

Alice Parker: Ibid., 553, 565–567, 271, 268 (Westgate), 573 (Bullock), 574 (Dutch), 575 (Shattuck), 567 (Warren), 566. Parker's trial may have continued to September 10.

Ann Pudeator: Ibid., 568.

William Procter: Ibid., 581–583 (grand jury).

Mary Esty: Ibid., 596, 602 (Arnold).

Sarah Cloyce: Ibid., 549, 579, 576, 809.

Giles Corey: C. Mather, *Wonders,* 250; Brown, "Case of Giles Corey."

William, Procter: Docs, 663, 776.

Giles Corey: C. Mather, *Wonders,* 250; Brown, "Case of Giles Corey," 282–299; Salem Church, *Records,* 218–219.

Mary Esty: Calef, *More Wonders,* 369; Doc, 654.

Mary Bradbury: Docs, 597, 431, 886.

John Alden escape: Calef, *More Wonders*, 355; Brattle, "Letter," 178.

Annie Putnam and ghost: Doc, 673; EQC, 6: 190–191; Chamberlain, *Notorious*, 86.

Giles Corey's death: Sewall, *Diary*, 1: 295, September 19, 1692; Calef, 367 (Calef's date of September 16 date is more likely when the court ordered the pressing); Docs, 899, 974.

September 22 hangings: Calef, *More Wonders*, 366–369; Sewall, *Diary*, 1: 297, September 22, 1692.

Corey's pressing: Calef, *More Wonders*, 367; Nelson, "Mary Tiffany," 145–146n20; Roach, *Salem Witch Trials*, 297.

Martha Corey's excommunication: Doc, 18; Calef, *More Wonders*, 367; Salem Village Church record, September 11 and 14, in Boyer and Nissenbaum, *Salem-Village Witchcraft*, 280.

Mary Bradbury's escape: Doc, 886.

Chapter 16: October 1692

Philip and Mary English in New York: Haefeli, "Dutch New York," 306; Bentley, *Diary*, 2: 25.

Dogs and Bradstreets: Calef, *More Wonders*, 372–373.

Threatened lawsuit: Ibid.

Cary and Obinson accusation: Brattle, "Letter," 179–180; Roach, *Salem Witch Trials*, 306.

Increase Mather: Brattle, ibid.; Cambridge Association, "Records," 268; I. Mather, *Cases*; Roach, *Salem Witch Trials*, 308–309.

Sarah Cole hearing: Doc, 683; Hale, *Modest Enquiry*, 132–133.

Andover children released on bail: Docs, 690 (Lacy), 691 (Sawdy), 688 (Faulkner), 689 (Johnson and Carrier); Roach, "Biographical Notes," 949 (Lacy), 957 (Sawdy), 940 (Faulkner), 948 (Johnson), 933 (Carrier).

Edward and Sarah Bishop escape: Calef, *More Wonders*, 370; Doc, 692.

Thomas Brattle: Brattle, "Letter," 165–190.

Samuel Willard: Haefeli, "Dutch New York," 303; Calef, *More Wonders*, 360.

Cotton Mather: C. Mather, *Wonders*, 212–213 (Stoughton); Roach, *Salem Witch Trials*, 317.

Capt. Nathaniel Cary: Haefeli, "Dutch New York," 307.

October 12 Andover petition: Doc, 694.

October 18 Andover petition: Ibid., 696.

Increase Mather and Thomas Brattle visit prisoners: Docs, 690, 699, 719; I. Mather, *Cases*, 70. The copy of the notes for this visit is dated October 19, 1692. However, Rebecca Eames stated on December 5 that although Mary Lacey and Abigail Hobbs had accused her of witchcraft, they disowned the charge "when mr Matther and mr Brattle were here." Mary Lacey Jr. was released on bail October 6. Although the vehemence of the accusations that Eames describes sounds more like the daughter, only Mary Lacey Sr. seems to have been in Salem jail by October 19. Increase Mather had visited earlier in the summer, when the prisoners he spoke with still held to their confessions, according to his *Cases of Conscience*.

Rebecca Eames: Doc, 712 (see above).

Act against fortune-telling and juggling: Ibid., 700.
Proposed fast: Ibid., 701; Sewall, *Diary*, 1: 299, October 26, 1692.
Samuel Parris's sermon: Parris, *Sermon Notebook*, 211.
Putnam child born: Parris, "Records," 15.
October 28, 1692 (William Stoughton): Sewall, *Diary*, 1: 299–300, October 28 and
    29, 1692; Tully, *Almanac*, "October Hath 31 Dayes," xiv.
October 29, 1692: Massachusetts Archives, "General Court Records," 245–246; Se-
    wall, *Diary*, 1: 299–300, October 29, 1692. Phips's answer here is given as a direct
    statement.
Capital crimes: Doc, 721; *Acts and Resolves*, 55–56.
Putnam and Tarbell baptisms: "Baptisms at the Church in Salem Village," 236.
Bishop confiscations: Calef, *More Wonders*, 370.

Chapter 17: November to December 1692
Afflicted go to Gloucester: Calef, *More Wonders*, 373; Docs, 704, 706–707.
Mary Herrick and Mary Esty's ghost: Calef, *More Wonders*, 369–370 (and note 1).
Abigail Faulkner petition: Doc, 711.
Andover men's petition: Ibid., 714.
Ipswich jail petition: Ibid., 702 (and note). This could have been submitted as early
    as October but no later than December 16.
Dorothy Good's release: Ibid., 719, 907.
Witchcraft law: Ibid., 721; "Helen Duncan."
Superior Court schedule: Doc, 693.
Order for blankets: Massachusetts Archives, 40: 626.
January trial date set: Doc, 724.
Public Fast order: Ibid., 727, 701.
Superior Court appointed: Ibid., 729.
Prisoners transferred: Ibid., 743.
John Alden in Boston: Ibid., 744, 975–976; Sewall, *Diary*, 1: 301, December 22, 1692;
    Haefeli, "Dutch New York," 308.

Chapter 18: January to May 1693
Parris's sermon: Parris, *Sermon Notebook*, 217–218; Matthew 25:40, 41 (Weigle, *Octapla*).
Essex County jurors: Docs 738–740, 254, 736, 449.
Superior Court in Salem, January 3, 1693: Doc, 747; Roach, *Salem Witch Trials*, 360.
January 4, 1693 trials: Docs, 752, 754–756.
January 5, 1693: Ibid., 760–761.
January 6, 1693: Ibid., 767, 763–764, 776.
January 10, 1693: Ibid., 779–781.
January 11, 1693: Ibid., 786.
Mercy Lewis and specters: Ibid., 792.
January 12, 1693:

    Philip and Mary English's trials: Ibid., 449, 789–792.
    Mary Post's trial: Ibid., 798.

January 13, 1693:

> Sarah Cloyce's trial: Ibid., 596 (and note), 602, 809–811; Rosenthal, *Records*, 40.
> Mary Lacey Jr.: Docs, 822, 918.

Hangings scheduled: Ibid., 836; Calef, *More Wonders*, 832 (the warrant's whereabouts is presently unknown); Roach, *Salem Witch Trials*, 371.

Elizabeth Procter gives birth: Perley, *The History of Salem* 2: 22–23. Perley is the only reference for this date and, unfortunately, cites no source.

January weather: Sewall, *Diary*, 1: 304–305, January 22 and 29, 1693.

Execution delay: Calef, *More Wonders*, 382–383; Doc, 836.

Nurse, Tarbell, and Wilkins vs. Parris and church committee: Salem Church records for February 7–16, 1693, in Boyer and Nissenbaum, *Salem-Village Witchcraft*, 279–283.

Fates of afflicted: Hale, *Modest Enquiry*, 132–135; Andover, "Vital Records," 2: 232, 2: 555; Roach, *Salem Witch Trials*, 363, 658n8; Pierce, *Foster Genealogy*, 130–131.

Rates committee: Boyer and Nissenbaum, *Salem Village Records*, January 15, 1692/3 meeting (so printed, but probably should be 17, as 15 was a Sabbath); Roach, *Salem Witch Trials*, 293.

Philip English and Phips: Doc, 840.

English daughters: Ibid., 975–976.

English's losses: Ibid., 902–903.

Edward Bishop remarries: D. Greene, "Bridget Bishop," 137.

April Superior Court: SJC 1: 36.

> Grace and Emerson: SJC, 1: 51–50.
> Arnold: SJC, 1: 38; Doc, 838.
> Alden and Green: SJC, 1: 52; Docs, 838, 678; Roach, *Salem Witch Trials*, 303.
> Watkins: Docs, 83, 841.

May 9, 1693 Superior Court: Ibid., 842.

> Tituba: Ibid., 844.

PART THREE: AFTERWORD

Rebecca Nurse

Parris on the dissenters: Salem Village Church records in Boyer and Nissenbaum, *Salem-Village Witchcraft*, 288 (October 23, 1693), 303 (November 13, 1693).

November 1694 meetings: Boyer and Nissenbaum, *Salem-Village Witchcraft*, 295–310.

Demand for Church Council: Ibid., 300–304.

Council of Mediators: Ibid., 306–308.

Francis Nurse's will: Hoover, *Towne Family*, 8.

1695 pro-and anti-Parris petitions: Boyer and Nissenbaum, *Salem-Village Witchcraft*, 260–263, 308–309.

Francis Nurse dies: Parris, "Records," 22.

Parris resigns: Boyer and Nissenbaum, *Salem-Village Witchcraft*, 311–312.

January 1697 public fast: Sewall, *Diary*, December 2, 1696, 1: 361–362 (and notes), January 14, 1697.

Suits against Parris and arbitration: Boyer and Nissenbaum, *Salem-Village Witchcraft*, 264–268.

Reverend Green mediates: Salem Village Church records in C. Upham, *Salem Witchcraft*, 668–669; Perley, History of Salem, 3:35.

Nurse farm paid off: *Suffolk Deeds*, 11: 50; Perley, "Endicott Lands," 379–382.

Petitions to clear names: Docs, 875–877, 879.

Annie Putnam joins church: Salem Village Church records in C. Upham, *Salem Witchcraft*, 671–672.

1706 bill against spectral evidence: Doc, 879.

1709 petition for restitution: Ibid., 881.

Isaac Esty statement: Ibid., 883.

Samuel Nurse statement: Ibid., 921.

1711 Reversal of Attainder: Ibid., 931, 933.

Reparations: Ibid., 930, 964, 954.

Rebecca Nurse's excommunication reversed: Salem Church, *Record*, 218–219.

Nurse Farm: Perley, "Endicott Lands," 380–382; Tapley, *Rebecca Nurse*, 100–101; W. Upham, "Account."

Danvers: Galvin, *Historical Data*, 37. Salem Village was called Danvers in 1752, and a township in 1757, which the Privy Council disallowed yet sent a representative to the Massachusetts House of Representatives from 1758 onward, was called a town in 1772 and made a town by an act on August 23, 1775.

Rebecca Nurse Memorial: W. Upham, "Account," 225; Tapley, *Rebecca Nurse*, 100–102; Eben Putnam, *History*, 1: 200–201.

Nurse Homestead: The homestead passed into the care of the Society for the Preservation of New England Antiquities (now Historic New England) and then to the Danvers Light Alarm Company (an eighteenth-century reenactment group, Light Alarm being the local minutemen).

Bridget Bishop

Thomas Oliver probate and Edward Bishop's house: Perley, "Salem, No. 14," EA 35–38, map opp. 22; Perley, "Part of Salem, No. 1," 167, map opp 167, 172–173; Thomas Oliver docket 20009.

Christian Mason dies and husband remarries: August 11, 1693 distribution in Thomas Oliver docket 20009; D. Greene, "Bridget Bishop," 138.

Edward Bishop, guardian to Susanna Mason: Essex Deeds, 10: 112–113.

Edward Bishop buys a house: Essex Deeds, 10: 3 verso; Perley, "Salem, No. 19," 79, and "Salem, No. 14," 36.

John and Susanna Becket: Perley, "Becket Genealogy," 15; Perley, "Salem, No. 22," 23, 25–26; Perley, "Salem, No. 19," 79.

Susanna Babbidge: Perley, "Becket Genealogy," 15–17; Bentley, *Diary*, 3: 90–91; C. Upham, *Salem Witchcraft*, 494.

Bridget and Sarah Bishop confusion: D. Greene, "Bridget Bishop," 131–137.

Mary English

Confiscation losses: Cheever, "A Sketch," 60–61; Bentley, "Notices," 232; Docs, 902, 840.

Mansion repairs: Cheever, "A Sketch," 160; Perley, "Salem, No. 21," 168.

Philip English's economic losses: LeBeau, "Philip English," 10.

Ebenezer English: Salem, *Vital Records*, 1: 282.

Mary English's death: Cheever, "A Sketch," 166.

English vs. Hollingworth lawsuits: James Duncan Philips Library, "Court of Common Pleas," 7: 41, 8: 57, 59.

Misc. English suits: LeBeau, "Philip English," 35n17.

March 31, 1696 suits: James Duncan Philips Library, "Court of Common Pleas," 8: 57, 61–62.

Philip English vs. George Corwin: Perley, "Part of Salem, No. 2," 69; George Corwin Probate, Essex County Probate docket #6949; "Seizing Corpses for Debt"; Roach, "The Corpse in the Cellar"; "Essex Institute ms. English Family Papers": Box 1, file 7: "Philip English (1651–1736) Papers/Legal Documents, 1675, 1682–1727, 1733."

Philip English's second marriage: Salem, *Vital Records*, 3: 337.

Susanna English: *Boston News-Letter*, September 30 to October 7, 1706, 6; Bentley, *Diary*, 2: 25.

Philip English recoups: LeBeau, "Philip English," 10; Schutz, *Legislators*, 215.

1709 Petitions: Docs, 881, 902.

1717 reparations: Ibid., 970–973.

St. Michael's Church: Miles, "*O, How We Have Loved Thee.*"

Philip English's decline: James Duncan Philips Library, "Court of General Sessions of the Peace," 4: 76–78; LeBeau, "Philip English," 10; "Essex Institute ms. English Family Papers," Box 1, file 8: "Philip English (1651–1736) Papers/Guardianship and Estate Papers, 1732–1744, 1751"; Essex Probate Records, 324: 182–183 (Touzel wills).

Philip English's last words: Hawthorne, *American Notebooks,* 75 (emphasis added).

Philip English's funeral: English, Essex Probate Docket 9083; Salem, *Vital Records*, 5: 231; Cheever, "A Sketch," 175–176.

Philip English probate problems and Susanna (English) Touzel's health: Doc, 978; Essex Probate Records: 324: 182–183.

Reverend William Bentley on Susanna English's embroidery: Bentley, *Diary*, 1: 23.

Reverend Bentley on English's mansion: Ibid., 2: 446–448.

Mary English's poem: Cheever, "A Sketch," 164.

Mansion's fate: Ibid., 160.

Horace Connolly and the English inheritance: Avery, *Genealogy*, 45–46; Eleanor Putnam, *Old Salem*, 81–82.

Mary (Hollingworth) English's sampler: Perley, *The History of Salem*, 1: 37–38; Curwen, "The Will," 252.

Ann Putnam

Thomas Putnam: Doc, 866; Boyer and Nissenbaum, *Salem-Village Witchcraft*, 255–256. The committee was Joseph Porter, Joseph Hutchinson Sr., Joseph Putnam, Daniel Andrews, and Francis Nurse.

Sarah Putnam born: Parris, "Records," 16.

Sarah Putnam dies: Ibid., 21.

Mrs. Mary Putnam's illness and death: Boyer and Nissenbaum, *Salem-Village Witchcraft*, 213–222.

Pro-Parris petition: Ibid., 262–263.

Seth Putnam born and baptized: Parris, "Records," 17; "Baptisms at the Church in Salem Village," 237.

Thomas Putnam and others protests Mary Putnam will: Boyer and Nissenbaum, *Salem-Village Witchcraft*, 215–216.

Thomas Putnam petitions probate court: Ibid., 216–217.

Mary Putnam estate testimony: Ibid., 217–220.

Parris quits: Ibid., 311.

Thomas Putnam sells Topsfield land: Ibid., 222.

Thomas Putnam sells home and moves: Perley, "Hathorne," 332–344.

Experience and Hannah Putnam baptized: "Baptisms at the Church in Salem Village," 237.

Meeting House seating changes: Salem Village Church records in C. Upham, *Salem Witchcraft*, 668.

Thomas Putnam dies: Salem, *Vital Records*, 6: 172.

Ann Putnam dies: Ibid., 6: 169.

Thomas Putnam estate: Boyer and Nissenbaum, *Salem-Village Witchcraft*, 223–225.

Putnam children: C. Upham, *Salem Witchcraft*, 671–672.

Ann Putnam Jr. joins Salem Village Church: Salem Village Church records in C. Upham, *Salem Witchcraft*, 672.

Ann Putnam Jr. dies: C. Upham, *Salem Witchcraft*, 673; Perley, "Hathorne," 342.

Tituba

Tituba's Salem jail bill: Docs, 857 (and note), 858. The number of months looks like a ten but is actually a one: ~~for tetabe Indan A whole year and 10 month~~.

Tituba's Boston jail bill: Ibid., 4, 481.

Robert Calef on Tituba: Calef, *More Wonders*, 343 (emphasis added).

Tituba's origins: Breslaw, *Tituba*, 3–62, 207n13, 14; Hoffer, *Devil's Disciples*, 105–210, 267–269 notes; Hansen, "Metamorphosis"; Tucker, "Purloined Identity"; Rosenthal, *Salem Story*, 10–31.

Mary Warren

Mary Warren's jail bill: Docs, 857–858.

Mary Warren's whereabouts: Ibid., 75, 216, 772.

Elizabeth Procter's petition: Ibid., 871.

Petitions and results: Ibid., 876–877, 879; Stevens, *Ancestry*, 1: 44.7, 44.12.

Procter Restitution: Docs, 935, 958–959.

Elizabeth Procter remarries: Stevens, *Ancestry*, 1: 44.4.

Afflicted blamed: Doc, 931, Calef, *More Wonders*, 384, 306.

Afflicted girls' later history: S. Noyes, Libby, and David, *Genealogical*, 429–430; C. Mather, *Diary*, 1: 261n, 382–383; Norton, *Devil's Snare*, 310–311.

BIBLIOGRAPHY

Abbreviations
CSM: Colonial Society of Massachusetts
Doc: Document number from Rosenthal, *Records of the Salem Witch-Hunt*
EIHC: *Essex Institute Historical Collections*
EQC: County of Essex, *Records of the Quarterly Courts*
EQC-VT: Verbatim transcription of Essex County Records, typescript
Essex Deeds: bound, handwritten copies of deeds
Essex, *Probate*: County of Essex. *The Probate Records of Essex County*, in print
Essex Probate & docket #: manuscript
Essex Probate Records: microfilm (at New England Historic Genealogical Society
    library, etc.)
GM: Anderson, *Great Migration*
GMB: Anderson, *Great Migration Begins*
MHS: Massachusetts Historical Society
NEHGS: New England Historic Genealogical Society
OED: *Oxford English Dictionary*
Register: *New England Historic Genealogical Register*
SJC: Superior Court of Judicature
SV: Salem Village
SV-VR: Parris, "Records of the Rev. Samuel Parris"
TAG: *The American Genealogist*

Quotations from the witch trial papers used in this book are taken from the defini-
tive *Records of the Salem Witch-Hunt*, Bernard Rosenthal, ed. To cross-reference the
document numbers given here with documents available in other, earlier editions,
readers might consult www.17thc.us/primarysources/Cross-Refs.

Unpublished Sources
Essex County Probate Court, Salem, MA.

    Corwin, George. Essex Probate Docket 6949.
    English, Philip. non compos. Essex Probate Docket 9082.
    English, Philip. Essex Probate Docket 9083.
    Oliver, Thomas. Essex Probate Docket 20009.

Essex County, South, Registry of Deeds, Salem, MA.

    Essex County, MA. Deeds, vols. 8–9, microfilm F/72/E7/E87, NEHGS Library.

The first one hundred volumes of deeds are accessible online at
   http://www.essexdeeds.gov.

James Duncan Philips Library, Peabody Essex Museum, Salem, MA.

"Court of Common Pleas, series 5, Salem Waste Book, vol. 7 (1692–1695), vol. 8
   (1695–1718/19).
"Court of General Sessions of the Peace," series 4, vol. 4 (1718/19–1727).
English, Mrs. Philip [Katherine Dana English]. "Facts About the Life of Philip
   English of Salem Collected by Mrs. Philip English, 99 East Rock Road,
   New Haven, Conn, 1943." Typescript. James Duncan Phillips Library,
   Peabody Essex Museum, Salem, MA.
"Essex Institute ms. English Family Papers":
   Box 1, file 7: "Philip English (1651–1736) Papers/Legal Documents, 1675,1682–
      1727,1733."
   Box 1, file 8: Philip English (1651–1736) Papers/Guardianship and Estate
      Papers, 1732–1744, 1751."
   Box 3, file 11: "John Touzel (bp. 1687–1737) Papers/Estate Papers, 1737–1746,
      1775–1778."
"Verbatim Transcription of the Records of the Quarterly Courts of Essex
   County Massachusetts." Typescript volumes compiled by the WPA under
   Clerk of Courts Archie N. Frost

Massachusetts Archives, Dorchester, MA.

"Council Records, 2 (1686–1698)," on microfilm.
"General Court Records (Records of the Governor and Council)," vol. 6, April
   18, 1689 to December 10, 1698, on one reel.
"Massachusetts Archives," scrapbook volumes on microfilm:
   81 (Minutes of the Council) 1689–1732.
   40 (Judicial) 1683–1734.
"Middlesex County Court Records 1683–1699."
"Superior Court of Judicature" 1 (1692–1695), 1892 transcript.

New England Historic and Genealogical Society, Boston, MA.

Essex County Deeds 8:338–41, #123 (Record books on microfilm), vols. 8–9,
   microfilm F/72/E7/E87.
Essex County, MA/Probate Records/Old Series (Record books on microfilm):
   Vols. 304–306, microfilm F/22/E36.
   Vols. 323–324/Book 23–24 (1737–1744), microfilm F/72/E7/976.

Published Sources
Acts and Resolves, Public and Private, of the Province of Massachusetts Bay, vol. 1.
   Boston: Commonwealth of Massachusetts, 1869.
Anderson, Robert Charles. "Bridget (Playfer) (Wasselbe) (Oliver) (Bishop): Her
   Origin and First Husband." TAG 64 (1989): 207.

————. *The Great Migration Begins: Immigrants to New England 1620–1633.* 3 vols. Boston: The Great Migration Study Project, New England Historic Genealogical Society, 1995.

Anderson, Robert Charles, George F. Sanborn Jr., and Melinde Lutz Sanborn. *The Great Migration: Immigrants to New England 1634–1635.* 7 vols. Boston: The Great Migration Study Project, New England Historic Genealogical Society, 1999–2011.

Andover, Town of. *Vital Records of Andover, Massachusetts to the End of the Year 1849.* 2 vols. Topsfield, MA: Topsfield Historical Society, 1912.

Avery, Lillian Drake. *A Genealogy of the Ingersoll Family in America 1629–1925.* New York: Frederick H. Hitchcock, 1926.

Bailey, Hollis R., ed. *Bailey Genealogy: James, John and Thomas and Their Descendants.* Somerville, MA: The Bailey-Bayley Family Association, 1899; facsimile, Salem, MA: Higginson Book Company, nd.

Bailyn, Bernard. *The New England Merchants in the Seventeenth Century.* New York: Harper Torchbooks, 1955 [paper ed.].

Baker, Emerson W., and John G. Reid. *The New England Knight: Sir William Phips, 1651–1695.* Toronto: University of Toronto Press, 1998.

"Baptisms at the Church in Salem Village, Now North Parish, Danvers." Communicated by Henry Wheatland. EIHC 15 (1878): 235–237.

Barclay, Florence Harlow. "Notes on the Hollingsworth, Hunter, Moore and Woodbury Families of Salem, Mass." TAG 40 (1964): 77–84.

Beckford, W[illiam], Jr. *Remarks upon the Situation of Negroes in Jamaica, Impartially Made from a Local Experience of Nearly Thirteen Years in That Island.* Whitehall (London): T. & J. Egedon, 1788.

Belknap, Henry W. "Philip English, Commerce Builder." *Proceedings of the American Antiquarian Society*, new series, 41 (1931): 17–24.

Bentley, William. "A Description and History of Salem, by the Rev. William Bentley." MHS *Collections*, 1st series, 6 (1799): 212–288.

————. *The Diary of William Bentley, D. D.* 4 vols. Gloucester: Peter Smith, 1962; reprint of Essex Institute edition, 1905, 1907, 1911, 1914.

————. "Notices of the Ancestry of Mrs. Susannah Ingersoll." EIHC 11 (1871): 228–234.

"Book of Sports." www.britania.com.

Boston News-Letter. September 30 to October 7, 1706, iss. e129, 6, http://infoweb.newsbank.com.

Boyer, Paul, and Stephen Nissenbaum, eds. *Salem-Village Witchcraft: A Documentary Record of Local Conflict in Colonial New England.* Belmont, CA: Wadsworth Publishing Company, 1972; Boston: Northeastern University Press, 1993.

————, eds. *The Salem Witchcraft Papers: Verbatim Transcripts of the Legal Documents of the Salem Witchcraft Outbreak of 1692.* 3 vols. New York: DaCapo Press, 1977.

Brattle, Thomas. "Letter of Thomas Brattle, F. R. S., 1692." In Burr, *Narratives of the Witchcraft Cases 1648–1706*, 165–190.

Breslaw, Elaine G. "The Salem Witch from Barbados: In Search of Tituba's Roots."
    EIHC 128 (1992): 217–238.
———. *Tituba, Reluctant Witch of Salem: Devilish Indians and Puritan Fantasies.*
    New York: New York University Press, 1996.
Brown, David C. "The Case of Giles Corey." EIHC 121 (1985): 282–299.
———. "The Forfeitures at Salem, 1692." *William & Mary Quarterly* 3rd ser. 50
    (1993): 85–111.
———. *A Guide to the Salem Witchcraft Hysteria of 1692.* Washington Crossing, PA:
    self-published, 1984.
Browne, Benjamin. "Youthful Recollections of Salem." EIHC 49 (1913): 193–209,
    289–304; 50 (1914): 6–16, 289–296; 51 (1915): 53–56, 297–305.
Burr, George Lincoln, ed. *Narratives of the Witchcraft Cases 1648–1706.* New York:
    Charles Scribner's Sons, 1914; New York: Barnes & Noble, 1946.
Calef, Robert. "From 'More Wonders of the Invisible World,' By 1700" [excerpt from
    More Wonders of the Invisible World. London: Nathaniel Hillier and Joseph Col-
    lier, 1700]. In Burr, *Narratives of the Witchcraft Cases 1648–1706,* 189–393.
Cambridge Association. "Records of the Cambridge Association." MHS *Proceedings*
    17 (1879–1880): 262–281.
Caporal, Linda R. "Ergotism: The Satan Loosed in Salem?" *Science* 192, no. 4234
    (1976): 21–26.
Chamberlain, Ava. *The Notorious Elizabeth Tuttle: Marriage, Murder, and Madness
    in the Family of Jonathan Edwards.* New York: New York University Press, 2012.
Cheever, George F. "A Sketch of Philip English—A Merchant in Salem from About
    1670 to About 1733–4." Part 2. EIHC 1 (1859): 157–181.
Curwen, George Rea. "The Will of George Rea Curwen." EIHC 35 (1900): 248–261.
Davis, Walter Goodwin. *Massachusetts and Maine Families, with Ancestry of Walter
    Goodwin Davis (1885–1966): A Reprinting, in Alphabetical Order by Surname, of the
    Sixteen Multi-ancestor Compendia (Plus Thomas Haley of Winter Harbor and His
    Descendants) Compiled by Maine's Foremost Genealogist, 1916–1963, Walter Goodwin
    Davis, with an Introduction by Gary Boyd Roberts.* Baltimore, MD: Genealogical
    Publishing Company, 1996.
Demos, John, ed. *Remarkable Providences: Readings on Early American History,* rev.
    ed. Boston: Northeastern University Press, 1972, 1991.
Dunton, John. *Letters from New-England.* Edited by W. H. Whitmore. Boston:
    Prince Society, 1867.
Essex, County of. *The Probate Records of Essex County, Massachusetts.* 3 vols. Salem,
    MA: The Essex Institute, 1917–1920.
———. *Records of the Quarterly Courts of Essex County, Massachusetts.* Edited by
    George Francis Dow. 9 vols. Salem, MA: Essex Institute, 1911–1975.
Equiano, Olaudah. *The Interesting Narrative and Other Writings.* Edited by Vincent
    Carretta. New York: Penguin Putnam, 1995; 2003 [2nd ed.].
Fairbanks, Jonathan L., and Robert F. Trent. *New England Begins: The Seventeenth
    Century.* 3 vols. Boston: Museum of Fine Arts, 1982.
Galvin, William Francis, ed. *Historical Data Relating to Counties, Cities and Towns
    in Massachusetts.* Boston: The New England Historic Genealogical Society, 1997.

Gragg, Larry. *A Quest for Security: The Life of Samuel Parris, 1653–1720*. Westport, CT: Greenwood Press, 1990.

Greene, David L. "Bray Wilkins of Salem Village, MA and His Children." Parts 1 and 2, TAG 60 (1984): 1–18, 101–113.

———. "Salem Witches I: Bridget Bishop." TAG 57 (1981): 129–138.

———. "Salem Witches II: George Jacobs." TAG, 58 (1982): 65–76.

Greene, Lorenzo Johnston. *The Negro in Colonial New England, 1620–1776*. New York: Columbia University Press, 1942.

H. B. [Benjamin Harris?]. *Boston Almanac for the Year of Our Lord God 1692*. Boston: Benjamin Harris and John Allen, 1692. Evans microtext 595, accessed from http://infoweb.newsbank.com.

Haefeli, Nathan. "Dutch New York and the Salem Witch Trials: Some New Evidence." *Proceedings of the American Antiquarian Society* 110, pt. 2 (2000): 277–308.

Hale, John. *A Modest Enquiry into the Nature of Witchcraft*. Facsimile of 1702 original. Bainbridge, NY: York Mail-Print, 1973.

Hammond, Laurence. "Diary of Laurence Hammond" MHS Proceedings, 2nd series, 7 (1891–1892): 144–172.

Handler, Jerome. "Archaeological Evidence for a Possible Witch in Barbados, West Indies." In *Witches of the Atlantic World: a Historical Reader and Primary Sourcebook*, edited by Elaine G. Breslaw, 176–180. New York: New York University Press, 2000.

Hansen, Chadwick. "The Metamorphosis of Tituba, or Why American Intellectuals Can't Tell an Indian from a Negro." *New England Quarterly* 47, no. 1 (March 1974): 3–12.

———. *Witchcraft at Salem*. New York: George Braziller, 1969.

Hawthorne, Nathaniel. *The American Notebooks*, vol. 8 of *The Centenary Edition of the Works of Nathaniel Hawthorne*, edited by Claude M. Simpson. Columbus: Ohio State University Press, 1972.

"Helen Duncan: The Official Pardon Site." www.helenduncan.org.uk.

Hoffer, Peter Charles. *The Devil's Disciples: Makers of the Salem Witchcraft Trials*. Baltimore, MD: Johns Hopkins University Press, 1996.

Hoover, Lois Payne. *Towne Family: William Towne and Joanna Blessing, Salem, Massachusetts 1635*. Baltimore, MD: Otter Bay Books, 2010.

Hutchinson, Thomas. *The History of the Colony and Province of Massachusetts-Bay*. 3 vols. Edited by Lawrence Shaw Mayo. Cambridge, MA: Harvard University Press, 1936.

Kittredge, George Lyman. *Witchcraft in Old and New England*. Cambridge, MA: Harvard University Press, 1929; New York: Athenaeum, 1972.

Konig, David T. "A New Look at the Essex 'French': Ethnic Frictions and Community Tensions in Seventeenth-Century Essex County, Massachusetts." EIHC 110 (1974): 167–180.

Jackson, Russell Leigh. *The Physicians of Essex County*. Salem, MA: Essex Institute, 1948.

Lawson, Deodat. "*A Brief and True Narrative*." In Burr, *Narratives of the Witchcraft Cases 1648–1706*, 145–164.

————. "Rev. Lawson's Sermon" [excerpt from *Christ's Fidelity the Only Shield Against Satan's Malignity*]. In Trask, *"The Devil Hath Been Raised,"* 64–106.

LeBeau, Bryan F. "Philip English and the Witchcraft Hysteria." *Historical Journal of Massachusetts* XV, no. 1 (January 1987): 1–20.

Levin, David. *What Happened in Salem?* 2nd ed. New York: Harcourt, Brace & World, 1960.

Love, William DeLoss Jr. *The Fast and Thanksgiving Days of New-England.* Boston: Houghton, Mifflin, 1895.

Ludlum, David. *The Country Journal New England Weather Book.* Boston: Houghton, Mifflin, 1976.

Lupson, Edward J. *Saint Nicholas Church, Great Yarmouth: Its History, Organ, Pulpit, Library, Extracts from Registers, Unique Combinations of Names, etc.* Yarmouth, UK: Edward J. Lupson, 1897.

Mahler, Leslie. "The English Origin of the Hunter and Hollingsworth Families of Salem, Massachusetts." TAG 78 (2003): 241–244.

Mather, Cotton. *The Angel of Bethesda.* Edited by Gordon W. Jones. Barre, MA: American Antiquarian Society and Barre Publishers, 1972.

————. "A Brand Pluck'd Out of the Burning." In Burr, *Narratives of the Witchcraft Cases 1648–1706,* 253–287.

————. *Decennium Luctuosum.* Boston: Samuel Phillips, 1699. In *Narratives of the Indian Wars, 1675–1699,* edited by Charles H. Lincoln, 169–299. New York: Charles Scribner's Sons, 1913; New York: Barnes & Noble, 1941.

————. *Diary of Cotton Mather.* 2 vols. Edited by Worthington Chauncey Ford. MHS *Collections,* 7th series, 7 (1911) and 8 (1912); renumbered as vols. 1 and 2. Reprint, New York: Frederick Ungar Publishing Co., nd.

————. "From 'The Wonders of the Invisible World,' by Cotton Mather, 1693" [excerpt from *The Wonders of the Invisible World*]. In Burr, *Narratives of the Witchcraft Cases 1648–1706,* 203–251.

————. "Memorable Providences, Relating to Witchcrafts and Possessions, by Cotton Mather, 1689" [excerpt from *Memorable Providences Relating to Witchcrafts and Possessions*]. In Burr, *Narratives of the Witchcraft Cases 1648–1706,* 88–143.

Mather, Increase. *Cases of Conscience Concerning Evil Spirits.* Boston: Benjamin Harris, 1693 [1692]. In Evans Microtext 658, accessed from http://infoweb.newsbank .com.

Miles, Dorothy F. *"O, How We Have Loved Thee, Church of Our Fathers."* Marblehead, MA: St. Michael's Church, 1976.

Murdock, Kenneth B. *Increase Mather: The Foremost American Puritan.* Cambridge, MA: Harvard University Press, 1925.

Nelson, Glade Ian. "Mary (Burrough) (Homer) (Hall) Tiffany." TAG 48 (1972): 145–146.

Norton, Mary Beth. *In the Devil's Snare: The Salem Witchcraft Crisis of 1692.* New York: Alfred A. Knopf, 2002.

Noyes, Nicholas. "An Elegy Upon the Death of the Rev. Mr. John Higginson." *Register* 7 (1853): 237–240.

Noyes, Sybil, Thornton Charles Libby, and Walter Goodwin Davis. *Genealogical Dictionary of Maine and New Hampshire*. Baltimore, MD: Genealogical Publishing, 1972.

Parris, Samuel. "Records of the Rev. Samuel Parris, Salem Village, Massachusetts, 1688–1696." Compiled by Marilynne K. Roach. *Register* 157 (2003): 6–30.

———. *The Sermon Notebook of Samuel Parris, 1689–1694*. Edited by James F. Cooper and Kenneth P Minkema. Boston: The Colonial Society of Massachusetts, 1993.

Perley, Sidney. "Becket Genealogy." EA 8 (1904): 15–17.

———. "Center of Salem Village in 1700." EIHC 54 (1918): 225–245.

———. "Endicott Lands, Salem, in 1700," EIHC 51 (1915): 361–382.

———. "Groton, Salem in 1700," EIHC 51 (1915): 257–270.

———. "Hathorne: Part of Salem Village in 1700 [No. 1]." EIHC 53 (1917): 332–344.

———. *The History of Salem, Massachusetts*. 3 vols. Haverhill, MA: Record Publishing, 1928.

———. "Northfields, Salem, in 1700. No. 1." EIHC 48 (1912): 173–184.

———. "Northfields, Salem in 1700. No. 3," EIHC 49 (1913): 186–192.

———. "The Nurse House." EIHC 62 (1926): 1–3.

———. "Part of Salem in 1700. No. 1," EA 2 (1898): 167–174.

———. "Part of Salem in 1700. No. 2," EA 3 (1899): 65–72.

———. "Part of Salem in 1700. No. 5," EA 4 (1900): 161–170.

———. "Part of Salem in 1700. No. 8," EA 6 (1901): 97–101.

———. "Rial Side: Part of Salem in 1700." EIHC 55 (1919): 49–74.

———. "Salem in 1700. No. 14," EA 8 (1904): 20–37.

———. "Salem in 1700. No. 19," EA 9 (1905): 72–86.

———. "Salem in 1700. No. 20." EA 9 (1905): 114–123.

———. "Salem in 1700. No. 21," EA 9 (1905): 162–171.

———. "Salem in 1700. No. 22," EA 10 (1906): 21–31.

———. "Salem in 1700. No. 29," EA 11 (1907): 58–168.

Phillips, Samuel. *An Elegy upon the Deaths of Those Excellent and Learned Divines; the Reverend Nicholas Noyes, A. M. and the Reverend George Curwen, A. M.* (1717?) [small printed pamphlet found in Phillips Library].

Pierce, Frederick Clifton. *Foster Genealogy*. Chicago: self-published, 1899.

"Plan of Great Yarmouth." Map. 1797. http://www.gtyarmouth.co.uk/html/map_1797.htm.

Pope, Charles Henry, and Thomas Hooper. *Hooper Genealogy*. Boston: Charles Henry Pope, 1908.

Procter, Leland H. *John Proctor of Ipswich and Some of His Descendants*. Springfield, MA: Research Associates, Genealogy Research Group, Genealogy and Local History Department, Springfield City Library, 1985.

Proctor, John. "Estate of John Procter Sr. of Salem." Transcribed and submitted by Gloria Konikoff. http://www.essexcountyma.net/Wills/proctorj.htm.

Putnam, Eben. *A History of the Putnam Family in England and America*. 2 vols. Salem: Salem Press Publishing and Printing Co., 1891, 1907.

Putnam, Eleanor [Harriet Bates]. *Old Salem*. Edited by Arlo Bates. Boston: Houghton, Mifflin, 1891.

Ramsay, James. *An Essay on the Treatment and Conversion of African Slaves in the British Sugar Colonies*. London: James Phillips, 1784.

Rapaport, Diane. "Turbulent Topsfield: A Tale of Two Ministers." *American Ancestors* 11, no. 1 (Winter 2010): 53–54.

Records of the Court of Assistants of Massachusetts Bay 1630–1692. 3 vols. Vols. 1 & 2 edited by John Noble; vol. 3 edited by John F. Cronin. Boston: County of Suffolk, 1901, 1904, 1928.

Richter, Paula, and Catherine Peabody. *Painted with Thread: The Art of American Embroidery*. Salem, MA: Peabody Essex Museum, 2001.

Roach, Marilynne K. "Biographical Notes." In Rosenthal, *Records of the Salem Witch-Hunt*, 925–964.

———. "The Corpse in the Cellar." *New England Ancestors* 8, no. 4 (Fall 2007): 42–43.

———. *Gallows and Graves: The Search to Locate the Death and Burial Sites of the People Executed for Witchcraft in 1692*. Watertown, MA: Sassafras Grove Press, 1997.

———. "Records of the Rev. Samuel Parris, Salem Village, Massachusetts, 1688–1696." *New England Historical and Genealogical Register* 157 (2003): 6–30.

———. *The Salem Witch Trials: A Day-by-Day Chronicle of a Community under Siege*. New York: Cooper Square Press, 2002.

———. "'That Child Betty Parris': Elizabeth (Parris) Barron and the People in Her Life." EIHC 124 (1988): 1–27.

Rosenthal, Bernard, ed. *Records of the Salem Witch-Hunt*. New York: Cambridge University Press, 2009.

———. *Salem Story: Reading the Witch Trials of 1692*. New York: W. W. Norton & Company, 1993.

Salem. *Vital Records of Salem, Massachusetts to the End of the Year 1849*. 6 vols. Salem, MA: Essex Institute, 1916–1925.

Salem, Church of. *The Records of the First Church in Salem, Massachusetts, 1629–1736*. Edited by Richard D. Pierce. Salem, MA: Essex Institute, 1974.

Salem, Town of. *Town Records of Salem*. 3 vols. Salem, MA: The Essex Institute, 1868, 1913, 1939, 1954.

Salem Village. "A Book of Record of the Severall Publique Transa[c]tions of the Inhabitants of Sale[m] Village Vulgarly Called the Farm[s]." *Historical Collections of the Danvers Historical Society* 13 (1925): 91–122; 14 (1926): 65–99; 16 (1918): 60–80.

Savage, James. *A Genealogical Dictionary of the First Settlers of New England*. 4 vols. Baltimore, MD: Genealogical Publishing Company, 1965 [reprint].

Schutz, John A. *Legislators of the Massachusetts General Court 1691–1780: A Biographical Dictionary*. Boston: Northeastern University Press, 1997.

"Seizing Corpses for Debt." In *Notes and Queries: A Medium of Inter-Communication for Literary Men, Artists, Antiquaries . . .*" September 12, 1874.

Sewall, Samuel. *The Diary of Samuel Sewall 1674–1729*. Edited by Halsey Thomas. 2 vols. New York: Farrar, Straus & Giroux, 1973.

Sibley, John Langdon. *Biographical Sketches of Harvard University in Cambridge, Massachusetts.* Cambridge, MA: Charles William Sever, 1873; New York: Johnson Reprint Corporation, 1967.

Stevens, Robert Croll. *Ancestry of Robert Croll Stevens and Jane Eleanor (Knauss) Stevens.* Pittford, NY: self-published, 1982.

Suffolk Deeds, vol. 12. Boston: City of Boston, 1900.

Swan, Marshall W. S. "The Bedevilment of Cape Ann." EIHC 117 (1981): 153–177.

Tapley, Charles Sutherland. *Rebecca Nurse: Saint but Witch Victim.* Boston: Marshall Jones Company, 1930; Danvers, MA: Danvers Light Alarm Company, 1979 [facsimile reprint].

"Textiles." British History Online, http://www.british-history.ac.uk/report.aspx?compid=58836.

Thomas, Keith. *Religion and the Decline of Magic.* New York: Charles Scribner's Sons, 1971.

Thompson, Neil D. "Hannah Fisher, First Wife of the Rev. George[2] Burroughs, Executed for Witchcraft in Salem, Massachusetts, 1692." TAG 115 (2001): 17–19.

Thompson, Roger. *Mobility and Migration: East Anglican Founders of New England, 1629–1640.* Amherst: University of Massachusetts Press, 1994.

———. *Sex in Middlesex: Popular Mores in a Massachusetts County, 1649–1699.* Amherst: University of Massachusetts Press, 1986.

Trask, Richard. *"The Devil Amongst Us": A History of the Salem Village Parsonage.* Danvers, MA: Danvers Historical Society, 1971.

———. *"The Devil Hath Been Raised": A Documentary History of the Salem Village Witchcraft Outbreak of March, 1692.* Danvers, MA: Yeoman Press, 1997; West Kennebunk, ME: Phoenix Publishing, the Danvers Historical Society, 1992 [rev. and enlarged edition].

———. "Legal Procedures Used during the Salem Witch Trials and a Brief History of the Published Versions of the Records." In Rosenthal, *Records of the Salem Witch-Hunt*, 44–63.

Trautman, Patricia. "Dress in Seventeenth-Century Cambridge, Massachusetts: An Inventory-Based Reconstruction." In *Early American Probate Inventories*, edited by Peter Benes. The Dublin Seminar for New England Folklife, Annual Proceedings, 1987. Boston: Boston University Press, 1989.

Tucker, Veta Smith. "Purloined Identity." *Journal of Black Studies* 30, no. 4 (March 2000): 624–634.

Tully, John. *An Almanac for the Year of Our Lord MDCXCII.* Cambridge, MA: Samuel Phelps, 1692. Evans microtext 630, accessed from http://infoweb.newsbank.com.

Ulrich, Laurel Thatcher. *Goodwives: Image and Reality in the Lives of Woman in Northern New England 1650–1750.* New York: Alfred A. Knopf, 1982; New York: Oxford University Press, 1980, 1982 [paperback ed.].

Upham, Charles W. *Salem Witchcraft with an Account of Salem Village and a History of Opinions on Witchcraft and Kindred Subjects.* Mineola, NY: Dover Publications, 2000 [one-volume edition; originally two volumes published in 1867].

Upham, W[illia]m P. "Account of the Rebecca Nurse Monument." EIHC 23 (1886): 151–160, 201–229.

————. *House of John Procter, Witchcraft Martyr, 1692*. Peabody, MA: Press of C. H. Shepard, 1904.

Weigle, Luther A., ed. *The New Testament Octapla: Eight English Versions of the New Testament in the Tyndale-King James Tradition*. New York: Thomas Nelson and Sons, 1962[?].

"Where I Live, Norfolk: Point 4–Row 114." http://www.bbc.co.uk/norfolk/content/articles/2005/07/05/coastwalk05_stage4.shtml.

Willard, Samuel [P. E. and J. A.]. *Some Miscellany Observations on Our Present Debates Respecting Witchcrafts, in a Dialogue Between S. & B*. Philadelphia, PA: William Bradford, 1692. Evans microtext #631, accessed from http://infoweb.newsbank.com.

"William Towne Estate." http://wwwessexcountyma.org/wills/townew.htm, and Essex, *Probate*, 2:358.

INDEX